DEEP SOUTH

DEEP SOUTH

A Social Anthropological
Study of Caste and Class

★

by A L L I S O N   D A V I S
BURLEIGH B. GARDNER
and MARY R. GARDNER

THE CENTER FOR AFRO-AMERICAN STUDIES

UNIVERSITY OF CALIFORNIA, LOS ANGELES

THE CENTER FOR AFRO-AMERICAN STUDIES

THE UNIVERSITY OF CALIFORNIA, LOS ANGELES

Reprint of the ed. published by
The Regents of the University of California
with a new foreword, 1988.

ISBN 0-934934-26-6
ISBN 0-934934-27-4 pbk.

Library of Congress Catalog Card Number: 41-23645

TO

EDWIN R. EMBREE

SOCIAL ENGINEER WITH A FAITH

IN THE

SCIENCES OF HUMAN BEHAVIOR

FOREWORD TO THE
COMMUNITY CLASSIC EDITION

DEEP SOUTH offers a window into everyday life and custom in an American community where black-white inequality was deeply institutionalized. Between the World Wars, some seventy years after the enactment of Constitutional amendments which declared the end of involuntary servitude and pledged equal protection of the law to citizens of all races, a new order had fully crystallized to maintain white dominance and black subordination. The authors aptly label this new order a caste system, and they make it the focus of their in-depth description and analysis, laying bare its ideological, social and economic components and showing how they are all inextricably interwoven.

Indeed, it is the clarity with which *Deep South* foregrounds the interrelationship between the economic and sociopolitical aspects of the American caste system that sets it apart and makes it a work of enduring significance. In its representation of conditions of life for many Black Americans in the South prior to World War II, its reputation as a classic has been well earned. It is therefore most fitting that *Deep South* has been chosen to introduce the new Community Classics Series of the UCLA Center for Afro-American Studies.

The foundations of American caste lie in the plantation economy of the antebellum South, a mode of production which figured prominently in the Caribbean and other parts of the New World between the sixteenth and nineteenth centuries. Africans who were forcibly imported to the Americas as slaves furnished the labor for the plantation system, in some areas up till the penultimate decade of the nineteenth century. In the American South and elsewhere, racism provided the ideological underpinnings for the social order that plantation slavery brought forth. In the ideological scheme of *Deep South*'s historical and cultural niche, the Negro race is not only the intellectual but the moral and aesthetic inferior of the White race. Interaction between the socially defined races is governed by customs which seek to secure white dominance in virtually every sphere of community life and which feature a range of rituals through which Blacks are forced in their everyday contact with whites to symbolize their subordination. Social boundaries between the races are rigidly maintained, despite the presence of mixed mating and the resulting mixed-race offspring.

Justice is also framed within the caste system; it may not be guilt or innocence which propels an inexorable march to execution but the seriousness of the threat to the caste system posed by even an alleged infraction. Whippings may be employed to sanction violations of the caste prescriptions that surround appropriate deference Blacks must accord to whites. The most serious caste infraction, however, appears to be the Black male's violation of the prohibition against sex relations with a white woman. If complicity is involved, the man may get off with a whipping, and both partners may be forced to leave town. If, however, it is charged that such relations have occurred by force, it is a capital offense and one which may not require the formalities of trial, sentencing and orderly execution by the state.

Deep South also examines the significant contrasts between the "Old City" that is the primary setting and its rural hinterlands. In the rural areas, the influence of the plantation system continues to exert itself in such a way that the black population remains for the most part also economically subordinate to the white population. Not so, however, in Old City, where urbanization has created the conditions for the emergence of economic differentiation within the black caste. A black business and professional class has evolved which, though small, in a number of respects parallels that class within the white caste. The resulting tension between the ascribed system of caste and achieved status system of class presages the open rebellion by Blacks against this oppressive system which captured the attention of the world in the 1950s and '60s and which brought forth new administrative, legislative and judicial measures to dismantle caste.

The research for *Deep South* was done in a manner that was relatively new in the study of American communities. The authors, scholars at the University of Chicago, lived for a year and a half as part of their respective racial castes in a small Mississippi town for which Old City is a pseudonym. And, as we learn in the Afterword contributed by the surviving author, Burleigh B. Gardner, living as members of their respective castes entailed such practices as semi-clandestine meetings between the researchers lest they fail to conform to caste norms and thereby compromise their research objectives. Through participant observation, a method then largely identified with anthropological studies of non-western societies, they observed the workings of this society from the inside and conducted their interviews of longtime residents as new neighbors rather than total outsiders. These discovery procedures and the quality of information they yielded are central to the texture and compelling character of this work, providing a counterbalance to the statistics and survey information which also support their analyses.

As anthropologist Margaret Mead said in her review of the book for the *New York Herald Tribune*:

> In a society where color caste profoundly divides white citizens from Negro citizens, and where the accident of sex also decrees that female citizens should display different attitudes from male citizens, and where the phenomenon of class stratification cuts across these basic divisions, each of us sees life from one highly constricted category, defined by caste, sex and class. Now we have a team of four workers, a white worker and his wife and a Negro worker and his wife, co-operating, sharing just those insights and those cross-caste statements which are usually most carefully hidden from outsiders, to produce a picture of the working of this city in the deep South—a picture at once more subjective and more objective than could otherwise have been arrived at.

The approach resulted in a wealth of anecdote and autobiographical detail, as well as verbatim records of first-hand accounts. It effectively allows the reader to vicariously experience life under this system in a way that only a qualitative ethnographic approach could.

Moreover, as Mead notes, this work asserts a moral tone, set by the authors as critical members of their culture. *Deep South*, "for that very reason, should prove an effective background for the kind of thinking which leads to social change; it will enlist the responsible ardor of those to whom democratic ideals appeal, and provide them with a most necessary disciplined type of social analysis to replace the loose use of phrases like 'race prejudice' or 'social snobbery' or 'the masses' which have too long hobbled our thinking."

In a review for The Annals of the American Academy of Political and Social Science written when the study was first published, reknowned scholar-activist, W. E. B. DuBois also gave the book high praise: "As a contribution to our knowledge of sociology and interaction of a small, deeply divided human group, this book deserves a high place."

The careful scholarship and insightful interpretation acknowledged in these reviews provides one motivation for the reissue of *Deep South*, which has been chosen to introduce the new Community Classics Series to be published by the UCLA Center for Afro-American Studies. *Deep South*'s contribution to illuminating American history and culture generally, and the Afro-American experience particularly, remains undiminished.

DuBois, like other reviewers at the time, also allowed that "in the study of the caste system, there is not much that is new." In this latter comment we find a particularly compelling rationale for making this work available to today's generation of college students. Racial inequality is a contemporary as well as a historical feature of American society; the various means by which white domination was achieved and perpetuated have profoundly shaped the economic and socio-political character of American society. Without question, understanding of the present can be enhanced by *Deep South*'s carefully drawn portrait of our past. To the extent that this subject matter continues to be neglected in social science and humanities curricula in higher education, our capacity to prepare students to understand and

FOREWORD

live in the modern world has been diminished. Only when works
such as *Deep South* are on the required reading list for all American students will we as educators meet our responsibility to
present an undistorted, well-rounded view of our society to our
students.

Not only has the legacy of segregation and slavery tended to
fade in popular consciousness, many of the crucial landmarks in
civil rights occurred before today's college freshmen were born.
For this reason, *Deep South* may prove more valuable today than
it was in its own time, keeping dramatically alive in the societal memory the roots of our contemporary social order. Despite
the disturbing legacy of racial subordination, a significant
proportion of Blacks alive today have not experienced *de jure*
segregation. Their white contemporaries tend to regard racial
slavery and segregation as part of a distant past. Worse still, as
they examine contemporary social issues such as poverty and its
varied social dislocations as well as intergroup conflict, they too
often lack a complete historical frame of reference. Given the
pressing need to understand the forces that sustain a black un-
derclass in a debased economic and social condition, *Deep South*
is an indispensable antidote to the kind of simplistic thinking
that would locate the sources of these conditions in Afro-
American culture itself. It also offers a valuable point of departure for a more critical evaluation of the "ethnic group" model,
which represents the Black American experience as a variant of
that of other immigrant groups. It may be noted that such treatment too frequently has become a basis for invidious comparison. Similarities notwithstanding, differences deserve to be
brought into sharp relief.

I can only conclude, as did Mead and DuBois, that *Deep South*
is essential reading for the socially literate. A place must be
guaranteed for it in the curricula of today and foreseeable tomor-
rows if new generations of socially literate citizens are to be
produced.

Claudia Mitchell-Kernan, PhD
October, 1987

xi

Allison Davis

Mary and Burleigh Gardner
Natchez, Mississippi, 1934

AUTHOR'S PREFACE

THIS research was carried out under the direction of Professor W. Lloyd Warner, formerly of Harvard University and now of the University of Chicago; it was made possible by a grant from the Committee on Industrial Physiology of Harvard University. The authors wish to express their deep appreciation to Professor Warner both for his teaching and for his organization of the research. Their indebtedness to him began with the conception of the study; it extends to all the benefits of his friendship and inspiration.

The field work was performed by the three authors, together with Mrs. Elizabeth Stubbs Davis and J. G. St. Clair Drake. To Mrs. Davis, our colleague during the whole period of the field work, we are indebted in countless ways, but especially for her skilful interviewing of the colored women in Old City and its plantation environment. The data concerning the Negro class system and miscegenation, as well as their interpretation, are in large part her contribution.

To J. G. St. Clair Drake we are indebted for much of the material on the clique structure of the Negro society, for the final cutting of the typescript by one-third, and for seeing the work through the press. The authors wish to express their sincere appreciation to him for his long-continued co-operation in this research.

Professor Earnest A. Hooton very kindly made available to us the services of the statistical laboratory of the Department of Anthropology of Harvard University for sortings of the agricultural data. To Dr. John Dollard, of the Institute of Human Relations of Yale University, we are grateful for stimulating discussions during the progress of the field work.

We also wish to thank the Julius Rosenwald Fund for having made possible the participation of Mr. Drake in this work. Without the help of this foundation and of Dillard University it would not have been possible to complete the study at this time.

We are also indebted to the Works Progress Administration for assistance in the preparation of the manuscript.

With regard to techniques, it is necessary to state here only the kinds of data which were gathered and the field methods employed. The operations themselves, by which the data were analyzed, will be illustrated or defined in the relevant sections of the book. As stated in an earlier report on the research:

A white fieldworker and his wife, and a Negro fieldworker and his wife lived in the society for a little over one and one-half years. All of the fieldworkers except the white woman had been born and reared in the South or in the border states, living there continuously except during their college or university training. In Old City they conformed to the behavioral modes of their respective castes; they participated chiefly with the upper and upper-middle classes. After about six months of residence, they appeared to be accepted as full-fledged members of their caste and class groups, and dropped their initial roles of researchers. Their observations of group behavior were therefore made in the actual societal context, in situations where they participated as members of the community, within the limits of their caste and class roles. The interviews also were obtained in this normal context, and except where matters of fact, such as factory or plantation management were concerned, few questions were asked. Every effort was made to adapt the principles of "free associative" interviewing to intimate social situations, so that the talk of the individual or group would not be guided by the fieldworker, but would follow the normal course of talk in that part of the society.

In this manner, both overt behavior and verbalization with regard to all the societal institutions were recorded for all color, class, age, and sex groups, down to the small, intimate cliques. The white and colored fieldworkers continually checked with each other all of their observations and interviews pertaining to Negro-white relations, so as to bring into the field of discussion their own initial caste dogmas, and to learn to see both sides of this behavioral relation. The methodological aim from the beginning was to see every Negro-white relationship from both sides of the society, so as to avoid a limited "white view" or a limited "Negro view." The same type of objective approach was sought to the study of class behavior; all interviewers participated in both formal and informal affairs, with all classes in their caste.

In addition to records of overt behavior and verbalizations, which cover more than five thousand pages, statistical data on both the rural and urban societies, as well as newspaper records of social gatherings, were collected.[1]

[1] W. Lloyd Warner and Allison Davis, "A Comparative Study of American Caste," in Edgar T. Thompson (ed.), *Race Relations and the Race Problem* (Durham, N. C.: Duke University Press, 1939), pp. 234, 235.

TABLE OF CONTENTS

PART I

CHAPTER I

INTRODUCTION: DEEP SOUTH—A SOCIAL ANTHRO-
POLOGICAL STUDY OF CASTE AND CLASS

BY W. LLOYD WARNER

THIS book describes the life of the Negroes and whites in a community of that area of the United States known as the "deep South." In order to study the area, a Negro man and a Negro woman, and a white man and a white woman, lived with the natives of Old City and Old County in Deep South for two years. In this book they have presented the results of their research on the culture of the community and the social life of its people. These four social anthropologists, all of whom received their training in anthropology at Harvard, have attempted to understand the social structure and customs of the Negroes and whites of Old City with the same perspective and minimum of bias which their fellow-anthropologists have used when they have told of the natives of New Guinea, the Indians of the Amazon, or the aborigines of Australia.

Old City is a small city of over 10,000 people, of which number over half are Negroes. It is a trade center for the large plantations of the cotton counties which surround it. These rural areas are about 80 per cent Negro.

Old City and Old and Rural counties are located in the heart of the "deep South," an area which can be defined roughly as the states of South Carolina, Georgia, Florida, Alabama, Mississippi, and Louisiana, overlapping into the adjoining states. Before the Civil War, great plantations flourished here. Many of the planters made cotton fortunes, built great houses, and lived in feudal grandeur. They became the

3

aristocracy of the white owning group and were known to be superior to all white freemen; and all white freemen lived in another and higher world from that "other species" of man, the black slave. When the South was defeated, the old social system of white master and Negro slave was destroyed, although they continued to raise cotton.

AMERICAN CASTE AND CLASS

But a new social system in Old City and its country side began to evolve out of the destruction of the old. It, too, organized the relation of Negroes and whites among themselves and with each other. It controlled the relations between Negroes and whites, and it regulated the social behavior of the different groups among the whites and among the Negroes.

The new social system also set apart from those jobs which were unpleasant and poorly paid the pleasant and well-paid jobs, a division of labor deemed necessary for the raising of cotton and the maintenance of daily life. The new system continued to place all Negroes in inferior positions and all whites in superior positions. It gave certain of the family groups among the whites superior positions to all other whites, and certain family groups the most inferior and least desirable places within the white society.

As the years have gone by, this new social system has become less like the old master-and-slave system out of which it was created. The Negro group has gradually changed its character, and new groups have formed within it. Its social life has become more like that of the larger white community of the rest of the country. All the pleasant and profitable jobs are no longer controlled entirely by the whites, and all the poorly paid and unpleasant jobs are not now done entirely by the Negro. The more desirable activities are now shared, although unequally in proportion, by both Negroes and whites. The educated Negro, the Negro professional men and women, and the store- and farm-owners recognize themselves,

4

and are recognized, as being different from those laborers and the domestics who now work for both whites and Negroes.

This difference between them is evaluated by all of them; the Negroes in business and the professions are felt to be superior, and the laboring group inferior, in status. Those Negroes who occupy an intermediate position are believed to be different from those below them and from those above them. The differences among them are recognized and evaluated as higher and lower not only by the Negroes but also by the whites. This new social order we have called a "class and caste system."[1]

One of the terms used in popular currency to express the feelings whites have for Negroes and Negroes for whites is "prejudice." The so-called "more liberal" whites say that certain of their members are "biased" or "prejudiced" against the other group, and some of the "more liberal" Negroes use these same terms when they refer to the attitudes of members of their own group. Both terms refer to the same social phenomena but, while expressive of certain of the attitudes felt by whites and Negroes about the other group, do not adequately represent the whole social situation to which they refer.

A man can have a prejudice against a certain individual or against things which he eats or wears; but when he and all the other members of his group express in their actions, feelings, and beliefs a large number of these "prejudices" about the members of another group in the community, it is necessary to re-examine the problem to determine whether our understanding of the problem—and the language used to refer to our understanding and to the facts—are correct. This need becomes increasingly strong when we find that the prejudices

---

[1] The presence of caste and class structures in the society of the deep South was reported upon first by a member of our research group in an article, "Formal Education and the Social Structure," published in the *Journal of Educational Sociology*, May, 1936, and later, in an article, "American Caste and Class," in the *American Journal of Sociology*, September, 1936.

have a core of sentiments which are emotionally held by all individuals who are members of the white group and that another body of sentiments in opposition to the first is carried by the Negroes. The sentiments are expressed in attitudes which place all Negroes in an inferior position and all white men in a superior position and which control the social relations of all individuals who live in the community of Old City.

This organized system of sentiments and attitudes is expressed in the social practices of the groups and in the beliefs they hold about themselves. We have called this part of the social system a "caste system."

THE CASTE SYSTEM

The second chapter of this book describes the caste system in detail and points out how the system is organized around the control of sex, with the placement of the offspring of inter-caste sexual relations in the lower caste, and those of intra-caste sexual relations in the group in which they are born. In the case of sexual relations between the castes, the community refuses the child and its parents a recognized family position in the upper caste and forces the child into the lower caste. In almost all such cases the mother is Negro and the half-caste child becomes a social Negro with white blood who lives with its mother; but if the mother is white, all the child's family relationships are destroyed by action of the community. The child may be given to a Negro family to raise, the father "run out of town" or lynched~by community action, and the mother also forced to leave town. In any case, the community maintains the caste relationship by keeping all children who have a Negro parent in the lower group and by refusing to recognize the relation of the white parent to the child.

The "purity of southern womanhood," even if it is fictitious, functions as one device by which the upper caste prevents a half-caste child from becoming a part of the upper caste and possibly destroying the group's unity. This device

6

also works to allow the ordinary "double-standard" sexual mores of our group to continue in a caste situation. The upper caste may have extramarital sexual relations with Negro women but not marital ones, and may never have fully recognized parental ties with the offspring of such unions. In the ideal caste situation the upper-caste woman is forbidden all extramarital relations; and since no women of that group can marry a Negro, all sexual relations between white women and Negro men are theoretically impossible. Sexual relations as "fun" are allowed to the men and not to the women; but should a man be serious enough about his cross-caste sexual relations to recognize the resulting offspring and accept the normal responsibility expected of a father in American society, social condemnation is his lot. So long as the factor of Negro-white relations is not involved, any white member of this community in the deep South immediately recognizes that such ethics are wrong and contrary to the general moral code of Americans. This contradiction between the general ethical and moral codes and the feelings aroused against a male white who recognizes his half-caste child indicates that the social system of the deep South provides a new code, a caste code. By this addition to the general moral code the members of the two groups organize thinking and behavior between themselves.

RELATION BETWEEN "CASTE" AND "RACE"

Another point must be made clear before we continue with our discussion. In popular and scientific speech in this country Negro-white relations are often spoken of as "race" relations. Many of the "white men" of Brazil and certain Caribbean countries, however, would be Negroes in Old City because the *social* definitions of what a Negro is and what a white man is are different in the latter locality. The awkward situation in Old City in which such a white-skinned man or woman is socially defined as a Negro is reversed if the social Negro moves to a new community and becomes a *social* white. If the word "race" were to have any meaning at all when applied to Negroes, it should indicate that Negroes produce Negro offspring. But some of the Negroes in Old City could not produce a "racial" Negro no matter how often and hard they might try. This is true for the very good reason that, by all the physical tests the anthropologists might apply, some social Negroes are *biologically* white and, when mated with their own kind, can produce only white children. Some Negro men and women may have a Negroid genetic structure, and some white men and women may have a Caucasoid genetic structure; but any physical relations of Negroes and whites in Old City are controlled not by their genetic structure but by social traditions organized into a social system which allows and forbids certain actions.

THE SOCIAL ANTHROPOLOGIST LOOKS AT THE DEEP SOUTH

Discerning the relationships between the biological and the cultural aspects of society is one of the anthropologist's main problems. Studying the culture of a society is the special province of *social* anthropologists. The methods of their profession are comparative. The social anthropologist looks at all the societies of the world, where he observes the similarities and differences in the social institutions, beliefs, and customs of the people he is studying. The present-day social anthropologist has added his own society to the others as part of his comparative scheme. We feel justified in being just as much interested in the life of our modern American communities as some of our colleagues are in the peculiar practices of the polyandrous Toda.

Since the modern social anthropologist does study his own society in the general framework of comparative sociology, it becomes necessary, for the purposes of coherence, to apply the same terms to the same kind of social phenomena or principles of social behavior, whether they be found in inner Tibet, this community of Old City in the deep South, or among the Andaman islanders in the Bay of Bengal. So it must be with Negro-white relations in the deep South.

A. L. Kroeber, professor of anthropology at the University of California, defining "caste" in the *Encyclopaedia of the Social Sciences*, states that "a caste may be defined as an endogamous and hereditary sub-division of an ethnic unit occupying a position of superior or inferior rank or social esteem in comparison with other sub-divisions." The social system of Old City (and, in all probability, of large parts of the South and some sections of the North) fits this definition of Kroeber's and of most of the ethnologists and social anthropologists.

THE CLASS SYSTEM

In the social organization of the deep South there seems to be not only a caste system but also a class hierarchy. Ordinarily, the social scientist thinks of these two different kinds of vertical structures as antithetical to each other. "Caste," as used here, describes a theoretical arrangement of the people of a given group in an order in which the privileges, duties, obligations, opportunities, etc., are unequally distributed between the groups which are considered to be higher and lower. There are social sanctions which tend to maintain this unequal distribution. This much of the definition also describes "class."

A caste organization, however, must be further defined as one where marriage between the two groups is not sanctioned and where there is no opportunity for members of the lower group to rise into the upper group or for the members of the upper to fall into the lower one.

In "class," on the other hand, there is a certain proportion of interclass marriage between lower and higher groups; and there are, in the very nature of the class organization, mechanisms established by which people move up and down the vertical extensions of the society.

Obviously, two such groupings are antithetical to each other, the one inflexibly prohibiting movement between the two groups and intergroup marriage and the other sanctioning intergroup movement and at least certain kinds of marriage between higher and lower classes. Nevertheless, they have accommodated themselves to each other in the southern community we are examining. Perhaps the best way to present the relationships between these two types of social stratification as they exist in the deep south is by means of the accompanying chart (Fig. 1). The diagonal lines separate the

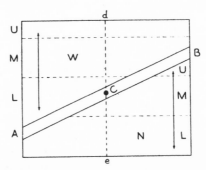

FIG. 1.—Relation between the caste system and the class system in the deep South. (This diagram and those which follow are not intended to portray quantitative relations between the groups. Rather, they indicate relative positions in vertical social space and permit a quick analysis of superordinate and subordinate relationships between the strata of the society.)

lower Negro caste (N) from the upper white caste (W), and the two broken lines in each segment separate the three general classes (upper, middle, and lower) in each caste from one another. The two double-headed vertical arrows indicate that movement up and down the class ladders within each caste can and does take place and that it is socially sanctioned, but that there is no movement or marriage between the two segments. It will be noticed that the parallel lines which separate the Negro and white castes do not run at right angles. Their arrangement expresses the essential skewness created by the

10

conflict of caste and class in the South. The gradual elaboration of the economic, educational, and general social activities of the Negro caste since slavery (and to some extent even before) has created new groups which have been vertically arranged by the society until certain fairly well-marked class groups have developed within the Negro caste. As the vertical distance of the Negro group has been extended during the years, the top Negro layer has been pushed higher and higher. This has swung the caste line on its axis (c), so that the top Negro group is higher in class traits than the lower white groups and is so recognized. (This recognition is expressed in circumlocutions and by unconscious actions, but at times it is also consciously and openly stated by the members of both the white and Negro groups.) If this process continues, as it seems to be doing at the present time, it is possible, and indeed probable, that the lines $A-B$ might move on the axis c until they approximate the hypothetical line $d-e$. (Theoretically, of course, this process could go farther, but it seems unlikely.) This tendency to bring the two groups out of the vertical opposition and organization into a horizontal arrangement is being reflected at the present time in such movements as "parallelism," a "solution to the race problem" expounded by many Negro and white leaders. Such terms, of course, are kinds of collective representations which have come into existence and which approximately express the social facts of the changing social structure, at the same time allowing the sentiments of some of the people who live in the structure to find expression also. Should the line $A-B$ reach the position $e-d$, the class situation in either group would be equivalent to that of the top white, while the lower classes in each of the parallel groups would also be equivalent. Even the present approximation of this gives the top Negro group certain advantages over his lower-class fellows which he is anxious to maintain.

It is interesting to speculate as to what might happen to caste relations if this process continues. It is possible that the

11

ordinary social sanctions which apply to cross-caste "social" relations might finally be weakened with the increasing differentiation in the Negro community and the disappearance of the caste differentials in power and prestige. Even the taboo on intermarriage might be relaxed. The children of such marriages would no longer necessarily be placed in the lower caste. They might conceivably take their place on either side of the caste line, thus progressively destroying the definitive nature of that division. Unless further sanctions were developed to maintain endogamy, the whole system of separate caste groups might disappear and new social forms develop to take its place.

On the other hand, the social skewness created by the present class-caste conflict, and which results in the process of changing the social location of the caste line, has placed the upper-class Negro in a decidedly difficult situation. The Negro who has moved or been born into the uppermost group (see Fig. 1) of his caste is superior to the lower whites in class but inferior in caste. In his own personality he feels the conflict of the two opposing groups, and in the thinking and feeling of the members of both groups there is to be found this same conflict about his position. He is known to be superior to the "poor white" (he is a doctor, say); but he is still a "nigger" or "Negro," according to the social context in which the words are used. Metaphorically speaking, he is constantly butting his head against the caste line. He knows himself to be superior to the poor white; yet to the poor white, the upper-class Negro is still a "nigger," which is a way of saying that the Negro is in a lower caste than himself. Furthermore, if it ever came to a crisis, the superordinate white class would maintain the solidarity of the white group by repudiating any claims of superiority by any Negro to the lower-class whites. The present and past political behavior of the South has to be understood in terms of the maintenance of the caste lines and as an effort to prevent the continued elaboration and segmentation of the class groups within the lower caste. The unequal distribution of the school funds and privileges are an excellent example of how the system tends to maintain itself through the changing generations. The operation of the courts and the activities of the police also reflect the same conscious or unconscious maintenance of control by the superordinate white caste. For that matter, all social institutions in the South, including the family, school, association, clique, church, and so on, are formed to fit the dominant-caste social situation.

An interesting hypothesis may be built out of the "skewed" social position of the upper-class Negro. It seems possible that the emotional instability of many of the individuals in this group (as compared, let us say, with the Negroes of the lower positions) may be due to the instability and skewness of the social situation in which he lives. He is always "off balance" and is constantly attempting to achieve an equilibrium which his society, except under extraordinary circumstances, does not provide for him.

In the chapters which follow, the caste and class attitudes are given in full. The family, clique, and associational organizations are carefully described, to demonstrate how caste and class are organized into the daily lives of the people who live in the community of Old City. The political and court procedures are fully described; and they, too, clearly demonstrate that, although the formal statements of the law books, on the whole, show no discrimination between the two castes, the actual practices, while taking into account the moral code expressed in the law books, usually reverse the democratic code of the law when dealing with whites and Negroes. The economic system is described in a number of chapters, and the problem of the division of goods from the community's labor is carefully related to the class and caste systems.

The intricate relations of this complex organization of human behavior are presented by the authors as a whole system, a system which represents a way of life that would seem as peculiar to the South Sea Islander as the South Sea

Islander's way of life does to a native of the deep South. It is but one more example of the almost infinite variety of social systems which man has devised to maintain ordered relations with the rest of nature and with his fellow-beings.

This book is one of several which are being published as a result of a number of years of research on modern American communities. The authors received their training in the study of American communities by the research they did for me on a New England community. The research on the New England community is now being published under the general title of *Yankee City*.

The Davises and Gardners have produced an excellent book. They have written a book which, it seems to me, gives us a keen insight into the human behavior of the deep South, and they have presented some of the facts necessary for a better understanding of the world in which we live.

University of Chicago, 1940

CHAPTER II

THE SYSTEM OF COLOR-CASTES

THE fundamental division in the social organization of Old City and Old County is that between the Negroes and the "white folks." This social cleavage is such that all privileges and opportunities, as well as duties and obligations, are unequally distributed between the two groups. The whites receive by far the larger portion of all economic and social rewards, while the Negroes have an undue share of the more onerous duties. Both Negroes and whites recognize the fact that the white group is superordinate in power and prestige, and they exemplify this awareness in both their behavior and thought. Furthermore, each of the groups is endogamous; that is, marriage between them is absolutely forbidden, and any children of extralegal sex relations are automatically relegated to the subordinate Negro group. Each individual is born into the Negro or white group and must remain in it for life. He may neither earn nor wed his way out. As has been pointed out in chapter i, such features of social organization are characteristic of a caste system; much of the behavior of both Negroes and whites, especially when in the presence of each other, can be called "caste behavior."

SANCTIONS FOR THE SUBORDINATION OF NEGROES

"Inherent inferiority."—The subordinate position of the Negroes is generally interpreted by the whites as being due to inherent differences between the two groups. Thus, to the whites, the subordination of the Negro is not merely a characteristic of the social structure, which might conceivably be subject to change, but is based upon immutable factors,

15

inevitable and everlasting. To them, the Negro is a lower form of organism, biologically more primitive, mentally inferior, and emotionally undeveloped. He is insensitive to pain, incapable of learning, and animal-like in his behavior.

The belief in organic inferiority of the Negro reaches its strongest expression in the common assertion that Negroes are "unclean." In spite of their widespread use as nurses and servants, there remains a strong feeling that the color of the Negroes is abhorrent and that contact with them may be contaminating.

There is generally a strong feeling against eating or drinking from dishes used by Negroes, and most of the whites provide separate dishes for the use of their servants. The idea of uncleanliness is also extended to any clothing worn by Negroes, as was dramatically shown when a Negro customer returned a coat which she had bought from a white clothing merchant. The clerk was unwilling to accept the coat and when the assistant manager accepted it, the clerk said to another clerk: "This is perfectly terrible; I think it is awful. We can't put that coat back in stock." The latter said: "I know it. Who wants a nigger coat? I don't feel like showing that coat to anyone; nobody wants to buy a nigger coat. Some little white girl will probably come in and buy it and not know it is a nigger coat." She hung it up very gingerly and didn't touch it any more than necessary. The assistant manager then said: "I think that is awful. We certainly couldn't make a practice of doing that, it would ruin our business if anyone knew about it. No one would come here to buy their clothes."

"The will of God."—Not only is the caste system believed by the whites to be based on inherent differences between the two groups, but it also carries sacred sanctions in their society. To them, it is the "will of God." This idea, expressed as a part of the whole pattern of white attitudes toward the Negro, was indicated by a physician, who stated:

The way I look at it is this way: God didn't put the different races here to all mix and mingle so you wouldn't know them apart. He put them here as separate races and He meant for them to stay that way. I don't say He put the Caucasians here to rule the world or anything like that. I don't say He put them here to be the superior race; but since they have a superior intellect and intelligence, I don't think God would want them to mingle with inferior races and lose that superiority. You know the Negro race is inferior mentally, everyone knows that, and I don't think God meant for a superior race like the whites to blend with an inferior race and become mediocre. I think God put all the different races here for a purpose, the Negro and the Indian and the Chinese, and all of them, and He didn't mean for them to mix. I think I am right in saying that, and my attitude is Christian-like.

There is just something about the different colored races that is a little bit abhorrent to me, not just the Negroes, either. I mean all the colored races, and I think that is the way with most white people; they all feel the same way. When I was in the University, I went to a meeting at one of those student-movement things, and there was a girl there from India. She was very dark-skinned, you know, black as a Negro. Well, she got up there and did a native dance, or sang a song, or something, and I guess it was good. But you know after she got through I said to a fellow who was sitting next to me, "You know, there's something abhorrent to me about her just because of her color." And he said he felt the same way. I think most people feel that way about it, and that's why I don't think God meant for the races to mix. He made them that way so they wouldn't want to mix.

"Unsocialized beings."—In presenting their views of the Negro's inherent inferiority, the whites frequently relate specific instances of Negro behavior as "proof" of their theories. Examination of many of these statements reveals that, to the whites, the Negro appears as an "unsocialized being," that is, he is thought to lack many of the social restraints and compulsions which form the pattern of approved white behavior. Thus, to them, he is lazy and will not work except under the compulsion of force or immediate need; he is irresponsible and does not anticipate and prepare for future needs; he is dependent upon the whites and prefers this dependence to the struggle of existing in the present society without their protection. One white woman related an incident in which her father had tried to get a Negro tenant to buy land. The Negro, however, assured his landlord that he

17

didn't want a "place of his own." He just wanted a buggy and a horse. The woman was convinced that "they don't want to be independent." She said: "Some outsiders have the idea that we bully the Negroes and try to keep them down. That isn't true. It's their own fault. Not one in a thousand wants to be independent!"

White people also feel that the Negro lacks respect for property and will steal with no feeling of guilt; he will also lie whenever it suits his immediate ends. It is believed also that he lacks emotional stability, is quick to laugh or to cry, and has fits of temper in which he will maim or kill without regard for possible consequences. In addition, he is thought to lack the white-man's concepts of sexual morality, continually practices sexual promiscuity, has no belief in chastity as a virtue, and allows his passions free rein.

"Childlike behavior."—For all the foregoing conceptions of the Negro the whites have one generalized description and interpretation, that is, the Negro is "childlike" and will never grow up. As various informants phrased it:

They are very much like children; they have no thought for the future and only think of their immediate wants.

They are really just like children. They can't be left to themselves; they don't have the ability to get along. They really need white people to direct them.

We have a Negro girl as our servant who has been with us about eight years, but she hasn't grown up any since we have had her. Even now if we scold her or say anything in a cross way she will start to cry. They are just children.

They are just children, especially about temptations. It is up to you to realize that and not leave things around to tempt them.

They are exactly like children, especially about Christmas. My cook is so wonderful lately, just because Christmas is so near and she thinks she will get more. My baby is just the same way; they are just alike. Children and servants are just the same.

THE SYSTEM OF COLOR-CASTES

In all these statements the behavior of the Negro is regarded as the behavior of a child, of an individual who has not yet become completely socialized. In the case of the Negro, however, such behavior is not considered a passing stage in the process of normal development but the final stage in his growth. Owing to his inherent inferiority, he can never become a mature individual, completely socialized according to white standards, and must remain forever a child.

Although, to the whites, this alleged childlikeness is indicative of inherent inferiority, it nevertheless arouses a certain amount of envy. Forgetting the powerful restrictions exerted upon Negroes by systematic social subordination, white people often think of the Negro as completely free from all irksome social controls and obligations; as living entirely in the present, with no regrets for the past or fears for the future; as enjoying to the fullest all physical satisfactions. The Negro can eat hugely with no thought of manners; he can laugh loudly; he can express his joy or his anger in direct verbal and physical action; and he can seek and enjoy his sexual experiences completely free from external restraints or personal inhibitions.

It is not unusual to hear a white person remark that he wished he could be "as contented as those niggers sitting in the sun"; or, as one white man expressed it:

I often think the Negroes are happier than the whites no matter how little they have. You always see them smiling and happy as long as they have a little to eat. One reason they are so carefree is that they have no morals to worry about and they don't have to keep up their good name.

One planter said:

Speaking of slaves, the Negro is no longer the slave, but the planter is. We have to worry over the crop, over financing the tenant and everything like that, while he just looks to us to take care of him and hasn't a worry as long as he is fed.

The most open expression of this envy of the Negroes' supposed "freedom" was made by a white woman, who confided to the interviewer:

> When I get drunk, I always start thinking I am a mulatto woman. You know I have had that mulatto-woman idea on my mind for a long time. I have always thought how nice it would be to really be one; you could just do anything you wanted and it wouldn't make any difference.

White "responsibility" for Negroes.—This belief in the irresponsibility of the Negro imposes a sense of certain responsibilities upon the whites, for, according to their beliefs, the whites cannot change the Negro's modes of behavior but must adjust to them. The housewife must "realize that the most faithful of them will steal from you and there is nothing you can do about it. It is no use firing them because the next one will be just as bad." Therefore, she must not leave temptation in their way. She must not leave the liquor unlocked, forget loose change about the house, or fail to keep a check on stockings, handkerchiefs, and food. If she fails in her duty and "things are missing," she may fire the servant, but the guilt is hers for having left temptation in a servant's path. In the same manner, the planter feels the responsibility for directing the work of his Negro tenants, inspecting their crops, seeing that they take care of their work animals. If necessary, he feels it proper to force them to do the work correctly.

There is thus, in Old City, a commonly shared body of beliefs about the status and capabilities of Negroes. This body of beliefs constitutes an ideological system which is used to justify the social relationships between the superordinate whites and the subordinate Negroes.

THE SYMBOLS AND RITUALS OF SUBORDINATION

Symbols of derogation.—"Blackness" is the master-symbol of derogation in the society, and the "typical" Negro characteristics of dark skin color and of woolly or kinky hair are considered badges of subordinate status, "disgusting" to the whites and disliked by Negroes. White persons often state that they prefer the lighter Negroes because "the black Negroes are much more primitive and animal-like in their actions and emotions"; and not infrequently a Negro will make some such remarks as the following: "You doan think it's so bad for a black nigger or a dark one to have no sense and act crazy, but you doan expec' a light one to ack ignorant!" One Negro remarked cynically of certain others: "Yeah, *they* are color-struck and so are the Yanceys. One boy married a dark-brown girl and the Yancey family like tuh died." This man claimed to prefer "healthy browns" to either light or black Negroes. Those Negroes fortunate enough to have light skin and "good" (that is, straight) hair are often the envy of their fellows, who sometimes strive to attain the same appearance through artificial means.

Throughout the society the term "nigger," which may be applied by any white person to any Negro, denotes the subordinate and inferior position of Negroes. Even though Negroes use the term in common parlance, their awareness of its derogatory nature is revealed when one Negro uses the word to insult another in a quarrel or to disparage his actions.

Spatial separation.—Spatial separation, too, is used to symbolize the separate and subordinate status of the Negro. In the jails and schools and on public conveyances provision is made by law for "separate and equal accommodations." (It is only in the jail, however, that "equal" becomes more than a verbal concession to the democratic imperatives of the United States Supreme Court.) "Segregation," too, is the rule in all moving-picture theaters, churches, and at other places where Negroes and whites occasionally meet. In such situations, signs and labels are unnecessary, as Negroes and whites both know their places and go to them, whether the situation be the nightly movie, the less frequent wedding or funeral at some white or Negro church, or the county courtroom.

21

Negro and white residential areas are not segregated by law; and Negroes live throughout the city, even in the more choice districts, where they occupy cabins along the bayous and back alleys. There are, however, several large concentrations of Negroes. Although the separation of the two groups is by no means absolute, there is considerable difference between the areas predominately Negro and those predominately white. In general, the Negro areas have fewer paved streets and side-walks (in fact, the only ones paved are those streets which carry a large amount of through traffic). Many of the Negro districts have no sewerage system; the streets are poorly drained and poorly maintained; and street lights are few or absent. In essence, this means that the Negroes generally occupy the least desirable residential areas and receive only a minimum of public services and improvements. Only whites of the lowest social status live in these neighborhoods, and in the white mind they become symbolic of the Negro's inferior status.

Deferential behavior.—As has been indicated, the system of Negro-white relations in Old City not only affects the dogmas of the society but also exerts a vigorous control over much of the behavior of the individuals. The most striking form of what may be called "caste behavior" is deference, the respectful yielding exhibited by the Negroes in their contacts with whites. According to the dogma, and to a large extent actually, the behavior of both Negroes and white people must be such as to indicate that the two are socially distinct and that the Negro is subordinate. Thus, the Negro, when addressing a white person, is expected to use a title such as "Sah," "Mistah," "Boss," etc., while the white must never use such titles of respect to the Negro but should address him by his first name or as "Boy." The Negro may go farther, especially in rural areas, touching his hat and greeting respectfully any white, even a stranger. The white person may return the greeting with a nod but will never touch his hat. In places of business the Negro should stand back and wait until the white has been served before receiving any attention, and in entering or leaving he should not precede a white but should stand back and hold the door for him. On the streets and sidewalks the Negro should "give way" to the white person. When going to a white house, the Negro usually knocks at the back door; or, if he should go to the front door, he must not ascend the porch to the door but should stand by the steps and knock. When his knock is answered, he then stands respectfully with his hat in his hand.

This deferential behavior goes beyond the mere observance of certain formalities; it extends to what the Negro may say and how he may say it. Under no circumstance may he contradict a white person except as a very humble offering of his opinion; and if the white man persists in his statements, the Negro must agree. In no event may he say or even insinuate that a white is lying. If the white is wrong, it can only be a mistake, never a deliberate untruth. Furthermore, under no provocation may the Negro curse white people, whatever the white may do or say to him. He must never express his antagonism through profanity or violence.

Not only must the Negro observe these rules of deferential speech and conduct, but he must observe them wholeheartedly and with no apparent reservations. It is not enough that he should conform reluctantly to the expected modes of behavior. He must show that he accepts them as proper and right; he must conform willingly and cheerfully.

The importance of deferential behavior as expressive of the social structure is clearly shown in the attitudes of the whites. A properly deferential Negro is a "good" Negro, and the highest praise offered is that a Negro is "humble and has the proper attitude toward the whites," that "he knows his place." On the other hand, the Negro who does not abide by these rules, who is not properly humble and deferential in his behavior, is "sassy," "uppity," and "bad," and is trying to "get out of his place." Thus the Negro who accepts and expresses his inferior social position is "good," while the one who

fails to express it is suspected of rebelling against it, is dangerous to the social system, and arouses the antagonism of the
whites. The following two comments exemplify these attitudes:

> Later Kenneth [Negro man] came back from the War and he was the
> proudest thing you ever saw in his uniform. Not that he wasn't per-
> fectly all right with whites, but he was certainly proud when with Ne-
> groes. He hadn't changed a bit though in his attitudes, he was still just
> as polite and humble with whites and not a bit uppity—a very fine boy
> who knew his place.

> Papa once had a Negro who was a big stout fellow, a fine worker and a
> good nigger around the whites. He was just as polite as could be and
> would do anything he was told. But he was Hell when he got out with the
> niggers. Papa first got him when defending him for killing another
> nigger. He got him off, and he took up with papa. He later killed an-
> other nigger, and Papa got him off again, but finally he killed a third and
> that was too much. He got fifteen years. However, all the white men
> said he was a good nigger, but they would admit he was a bad one among
> the other niggers.

While the burden of deferential behavior rests upon the
Negroes, it also imposes certain restrictions upon the white
people. A white must not use terms of respect in addressing
Negroes, and he must not offer to shake hands upon meeting
them. In general, he must not apply to them any of the symbols of equality commonly used between whites; and if he
disobeys these rules of conduct, he encounters the disapproval
of the white world. If he persists in flaunting custom, he may
even become an outcaste.

ENDOGAMY—KEYSTONE OF CASTE

The practice of endogamy is the most significant social
control in any caste situation. In Old City it is the most
rigidly enforced aspect of Negro-white relations and carries
more emotive content than any other. While some individual
Negroes may achieve a high economic position, receive recognition of their high intellectual abilities, or may even oc-

casionally transgress the rules of deference, no Negro may ever marry a white person. All other rules may be, and at times are, broken; this one never. Thus, social mobility between the white and Negro societies becomes impossible, for there can be no legal family life involving a Negro and a white. The two in-marrying groups are perpetuated as *castes* whose differences are regarded as inherent, "in the very nature of things."

Negro men and white women.—One control which acts to maintain the endogamous system is the taboo existing on relations between Negro men and white women. Not only is there a formal law which prohibits intermarriage, but the society also seeks to prohibit any sexual intercourse outside of marriage between white women and colored men. Any Negro man who makes advances toward a white woman, even though she be a professional prostitute, has broken the strongest taboo of the system and risks a terrible punishment. Furthermore, since he is regarded as a primitive being, emotionally unrestrained and sexually uncontrolled, the Negro man is thought by the whites to be always a potential rapist. Thus, white women are expected to fear strange Negro men, and they usually feel it unsafe to go alone in Negro districts or to stay alone at night in isolated houses. So ever present is this fear, that Negro men are often afraid to approach strange white houses where there may be a woman alone, or even to approach too near a lone white woman on the streets at night. One Negro man who delivered Negro newspapers in a mixed neighborhood complained of his difficulties as follows:

> I can't tell which houses to go to in some blocks. It's dangerous, too, if nobody but a woman is home. The other day I went to a house and a white woman came to the door. There wasn't anything for me to do but stand there. I said, "Paper?" and showed her the paper, and she said, "No." I was glad to get away from there!

"Rape."—The most flagrant infraction of this taboo on relations between Negro men and white women would, of

course, be rape. It is not surprising, therefore, that this potential violation of customary caste behavior on the part of Negroes is frequently visualized and sometimes alleged, although actual rapes in Old County are rare. Even cases of voluntary sex relations, however, are sometimes called "attacks," as in this reference by a prominent white man to several Negroes who were run out of town: "They were bad niggers and were getting biggity . . . . they had been 'attacking' some white women around here—prostitutes—not any decent women."

Shortly before the researchers arrived in Old City, a case occurred in a neighboring county which illustrates the working of this taboo. A Negro man had been accused of raping a white woman. In spite of considerable doubt that the woman had been attacked at all, the mere charge was sufficient to cause an attempted lynching, a trial, a conviction, and legal hanging—all within a few day's time. The incident was described in detail by white informants, one of whom stated to an interviewer:

I remember the case you mention and I saw most of it. It happened out in the country here. There is an old woman who lives all alone out here who is rather queer. I think possibly those two Negroes went to her place with the idea of robbing her but I doubt if they really attacked her—in fact, I never did think they did that. The day it happened I got word that these two Negroes had attacked this old lady and I went out and soon there was a big mob out from the city hunting for these Negroes and telling what they were going to do when they caught them. Now this woman is queer and hard of hearing and has a habit of saying "Yes" to anything you ask her. Ted was one of the big talkers in the mob and was active in stirring things up. I expect he went there all excited and asked her if she had been raped and she said "Yes" without knowing what she was saying. Anyway, the doctors were said to have examined her and found she had been attacked, but I never did believe she had.

This mob raved around about what they would do if they could lay their hands on this nigger and were going to hunt him down. I didn't want to get mixed up with it so I said I would wait at the store and maybe the nigger would show up, as he lived close by. So I sat on the porch with a rifle and along toward morning the Negro walked up within fifteen feet of me before he saw me. I covered him and called another fellow over, young Ted, who had been "talking big" about what he would do when he caught the Negro. I told him that here was his man and he could take him, and then he took him and turned him over to the sheriff, who took him to jail. After all the talking Ted had done, he walked through a quarter of a mile of woods with the Negro and never did a thing; so I figured it was mostly talk. They might have done something if the whole crowd had been there, but by the time they knew about it, the Negro was in jail. They did go to the jail but I figured that was just a bluff like all the talking this young fellow had done. I could have killed the nigger, but I didn't believe all the story. I might have done it, if I had known of my own knowledge that it was true, but I wouldn't kill him on the basis of such evidence as they had. Of course, they hung him legally after the trial. There was so much feeling that he was bound to hang. You couldn't get a jury *not* to convict him.

Another white informant, when asked about this hanging in Old City, stated:

That was a few years ago; it was a nigger supposed to have raped an old white woman. I never did believe that he attacked her. She was pretty old and sort of weak-minded. Maybe the nigger scared her, but I don't believe he actually touched her. But they had to hang him; there was nothing else they could do under the circumstances.

The Negro had been working for a white woman. After an argument, she claimed that he had attacked her. So they arrested him and brought him to jail here. Some of these "red necks" out here got together to lynch him and came to town after him. When they got to the jail the sheriff told them they might as well go back because we didn't have anything like that in Old City.

The interviewer asked what happened to the Negro, and the informant said: "He was hanged. They tried him, though."

Infractions of sex taboo.—In spite of the strength of the taboo and the ruthlessness displayed in the enforcement of it, cases of sexual intercourse between Negro men and white women do occur. According to Negro accounts, it is quite common for white women to "have" Negro men: "plenty of 'em, and those white women crazy about 'em." On the other hand, the whites are generally horrified by any such suggestion and tend to deny that it occurs at all frequently. Thus, both groups express their attitudes toward the caste lines, the Negroes watching eagerly for any breakdown of the restrictions, and the whites asserting the strength of the system—with existing conditions being something between either extreme. Actually, there are a number of cases in which an infraction of the taboos has occurred, and undoubtedly there are others which were kept from the knowledge of the white group. One of the most authentic of these was cited by a white man. According to him:

There was a case a few years ago; a white man from a good family. He was raising his grand-daughter because her father and mother were dead. And he had gotten so queer that he wouldn't let her get any education or do like the others. He just kept her in rags and half dressed and she got to playing around with Negroes. She was seen going around with Negro men. Finally people got together and hung a Negro man, and told this white man that he would have to send her away and leave himself.

A Negro told a revealing story of his own experience as follows:

No, Tom wasn't mixed up with those foreign girls; these were some white girls in the other part of the city. And you know, he came near getting me in that thing. He came up on the porch one night and said to me: "Come on and have some fun with me tonight." I said: "What fun you mean?" He said: "I got two white girls and they wantah go out tonight an' you can go with me." I said: "No, man, not me. I'm not taking any chances like that." You know I felt real weak.

The next day he came in and tol' me: "Man, you know those people have caught up with me about those white girls." I said: "What you mean? They caught you?" He said: "No, but Chief Sutton sent for me to come down to the station this morning, and I went, an' he tol' me they'd found out and he'd protect me until night, an' if I hadn't left town then, he wasn't going tuh try to stop them from gettin' me."

So I said: "You bettuh get the firs' train outtah here." But you know he hung around that house all day, an' every five minutes we'd see the Chief uh Police ride up and down in front of the house. But as soon as it got about seven o'clock, the Chief stopped ridin' up and down. About 7:15, ol' Tom went across behind Mack's coal yard and hopped the train there.

You know, the train had no sooner left town, than they came here after him—a gang of men and the Chief hisself leading them. When they saw he wasn't here they went away. And you know those white girls were on the same train! They made them leave too.

A prominent white citizen described one method of handling such cases:

> You probably heard about that case out in the country of the white girl who had a baby by a Negro. It was all handled quiet and no one knew about it. We got a Negro woman in another city to adopt the baby; the supervisors paid her $100 to take the child. You won't see it in the records, as we don't want things like that spread before the public. We want to keep them quiet. We sent the girl to a reform school.

The interviewer asked about the fate of the Negro, and the informant said: "No one has seen him since. He has left the 'country.' McIlroy and that bunch are watching for him. If they keep quiet about it, he will probably show up again and they will get him and give him a good whipping." When asked if they wouldn't kill him, he said: "No, it is better to just whip them and tell them to leave the 'country' and then if they come back, hang them. They won't come back though."

The white women and Negro men involved in cases of sex infractions.—Although little information is available concerning the individuals involved in such cases, the evidence indicated that, on the whole, the women were largely isolated from the white group and little affected by the normal social controls. As was shown in one of the interviews above, the girl's father was "queer," had withdrawn from the white group, and prevented his daughter from participating within it. A social worker described another case in which these same factors were operative:

> .... There are two of these white girls, one about eighteen and one twenty-five. They live with their father; their mother left them some years ago. They are having babies and are not married. We have tried everything we can with them but we can't do anything. They are just ignorant people and we can't get them to go to school. We have tried to get them to our adult school, but they just won't take an interest. We even sent the bus up there to get them but they won't come. They just live this life and have children without having any husbands.

I went out several times and tried to get to talk to the father. Finally, I went back where he was hoeing and talked to him out there. He was the very emotional type, cried when he talked about his wife, and carried on about he couldn't take all the responsibilities he has with a big family and everything. . . . . I suggested the church, of course, but he said no, he didn't want to send them to church and they didn't want to go. I told him we could arrange it right there at his house, and we could send Miss Cole out, and have the school and church all in one. He finally agreed but he never did do it. We couldn't get to see him for a while after that.

That isn't the end by any means. I don't think I'm prejudice-minded and I hope I'm not dirty-minded either, but somebody told me that this older girl was sleeping with the father. . . .

After the recitation of the case, when the social worker was out of the room, a woman whispered to the interviewer: "Mrs. Wilson says *those girls have Negro men, too*, but Miss Trent [the supervisor] won't let her say anything about that. Mrs. Wilson says she has proof of it. *Isn't that awful?*" It is significant to note from this interview that the incest situation was viewed with less horror than infraction of the caste sex taboos.

Much less information is available concerning the Negro men involved, but there is nothing to indicate that they were isolated from their own group or considered queer. In fact, some of them, as has been indicated above, were on intimate terms with other Negroes who knew what was going on. It appears, then, that these cases involve women who are isolated from their own group, who either refuse to participate or are prevented from participating in the normal ways, and who, instead, develop sexual relationships with Negroes, thus breaking the strongest taboo in the society. The Negro man, on the other hand, may have normal social relations within his own group. His behavior may not be a symptom of maladjustment to the class system within the Negro society but rather a rebellion against the caste structure. He enjoys the forbidden pleasures and at the same time flaunts the caste taboos, thus secretly defying the power of the white group. So powerful is this taboo, however, that the individual Negro man may be unable to throw it off even upon leaving the South, and may carry it with him wherever he goes. As one Negro said, when telling of an experience with a white girl at a northern university who was friendly to him: "I didn't feel right. I guess I thought I was still down South."

This taboo is not merely imposed upon the Negro man but is equally effective for the white woman. Any white woman who has sexual relations with Negro men or even encourages advances is open to punishment and expulsion by the white group. Even white prostitutes are not allowed to accept Negro business; and, should they do so and be discovered, the Negro is likely to be whipped and the prostitute run out of town.

Sexual relations between white men and Negro women.— In the case of white men and Negro women, the situation is entirely different. There is no taboo preventing sexual intercourse, despite the inflexible taboo upon marriage or upon any action which might tend to introduce their offspring into the white group. The sanctions of the white group, however, require either that such affairs be conducted with a certain amount of discretion or that the man relinquish many of his relations within his own group.

The effect of openly acknowledging this type of sex relationship is illustrated in the following story. In answer to the question "Would a white man be ostracized if it were known that he had a Negro mistress?" a white woman answered with a story of a white married man she knew. When the house of his Negro mistress was burning down,

this white man was standing in the crowd. His wife was standing right beside him but I guess he didn't know or didn't care. Anyway he broke through the crowd and called out, "Let me in to save my children!" He went into the house and came out with all those little black children. Well, his wife just left him; she never went back to him. He had grown-up white children too. Nobody ever had anything to do with him after that.

Temporary sexual relations involving white men and Negro women.—In spite of the necessity for discretion, there are a considerable number of cases involving sexual relations of white men and Negro women known to both Negroes and whites. Most are of a temporary nature, such as a white man visiting a Negro prostitute, having relations with a servant in his house, or picking up a Negro girl on the streets.

The most usual procedure in the latter case seems to be for the white man to pick up the girl in his car and drive out into the country with her. One Negro informant described the process of "pick-ups" by stating to an observer:

> You see those two girls walking down the street? You'll see young girls like that always walking up and down those business streets. That's the way they have of getting white men. That's what they're doing now. That's the only way most of them can get in touch with a white man.

Negro women, too, often referred to the advances of white men or to the methods of dating white men. A case of the latter type was mentioned as follows: "Once Katherine and I started to walk into town after school and a white fellow offered to bring us, so we came. Right then and there, with me in the car, Katherine made a date with the man and she had never seen him before."

In some cases a white man working on the river or in levee camps maintains a Negro woman, pays her a few dollars a week, and visits her when he can. These relationships, however, are of a transitory nature and involve little beyond the sexual act and payment therefor. They do not become relationships involving more extended reciprocal duties and rights. As one Negro prostitute at a construction camp phrased it:

> A nigger don't treat you with as much respect as a white man. The white man treat you courteous-like, and leave you free to yourself most of the time. Those white men will pay you five and ten dollars and likely won't bother you but once a week. That's all they want, and they don't think they have the right to beat you when they want to.

The extent of these relations is impossible of accurate determination, since the Negroes tend to emphasize, and the whites to minimize, them. In general, the white informants, especially those of middle- or upper- class status, claim that such relations are decreasing in number and, although still frequent, are not nearly so common as before the World War. Certainly, since about 1920 the brothels have declined in number and importance, and the elaborate establishments, described as common formerly, no longer exist. On the other hand, the Negroes complain that the white men have "all" the attractive Negro girls—"All the bes'-looking ones—you know about that? The white men git them or they go down on Monroe Street [prostitute area]"; or, "If a decent cullud girl here ain't got a white man, it sho ain't her fault, 'cause anybody can go and pick one up. They jus' hangin' 'round like flies 'round molasses, waitin' for somebody to give 'em a sign."

Permanent sexual relationships involving white men and Negro women.—Another type of sexual relationship between white men and Negro women is comparatively permanent in nature. This occurs when a white man maintains a Negro mistress and supports her and their children. In some cases he may give her a house and even go so far as to live there with her. In no case, however, may he marry her or incorporate her children into the white society. While such unions are more rare than the temporary relationships, a number of them are now in existence and, needless to say, are of considerable interest to both groups, especially to the Negroes. The bond between the man and woman in these cases becomes very close and tends to take on many of the characteristics of a husband-wife relationship with all the usual emotions and sentiments. Furthermore, the white man accepts the children as part of the relationship; he cares for them and exhibits much the same affection as if they were legitimate. Thus there is formed a family group which, at least within the home, ignores the caste restrictions. The attitudes of the people involved are shown in the following statement by the Negro partner in such a relationship:

I love Jim's daddy [her son's white father], 'n Jim's daddy loves me. Nothing else matters. We were boy and girl sweethearts 'n we're sweethearts today. So the rest of the world can go by. When he made money we had it; now business is bad, we don't have so much, but we've still got love. A few words of marriage ceremony, what do they mean? I feel I'm living a great deal more decently with a union based on love than some who are married before the law. And I don't feel that I've heaped any disgrace on Jim. He's got a dad and a good one who is doing everything possible to be a good dad to him. And we live here in our little shack, happily, and according to my standards, decently.

A few other incidents will be cited to illustrated the extent to which such "affairs" may become permanent relationships. A Negro resident pointed out a house to an interviewer where he said a white man stayed with a Negro woman almost every night:

He's been practically living with her for a number of years. At first, he used to wait until late at night to go there, but now he walks up as big as day any time. A few years ago, when the Klan was flourishing, they went to him and threatened to get him if he didn't leave her. You know that booger faced them and told them where they could go! He told them: "I've been living with that woman almost ever since I've been a man, and she's just the same to me as my wife could be. I'm not going to leave her for anybody, and if you want to try and make me, you come on and try." And they let him alone too. He went on with her, just as he had been.

A crisis situation sometimes throws such relationships into vivid relief, as in the following incident, overheard by one of the observers, while in an Old City barber-shop. This is first-hand evidence of the strong emotional ties which sometimes exist between a white man and his Negro mistress.

While Mr. Price was cutting my hair, a great shouting and cursing began in the other half of the building, which is separated from the barber shop by thin boards with cracks straight through in many places. Most of the shouting was quite easily understood. . . . .
Mr. Price and the other barber said that the person shouting was Mr. Anderson, the white man who kept a restaurant with his cousin next door. He was shouting and cursing at his cousin. Mr. Price said: "He's been living with a colored woman for over thirty years, to my knowledge, an ordinary looking colored woman, too. But he thought the world of her.

THE SYSTEM OF COLOR-CASTES

She ben sick, and she died last night, and he's missing her this morning. He's started up again now. That's his cousin he's cussin' and maybe his cousin's wife. He cusses them out any time they say anything about her. Some of them done said something about her now. That's what's the matter with him. He comes in here sometimes raising hell. . . . . Listen to him now."

I heard him raving again: "—— —— ——, don't none of you white —— —— —— say anything to me. Don't say anything. —— —— ——, she's gone!" He began sobbing and moaning and weeping.

"That's him all right," said Price. "He's raving today. . . . . Oh man, he thought the world of that woman. He's been carrying on like that ever since she ben sick, and he had Dr. Barnes to attend her. He told Dr. Barnes to go every time she needed him, and the money was right here for him."

Caste sanctions and the permanent Negro-white sexual relationship.—As may be seen from the preceding quotations, the Negroes continually insist that the relation between the white man and his Negro mistress is essentially a *family* relation, with the man assuming all the usual family obligations. Even the children of such couples maintain this view, as in the case of one who said:

No indeed, don't you ever believe that a child has no father just because he's white. You have your family just the same. My white father and colored mother lived together just like Paul and I do, but my mother died when I was a baby. But our home went on just the same. When I was old enough to go to school, my father brought me along with my sisters and brothers over here to school during the week. Then, on Friday, he would come for us, and he'd always hold me on his lap, driving home. When he died, he left his brother as our guardian and he treated us just like my father had.

Although within such a family the caste line may be ignored in the relations of the family to the outside world, as a rule, the taboo is not so openly broken. Outside the home the man is white, and the woman and children are Negroes. Outside, each must behave as prescribed by the caste regulations. This prevents them from appearing publicly as a family group or from participating as such within either caste. Any other relations of equal to equal which the woman or children may have are within the Negro group. Their relationships to other whites tend to be subordinate occupational relations. All other relations of equivalence which the man has are within the white group; his other relationships with Negroes are those of a superordinate. In all cases known, the white man was, to a large extent, isolated from his own group, especially from any form of social participation in mixed groups of men and women. He usually retained his occupational relations, and certain informal relations with other men; but, on the whole, his activities with whites were considerably limited. One white woman described the case of Prescott, who "has a Negro family, has had for years." She said: "Everybody knows about it. . . . . He just doesn't go anywhere at all. . . . . Why, I doubt if he even goes to his sister-in-law's house. I don't believe she would have him in her house."

With the Negro woman, the situation is different in Old City. She has associated herself with a member of the superior caste; she has acquired a measure of security far greater than is common among her group; she has a protector who will guard her in her relations with the white group. All this is reflected in her relations within her own caste. Instead of being isolated socially, as is the white man, the woman frequently has an active social life outside her home. The white man does not enter into this social life, however, nor does the woman entertain her friends when he is home. Otherwise the relationship imposes few restrictions. She may be active in Negro church and club affairs and may give generously of her time and money to their enterprises. In a few cases the woman may be a leader in clubs and social activities, with complete acceptance on the part of the Negro group. According to one upper-class Negro man:

> Usually colored women who are mistresses of well-to-do white men have quite a social position because of their connections with good white families and because they have money at their disposal. And frequently

they get money for the Negro churches, the Christmas tree, and anything for which Negroes happen to be raising money.

This same attitude was expressed in various ways by other Negroes, some of whom stated: "Oh, well, if she's got a white man, she mus' be sumpin', 'cause if yo gotta white man, yo got evahting. Yes, indeed, yo' got evahting"; or "You know, I can name many colored mothers here who have actually made, or encouraged, their daughters to take white men. They think it's better for them than to marry a Negro who can't support them on six, or nine dollars a week. They think they'll be much better off economically. There's really nothing a colored man here can offer them." Comparisons between Negro and white men can even become a joking matter among Negro women, as in the case of a girl who laughed and said: "Caroline says she's sorry she didn't take her a white man instead of a black one, 'n having a whole lot of black children." The interviewer later asked Caroline about it, and she said: "Wal, a cullud man, none of 'em kin give you mo' dan fo' bits or a dolluh. I tol' my husband dat, 'n he says: 'So yo wants a white man?' I tell him I done make my choice."

Attitudes of Negroes toward miscegenation.—The situation is, thus, such that the Negro mistress of a white man has not only a home and family but also economic security and a measure of prestige within her own group. The foregoing statements suggest that, at least in some cases, the role of mistress to a white man was greatly to be desired, that some women expressed regret at marrying a Negro rather than accepting the advances of whites, and that mothers have been known to openly encourage their daughters to accept white men. The white men thus find Negro women available to them as sexual partners, and the choicest Negro girls may even be unavailable to the Negro men. One colored man gave examples of colored girls in Old City "who have been sent to college, at great sacrifice, by their parents" and who have got new ideals and ways of thinking, new tastes and standards. Then they come back here and find there is no work of the kind they have been taught to do. So they end up by getting a white man. White men are always after them. A white man can give them the clothes and leisure and money that they have been taught to want in college.

Such examples, though not numerous, were frequent enough to warrant comment.

Although many of the Negro women regard this situation as one which offers them considerable opportunity, the Negro men are uniformly antagonistic. One young Negro man said with obvious exaggeration:

It's rife in this school here. Teachers and students too. Course, there's a few exceptions, but quite few. But I hate that kind of business. It makes me sick in my stomach to think of it happening. It really does make me sick. I don't see any excuse for it; they just want the money and dresses some white man can give 'em.

A typical male attitude was expressed with vehemence by a Negro who said: "I can't stan' dese white men gittin' cullud girls. It steams me up, I guess. I gits mad all ovuh."

It appears, then, not only that the Negro man is subordinated in all his relations to the whites but that his subordinate role weakens his relations with women of his own group. If he marries, his wife may at least sometimes compare him with that potential ideal, a white lover. If he seeks after the more attractive girls, or those educated or better dressed, he must compete with the white man who can offer money, prestige, and security. The hopelessness of the situation was shown in a story told by an upper-class Negro girl about a Negro boy who approaches her in behalf of his white employer. When she berated him for his action, he replied: "I'd like you myself, yes indeed, I'd like you fo' myself, but I works for him."

Effects of miscegenation.—The offspring of these unions of white men and Negro women introduce a significant element into the Negro group. Although the caste controls relegate them to their mother's caste, their biological inheritance reduces the differences in physical appearance between them and the white group. Even casual observation reveals that a very large percentage of the Old City Negroes have white blood, and reliable informants claimed that the extent of intermixture appeared to be much greater there than in other communities in the state. This intermixture has resulted in a very wide variation in the appearance of the Negroes, ranging from those showing no indications of any white blood to those who cannot be distinguished from the whites in appearance.

It is the belief of many Negroes in Old City that the extensive miscegenation has definitely affected the general relations between the two groups. They insist that the caste rules are not so rigidly applied and that the Negroes are not so strongly subordinated as they are elsewhere in the state. As they express it, the two groups "get along well." The popular belief in the function of miscegenation as a softener of the rigors of caste was voiced by one Negro:

> I'll tell you why they get along well here. It's easy to see why. So many of these white men got colored children and families. Why there are two white men who *live* with their colored families. And there are gangs of them who live with colored women or got colored children. That's why they don't start hurting people. They don't know who they'd be hitting. They might hit some of their own children.

Another Negro man thought that "if any violence starts, a white man who has a colored son or daughter will think about this colored child of his, and he'll be against violence." When a colored interviewer asked, "Why is Old City better for Negroes than these other places?" one man laughed and said:

> You know why. So many white men have colored children or run with colored women. Do you think they can be so hard on Negroes when they always run with colored girls? You know they can't be with colored women all the time and still be nasty to them. That's what accounts for the way these Negroes get along here.

White interest in Negro kin.—Negroes tend to emphasize the ties of blood kinship extending across the caste barrier as a factor affecting caste behavior. Since the caste controls prohibit any open acknowledgment of kinship, however, it is to be expected that the whites would deny such an influence. Nevertheless, the Negroes assert that the whites show considerable interest in their Negro kin. One Negro nurse volunteered the following comment: "Oh my gawd, yes. Dey sho owns dere cullud kin. Dey int'rested 'n' always askin' 'bout 'em, 'n' dey'll do fo' 'em if dey gits in need. Dese white folks almost proud of dere cullud kin. It's funny, aw right, but it's true." Such a comment may be overenthusiastic, but a colored woman told an interviewer how a white woman stopped her on the street one day and asked how Ellen was, saying: "You know she is one of our own and she looked rather badly the last time I saw her. We wouldn't want anything to happen to her."

In the case of the Negro children of white men, it is certain that many gain some benefits from their relationship to the white caste. As was indicated in preceding statements, the men often fulfil the role of father as far as the caste system will permit. They care for their children, clothe and educate them, and may even live with them. In some cases the white fathers send their Negro children away to be educated, and in a number of instances have provided for them in their wills. One white man told how "in the early days a man here had a big plantation and when he died he left half to his white children and half to his colored children." He then said: "That was only fair. Those niggers still have their place; they are good niggers. But the white children have let theirs get away." The advantages of having a white father are clearly recognized by many Negro children. One colored school child made the wistful statement: "Ollie's father is white and she can git anything she wants. Guess I could too if I had a white daddy."

Attitudes toward mixed bloods.—The possession of a noticeable amount of white blood tends to affect the relations of an individual with both Negroes and whites. All the stigmas of the Negro group, as previously mentioned, are associated with physical appearance; and it is the black Negro who is regarded as mean, ignorant, primitive, and animal-like. The light-colored Negro, however, is conceived of as "smarter," more intelligent, more "civilized" (more "like the whites" in behavior and ability). These beliefs are not restricted to either group but are frequently expressed by both Negroes and whites. Sometimes the comment of Negroes is very extreme, as in the case of two Negroes overheard discussing "blackness." One of them said: "A black nigguh is the meanes' rascal God evah made! I mean it. A black nigguh is jes' natchally mean. He always suspects you of trying to beat him out of something or take something from him." His companion corroborated his opinion: "My grandmother raised me. My mother didn't do nuthin' fuh me 'cept born me. My grandmother wuz uh little black woman, an' she wuz one of the evilest black women God evah made! Dat's de truth. He's right about dat. Dey really evil!" Cases were known where light-skinned grandparents trained their children to condemn a black parent, the child saying of her mother: "Oh, she's black!"

Although the whites attribute superior qualities to the Negroes of mixed blood, there tends to be a general antagonism toward them. Such Negroes are constant evidence that, in spite of the principles of caste endogamy, the informal processes of intermixture are slowly lessening the physical differences between the two groups, eliminating those very physical differences which the whites make the basis of the subordinate position of the Negro group. Since the mixed bloods are conceived of as having white characteristics, moreover, they are suspected of being rebellious against the restrictions of the caste structure. They "want to get out of their place." Whites state that they "never have any trouble with the black ones but most of the trouble is with the mulattoes .... the white blood makes them bad," or that, "as soon as they get enough white blood to be more ambitious, they are liable to give trouble." Such "bad niggers" face the antagonism and even the hate of whites.

"Passing for white."—The extent to which the social gulf separates even *biologically white* members of the lower caste from the other "white" persons in the upper caste is vividly illustrated by the practice of "passing." There are many Negroes in Old City whom even a practiced eye could never distinguish from the "whites." To these individuals of mixed blood the avenue of complete escape from the caste stigma is opened, that of moving entirely out of the Negro group and of "passing for white." To "pass" successfully, it is necessary that the individual be indistinguishable from whites in appearance. This necessity limits the possibility to a comparatively small proportion of the Negro group. In the area studied, moreover, it is necessary for the individual to move to another community where he is unknown and where his identity with the Negro group has not been established. Finally, he must sever all connections which might identify him with his past position. He must abandon all relations with his former friends and kindred and must conceal himself so completely from them that they will never see or know him again. Failing to do this, he lives in continual risk of having his past revealed, either through malice or accident.

It thus appears that "passing" has the characteristics of sociological death and rebirth. The individual completely severs all relations with his past life and conceals himself from all who knew him, so that he is as completely removed from his former social relations as if he were actually dead. Once having left his past life behind, he must then re-establish himself in a new life and in a new pattern of behavior. He must be a white, must act as a white, and must become completely identified with the white group. He must be reborn as a new social personality.

To be successful, such a change depends not only upon a complete readjustment of the behavior of the individual but also upon a large number of chance factors entirely beyond his control. It is not surprising that "passing" is much more frequent in the northern cities, where the individual can most easily lose all contact with his past and where the penalties for discovery are not so great. In the larger cities it is fairly common for individuals to pass for white occupationally and yet to retain their social contacts with the Negro group. This practice was mentioned by girls in Old City who had formerly worked in white department stores in Chicago but had never cut themselves off from the Negro group. Such conditions could not exist for any length of time in the smaller southern communities, where the entire pattern of behavior must be either Negro or white and where every white feels a responsibility for keeping the Negroes in their "proper" place. The latter behavior is illustrated by the story of a local white man who noticed a Negro girl from Old City "passing" in a town of another state. He immediately notified the police in the town.

A similar case occurred in Old City when a local Negro man, son of a prominent white, returned after an absence of several years and attempted to "pass." At first he was successful and obtained a job on a government boat, a "white man's job." He was reported also to have been going with white girls. After a few months he was drowned, accidentally, according to the official reports. It was rumored, however, that the white men with whom he worked had discovered that he was a Negro, had knocked him in the head, and thrown him overboard.

In this case it was interesting to note the behavior of the whites after the drowning. The boat captain first reported that the man was white, so that the newspapers handled the story as "white," giving it headlines on the front page and not mentioning the man's color. This was the usual method of reporting the death of a white person. The story ran for several days while a search was conducted for the body, which had floated downstream. As soon as the editor discovered that the man had been a Negro, however, the story was immediately relegated to an inside page, shortened considerably, and it was stated that the dead man had been a Negro. After the body had been recovered, the mother tried to have her son buried in the white cemetery, but the officials refused and forced her to bury him in the Negro cemetery. It was apparent that from the moment it was learned that the man was socially a Negro the whites immediately treated him as such in every respect, from the form of the news story to the burial of the body. The white group, generally, took the attitude that, regardless of the truth of the rumor about the circumstances of his death, violent action was only to be expected and would have occurred eventually. The Negro had completely flaunted the caste taboos and therefore deserved to die.

It is evident, then, that endogamy reinforces the social subordination of the Negroes. Although there are some sexual relationships across the caste line, in no cases do they alter the endogamous pattern. All offspring automatically become Negroes. Such relationships cannot be legalized, nor do the caste sanctions allow a mixed Negro-white family to function as a normal family unit. When a Negro attempts to "pass," he has left the social position where his family "placed" him and must be punished. Endogamy is the keystone of the caste system.

"KEEPING THE NEGRO IN HIS PLACE"

"Caste" is, then, no mere conceptual device for analyzing Negro-white relations in Old City. It is a vigorous reality, as the sanctions for the subordination of the Negro and the maintenance of endogamy have revealed. The caste system is at work in every aspect of life in Old City; and Part II of this volume deals, in detail, with the operation of the caste controls in the distribution of economic and political power. The caste division also is directly responsible for the existence of two separate and distinct systems of social classes among Negroes and whites, both of which will be analyzed in subsequent chapters.

All the social structures in the society operate to reinforce the caste system—associations, churches, the courts, even the schools and the Negro class system—for none of these challenges the fundamental separate, endogamous nature of the two caste groups. Relations between Negroes and whites generally proceed smoothly, with each group playing its "proper" role. Habit and the law are not the only sanctions for conformity, however; upon occasion, direct physical punishment is used "to keep the Negroes in their place."

Direct punishment of Negroes.—Examination of the behavior of both Negroes and whites shows that there is considerable variation from the behavior demanded by the dogma of caste. Nevertheless, there are limits to the extent to which variation is permitted; when these limits are reached, the white group asserts its superior position and punishes the offender by either legal or extralegal means. In cases of infractions of the rules of caste behavior the whites often act directly in punishing the offender, as has been indicated in several examples cited above. In fact, it is considered entirely correct for the white person to resort directly to physical attack upon the Negro. Thus, if a Negro curses a white, the white may knock the Negro down; and failure to do so may even be considered as a failure in his duty as a white. The white must always be ready to maintain his superordinate position, even by physical violence. Speaking of some trouble he had once had with a Negro over an account, a white man stated:

> I looked up his account and it had a pair of shoes charged to him. He claimed that he hadn't bought them but I told him someone must have bought them on his account as we didn't usually make mistakes. He got mad and said I was lying and I hauled off and hit him in the mouth and cut my finger. He then started to hit me and someone ran up and hit him. He turned to the other fellow and chased him down in the cellar. When that nigger came out of the cellar he was the bloodiest thing I ever saw, there must have been fifty people who took a poke at him.

Another white businessman had a similar story:

> I remember one time down at the mill, I was paying off and I had twenty-five dollars in quarters. You know the kind of bag they come in? Well, this nigger came in; he didn't do anything, but he had that insolent

kind of manner about him that always did make me mad. So he said something to me in that kind of sassy way of his and I just picked up my twenty-five dollars and hit him over the head with it. It was a pretty good thing to hit with, but just as I was going to hit him a second time I thought, "what if I should break the bag over his head?" Then where would I be with all my quarters on the ground? So I decided it wasn't worth it and I slapped him with my hand the second time.

In some cases, where individual action is not taken, either through fear of the consequences or for other reasons, the white man may organize a group which visits the Negro later and punishes him. Although such actions are entirely extra-legal, the whites frankly admit that they occur, one man stating that in Old City "we don't often have any trouble. They do sometimes run some Negro out who gets too sassy with a white man. They just tell him to leave or give him a whipping and put him on a train."

It is a common belief of many whites that Negroes will respond only to violent methods. In accordance with their theory of the "animal-like" nature of the Negro, they believe that the formal punishments of fines and imprisonment fail to act as deterrents to crime. As one planter stated it:

The best thing is not to take these young bucks into the courthouse for some small crime but to give them a paddling. That does them more good than a jail sentence. If I catch a Negro stealing a hog or some chickens, what is the use of taking him into court? He would get a fine or jail sentence and unless I pay him out he will lie up in jail and when he gets out he will keep on stealing.

In accordance with this belief, it is a very common practice in the rural areas for the planters, themselves, to judge and punish the Negroes for petty crimes as well as for infractions of the caste rules. This is so well accepted as a practice that a white justice of the peace reported that "most of the planters when they catch one of their hands stealing . . . . will take them out and give them a beating and that's the end of it. It never gets into court." Not only is this practice generally recognized, but many of the judges and lawyers thoroughly approve of it, one justice of the peace stating that he believed "in the whipping-post for these petty crimes—it would do a lot more good than anything else." He mentioned a "malicious-mischief" case in which he gave the Negro prisoner a choice of "six months" or a whipping; "he took the whipping and has been a good Negro ever since." In other cases Negroes were whipped and ordered out of the county.

Punishment for infractions of sex taboos.—As might be expected, infractions by Negroes of the taboo on white women evokes the use of violence more readily than any other caste violation. The Negro man who dares such violations risks a terrible retribution. In the case of rape, the Negro, if caught, faces certain death and probably death by torture at the hands of a mob. In the case previously noted it was shown that, despite the fact that many whites doubted the guilt of the Negro, he was saved from a mob only to be given the forms of a legal trial, conviction, and death sentence: "They tried and then hung him; that was the only thing they could do."

When a white woman acquiesces to an affair with a Negro, the punishment is generally not so open or dramatic. The usual procedure is for a group of whites to waylay the couple, whip the Negro, and make them both leave town. In some instances the Negro may be killed, but this is unusual. Generally the whole affair is kept under cover. White men occasionally mentioned incidents such as "a case about two years ago," when "a waitress at the hotel was going out with this Negro man. A bunch laid for them and caught him but she got away. They whipped him and told him to leave and he hasn't been back. She never has been back either." In one case:

A couple of years ago, some of the fellows around here took out six or eight Negroes, beat them, and made them leave town. They had a broad leather strap with holes in it and every time they hit one it would bring blood. They would beat them and then take them out on the road and turn them loose, and they just kept right on going and never have come back here. One of them, they beat until he couldn't stand and they took him and put him on the train. There hasn't been any trouble since, but some are getting pretty sassy now.

Every whipping is designed to teach the other Negroes a lesson. One white man described the educational effect of a whipping as follows:

We often have to whip one of them around here who gets too uppity or insolent or does something. We don't run them off, because it usually does more good to let them come back to work so the other niggers will know about it. You may have noticed that tall yellow Negro who works at Buford's. We whipped him one time till I thought he would die, we laid it on so. There were some white whores who had them a fine place down on Duncan St., and we overheard him one night calling them and making a date with them. We phoned around and got a few men we knew together and went down there and waited for this nigger and the other who was with him. They came along and the other suspicioned something and broke and ran. We shot at him a few times but he got away and never has been back. We took this one out and whipped him and told him to be back at work the next day. Ever since then, whenever he sees me he tips his hat and has been a good nigger ever since.

Periodic "trouble" between the castes.—Although the whippings described above appear to be more or less routine punishments of Negroes for some specific violation of the caste rules, in many of them there is another factor involved. Periodically there seems to develop a situation in which a number of Negroes begin to rebel against the caste restrictions. This is not an open revolt but a gradual pressure, probably more or less unconscious, in which, little by little, they move out of the strict pattern of approved behavior. The whites feel this pressure and begin to express resentment. They say the Negroes are getting "uppity," that they are getting out of their place, and that something should be done about it. Frequently, the encroachment has been so gradual that the whites have no very definite occurrence to put their hands on; that is, most of the specific acts have been within the variations ordinarily permitted, yet close enough to the limits of variation to be irritating to the whites. Finally, the hostility of the whites reaches such a pitch that any small infraction will spur them to open action. A Negro does something which ordinarily might be passed over, or which usually provokes only a mild punishment, but the whites respond with violence. The

Negro victim then becomes both a scapegoat and an object lesson for his group. He suffers for all the minor caste violations which have aroused the whites, and he becomes a warning against future violations. After such an outburst, the Negroes again abide strictly by the caste rules, the enmity of the whites is dispelled, and the tension relaxes. The whites always say after such an outburst: "We haven't had any trouble since then."

In spite of the number of such incidents described by both Negro and white informants, it should be made clear that these are relatively rare occurrences. The informants prefaced their accounts by such statements as "It happened several years before," or "During the yellow fever epidemic," or "Just after the war." Regardless of the actual frequency of such brutal punishments, however, they do occur, and they stand as a warning to the Negro. Thus he lives under the shadow of an ever present threat. He is a Negro, and woe unto him if he forgets; if necessary, the whites can and will enforce their authority with punishment and death.

VARIATIONS IN CASTE BEHAVIOR

Variations incident to social class.[1]—Although the general etiquette of caste behavior for both Negroes and whites is fairly rigidly defined by the caste sanctions, a number of factors tend to cause limited variations. It has been seen that, in permanent sex affairs, much of the normal caste behavior in sexual matters may be altered or replaced by a family type of behavior. In the same manner, many occupational relations, especially the employer-servant relation, permit considerable variation from formal caste behavior. Moreover, the relative class position of the individuals involved has some effect upon their caste behavior. Not only does an upper-class Negro have a pattern of caste behavior somewhat different from that of a

[1] Chapters iii–v will develop the class pattern of the Negro and white castes in detail. At this point it is sufficient to note that well-defined upper, middle, and lower social classes exist within each caste. Each of these classes has its distinctive pattern of familial, recreational, and general social behavior.

lower-class Negro, but also the actions of each are further altered by the class position of the whites with whom they are in contact.

Within each caste, each social class is subordinated by the classes above it in the social hierarchy, although the pattern of class behavior is neither so clearly defined nor so rigidly enforced as that of caste behavior. The members of each class express their superordination and subordination in their relationships. In fact, the behavior of lower-class whites to upper-class whites is frequently very similar to the deferential behavior of Negroes to whites. At times, social class loyalties are sufficiently strong to cut across the caste line to a certain extent. Thus, in some economic situations the behavior of individuals on opposite sides of the caste line may take on the characteristics of class behavior, and a lower-class white may treat a lower-class Negro as an equal, or he may actually subordinate himself to an upper-class Negro. Always, however—and this is crucial—he may demand that the Negro act his caste instead of class role.

Lower-class whites and Negroes.—Examples of the effect of class behavior in modifying caste controls were frequently seen in the case of lower-class whites and Negroes. In many instances it was noticed that lower-class whites living in Negro neighborhoods treated their Negro neighbors in much the same way as they did their white neighbors. There were the usual gossiping, exchange of services, and even visiting. Extensive contact with lower-class whites on the part of the observers sometimes elicited comments such as this one, of a lower-class white woman:

There ain't nothing wrong with the niggers anyway. I always liked them, and I always had a lot of niggers for friends wherever I been. I just say if you treat them good, like they was real people, they'll be just as good with you as any white ones. I reckon I got as many colored people for friends as I got white right now. Out there on Jones Street where I was, I had lots of nigger friends. They was all crazy about me, up and down the street there. I always treat them good, you know.

THE SYSTEM OF COLOR-CASTES

I say it's just how you treat them. They always been good friends to me and I ain't got a word to say agin 'em. I think they ought to have their recognition just like white people. They feel the same about things and they ain't no different from us. They ought to be considered just the same. They all been here a long time and it ain't like we didn't owe them nothing. If it hadn't been for the niggers, the South wouldn't a been where it is now. It's all on account of the colored people we got where we is. You and me and everybody owes a lot to the niggers all right and they ought to have their recognition.

Evidences of neighborly relations were also apparent in comments by whites in rural areas, of which this is a sample:

Oh, they's just colored people all around us but we don't mind that none. They's right nice and friendly and we get on good with them. There's some white people on the next farm but they don't amount to nothin'. We don't have nothing to do with them. They're just ugly and ain't good neighbors at all. They ain't done nothing to help Bill at all, they ain't said a word nor asked him nothing about how he was going to do nor nothing. We been here since Saturday and they ain't never come near us at all, ain't been to the house here once. But them niggers there, they been just as nice; they come over and asked was there anything they could do, and they went out and helped Bill plow his field and all like that. It don't bother me none if there ain't no white people living near me. I'd a heap rather associate with that kind of niggers than with some white people. It don't make no difference to me if they's black or white, just so's they treat you decent.

Lower-class whites, surprisingly enough, were sometimes friendly in their attitudes toward middle-class Negroes, as in the case of a woman who said:

The niggers isn't such bad neighbors either. I thought I wouldn't like it at all when he rented them houses across the street to niggers, but they ain't bad. Like right across from us here, there is a perfesser. He is a perfesser up to that nigger college, you know. They're right high-up niggers and just as nice too.

They are right good neighbors, just as friendly and nice. Like when my daughter was so sick here before she died, the perfessor come over here to my husband and said if there was anything they could do to help us they would be glad to do it. I declare I thought that was right nice; that's real neighbors. There ain't so many white folks'll do like that when you're in trouble that way.

DEEP SOUTH

Middle-class whites, on the other hand, even though living near Negroes, never developed neighborly relations and were generally antagonistic. A case of a Negro woman and child who moved into a lower-middle-class white neighborhood illustrates the prevailing attitude of middle-class whites.

The observer was chatting with a lower-middle-class white woman who began to discuss Negroes:

We got some new neighbors in there yesterday, some colored people, and everybody is up in arms about it. Everyone in the neighborhood who rents from Mrs. McCulloch has been in to see her about it and I went too. Well, anyway, Mrs. McCulloch told me that it was just an old colored mammy and her little grandson, a little boy four years old, and they wouldn't bother us any. She was right nice about it, said they's have to keep the little feller out in the back and not let him bother us. She said if any of us had any complaint, after they'd been here awhile, then she'd just have to put them off. I didn't feel so bad when I found it was just an old mammy and the little boy, but when I seen all them Negroes over there yesterday I didn't know what was going on. I thought if they had children I didn't know what I was going to do. I didn't want the children out here playing with my children. I suppose the little boy will be all right if they keep him out back but there isn't any place for him out there really. She can't keep him back there, right on the bayou all the time. Yesterday he was out front with three or four other little darkies playing on my front walk. I don't know what she will do with him when others come out to play with him, because of course he can't just be by himself all the time.

Later, in answer to an inquiry about the welfare of the new neighbors, she said:

Oh, they moved out. They was only there about a week, I guess, and moved off. The lady had them move, she couldn't have them there. There was the old colored mammy and her grandson, I guess he was about seven or so. Well, the lady who rented the place, she has a daughter about eight or nine, and she was playing with the colored boy all the time. Of course, she just couldn't stand for that, so she just had to ask them to go. She couldn't put up with that, of course. But you know it was awful having them right there so close by. It wasn't like they was a little way off, you know, but they was living right there among us that way, right in our very middle!

52

THE SYSTEM OF COLOR-CASTES

Treatment of upper-class Negroes.—In some cases it was observed that white filling-station attendants would speak to upper-class Negro customers and even touch their hats as they did to upper-class or upper-middle-class white customers. In referring to at least one prominent Negro woman, the upper-class whites sometimes used the term "Mrs." In some instances this seemed to be an *unconscious* recognition of her class position, since the whites seemed unaware of what they had said, and when questioned would deny their behavior vigorously! In other instances this woman was addressed as "Mrs." by white store clerks, a direct reversal of the proper caste behavior. It appears, then, that whites sometimes ignored minor aspects of caste etiquette and, both consciously and unconsciously, followed correct class, rather than caste, behavior in relation to upper-class Negroes.

A similar occurrence was described by an upper-class white from the neighboring Rural County, who said:

I called on a nigger in Old City to see about buying some timber from him. He has an office there; when I went in, he got up and offered to shake hands! I didn't know just what to do and wondered what I was getting in to, but I shook hands with him. After I told him who I was and what I wanted, he was all right and never did try that again.

Such a gesture on the part of a lower-class Negro would have evoked an immediate response from the white in the form of a "cussin' out" or a blow. Coming from an upper-class Negro, however, this action left the white undecided and uncomfortable, and he actually shook hands. According to the white man, when the Negro learned his identity, he never again attempted to overstep the bounds of proper deference toward an upper-class white man.

Sometimes, however, solidarity between upper-class Negroes and upper-class whites seems evident. A leading Negro told of instances in which the upper-class and the upper-middle-class whites had promised him protection against lower-class whites. In one case, a lower-class white woman first threatened him with a gun and, after being disarmed, accused him of striking her and tried to rouse a mob. The chief of police and other whites promised the Negro man protection; when the white woman took the case to court, the judge threw it out. On another occasion, an upper-class Negro pharmacist accidentally ran down a drunken white, who died. The leading whites offered their assistance, and even a group of white women called on him and said: "We want to tell you how sorry we are that you should have this trouble, and don't worry one bit. We know it wasn't your fault and we don't intend to let anything happen to you. We want you to stay here in Old City." This could never have occurred in the case of a lower-class Negro.

Rural and urban variations in caste behavior.—The whole pattern of caste behavior and controls is also significantly affected by the differences between rural and urban situations. It is commonly recognized, for instance, that the rural Negro is more subordinated in his behavior than the urban Negro. In fact, the rural Negro frequently follows the formal pattern of caste etiquette exactly. He is exceedingly polite in all his dealings with the whites; he always says "Yas sah" and "No sah"; he pulls his team to the side of the road to let the white man pass; he greets even strange whites who may pass on the road with a tip of his hat and a polite word; he stands with his hat in his hand when talking to a white; and he generally acts the humble and obedient servant.

This rural behavior differs greatly from the ordinary behavior of the Negro in Old City, who, unless he has an established, direct relationship with a white, frequently exhibits only a minimum of deferential behavior. The urban Negroes often crowd whites in the stores, ignore them on the streets and sidewalks, and frequently are accused by whites of "seeing how far they can go." The whites are well aware of this difference in behavior and often speak with wistful approbation of the politeness and "good manners" of the country Negroes, as compared to those in the city. The whites in a neighboring county frequently complained that the whites in Old City are too lenient with the Negroes and "don't keep them in their places."

This difference can be understood in terms of the different structure of relations between Negroes and whites in the two areas. In the rural areas the whites are principally middle-class and upper-class planters, and the Negroes are predominantly lower-class tenant-farmers. The relations between the two groups are, therefore, almost entirely relations between lower-class tenants and the highly superordinate white landlords. The relations between tenant and planter are generally of such a nature that the planter exercises continuous and detailed control over much of the Negro's activities, and under such conditions it is not surprising that the subordinate deferential lower-caste patterns become well established and extend to all contacts with white people.

In the city, on the other hand, the relations between Negroes and whites are much more varied, just as the class positions of the individuals are more varied. Thus, the upper-class and upper-middle-class whites frequently have little direct relations with any Negroes except house servants or, possibly, a few laborers. The lower-middle-class whites, however, have contact with all classes of Negroes through various occupational relationships in stores, as foremen or laborers, and so on. Urban lower-class whites often work beside Negroes in factories or on the river and may have Negro neighbors with whom they are friendly. This diversity of relations tends to prevent the formation of simple and uniform behavior patterns such as the rural Negroes show.

The matter of controlling the Negroes through direct force also shows rural and urban differences. In the rural areas the punishment of Negroes is largely in the hands of white planters. They whip Negroes both for infractions of the caste rules and for minor crimes, such as fighting or theft. Furthermore, the planter for whom the Negro works either participates in the punishment himself or gives his permission. Some planters assert that they are solely responsible for their own Negroes and that no one else has any right to punish them. Here one finds a situation in which there is a paternalistic control and responsibility on the part of the planters, who personally direct, control, and punish the Negro tenants. The planter group is extremely antagonistic, however, to any whipping or punishment of Negroes by the lower-class or lower-middle-class whites and resents their appearance at any such affairs conducted by the planters. In the city the situation is different. Here upper-class individuals do not have the extensive direct relations with Negroes found in the rural areas, and their paternalistic responsibilities and controls are lacking or weakened. Coincident with this, we find that upper-class and upper-middle-class people rarely participate in the whipping of urban Negroes. Those who own plantations may be active in controlling the Negroes on their own and neighboring plantations, but in the urban situation these activities are left to others. Although the rural Negroes are frequently whipped for theft and other minor crimes, in the city the informal controls over these violations are replaced by the formal controls of the police and courts. Instead of receiving a whipping, the Negro is tried and sentenced. Generally, the urban Negro is subjected to informal punishments by the whites only for infractions of the caste rules, not for legal crimes.

While the upper-class whites agree with the principle of punishing the Negroes for caste infractions, especially for infractions of the sex taboo, nevertheless they rarely participate themselves. In general, it is the lower-middle-class whites who take it upon themselves to control the urban Negroes and to "keep them in hand." Complaints about the behavior of the city Negroes, the suggestions that "something should be done about it," and expressions of antagonism to any small infractions of the caste rules usually come from the lower-middle class. Also, in all recent whippings which were studied in Old City the leaders and most of the participants were from this class. There was, in fact, one group of lower-middle-class whites who seemed to take upon themselves the whole burden of controlling the Negroes and derived much pleasure from such "affairs."

It was noted, also, that, while members of the lower-middle class occasionally had Negro neighbors, they never developed a neighborly relation with them and were generally antagonistic. Lower-middle-class individuals, in their everyday activities and occupations, seldom develop direct superordinate relations to many Negroes and frequently are placed in the subordinate position of serving as clerks to Negro customers. They achieve their superordination through direct force. Such aggressive behavior also has an additional function, in that their efforts to "keep the niggers in their place" not only reinforces their own social position but also that of the whole white caste. They are performing a "duty" in defending the highest ideals of the southern whites.

SUMMARY

The caste system, as has been shown, controls and defines the relations between the two color groups and is the principal factor in the interactions between any Negro and any white. It is expressed not only in behavior but also in the concepts and ideologies of the groups. Furthermore, the caste system limits the variation from the caste dogmas and enforces the systems of control by which extreme variations are prevented or punished. It thus provides a very definite code of behavior by which every individual knows how he should act and what he can expect in his relations with the other group. Although the principal pressures of the restrictions and the controls bear upon the Negro group, they are not unorganized and unpredictable restrictions, and the Negro who accepts and abides by them may achieve a high degree of security in his relations to the whites.

This caste structure, however, does not exist separate and apart from the total society. It is only one element in the total structure and, although the most clearly defined, is affected by and, in turn, affects all others. Thus sexual relations, occupational relations, the class structure, etc., all introduce factors which modify behavior in specific situations. An increase in the number and frequency of such modifying factors results in an increase in the variations of behavior from the caste dogmas defining the appropriate behavior for Negroes. As a result of this fact, the relatively simple rural and the more complex urban areas show striking variations in behavior and systems of control while adhering to the same general principle and concept of caste. One of the most important factors in modifying caste behavior is the class structure of both the Negro and white castes. The chapters immediately following will deal with these class divisions within each caste group.

CHAPTER III

THE CLASS SYSTEM OF THE WHITE CASTE

THE "caste line" defines a social gulf across which Negroes may not pass either through marriage or those other intimacies which Old City calls "social equality." A ritual reminder is omnipresent in all relationships that there are two separate castes—a superordinate white group and a subordinate Negro group. Within each of these separate social worlds there are other divisions: families, religious groups, associations, and a system of social classes.[1]

The most fundamental of these divisions within each caste is that of social class; and the researchers, both white and Negro, were initiated into the intricacies of class behavior at the same time that they were being taught how to act toward persons of the opposite caste. Whether it was a matter of accepting an invitation to a party, deciding to visit a family, or planning to attend a church, the participant-observers, who had been "adopted" by people of relatively high social status within their respective castes, were advised upon the important matter of "who" and "where." Certain people were to be approached, not as equals, but as subordinates. There were places where one "could not afford to be seen" having a "good time," or even worshipping, without loss of status unless it was for purposes of research.

---

[1] As here used, a "social class" is to be thought of as the largest group of people whose members have intimate access to one another. A class is composed of families and social cliques. The interrelationships between these families and cliques, in such informal activities as visiting, dances, receptions, teas, and larger informal affairs, constitute the structure of a social class. A person is a member of that social class with which most of his participations, of this intimate kind, occur.

There were many clues to assist in the "placing" of people within broad limits, some easily observable, such as peculiarities of speech, type of clothing worn, the manner of drinking and "carrying" liquor, or occupation. (Among Negroes there was the added factor of color evaluation.) Other criteria were far more subtle—genealogies and inner thoughts—which were ascertainable only after prolonged acquaintance with the society. "Stratifying" the inhabitants of Old City was, thus, one of the major research problems, that is, finding out the values cherished by people of varying circumstances, checking their behavior against their beliefs about status, and finding a systematic way of describing the class structure of the society. First, we shall examine the class divisions within the white society and, later, those within the Negro caste.

SOCIAL STRATIFICATION

As one becomes acquainted with the white people of Old City, he soon realizes that they are continually classifying themselves and others. There are "Negroes" and "whites"— the caste groups—a relatively simple dichotomy. There are also "leading families," "fine old families," "the four hundred," "the society crowd," "plain people," "nice, respectable people," "good people, but nobody," "po' whites," "red necks," etc.—all terms used to refer to different groups within the white caste. Not only do the whites frequently refer to these subdivisions within their own caste group, but they do so in such a manner as to indicate that they think in terms of a social hierarchy with some people at the "top," some at the "bottom"; with some people "equal" to themselves, and others "above" or "below" them. There are recurrent expressions such as: "He isn't our social equal," "She isn't our kind," "They are just nobody," "Those folk are the way-high-ups," "They're nothing but white trash!" "Oh, they're plain people like us." These expressions refer not only to individuals but also to groups, so that one may speak of superordinate and subordinate groups within the white society. And, most important of all, people tend to act in conformity with these conceptions of their "place" and the social position of others in the society.

When the individuals and groups so designated are studied, striking differences between them with regard to family relations, recreational behavior, standards of living, occupation and income, education, and other traits are immediately apparent. On the basis of these differences, it is possible to define the social classes within the white society and to describe them in detail. It was soon evident that people at all levels were thinking in terms of, and often referring to, three broad social classes—"upper," "middle," and "lower"— although, when designating particular individuals, there were divergences of opinion as to their social position. There was some difference of opinion, too, as to the things that made one upper, middle, or lower; but an analysis of the relative social positions of the informants showed that these variations in conceptions of class status were, themselves, related to the social position of the informant. Thus, a "po' white," as defined by persons of the higher classes, conceived of the total structure in a somewhat different manner from an upper-class planter. In other words, the social perspective varied with the social position of the individual. People in the same social positions agreed, in the main, however, on the traits which characterized the classes, although the class traits did not apply to everyone within a class in absolute fashion. Thus, a member of a group defined by consensus as "superior" might have a few characteristics in common with a person of an "inferior" group; but when each group was considered as a whole, the differences were large and significant. Thus, "the society crowd," as a group, owns more property than the "po' whites," although some "society folks" own none at all; the "poor, but respectable" people, in the aggregate, are more church-minded than "trash," though some are not affiliated with churches.

The researchers were able to describe the structure of the

society by interviewing a large number of informants drawn from various occupational, associational, and other status groups who "placed" individuals and stated their conceptions of class criteria. The observers were also alert to "off-the-record" remarks and to behavior in public places and in crisis situations, in order to ascertain the bearers of prestige, the wielders of power, and the persons who associated together on various occasions. The resulting picture of the society is that of a class system in operation, with a description of the way it appears to the people within it.

While generalized conceptions of the class structure were readily obtainable from interviewing, a detailed study of class characteristics depended upon a method of determining the social position of specific individuals. The first step was to establish a series of individuals distributed from the "top" of the society to the "bottom." This was done through interviewing, since almost any member of the society could point to some other individuals or groups whom he considered at the very top, at the very bottom, or "in between." Interviewing and observing the people who were thus placed resulted in the identification of a group of individuals who considered themselves either superordinate, subordinate, or equal in relationship to one another. Continuous interviewing of these informants made possible a detailed study of their ideology and behavior. Wide discrepancies in placement were studied as special cases, with the purpose of relating them to the system of relationships which was gradually emerging, and of accounting for the differing opinions of their social position. Thus, over a period of eighteen months, interviewing, coupled with observation of overt behavior, permitted the researchers to establish with certainty a sample of the personnel of the different social classes.

After identifying these individuals within the classes, it was possible to study their relationships and characteristics in detail and to correlate traits such as income, property, education, and church and associational memberships with social position and general behavior. An additional check was provided by interviewing for the "values" which people attributed to various types of behavior and class traits when they talked about them. It was thus possible to relate ideology to social class.

Because of the limitations of time, it was impossible to stratify every individual in the society by the interview-observation technique; but once the characteristics of the known individuals had been determined, criteria were available for placing any individual about whom some important facts were available.

Thus, when a person's participation could not be checked, if some pertinent facts about his job, his family, his education, and his children were known, one could state the participation potentialities which his social personality bore.

On the basis of the attitudes of many informants of various social positions, together with observations of many kinds of social behavior, the researchers concluded that the three main class divisions recognized by the society could be objectively described. Each of these was characterized by its particular behavior pattern and by a distinctive ideology. Closer study revealed the existence of subclasses within each of these three larger groups, and these are referred to in this study as the "upper-upper class," "lower-upper class," "upper-middle class," "lower-middle class," "upper-lower class," and the "lower-lower class." We shall examine, first, the conceptions of class which each of these groups holds, for the very way in which people conceive of the class divisions varies with their social position.

CLASS PERSPECTIVE AND THE CLASS STRUCTURE

The upper-upper class.—It was evident from the outset that certain persons were at the very top of the social hierarchy. They were accorded deference in nearly all types of relationships; people were anxious to associate with them; they belonged to the exclusive churches; their names were sought for patron's lists; they lived in imposing mansions inherited from Old City's "antebellum past" (or at least their parents did); and, on ritual occasions of high import, they dominated the scene and tended to organize community behavior. They were, without doubt, in almost everyone's eyes, members of the "upper-upper class." Neither whites nor Negroes questioned their position even when they resented it; and resentment, itself, tended to dissolve when they were functioning as symbols of the total community on such occasions as the annual Historical Week, when visitors from the entire nation came to Old City. It was this upper-upper class which made the finest distinctions when ranking or "stratifying" other people.

Members of this highest status group recognize five class divisions in the society (see Fig. 2). They visualize themselves at the top of the society, an *"old* aristocracy" whose superordination has its origin and stability in "time." They consider themselves the highest group in the society by inheritance, because, as they phrase it: "Our families have always been the best people." Immediately below them on the social scale the members of this class point out another group, which has been designated the "lower-upper class." These are people with whom the "old aristocracy" is willing to participate in informal relationships, whom they know intimately and recognize as fundamentally no different from themselves in income, consumption standards, education, intellectual interests, and general behavior pattern. But they are not *"old* aristocracy"; they haven't been upper class long enough. An analysis of these two upper groups indicates that the division between them is reflected hardly at all by differences in overt behavior or other characteristics. It is a subjective division which finds objective expression only in certain very intimate situations when antagonisms between the two groups are verbalized.

Beneath the lower uppers, the upper uppers see the "nice, respectable people" (the upper-middle class) who have "never been prominent at all." They know these people by name,

UPPER-UPPER CLASS   LOWER-UPPER CLASS

Upper-Upper		Lower-Upper
"Old aristocracy"	UU	"Old aristocracy"
"Aristocracy," but not "old"	LU	**"Aristocracy," but not "old"**
"Nice, respectable people"	UM	"Nice, respectable people"
"Good people, but 'nobody'"	LM	"Good people, but 'nobody'"
	UL	
"Po' whites"	LL	"Po' whites"

UPPER-MIDDLE CLASS   LOWER-MIDDLE CLASS

Upper-Middle		Lower-Middle
"Society" { "Old families"	UU	
"Society" but not "old families"	LU	"Old aristocracy" (older) | "Broken-down aristocracy" (younger)
"People who should be upper class"	UM	"People who think they are somebody"
"People who don't have much money"	LM	**"We poor folk"**
	UL	"People poorer than us"
"No 'count lot"	LL	"No 'count lot"

UPPER-LOWER CLASS   LOWER-LOWER CLASS

Upper-Lower		Lower-Lower
	UU	
	LU	
"Society" or the "folks with money"	UM	"Society" or the "folks with money"
"People who are up because they have a little money"	LM	"Way-high-ups," but not "Society"
"Poor but honest folk"	UL	"Snobs trying to push up"
"Shiftless people"	LL	**"People just as good as anybody"**

FIG. 2.—The social perspectives of the social classes

65

speak to them on the street, and may converse with them at church or associational meetings; but they do not participate with them at social affairs of the more intimate kinds.

The upper-middle class is contrasted with the "good people" who are "just nobody" (the lower-middle class). With the lower-middle class, the upper uppers have only formal and definitely limited relations, usually economic in nature, such as those of employer-to-employee or merchant-to-customer. The type of behavior in such relationships is explicitly delimited; and, in general, upper-upper individuals resent the social mobility of lower-middle-class persons, probably because such a movement involves a change in these relatively impersonal economic relationships and the corresponding traditional behavior pattern.

Finally, at the very bottom of the society are the people whom the upper uppers call the "working class," "the poorer class," or just "po' white." They have little contact with this group, tending to ignore their existence. They make no distinction between tenant-farmers, fishermen, factory workers, as these people, themselves, do. Nor do they distinguish between other variant behavior patterns within this lower-class world.

The lower-upper class.—The lower uppers, whom the upper uppers call "aristocracy, but not *old*," make the same general distinctions between social groups. They do not emphasize the distinction between themselves and the upper uppers so much as the upper uppers do, however. This may be attributed to the fact that most of the members of this group have, during their lifetime, been socially mobile, and they have moved into the upper class from the upper-middle group. Consequently, while they recognize themselves as a group apart from, and below, the upper uppers, they tend to ally themselves with this group and to minimize the value of family background. Their actual status is evident, however, in their individual relations and in their verbally expressed antagonisms toward the upper uppers on certain occasions. In several cases, lower uppers resisted subordination by upper-upper individuals through face-to-face criticisms of their ancestry. Thus, Mrs. Bowley, upper upper and proud of her family, was both hurt and indignant at lower-upper Mrs. Duncan's remarks about her ancestry:

I said something to Mrs. Duncan about being related to the Montgomerys. She said; "Well, that is nothing to be proud of. I wouldn't brag about it!" I said I didn't see why not; my father had always taught me to be proud of the Montgomery blood in my veins. Then she said that the first Montgomery was nothing but a gambler, and that that was nothing to be proud of. Well, that isn't true! He wasn't *really* a gambler . . . .

Similarly, the lower uppers' definition of the upper-middle class, as a group, is both vague and reluctant. Directly questioned, they frequently deny that persons stratified as upper middle are really below them on the social scale, or they will attempt an evasion. (Their overt behavior, however, belies their words.) They will say, for instance: "I don't mean that Mrs. Atkins and people like that aren't nice and all that. She is. She is very nice and well-thought-of here. We just don't happen to know her very well, and *she doesn't enjoy the same things we do.*" This hesitancy about actually identifying persons as upper-middle class is probably related to the fact that they, themselves, have rather recently moved out of the upper-middle stratum, and many of them still have kinsmen in this social position. (Equally logical, perhaps, are attempts by some persons to overestimate the social distance between themselves and the class from which they came.)

The lower-middle class, on the other hand, is clearly defined by these ascending uppers. In general, they have the same limited contact with the lower-middle class as the upper uppers have; but they seem less inclined to resent the rise of lower middles into the upper-middle class, or their economic improvement. This is, perhaps, due to the fact that specific limited relations with these persons, and a corresponding behavior pattern, are less well established and less fixed by tradition than in the case of upper-upper relations with the lower middles.

Toward the lower class, as a whole, lower uppers present the same indifference and lack of precise definition that their upper-upper associates display.

The upper-middle class.—Stratification of the society by persons immediately below the upper class (here designated the "upper-middle class") is frequently associated with an expression of moral attitudes and with definite conceptions of the positive value and important role of wealth. These persons are often unable to reconcile the existing social hierarchy with a hierarchy that "should be." In their thinking, their own class group "should be" the highest group in the society, since it is the wealthiest group and the one whose behavior reflects most precisely the traditional teachings of the Protestant church. In spite of this condemnatory attitude, however, they conceive of the upper class as a group separate from themselves. Its superordination in the existing scheme of things is generally acknowledged, albeit somewhat reluctantly. Occasionally, certain persons whom upper uppers place as lower uppers are not included in this group by the upper-middle class. But the *"old* aristocracy" is quite definitely assigned its place at the top; its ascendancy is resented; and the group is condemned for its "immoral behavior."

Upper-middle class individuals who are attempting to rise in the social scale point out beneath them the "lower middles" as a separate class group and almost invariably attempt to exaggerate their social distance from it. Behavior and attitudes of these mobile middle-class individuals toward the subordinate lower middles are similar to those of the upper class, and their relationships with this group tend to be formal and economic. Stable upper middles, however, know many lower middles and sometimes participate with them informally, especially in the younger age ranges. In general, they attribute this differentiation more to the lower economic position of these people than to other traits. They do not try to maintain great social distance between lower middles and themselves.

Like members of the upper-class groups, upper middles make no distinctions within the lower-class group, although they seem somewhat more aware of the presence of this group at the bottom of the white society. While they do have somewhat more frequent contact with them than uppers, especially in employer-employee relationships, all of the lower class is thought of as "just the working class," the "poorer class."

The lower-middle class.—"We poor folks" and the "other poor people like us" make up the lower-middle class. But, "it shouldn't be that way," they think. "The people who are up are there mainly because they have money," they insist. Persons in this group have rather strong class feelings. Above them they see the upper middles, people like themselves, but with more money. Above the upper middles, they recognize an "aristocracy." Within this "aristocracy" (upper upper and lower upper together) they distinguish between the older persons who have established their superiority through the possession of great wealth in the past and younger individuals, on the other hand, who are not now wealthy or who never have been. These latter have no claim to the position of "upper class," they say; yet they are there. They are just a "broken-down aristocracy." Lower middles think in terms of "younger" and "older" aristocrats, rather than in terms of an upper-upper and lower-upper class, with all age ranges within each group.

Toward the upper middles they level a frequent taunt, "They think they *are* somebody"; and as a group, lower middles prefer not to recognize the social distance between themselves and such people. They resent all attempts by this class to express any social distance. In general, too, they seem to resent mobility from the upper-middle class into the upper class more than they do mobility from their own ranks into the upper-middle class.

Here, for the first time, a group subdivides the lower class.

There is one group, immediately below them, for whom the lower middles have pity but whom they do not condemn or scorn. These are people "even poorer than us," the upper lowers, who are definitely distinguished from the "po' whites," the "no-count," and the "worthless"—the lower lowers.

The upper-lower class.—Members of the upper-lower class have a sense of solidarity and speak often of "people like us" as distinct both from the lower-middle class above them and the lower lowers below them. Like the middle classes, they think of social stratification in Old City as an absolute hierarchy of wealth. (They are less accurately informed of the actual economic status of individuals above them, however, than one would infer from their conversation.) Their interpretation of class differences is less often tinged with moral concepts than in the case of the middle class.

At the top of the social world, as they see it, is "Society," composed of nearly all those persons who are upper upper, lower upper, and upper middle. All these people are said to be "wealthy." Their high social position is thus recognized and accepted as a fact. Beneath "Society," the upper-lower class recognizes the members of the lower-middle class, whose assumption of social superiority they resent. They are sure that these people occupy a superordinate position simply because they have more wealth.

Between themselves and the lower-lower class, upper lowers make a very careful distinction in their verbalizations, although in actual overt behavior little social distance is maintained. They visit and borrow, exchange domestic services, and converse on the street and in the stores, although such relations are not so frequent as with members of their own group. Thus, while they participate as equals with lower lowers in many one-to-one, face-to-face relations, they do not, as a group, wish to be identified with those whom they consider inferior, unkempt, and improvident.

The lower-lower class.—The lower lowers, like the upper lowers, also see "Society" at the top, a vague category for persons above the lower-middle position. Lower-lower-class women occasionally refer to the "very wealthy ladies" in this group. Sometimes, even a few lower-middle-class individuals are included in "Society"; more often, however, lower-middle-class individuals are recognized as a separate group with "some money, but not Society." The small shopkeepers with whom they trade, some policemen, artisans with whom they have some contact, and other members of the lower-middle class are spoken of as "way high up" but distinct from "Society." Lower lowers resent the position of the upper-lower class, the members of which are thought to be socially ambitious and snobbish. Their attempts at refinement are generally ridiculed. The upper lowers' claim to a higher social position is thought to be unjustified and to be based entirely on their economic superiority, their better jobs, and more adequate housing.

Summary.—Members of any one class thus think of themselves as a group and have a certain unity of outlook. This is indicated by their frequent reference to "people like us" and to persons "not our kind." Expressions of this group solidarity are particularly prevalent when individuals are discussing groups immediately above and below them. When expressing resentment at exclusion from the class above and antagonism toward mobility from the class below, social classes betray unconsciously their sense of solidarity and "we-ness." It will be seen subsequently, too, that members of these classes and subclasses have a further unity through a common set of beliefs, a common pattern of overt behavior, and other traits which function as symbols of status.

While members of all class groups recognize classes above and below them, or both, the greater the social distance from the other classes the less clearly are fine distinctions made. Although an individual recognizes most clearly the existence of groups immediately above and below his own, he is usually not aware of the social distance actually maintained between his own and these adjacent groups. Thus, in all cases except that of members of the upper-lower class the individual sees only a minimum of social distance between his class and the adjacent classes. This is illustrated by the dotted lines in Figure 2. Almost all other class divisions, however, are visualized as definite lines of cleavage in the society with a large amount of social distance between them.

In general, too, individuals visualize class groups above them less clearly than those below them; they tend to minimize the social differentiations between themselves and those above. This difference in perspective is partly explained by the fact that class lines in the society are not permanent and rigid and that upward mobility is fairly frequent. It is, further, due to the natural tendency in such a status system to identify with "superiors." In view of this situation it is not surprising that individuals in the two upper strata make the finest gradations in the stratification of the whole society and that class distinctions are made with decreasing precision as social position becomes lower.

Not only does the perspective on social stratification vary for different class levels, but the very bases of class distinction in the society are variously interpreted by the different groups. People tend to agree as to where people are but not upon why they are there. Upper-class individuals, especially upper uppers, think of class divisions largely in terms of time—one has a particular social position because his family has "always had" that position. Members of the middle class interpret their position in terms of wealth and time and tend to make moral evaluations of what "should be." Both middle-class groups accept the time element as an important factor in the superordinate position of the "old aristocracy," but for the rest of the society they consider only individual wealth and and moral behavior as differentiating factors. Lower-class people, on the other hand, view the whole stratification of the society as a hierarchy of wealth. The lower lowers think that all those above them on the social scale are progressively wealthy and that their own subordination is dependent upon this economic factor alone. While upper lowers have a similar idea of those above them, they frequently add a moral note in explaining the subordinate position of lower lowers.

The identity of a social class does not depend on uniformity in any one or two, or a dozen, specific kinds of behavior but on a complex pattern or network of interrelated characteristics and attitudes. Among the members of any one class, there is no strict uniformity in any specific type of behavior but rather a range and a "modal average." One finds a range in income, occupation, educational level, and types of social participation. The "ideal type" may be defined, however, for any given class—the class configuration—from which any given individual may vary in one or more particulars. Also, two individuals may belong to the same association, fall in the same occupational category, belong to the same church, or have the same ideas about local politics; but identity in any one or two such particulars does not necessarily indicate that both individuals belong to the same social class. Class position is determined rather by the configuration of traits which an individual possesses.

An important aspect of this configuration is "ideology"— the set of concepts and the complex of attitudes toward individuals and institutions which individuals exhibit. The members of any one class or subclass share the same general attitudes and beliefs—that is, the same ideology. The conceptions of class which have been described in this section represent one aspect of the class ideologies; and while no systematic cataloguing of the beliefs and attitudes of each class toward all social structures is given in this study, the ideology of each class will be characterized in terms of one or two distinctive and fundamental concepts which dominate the thinking of each group. These will then be related to the other traits in the class configurations.

THE UPPER-CLASS CONFIGURATION

The idealization of the past.—The ideology of the upper class, as suggested above, is colored particularly by the concept of time. Stability in time is of supreme value to members of this class, and they conceive of the class structure as having its basis in lineage, in the stablity of a family's social position. An individual is thought to have a certain class position because his family has always occupied that position. This emphasis on the past may be seen, furthermore, in almost all aspects of upper-class behavior. They display little interest in the community, today, except where particular activities reflect the past.

Although upper-class people, today, enjoy a certain amount of economic security, they are not all "wealthy" individuals, nor are they the most affluent group in the society. Most members of the upper-upper class, however, have been wealthy in the past, or at least their families have been. Their families, a generation or two ago, were a group whose economic position and standard of consumption far surpassed that of the rest of the community. Mostly large planters, owners of great tracts of land and of many slaves, they lived extravagantly, spent money freely, and entertained elaborately; and upper uppers, today, in spite of their diminished resources, try to preserve, as far as possible, this old pattern of behavior which their families established during a past period of opulence. Houses and furnishings reflect their erstwhile riches, and this particular reflection of the past is highly valued by them. Whenever it has been economically possible, the members of the "old aristocracy" have retained their plantation homes; and they take great pride in keeping them intact—just as they were in "the old days." Newly acquired furnishings are generally old, preferably "antebellum" rather than new and modern. In fact, one proof of their superordinate position is that members of the lower-upper class whose lineage would not, in itself, engender such reverence for the past, tend to pattern their behavior after that of the upper-upper class and to cultivate an appreciation for time, as a part of the process of seeking mobility into the upper-upper group.

Lack of interest in the community.—As a group, members of the upper class seldom participate actively in contemporary community organizations or activities. There is almost no political activity among them, or even any pronounced effort to observe with care the laws of the community. Their regular attendance at church is apparently just a part of the ritual of upper-class behavior and does not signify any interest in theology or religious teachings. Their associational activity is limited almost entirely to participation in the Historical Club, the primary function of which is preservation and honoring of the past. Most of their informal social participation is in small groups whose memberships, especially in the older age ranges, often include upper-class persons exclusively.

Primacy of lineage.—It is apparent from this brief summary of the upper-class configuration of attitudes and behavior that their concept of time, their value of the past, is a very important element in their ideology and one which has a very definite relation to specific behavior. Closely linked to this time concept, and an integral part of it, is the upper-class preoccupation with lineage. It may be said that an upper-class person is primarily a member of a group and is only secondarily an individual. He is a member of a kinship group and, as such, a bona fide member of his class. Variations in his individual behavior have little effect upon his membership or position in either his family or his class. Because of the high value placed on lineage, he maintains his position no matter what his individual pattern of behavior may be. Social control, pressure by the group to maintain uniform patterns of individual behavior among its members, is, therefore, at a minimum in the upper class. An individual is a member of the upper class because of the past—his family's past—and not because of what he has or what he does.

THE MIDDLE-CLASS CONFIGURATION

Importance of wealth and morality.—The middle class, on the other hand, may be looked upon as a group in which special value is placed upon individual wealth and upon the observance of religious and moral precepts in individual behavior. Middle-class ideology is colored not by the past behavior of the individual's forebears but by his own present behavior, especially as that behavior reflects economic status and moral and religious attitudes. Not only the number of possessions, but their cash value also, is of significance to this group. It is here, especially in the upper-middle class, that "appearances" are particularly important. Both of the middle-class groups, while interpreting the class structure of the society primarily in terms of contemporary wealth, at the same time concede that the superiority of the upper class has its basis in past affluence. Also embodied in their interpretation of the society's stratification is a preoccupation with religious teachings, a concern with moral concepts of "right and wrong," "good and evil." These concepts, then—the high value of contemporary individual wealth and "moral" behavior—profoundly influence middle-class behavior.

In general, the configurations of upper-middle and lower-middle class are sufficiently similar so that they may be discussed together. Differences between them in regard to any one characteristic of behavior are generally differences in degree, so that upper middles are usually superordinate to lower middles only in a specific type of behavior or in a specific type of relation. Economic security is enjoyed to some extent by both groups but is achieved to a much higher degree in the upper-middle class, although lower-middle-class persons generally have a certainty of sufficient income to meet their physical needs. Members of the upper-middle class, however, on the whole, control more wealth, receive higher incomes, and are in occupations which have more prestige, thus giving them a security beyond the mere ability to care for fundamental physical needs. Upper-middle-class men are most frequently found in independent or supervisory occupations, as professional men or as employers and owners or managers of large businesses. Lower-middle-class men are much more often employees or the owners of small enterprises. The greatest wealth in the society today is centered in the upper-middle class, and it is in this group that the greatest emphasis on the display of wealth is found. Fine clothes, new cars, well-kept homes, and expensive furnishings are the rule. In neither middle-class group, however, do possessions suggest the time values of the upper class. Rather, there is an emphasis on modern styles and values, with concern for "quality" among upper middles and for "quantity" in the lower-middle group.

The informal social participation of the middle class is often characterized by organization into card clubs, a type of association not often found among the upper class and entirely absent from the lower-class configuration. Behavior in these informal groups is usually more restrained and more limited to a specific recreational activity than among the upper class, whose recreational behavior is condemned by the middle group as "indecent" and "immoral." Middle-class people refer to their own members as "good clean people," emphasize the fact that they "don't drink," often mention that their "women don't smoke," and are particularly vehement in stating that their married couples don't "carry-on" with one another's mates in the manner of the upper class.

"Self-improvement."—In the middle class, furthermore, it is also important to "improve one's self," an attitude which has special significance for those individuals who are aware of the possibilities of social mobility. Every middle-class parent who is financially able attempts to educate his children beyond secondary school, at least to some extent. Specialized study, talent achievement, and organizations around talent, such as music and study clubs, flourish on this social level. It is primarily the mobile middle-class individuals who want to "improve" themselves through study clubs and exercise of talent, although even the more stable members of the middle class attach considerable importance to self-improvement as a means of maintaining status (usually defended as a means of achieving a "better" community through "better" individuals).

"Community improvement."—Community activities and organizations are the great participation field of this class. Both middle-class groups are active politically (the upper middles usually occupying the superordinate positions), and both groups feel it their "duty" to take an interest in this particular function of the community. Laws are taken much more seriously by them than by the upper class. Very active in churches and church associations, middle-class people are not content merely to participate but tend to concern themselves with discussions of theology and with a strict observance of religious teachings.

It is this group which supplies the majority of the members in formal associations, the upper middles usually occupying the positions of authority in them. A large proportion of these associations—men's and women's organizations alike,—profess to function in the interests of the community as a whole and concern themselves with various types of civic improvement, such as, promoting "better" business relations, "better" schools, and more "beautiful" public parks, streets, etc. Emphasis is pre-eminently on the community of today, and almost no middle-class associations are primarily interested in the past, the chief preoccupation of the upper-class Historical Club. In all their organized activity there is a moral note. It is one's "duty" as a member of the community to function actively in the Rotary Club, the Woman's Club, the Parent-Teachers Association, or in some associations concerned with "bettering" present conditions.

Social conformity.—The importance of wealth and "moral" behavior is stressed with emphasis upon the individual and his expression of these values. In the middle class, a person's position is directly dependent upon his pattern of behavior, especially his appearance of wealth and his moral attitudes. His social status is not an inherent quality, as is that of an upper-class individual, but is dependent entirely upon his actions. He retains his position in the group only so long as his behavior conforms to the rules which the middle class has established. It appears, therefore, that behavior in this class is highly organized and closely controlled; and, much more than in any other group in the society, the members of this group complacently accept and abide by the "rules." The high development of associational behavior is the one outstanding expression of these controls, and the whole associational structure reflects the moral concepts of the middle class.

The middle class may, then, be interpreted as a group in which a high degree of organization and moral rules act to limit the amount and effects of individual variation. In other words, in a class where membership may be directly influenced by variations in individual patterns of behavior, the many rules and the extreme group pressure for enforcement may be seen as a technique for limiting individual variations and so strengthening class solidarity through enforced uniformity. Similarly, the large amount of organized activity in the middle class—in churches, associations, politics, etc.—is a means of controlling and limiting the disruptive effects of middle-class individualism.

THE LOWER-CLASS CONFIGURATION

Lack of integration into the community.—In contrast to the upper class, the lower class is a relatively new group in the community. This is not to infer that the presence of some type of lower class is new but, rather, that it has only recently become a significantly large group and is composed of a type of people relatively new to the community. Now comprising about a third of all the white population, the lower class is composed mainly of mill and factory workers who have come into the community during the last thirty years. They are primarily an industrial group, a new occupational grouping in the society, and one which, as we have already pointed out, is generally ignored by the higher social classes.

The lower class in Old City does not take part in the formal associational activity found in the middle class. There are few associations and formal groups among them. They take no part in the organizations and group activities of the other classes or of the community as a whole, and seem but slightly interested. They participate but little in community politics except as voters; and the lower lowers, especially, have a conscious, thorough disregard for the laws of the community. Crimes of violence, public drunkenness, disturbing the peace, are frequent offenses among them. Lower-class people, too, generally have little church participation, although upper lowers do attend church services occasionally. By and large, lower-class behavior and ideology may be said to be characterized by a disdain for all the values of the higher classes, a disdain for the government and laws which they see as creations of the upper class and middle class, a disdain for churches and associations and for the moral and religious values. This contempt for all the mores and institutions of the upper classes, especially for those of the middle class, reaches a much higher intensity in the lower-lower group than among upper lowers. The latter group is more aware of the social position of the middle class, feels less socially distant from its members, and, in many cases, sees the possibility of mobility into this class.

Economic insecurity.—Lower-class people generally do not have a high degree of economic security. Usually employees, working for wages by the hour or by the day, they have little certainty of sufficient income over any period of time to care for their physical needs. This insecurity is reflected in the number and type of their possessions and in their attitude toward them. One lower-lower-class family, for example, exhibited as its most prized possession a colored paper poster advertising some commercial product. One adult member of the family had found it in the city dump and had brought it home as a gift for his younger brother. There is a great deal of instalment-plan buying, and emphasis is entirely upon quantity without regard for quality. While upper-lower-class people take some interest in caring for such possessions as they have, lower-lower-class individuals are quite consistently improvident. They have little consideration for their future welfare; and they find it impossible to provide for the future, since immediate needs are so rarely satisfied.

Primacy of the job.—The meaningful solidarities among the lower classes are neither those of association nor those of church, but rather those of occupation and neighborhood. Roughly, these "new people" divide themselves into three groups on the basis of their industrial affiliation: that is, workers in cotton mills, sawmills and planing mills. Members of each of these segments of the lower class have a certain amount of solidarity through their occupational relations and consider themselves somewhat different from members of the other occupational groups. This differentiation among themselves has some basis, too, in the backgrounds of the various groups, for cotton-mill workers (who, in actual fact, have had no common bond of employment, since the cotton mills closed some ten years earlier) came to the community mostly from other industrial cities in the eastern part of the state; planing-mill workers and many sawmill workers, on the other hand, are largely people of farming background—tenant-farmers and small farmers—and farm laborers from the surrounding territory. In addition to these industrial people who form the bulk of the lower class today, there are also some fishermen, artisans, and small shopkeepers. There are also a few tenant-farmers and small farm-owners who do not actually have a "place" in the urban society but who may have extensive urban contacts. Members of these latter urban occupational groups do not have occupational solidarities among themselves, as the industrial groups do. They do, however, have membership in other lower-class groupings based on the locality in which they live.

Importance of residential areas.—Superimposed upon the industrial groupings in the lower class, and closely related to them, are distinctions made on the basis of specific localities in which individuals live. These localities are larger than neighborhoods, as that term is generally applied; and residents do not necessarily have the complex of one-to-one, face-to-face relations with one another which constitute the conventional neighborhood relation. There is, however, a certain solidarity among residents of the same district, a distinction between themselves and members of their class who live in other parts of town. Thus, Dunlap Street, on the "east side of town" near the planing mill, and the side streets and alleys running into it, constitute a locality whose residents have a sense of solidarity. Inhabited mainly by planing-mill workers, this district's solidarity embraces some residents who are not employed by that factory. Similarly, Crowder Street, inhabited largely by people who once worked in the cotton mills, is not limited to them entirely. A third, quite well-defined locality is that which includes factory workers and fishermen who, together, have a certain amount of solidarity because of common residence in this district. Sawmill workers generally live outside the urban area.

Not only does the lower class make distinctions and form groups on the basis of these industrial differences and locality differences, but there is also a definite ranking of residential areas.

This reflects a significant difference, for Crowder Street residents, and perhaps the bulk of cotton-mill workers in the community, have a general pattern of behavior somewhat different from the other lower-class population, a pattern which is upper-lower rather than that of the lower-lower-class people on Dunlap Street and the river front. The upper-lower-class people have a little church of their own, somewhat better housing, an interest in caring for their real and personal property, and a more complex code of ethics. Even within the lower lower-class there are distinctions in rank. Dunlap Street ranks higher than the river front; planing-mill workers are considered definitely above fishermen and houseboat dwellers. One woman, whose several husbands had been variously employed in several different industries and who had lived in almost every lower-class locality in Old City, felt that she had really reached the lowest rank when her husband moved her into a houseboat on the river front.

> I ain't never had to live like this and I ain't never going to do it for no man. I seen some mighty hard times, but I ain't never see nothing like this. He's just been trying to pull me down lower and lower ever since I took up with him. I'm down low enough, and I ain't going to have him nor no man pulling me down lower. . . . . I told him just how it was, and I says to him, I says:
> "I'd jest as leave get out and scratch dirt with the chickens as live here like this with you!" And I would, too. . . . . I ain't never had to live like this. I just ain't going to put up with it. No, Honey, I ain't never had to live here before. I never did like it none down here. I seen some mighty hard times, but I always was able to get me a house up in the town.

Summary.—The inhabitants of Old City recognize the reality of class division within the society and, from their varied positions in the social structure, evaluate the class system from different perspectives. A synthesis of these perspectives and a study of overt behavior reveal three well-defined classes and three subclasses. The classes may be characterized by general patterns of behavior. The past is of prime importance to the upper class. Wealth and "morality" mark the aspirations of the middle class, as well as concern with making themselves and the community "better." Poverty, lack of formal organization, and isolation from the other classes distinguish the lower class, and the "job" and area of residence serve to differentiate segments within it.

Class distinctions are reflected most clearly in the face-to-face relationships of individuals, particularly those of the family and intimate friendship groups. Therefore, the next three chapters deal with one of the most fundamental structures in the society—the family—analyzing the patterns of family behavior within each class. Subsequent chapters will demonstrate the relationship between class behavior and the formal and informal participation groups in the white society, and the role of the social classes in the economic and political life of the community.

CHAPTER IV

THE WHITE UPPER-CLASS FAMILY

TO UNDERSTAND the upper-class family in Old City, one must first understand the extreme reverence for the past with which each "old family" is a link. The upper-upper class may be said to recognize three important kinds of kin relations, in three different types of kinship groups: the immediate family, the laterally extended family, and the lineage group. Every individual in the upper class has a series of duties and privileges, associated not only with his parents, brothers, and sisters but also with his extended kin (his aunts, uncles, and cousins), and, most important of all, with his direct, lineal ancestors—symbols of the past.

Veneration of the local past.—Upper-upper-class reverence for ancestral generations, however, does not generally extend indefinitely into the past. It confines itself, for the most part, to the local scene, although knowledge of one generation before the first settlers in the local community is sometimes cherished. In the thinking of the upper-upper class, their aristocracy began in Old City and will forever maintain itself in Old City. They do not concern themselves with tracing their ancestry to Old Virginia, New Orleans, or France but are content that certain individuals in their lineal-kin groups were the original wealthy planters, and so "the aristocracy," in the local community. As an explanation of this attitude, it is probably significant that, for the most part, their ancestors, before they appeared on the local scene, had little claim to wealth or high social position. The founding of the local community, the establishment of large plantation holdings, and the elaborate and extravagant living of those early days represent the highest social achievement of most upper-class ancestral lines. This opulent era, "the old days," is seen as the far-off beginning wherein the aristocratic lineal-kin groups were born. In each kinship group the first wealthy planter in the local community is considered the original ancestor, the founder of the family line.

Descendants of this "old aristocracy" are not, of course, unaware that these original "old planters" came from somewhere beyond the local community and that they were, for the most part, inconspicuous citizens in those earlier environs. Among themselves, however, they prefer to ignore the earlier commonplace history of their families, do not discuss it, and do not revere its participants. They are, nonetheless, vulnerable concerning this earlier period when it is inescapably brought to their attention by resentful individuals or by jealous aspirants from mobile groups below them. The greatest possible insult to an upper-upper-class person is the defamation of his "original ancestor," the founder of his local family line. In most instances the easiest and most obvious means of defaming him is to call attention to the inconspicuous, or even ignoble, role of this "original ancestor" (or his parents) before he became a wealthy planter in the local community. The descendants of an old family can ignore the fact that their founders, or the founders' forebears, were merely artisans, or pirates, so long as the fact remains unspoken. Once it has been mentioned, however, it becomes an insult and a statement to be denied heatedly and blindly or to be explained away defensively.

Quarrels between upper-upper-class individuals almost inevitably result in the hurling of these ancestral insults. One informant, a "newcomer" who participated in upper-class groups but had lived in the community for "only" fifteen years, told of one such typical squabble, in which

> Ruth and Josephine took up the fight, and went back generations telling each other things about their families, digging up things that nobody wants to hear about. That is the way people do here. If they once get mad with you, they don't just be mad with you—they go back

as far as they can—telling stories on each other's ancestors. Ruth was the one to blame in this case I think; she dug up all kinds of things about Josephine's family.

Similarly, the pre–Old City period of the inconspicuous or infamous ancestors is the one point on which mobile upper-middle-class and lower-upper-class individuals may effectively attack the descendants of the "old aristocracy." These aspiring individuals—upper middles who are attempting to rise in the social scale, and lower uppers who have partly "attained" —generally express a reverence for "the old days" patterned after that of the upper-upper class. This is part of their mobility adjustment. If sufficiently goaded, snubbed, or directly subordinated, however, they invariably point out that the founders of "old aristocratic" lines were only commonplace individuals, that the upper-upper class is therefore "no better" than themselves, that it has no greater claim to aristocratic background and high social position. Upper-upper-class individuals do not ignore such attacks; they meet them as united family groups, and sometimes as a united class, rallying all descendants of all aristocratic lines to the defense. Regardless of the facts, they blindly deny all accusations and, at the same time, pose a counterattack by pointing out not only that the insulter's forebears were of more degraded and questionable character but that they have been so in more recent generations, too. Description of one of the many instances observed will perhaps suffice to demonstrate the highly charged situation which results.

A lower-upper-class woman, Mrs. Duncan, whose parents had achieved some measure of recognition by the upper-upper class, felt that she was being snubbed by the "old aristocracy" and was not properly accepted as an equal among them. She attacked the Montgomery family by calling their founder "nothing but an ordinary gambler." A younger member of the Montgomery line of direct descent, Mrs. Bowley, to whom this insult was originally addressed, met the attack on the spot by denying the accusation and implying that "gambling was not necessarily disgraceful, anyhow." Later she reported the incident to older members of her lineal and laterally extended groups. All were incensed and warmly denied the charge of gambling. One older cousin, Louise, also a direct descendant of the founder, undertook an elaborate search to uncover some devastating facts about Mrs. Duncan's family background. At an afternoon tea Mrs. Bowley described the Montgomery family's reaction:

> When I told Louise what Mrs. Duncan said about being ashamed of the Montgomerys, she was just furious. She's been mad ever since, and she has been looking around trying to get something on Mrs. Duncan. So just a few days ago she came to me very gleefully and said she had found out that Mrs. Duncan's grandmother ran a country store, and she is just waiting to get hold of Mrs. Duncan to tell her.

Louise joined the group at this point, and said:

> Yes, I am certainly going to tell Mrs. Duncan about her grandmother the first time I see her. The nerve of her saying the Montgomerys were gamblers! I'd like to know what her family have ever had to brag about! The Montgomerys were not gamblers! Old John Montgomery was a fine old man, and came from a fine old French family. I don't care if he had been a gambler. I wish he had been a gambler, but he wasn't, and if there is anything I like it is the truth. . . . . As for Mrs. Duncan, I know a lot of things about her family that I wouldn't repeat to anyone, but she better be careful. I have found out something even better than the country store now. Her grandmother was a nurse! Just wait till I tell that one to Mrs. Duncan, and then see what she has to say about the Montgomerys being gamblers. I think that will keep her quiet for a while. And I am going to tell her too! A nurse!

THE UPPER-UPPER CLASS AS AN EXTENDED KIN GROUP

Almost all members of the upper-upper class today are members of one laterally extended kin group. They form a unified group which maintains solidarity not only through a common social position and way of life but through common kinship. The number of "cousins" an upper-upper-class individual knows and recognizes in the community seems almost unlimited. Older members are able to point out their exact relationship to each of their many kinsmen. This inclusion of almost the entire upper-upper class among the kin of any one individual is largely explained by the fact that, until quite recently, the upper-upper class was almost strictly an endogamous group. Children of one "original ancestor" married children of another "founder"; the third generation intermarried among themselves; cousins married cousins until all were intertwined in an intricate kinship pattern. The solidarity of the upper-upper class today as an extended kinship group is further explained by the fact that all degrees of kinship are recognized, beginning with the era of the "founding of the family."

For the most part, there cannot be said to be any noticeable differentiation in kin behavior based upon the degree of kinship. With his aunts and uncles and with his first cousins, an upper-upper-class individual is generally expected to exhibit a solidarity and intimacy somewhat greater than with other members of the laterally extended family. Even relations with these kin, however, are not viewed as isolated relationships. These relatives are essentially part of the large laterally extended family; and, as such, behavior toward aunts and uncles is little different from behavior toward cousins of all degree. The upper-upper class is, itself, a group of kinsmen.

Age-grading in the kinship group.—Age-grading is far more important than degree of kinship in determining behavior. The individual recognizes a greater obligation, a more significant relation, with a "cousin" of his great-grandmother's generation, whatever the degree of kinship, than with kinsmen more nearly his contemporaries who may have a less distant kin connection. Because of this age-graded behavior and because the whole class group is related through blood ties, very old individuals are the focus of all upper-upper-class kinship relations. Old men and women in their eighties and nineties are reverenced not only by their direct descendants, the members of their lineal-kin groups, but by all the younger persons of the upper-upper class as well.

THE WHITE UPPER-CLASS FAMILY

A very old woman may be said to be a symbol of the upper-upper class as a group. While she lives, she is the veritable ruler of the whole class group; she is the final authority on historical facts and traditional patterns of behavior. The whole clan bows to her, obeys her every command, grants her every request. The ritual and deference surrounding her attendance at a group gathering—generally limited, by her great age and physical incapacity, to afternoon teas—is suggestive of royalty. Her entrance is heralded among the guests; she is given a seat of honor among the group; and each guest individually feels an obligation to greet and converse with her before departing. She is a symbol of the group's aristocracy—a cherished link with the past, a living symbol of "the old days."

In view of the fact that the upper class is one large kinship group, it is not surprising that the immediate family, whether of procreation or of orientation, is considered secondary in importance to the extended family and that the extended family achieves a unity in which individual kin relations are subordinated to the total kinship pattern. It is considered more important, for example, that an individual be a descendant of the Mandeville *family* than that he have specific kin relations with other Mandevilles in the society today—with his individual aunts, uncles, or cousins, for instance. Among all the members of his extended family, among all descendants of a given family, there is a general pattern of behavior.

In the middle-class and lower-class kinship structure, on the other hand, the immediate family is the focal point, so that other relationships become progressively less significant as they are farther removed from the immediate family. In the upper class the whole kinship structure does not radiate from the immediate family as a unit; rather, the whole line of direct descent from an idealized past, of which the immediate family is only a part, constitutes the focal point of loyalty. In upper-class ideology, the immediate family is subordinated to lineage and is significant primarily as a means of maintaining the continuity of the ancestral line. This is the essential difference between upper-class kinship structure and that of other class groups. In the middle and lower classes a significant degree of unity is found only in the immediate family and among members of the household; the extended family represents hardly more than a series of individual kin relations. In the upper class the whole group of descendants from a common ancestor is a closely united group; and to a somewhat lesser extent, but more than in other class groups, the whole extended family in all its lateral ramifictions has solidarity as a group.

THE UPPER-CLASS HOUSEHOLD

Husbands and wives.—In their overt behavior upper-class husbands and wives have, roughly, a relationship of equivalence. There is no clear-cut division of labor between them, as in the other classes. Most upper-class husbands, however, rule the economic sphere of home life, earn the living, and hold the purse strings. Most wives concern themselves with the direction and supervision of the care of the house and children. In many instances, however, the husband's control of the economic sphere is weakened by the fact that the wife has also found employment and is contributing to the family income. The presence of servants, furthermore, especially the old family retainers of the upper-upper class, makes the wife's function as housekeeper and baby-tender comparatively unimportant. The general equivalence in the husband-wife relation in the upper class is also indicated by their joint social participation. Whereas men and women in the middle and lower classes tend to have a separate recreational life, informal participation in the upper class is generally by couples together. Although there is some social activity, during the daytime, of the sexes separately, this entertainment is not considered so interesting, nor does it occur so frequently, as mixed evening gatherings.

Although the upper-class man and woman are, ideologically, essentially equivalent in the husband-wife relation, their comparative status is in large measure dependent upon their individual kinship with the past, their lineage. In the thinking of the upper class, as a whole, and to some extent in the actual behavior of married couples, the partners are equals only if they have similar kinship relations with an "old family." Thus, the marital partner who is related to the past by direct descent is superordinate to the partner whose relation exists only through cousins. A partner who has no kin relation at all with an "old family" is subordinated to one who has.

The children.—In a class where social position depends upon birth into an "old family" and not upon individual behavior patterns, children must be impressed with their responsibility to the past. The child is not considered as an individual or primarily as a member of the immediate family group. Rather, he is but one of many links in a long chain of upper-class social personalities. He is primarily a member of a large extended family and, as a member of that group, must conform to its traditional pattern of behavior in order to maintain the continuity of the ancestral line. The upper-class child is taught that he must behave in a certain way not so much to maintain his own social status as because he has an obligation to his whole extended family group to do so, and thus to the entire upper class. Unbecoming conduct on the part of one member of a family group usually indicates a lack of respect for the family name, a lack of reverence for the past, and a breaking of highly valued ties with his ancestral line. The whole class brings the weight of its disapproval down upon him, and he becomes an individual "without a place" in the society.

Negro servants and the training of children.—In the upper-upper class especially, a large part of the training of the child devolves upon Negro servants, often old family retainers. Most children of this class level actually have more contacts and more intimate relations with their Negro servant than with their parents. The servant not only takes care of them physically but also supervises their play, selects and censors their companions, and, in general, teaches them behavior becoming to "ladies and gentlemen," that is, to descendants of the "old aristocracy." Parents, of course, have the ultimate authority over these nursemaids and direct them, to some extent, in this training. For the most part, however, they see their children only formally, as when they take them calling or bring them in to meet guests, and at formal meals.

When the servant is an old family retainer, one who has been with the family for several generations, her role as a socializer of the children may be seen as fitting into the upper-class reverence for the past. For example, a Negro, who was a servant in the household of the child's grandfather and who took part in training the child's parent is considered a direct link with the past. As such, she is considered very well suited to initiate the child into the cult of traditional upper-class behavior. In one instance observed, an old Negro servant who had such a direct connection with the family past became the veritable ruler of the white household. The white woman, whom she had nursed as a child, was still called "Baby" by the old woman. Although she was in her late thirties at the time of this study, she was still treated as a child by the old servant. The old servant managed the household affairs and the other servants and took charge of the children's welfare. The white mother was often away for days at a time, leaving the colored woman in complete charge; and the latter frequently took the children to her cabin in the country for visits. She selected their clothing, walked with them to school, chose their companions, and generally supervised their social behavior.

Often servants who have a less direct connection with the family ancestors are also considered very desirable nurse-maids if they have some connection with the white family through their own kin. For example, a Negro whose mother, or even whose aunt, worked in the household of the white children's grandfather, is thought to have a close connection with the white family's background and is therefore regarded as a more suitable nurse than a Negro who has no such indirect but significant ties with the family. In a sense, then, upper-class whites extend their concept of kinship and lineage to the Negro servants whom they employ.

The "mammy."—More than any other servants in the white household, the Negro nurse who takes care of the children is part and parcel of the white family, although, to a certain extent, any servant who has been with the family for a long time achieves this psuedo-kin relation, is said to be "just like one of the family," and is often called by the kinship terms "aunty" or "uncle." The Negro nurse, however, functions as a member of the immediate family. It is significant that she is often called "Mammy," a term reserved for nurses alone and applied to them only by the children whom they have nursed. The nurse, or "Mammy," performs many of the functions which the real mother assumes in other class groups. Often she has a more intimate and affectionate relation with the white children, greater contact, and more direct authority than the real mother, although the term "Mother" is never applied to her. She is a pseudo-mother, however, and, as such, she is given a title which is derived from the kinship term "Mother." It is not surprising that, with the encroachment of the servant upon the mother's role in the kinship structure, the mother-child reciprocal is relatively weak in the upper class.

Mother and child.—In spite of the fact that the mother-child relation in the upper class involves scant contact and little intimate behavior, in the ideology of the upper class this is still the most important single relation in the kinship structure. The relation between a mother and her child is highly sentimentalized and is expected to carry a great degree of emotional force, although in fact the affection between a mother and child is exhibited more in verbal expression than in overt behavior. Upper-class women, for the most part, do not concern themselves with taking care of their children, entertaining them, or being entertained by them. Nevertheless, they guard jealously their reputations as "good mothers," a role which consists primarily in expressing verbally before others their "interest" and "love" for their children. To be accused of not being a "good mother" is an insult second only to having aspersions cast upon one's ancestors. Among one group of women, for example, a series of antagonisms had developed. When one woman accused another of not being a "good mother," the defense and further condemnation of this and other mothers in the group became the focus of the whole quarrel, although the function of a mother had had no part in the original rift. One woman said, heatedly:

> I think it is a shame the way they are all down on Nancy. She is really a wonderful mother to those children. I don't see how Doris and Sophie can talk about her the way they do, and I don't see how they can say she isn't a good mother. She is a wonderful mother. She reads to them and gives them music lessons and takes care of them. Anyway, I don't see how Sophie can talk. She is about the worst mother I ever knew. She certainly doesn't think she has raised her children. . . . . Old Sarah [Negro servant] has raised all her children and she never lifted a hand for them. I don't know what call she has to say Nancy isn't a good mother.

Another antagonist was just as heated in her accusation of Nancy:

> Nancy pretends to be such a wonderful mother. She doesn't take a bit of interest in those children. Why she runs off to Atlanta when they are sick. . . . . I remember one night we were all on a party up here at the hotel and I heard her telling some newcomer what a wonderful mother she was and how she just loved her children more than anything and they always came first. Really it almost made me sick!

Just what behavior is thought to be involved in performing the role of a "good mother" was never stated. In fact, the actual overt behavior of mothers in the controversy was less significant than the storm evoked by the accusations and the ardor with which the mother was defended. This situation, one of many similar disputes observed among upper-class women, indicates that ideologically a very high value is placed upon the mother's role. In spite of the fact that contact between mother and child is comparatively infrequent and that overt behavior between them is limited to formal participation, there is a strong emotional force and a feeling of mutual obligation in the mother-child reciprocal which are maintained and enforced by the reverential attitude of the upper-class group toward motherhood.

THE BOND OF LINEAGE

Although the mother-child relation has a high value for the upper class—although it is, in fact, the most valued of the single one-to-one relations in the kinship structure—it is, nevertheless, subordinated to kinship groups, particularly the lineal-kin group, as are all specific individual relations. The upper-class child cannot be said to "belong" primarily to his mother, as in the lower class, or to his parents jointly, as in the middle class, or even to his immediate family. He is first and foremost a member of a lineal-kin group, and as such he "belongs" to *all* his forebears. In this kinship group there is a very marked hierarchy of age, so that progressively older generations are progressively superordinate to one another. Thus, upper-class parents are not the only, or the final, authority over their children. In their control of their children, parents are responsible to grandparents and to great-grandparents. This authority of the older generations, furthermore, does not cease with the death of a forebear. In a sense, it becomes more binding in that it then becomes unalterable.

The parent-child relation in the upper class has, so far, been seen as a relatively weak reciprocal in view of the small amount of contact and the behavior of parent and child in relation to each other. As a part of the lineal-kin group, however, the parent-child relation is a strong relation in that it is enduring. It is a relation which lasts forever, is forever reverenced and unchanged, regardless of the age or death of individuals. As members of a particular line of descent, upper-class parents and their children maintain an almost uniformly high degree of sentimental and emotional solidarity even after the children marry and become parents or grandparents.

Kinship ties after marriage.—Although upper-class children as members of their family of orientation are less dependent upon their parents and less directly related to them in their behavior than children of other classes, yet, as married adults in their family of procreation, they are much more bound, much more dependent upon their parents' authority and approval than are children of the middle class and the lower class. The large number of upper-class children who continue to live with the parents of one partner after marriage and after child-bearing may be seen as an indication of the strength of this tie. Various explanations are given by parents and children. The most frequent explanation is that of economic necessity; others say simply that they "couldn't leave," or "*Of course* my son and his family live with me." One married woman in her thirties, the mother of a three-year-old child, said: "Oh, I just couldn't bear to live anywhere but Old City. If I had to leave, I know I should die. I guess it is on account of living with Mother. You see I have always lived in the same house with her, and I just can't imagine living anywhere else. It makes such a difference." This young married woman still lived as a child in her mother's house. The older woman continued as head of the household, as authority over her daughter, son-in-law, and grandchild. This situation is typical, for when the married children continue to live in the parental home, they have a child's place in that home.

Living at the family home.—On the face of it, this situation appears to indicate the great dependence of the adult child upon his parents, the great strength of the parent-child relation as such. More subtly, it represents, in reality, the strength of the lineal kin group, of which the parent-child relation is only a part. It is not so much that adult children cannot leave their parents as that they cannot leave the larger kin group, their lineage, as symbolized by the parental home. This explanation is borne out by the fact that, whatever the problem, whatever the reason for living with the parents, it is always the child who lives with the parents and never a case of parents living with the child. It is significant that, although well over one-half of married upper-class children were observed to be living in the home of one partner's parents, in no instance was a parent found living in the home of a child. That only ancestral or parental homes are involved in this living together, points to the fact that the bond lies in lineage, in the whole ancestral line, rather than in the parent-child reciprocal *per se.*

The role of grandparents.—In most instances grandparents do not have direct authority over their grandchildren but have an indirect influence through their continued authority over their married children, the parents. In some few cases, in which all three generations lived together in the grandparent's home, grandparents were observed to supervise the behavior of their grandchildren directly, or through their nursemaids, without regard for the parents' intermediary role. More generally, however, even when the married children, the parents, lived in the ancestral home and held the position of children in that household, grandparents directed the behavior of their grandchildren by bringing pressure to bear upon the parents, who, in turn, brought pressure upon the nurse of the children. Although this seems a roundabout method—through parents, through Negro nurse, to children— the grandparental influence and authority is effective. One upper-upper-class girl in her early twenties said of her dead grandmother: "She was the one who really believed in the fine old families. She wouldn't have allowed me to do lots of these things and to go with these people. Mother did everything she said. Mother listened to her in everything." Speaking of a middle-class beau of whom her parents ineffectively disapproved, she went on: "I know this: If my grandmother was still alive, I certainly wouldn't be going with Tom. She was even stronger in her opinions than Mother is. And, to her, his family were just the limit, and it was hardly respectable to go with them."

These statements, and others similar, indicate that the grandmother, while living, maintained an authority over the mother and so influenced the behavior of the grandchildren. The case of this particular family is, however, unique in that the grandmother failed to maintain her authority after death, or at least did not have sufficient influence to keep the granddaughter from doing things of which she disapproved. However, even here, it will be observed, the girl was still acutely aware of the dead grandmother's disapproval. In spite of this awareness, the girl did not conform to the family pattern of behavior. She felt uncomfortable and guilty, however, in not doing so. When asked how she happened to belong to a clique of varied social composition, she said: "Do you mean mixed as regards families? Well, we got that way over the bodies of our families, and we are still trampling over their bodies." Speaking of her middle-class beau, she went on:

> Take Tom—I didn't know him until I was about seventeen, and then I started going with him some. The family nearly had a fit over that, and I really almost hated him. You know how it is. When your family think a person is too terrible, you feel that it is wrong to go with him. That is the way I felt. I didn't want to be seen out with him.
>
> .... I know this, I would never marry Tom and live here. . . . . My family would all be opposed to it.

In most cases children are unable to resist strong pressure from their elders for conformity to the traditional pattern of behavior. Upper-upper-class children can generally be forced to relinquish "unsuitable" companions and to cease "unbecoming" conduct. Parents can call upon the attitude of their grandparents, living or dead: "What would your grandmother say!" or "Your grandfather would rather see you dead!" This technique is employed effectively, though more indirectly, in bringing pressure from even more distant generations. A mother seldom asks a child to consider what his great-grandfather would have thought of his behavior, but the influence of this forebear is felt indirectly, for the grandparent may force the mother to greater effort in controlling her children by recalling her grandfather's attitude. So great is the reverence for the past, so strong the solidarity of the lineal-kin group, that indirect control by long-dead generations is still remarkably effective.

THE PERVASIVENESS OF KINSHIP

Concepts of kinship and the family color the whole life of the upper class. The family name is the capital stock of the upper class and must be conserved. Those who enter this expanded group of kinsmen by marriage must do so on the terms which the upper uppers lay down. Marriage becomes far more than a legal rite; it becomes an initiation into a local kinship group with its own traditions and customs. Lower uppers who lack the proper lineage are a generation themselves debarred, but their children may possibly enter, in the days to come. The problem of the continued existence of the upper-upper class is thus bound up partly with the process of mobility from the lower-upper class and partly with the supply of eligible "cousins" in the large extended kin group.

CHAPTER V

THE WHITE MIDDLE-CLASS FAMILY

PRIMACY OF THE IMMEDIATE FAMILY

B OTH upper-middle-class and lower-middle-class husbands and wives recognize the raising of a family as the primary function of their relationship, more important than the sexual enjoyment of the partners, their economic security, or their general physical comfort. Children are trained to a definite pattern of behavior; middle-class husbands and wives take their function as parents seriously; and the relations within the immediate family are colored and dictated by the parents' moral attitudes and their respect for group controls.

More than within any other class, the marriage relation is here looked upon as permanent union. Condemned by the religious teachings, divorce is frowned upon; separation, too, is uncommon. Middle-class individuals marry "for better or for worse" and "till death do us part." As is to be expected, practically all marriages are legalized, and the great majority are performed with a religious ceremony. Absolute constancy in sexual relations is the rule of marital behavior, a rule which seems to be generally obeyed. Habitual extramarital relations, which are apparently quite rare, are condemned. The extent of premarital sexual relations cannot be determined, although this behavior is condemned by the group, vehemently by adults, less markedly so by adolescents. The fidelity demanded of married couples forbids not only adultery but also sexual innuendo, flirting, or kissing. This extended fidelity is required primarily of wives and is applied somewhat less rigidly to husbands. Wives may not accept advances from men, and to seek or invite advances is condemned not only by the husbands but by the entire group. Husbands, on the other hand, may engage in discreet flirtations, especially outside their social group. Occasional extramarital sexual relations may even be overlooked or forgiven if the husbands are discreet and do not make a habit of having "affairs."

Husbands and wives.—As in all the class groups, there is in the middle class a fairly distinct division of labor between the husband and wife. Middle-class husbands are remuneratively employed and support their wives and children, furnishing money for the home, for food, clothing, recreation. Wives, in their turn, care for the house and children. In the lower-middle class, women do housework and care for the children, themselves; in the upper-middle class, they more often direct servants in these duties. In the lower-middle class, wives who are remuneratively employed are not uncommon but are not the rule. With the arrival of children, working wives usually end their occupational activity. In the sum total of their behavior, middle-class wives are subordinated to their husbands; but in specific behavior, the husband and wife each has a sphere of domination. Wives generally have authority in the care of the house and in matters related directly to the house and possessions. They direct the husband in his behavior within the home, in such activities as his treatment of the furniture or his eating. In general, the husband may be said to be subordinated to the house directly; that is, his physical comfort is considered of less importance than the careful preservation of possessions. He may not lie down and disarrange the cushions; he must not let his ashes fall on the floor; he has to wipe his feet before entering the house; he may not put his feet on the furniture. Although the wife does most of the purchasing, the husband, nevertheless, is the authority in money matters, directing and limiting her spending. Large purchases, such as houses and cars, are usually made by the husband himself. Through this domination in money matters the husband has a certain authority over the house, despite the fact that it is the woman's sphere of influence.

In their leisure-time pursuits middle-class husbands and wives have considerable joint participation. Much of the social participation of a couple, however, is by the sexes separately, especially in the lower-middle class. Middle-class participations are largely female events—afternoon bridge parties, teas, wedding parties, club meetings, etc. Wives usually engage in recreation with other wives in the afternoon, participate in associations, church clubs, and informal group activities. Husbands enjoy some recreational activity with other men during working hours; and they play poker, drink, or attend associational meetings with other men in the evenings. Middle-class couples, however, spend many evenings at home alone, reading, sewing, conversing. Occasional mixed parties in the evening are not uncommon, being more frequent in the upper-middle class than in the lower-middle class.

More than within any other class, husbands and wives in the middle class achieve an identity in social personality. In the middle class particularly, this identity goes even farther. Individual relations between an outsider and one mate also involve obligations to the other mate. Friendship between two husbands involves friendly behavior toward each other's wives, and vice versa. An antagonism toward one partner is extended to the other partner. This situation occurs to some extent in all class groups, but it is the most extreme in the middle class, where the marital relation is most permanent and highly sanctioned. From various preachers in the community we learned that individuals of different churches usually join the same church after marriage, thus increasing their social identity. Wives of Masons usually join the Eastern Star; wives of American Legionnaires, the Legion Auxiliary; etc. We shall see subsequently that the mate's kin are generally adopted into the same pattern of kinship behavior as blood relatives.

SOCIALIZATION OF THE MIDDLE-CLASS CHILD

Class indoctrination.—Middle-class children may be said to "belong" to both parents jointly, although, because of her greater contact with them, the mother is more concerned with constant enforcement of the children's training program. It is she who is more directly responsible for their training. The father, however, feels a large amount of responsibility, discusses training problems with the mother, and may insist that she apply certain techniques or principles. Frequently, the father is the final authority, although in such a case the mother carries out his wishes. The father is also called upon to administer physical punishment to the children rather than to have the mother punish them directly.

In the earlier discussion of class configurations it was pointed out that the middle class, more than any other, is a rigidly controlled group in which the pattern of individual behavior is particularly significant. It follows, then, that the socialization of the child in the middle class, that is, the training of a child to take an adult's position in middle-class society, is a well-defined and consequently rigorous process. There are definite rules to be taught and obeyed; and a definite ideology, and respect for these rules, to be imbued. As in other class groups, middle-class parents attempt to teach their children to hold the same values that they themselves hold, to obey the same rules of individual behavior that they themselves respect. Middle-class children are therefore taught, directly or by intimation, to conform to that behavior which is formalized in religious teachings, to lead "good" and "moral" lives, to "honor thy father and mother," to "do unto others as you would have others do unto you," to value the opinion of the group, to accept social controls, to respect possessions, and to prize individual wealth. Although middle-class children are subject to socialization from their school and church contacts, the burden of their training lies with their parents. One preacher pointed out that, although middle-class parents send their children to Sunday school and often to church, in the great majority of cases children follow "the teachings of their parents and not those of the church." They absorb their religious ideology not from the church directly but from their parents.

DEEP SOUTH

Active supervision of children.—Middle-class parents, mothers particularly, attempt to participate in, and to direct all of, the child's activity. The child is sent regularly to Sunday school and to church. His progress in the public schools is watched with interest by both parents. Individual mothers frequently visit the school to discuss the child's progress with his teachers, and mothers from this class constitute the majority of members of the Parent-Teachers Association. The child's recreation and play are supervised as well. Children old enough to go to school are, of course, not actually chaperoned by their parents in their play; but where they are, what they are doing, and with whom they are playing, the mother attempts to know at all times. Especially in the upper-middle class, a child's companions are selected and limited by the mother to a large extent. In general, parents limit their children's companions to other children who have the same training, to children who follow the same rules of behavior and possess the same ideology. "Strange" children, children unknown to the parents, are viewed with suspicion and generally "investigated." In some instances in upper-middle-class circles, parents allow their children to play only with children whose parents are known to them and are their friends. Failure by parents to keep constant check upon their children is vociferously condemned, as in the case of a woman who told of the child of a new neighbor:

There's one little boy, about four or so, comes down to the house all the time and calls to Charles [her son] and says, "Little boy, little boy, come on out and play with me," till I almost go crazy. He just hangs around all the time. He came over one day and stayed and stayed, and finally I heard him say he was going to eat dinner with us. So I just said, "Oh, no you're not, you're going home to dinner. Your mother would be worrying about you." But he just said, "Oh, no, she won't care. My mother doesn't care where I eat dinner." Well, after that I just told him to go home. I didn't worry about hurting his feelings. I just decided they were the kind of people that wouldn't know anything and you can't hurt their fellings if you try..... His mother doesn't pay any attention, doesn't seem to care where he is..... I don't know who they are, just common people, riffraff, that's all.

THE WHITE MIDDLE-CLASS FAMILY

Children's parties, a quite frequent occurrence in both upper-middle and lower-middle classes, are directed almost entirely by the mother until the children go to high school. The mother selects the guests to be invited from among the children of her own friends. She may include a few friends of her own child if the latter insists and if the other child's parents and pattern of behavior are not too deviant from middle-class standards. Usually the mother invites the mothers of the little guests to attend the party and so makes it into a joint adult and subadult event. In essence, mothers of middle-class children attempt to confine their children's intimate associates to the children of their own friends. In the matter of organized parties, this attempt is fairly successful, although young children in their casual contacts with one another most frequently select their close neighbors as companions, regardless of their mother's desire to make her children's circle conform to her own.

Supervision of adolescents.—With adolescents, parents are somewhat less successful in directing and limiting their sphere of companionship. Apparently, this results both from a conscious slackening of parental supervision and from the fact that adolescent children have begun to develop social personalities as individuals. High-school groups do not emphasize class distinctions so much as their parents do. There is some evidence to indicate that this comparative lack of discrimination is disapproved by their parents, who attempt to maintain their right to select friends for their children even after they become adolescents. In one instance, several upper-middle-class parents became very indignant when a child from a lower-middle-class family was included at a party which their children attended. Subsequently, however, this same lower-middle-class child gave a party, and these upper-middle-class children were present.

In their relations with others of the opposite sex, in their courtship and quasi-courtship relations, adolescents and adult children living at home receive some direction from their parents. The beaux of their daughters (not so frequently "girls" of their sons) are "investigated" before parents consent to joint participation. Daughters, however, may go about with boys who are disapproved of by their parents, if they wish to risk defiance of the conventional parent-child relation and to resist the pressure put upon them for obedience.

Deference and obedience expected of children.—Middle-class children of all ages are expected to obey and defer to their parents, although the degree of obedience and deference decreases as children reach adolescence and adulthood. The authority of parents over married children is comparatively small. Although parents are generally unable, and unwilling, to manifest their authority over their grown or half-grown children by physical force, they generally expect to be obeyed because of the force of childhood training, the strict pattern of behavior established over a period of years. Thus, most adolescents and adult children, with childhood background of strict parental authority and supervision, are reluctant to go against the wishes of their parents, although the latter generally have no techniques for enforcing their wishes beyond the verbal expression of their disapproval.

Attitudes toward children's marriage.—In general, middle-class parents disapprove of their daughter's beaux, and to some extent their son's "girls," when these are of a social position below their own. While mobile parents may encourage friendships with boys and girls of a higher social position than their own, most of the stable middle-class parents, especially upper-middle-class parents, disapprove of association with upper-class boys and girls. In this situation their objection is based upon a general disapproval of the upper-class pattern of behavior, a pattern quite different from, and contradictory to, the middle-class configuration. One upper-middle-class mother voiced her disapproval of her daughter's upper-class beau, mentioned her technique for discouraging the affair, and spoke of her approval of the middle-class man whom the daughter subsequently married:

THE WHITE MIDDLE-CLASS FAMILY

When I saw what the upper-class people were like, I made up my mind that I didn't want to know them so much, and I certainly didn't want my daughters to marry into any of the old families. They just weren't clean and moral, that is all. They weren't good for anything. One of my daughters did have a beau from one of the best families. He wanted to marry her. I was just sick about it. I really think I would rather have seen my daughter dead than married into one of those old degenerate families. Anyway, I just made fun of the affair and I finally managed to break it up. I just ridiculed the boy all the time until Beatrice finally got sick of him. He was a young man whose family had lost most of their money, but they *had* had a great deal. He had nice manners and all that, but I had heard things about him that I didn't like and I just wouldn't let Beatrice marry him.

Now Duncan [the daughter's husband] is different. He is queer in some ways but he is a dear when you get to know him. . . . . He is just as good and clean as he can be . . . . and when she married him he was already settled down. He is a fine fellow and absolutely moral.

This expression may be taken as typical of the attitudes of upper-middle-class parents toward their children's mates. They desire, for them, mates who have similar concepts and patterns of behavior, "clean and moral" individuals, according to middle-class standards. This particular informant did not, exercise extreme parental authority in breaking up the affair of her eighteen-year-old daughter, however. She did not forbid the girl to see the young man but resorted to an indirect method of control and voiced her disapproval through ridicule. This same mother, however, in controlling a younger daughter, a girl of fifteen who had a proposal of marriage from the same disapproved upper-class suitor, interfered directly. Apparently she did not forbid the girl to see him, but she told the young man directly "never to come to my house again as long as I live."

Married children.—Middle-class parents generally relinquish most of their authority and supervision over their children when the latter marry. The fundamental pattern of parent-child relations, however, still remains. Although parents do not attempt to supervise the behavior of the married child and do not interfere in relations with the mate or demand consistent obedience, the child still continues to defer to the parents. In some specific actions behavior is modified "out of respect for" the parents. Thus, one upper-middle-class son of a Catholic mother married a Baptist girl. He ceased to attend the Catholic church but did not join a Protestant church, "out of respect for his mother." In another instance, a married son of an upper-middle-class family disapproved the year of mourning imposed upon him when his father died. But he conformed to this custom, as his wife said, "out of respect for his mother's wishes."

Married middle-class children generally do not live in the same household with their parents except in the case of economic necessity. Living in the same neighborhood, however, or on the same street and block, and even in the adjoining house with either or both parent, is very common. In both the upper-middle and the lower-middle class there are many instances of this clustering of households around the parental home, married sons often buying (upper middle) or renting (lower middle) houses very near to those of their parents. With noticeable frequency, young married couples are accommodated under the same roof with the parents of either partner. This occurs more frequently in the lower-middle class and is generally a temporary arrangement, one which lasts only for a year or two after marriage. In this situation the young couple are not usually regarded as actual members of the parental household. They generally have a part of the house as their own, in which they have their own specially designated rooms. Although they do not necessarily have a separate entrance or complete privacy from the parental household, they do, themselves, constitute a separate household, have their own dining-room and eat separate meals.

HOUSEHOLD RITUAL

There is considerably more ritual surrounding the behavior of the immediate family in the middle-class household than is found in the lower class. This is most evident in upper-middle-class homes, where the increase in ritual over that found in the upper-lower class appears to be closely associated with the increase in number and differentiation of rooms. Although each member of the family in the lower-middle class does not generally have his own part of the house or his own room, there are more specialized rooms than in upper-lower-class homes. In the great majority of lower-middle-class houses there is a living-room, serving as a room for the whole family and their guests; a dining-room, a room where the whole family participates in group repasts; a kitchen, where the food is prepared; a sleeping-room for the parents; and one or more sleeping-rooms for the children. With the designation of a particular room for eating in the lower-middle-class households, meals can be more ritualized than in the lower class, and eating becomes definitely a group activity for which each member of the family makes some preparation. Children wash their hands; the father often dons a coat; and the mother usually removes her apron. Each person has his particular place at the table, and definite formalities are observed in the order and manner of serving and eating the food. The general lack of servants in the lower middle class, however, makes eating still an essentially informal activity.

Upper-middle-class variations.—Increase in the size of house and the presence of servants allows a greater amount of ritual in the behavior of an upper-middle-class household. Living-room, dining-room, and kitchen are a uniform part of upper-middle-class houses. As in all classes in the community, husband and wife share the same bedroom; but each child generally has his own room for sleeping. Here, too, single beds come into prominence. In upper-middle-class homes there are usually other rooms designated for particular usage or for particular members of the family, such as a sewing-room for the wife and mother, a den or smoking-room for the father, and a playroom or workshop for the children.

The presence of a servant, usually a cook who also acts as waitress, allows for greater formality at family meals. The upper-middle-class mother is not required to participate in the preparation and serving of the food. In this class group, very young children are usually excluded from the family meals, being served in the kitchen by the servant or the mother before older members of the family partake. At the table polite usage is observed. There is increased ritual and restraint in serving, in the requesting of food, in the choice and handling of utensils, and often even in the type of conversation.

STRENGTH OF FAMILY SOLIDARITIES

Brothers and sisters.—Between children of middle-class families there is often an affectionate relationship while they are members of the same household. They are expected to feel and to express a solidarity with one another greater than their solidarity with their friends or kin of other degree. One upper-middle-class girl, for instance, told of a lower-class girl who reviled her brother for killing her fiance. "Isn't that an awful thing, though," she said, "for her to turn against her own brother that way!" Discrimination by parents toward their children on the basis of age, that is, the favoring of the first-born or the youngest, often results in jealousies and antagonism among children. Outside the household, however, these antagonisms are often disguised; and once the children marry and leave the household, they may be dissolved.

Married brothers and sisters usually maintain their solidarity, and sometimes achieve a greater degree of solidarity, since intimate contact in the household and parental discrimination is at an end. Although children of the same household, as adolescents or as adults, do not usually become members of the same friendship groups, they do have a large amount of social participation with one another. When married, they may be said to have entree into one another's intimate social circles; they become potential members of each other's "cliques." A married girl, for instance, generally includes her sister when she is hostess at a party, although the latter is not a member of her "set," and a "clique" may include a member's sister when the former is being honored at a party. Often, married sisters "assist" one another in entertaining; that is, the nonmember sister is not only invited as a guest but officiates as assistant-hostess. Between married brother and sister there is less social participation directly, since mixed social participation is not a frequent type of activity in the middle class. Their relation, however, is projected to their mates, so that a woman includes her brother's wife in her activities almost as frequently as she includes her own sister. Married sisters visit each other frequently, and the brother's wife is included in this activity. Where servants are not kept, sisters assist one another with child care, errands, and household tasks, as well. Married brothers, too, maintain friendly relations with each other but are less intimate and have less contact than married sisters. This situation may be explained largely by the fact that men are seldom hosts in their own right and seldom entertain other men without their wives' supervision and direction.

Middle-class men do not often give parties for other men, and even mixed parties are initiated and directed by wives; so brothers appear to have little opportunity to take the initiative in including each other in their activities. Their relation and solidarity with each other is expressed more often through the joint activities of their wives than between themselves directly. The wives of two brothers often include one another in their cliques and clubs, or they may exchange calls and invite one another to dinner.

Aid in crises.—Neither in the brother-sister relation nor the parent-child relation of middle-class adults is the obligation to provide mutual refuge as apparent as we shall find it to be in the lower class. This difference may be explained in large part by the increased economic security and greater permanence of the marital relation in the middle class. Middle-class parents and their married children turn to one another for aid in economic crises, however, and feel an obligation to help one another when they are able. Both economic and domestic crises (separation and divorce, for instance) are comparatively infrequent, so that individuals are not often called upon to fulfil obligations arising from such emergencies. In our observation of this community not enough instances of middle-class parents having to aid their married children were observed to determine whether the husband's or the wife's parents were called upon more often. Between brothers and sisters there is some feeling of mutual obligation in economic crises, but it is not so strong as in the parent-child relation. In economic crises brothers call upon one another for aid more often than sisters, and younger brothers ask help from older brothers more often than vice versa.

Extended kin relations.—Other extended kin relations (that is, those outside the immediate family) are recognized by the middle class within certain limits and involve definite patterns of behavior. The extended middle-class family does not constitute a group in itself, however, as in the upper class. It is, rather, a series of relations in which the individual functions in a network of kinship ties through various other individuals who do not necessarily form a group with an all-embracing solidarity. Extended kinship usually does not include relations more than three degrees removed from an individual. It includes particularly the members of his immediate families of orientation—that is, his grandparents and his aunts and uncles. It includes also his first cousins and, to a lesser extent, his great-aunts and great-uncles and their children (his parents' first cousins). These are the significant relations when the individual is a child in his immediate family of orientation.

With his maternal grandparents and his paternal grandparents the child usually has an identical relation; and although an individual child may show a preference for one particular grandparent or one particular type of relation, the middle-class family does not emphasize relations with one grandparent as against another. Often diminutives are applied to grandparents, or their surnames are used with the title "Grandfather" or "Grandmother."

THE WHITE MIDDLE-CLASS FAMILY

Solidarity of alternating generations.—The grandparent-grandchild relation is generally an affectionate, close one. Grandparents sometimes attempt to defend the child against the authoritative demands of the parents; and, in cases of the extreme exercise of parental authority, children may seek refuge in the home of their grandparents. Middle-class children frequently visit their grandparents' homes, where they are much less subordinated than at home. This great solidarity between grandparents and their grandchildren is often expressed as solidarity directed against the children's parents. Such grandparent-grandchild alliances are not sanctioned by middle-class ideology, although they are definitely a part of the behavior. In a sense, grandparents feel that they have a secondary ownership of their grandchildren, an attitude accepted by the grandchildren while they are young, but not usually recognized by the parents. Also, between the maternal and paternal grandparents, antagonisms occur if a child openly expresses preference for one or the other or if his parents show such favoritism.

Relations with aunts and uncles.—The father's and mother's brothers and sisters, as well as their respective mates, are all called "aunt" and "uncle" by the child, and he has an identical relation with all of them. In the middle-class kinship ideology, aunts and uncles are generally accorded a relatively high place in the hierarchy of kin solidarities. Actually, a person's behavior in relation to them is usually less intimate and less affectionate than that with his grandparents. He knows that they are his kin, but his behavior differs little from his behavior toward other friendly adults with whom his parents are intimate. He is expected to be deferential in his contacts with them and to show them the same courtesy which he must accord all friendly adults. In practice, aunts and uncles exercise little authority over him and demand obedience of him only when he is in their house or placed directly under their supervision by his parents. As a rule, a child's concern with aunts and uncles is related only to the fact that they are the parents of his cousins, whom he knows and plays with if they are his age and live in his neighborhood. He may visit their homes with a certain amount of freedom; and they, in turn visit his. In the middle class, where extended family parties and dinners are common, he generally has a certain amount of contact with his aunts, uncles, and cousins, even though they do not live near him.

Unmarried aunts and uncles, or those who have no children of their own, may have relationships with a child which resembles those of a grandparent. These childless aunts and uncles often lavish gifts upon the child, humor him, have him visit their homes, demand little or no obedience of him, and treat him with extreme affection. In his turn, the child is not confused, since they exercise no parental control, as do the parents of cousins his age. He may, therefore, accept them as especially indulgent adults, toward whom he shows affection and with whom he has a certain amount of solidarity.

Although the middle-class child does not have any particular affection for, or particular pattern of behavior toward, aunts and uncles who are also parents of his counsins, these kin often have an affectionate interest in him, devoid, however, of any sense of "secondary ownership" of the child. They take a personal pride in his achievements, in his school honors, Boy Scout honors, and similar accomplishments. They feel some personal responsibility and shame should he not be promoted with his school grade or if he fails to "speak a piece" properly at a public recital.

With individuals more distantly related than grandparents, aunts, uncles, and first cousins, a child cannot be said to have any well-defined behavior pattern. As a rule, he has fewer contacts with them. His great-aunts and great-uncles and their children are generally recognized as kin (as are second cousins, also); but these are generally viewed as less intimate aunts, uncles, and cousins, than first cousins and their parents. They are accorded but little consideration and affection. They are all, however, called by kinship terms, with the exception of third cousins who are of the same generation as themselves. Great-aunts are called either "aunt" or "great-aunt," and parents' first cousins are usually called "cousin" with the first named attached. Beyond these kin relations, however, the child does not recognize kinship, nor is he expected to. For the more extended kin relations he has no kinship terms at all. In the upper class, however, all such persons would be claimed as relatives.

The three significant generations.—In general, extended kinship relations in the middle class include only three generations. Although any given individual in his lifetime actually may have relations with six generations of kin—from his grandparents to his grandchildren, there are usually not more than three generations living and active in kin relations. Relations with his parents and grandparents, his brothers and sisters, his first cousins, together with one or two degrees of lateral extension from these, are the extent of one's extended kin. A great-grandparent, while living, is definitely recognized; but extensions of kinship through to second and third cousins have no significance, nor is a great-grandparent cherished and honored after death. Extended kin include only individuals whose kinship may be traced through other individuals living during one's lifetime. There is little interest in tracing ancestry and claiming kinship with individuals who may be kin through great-grandparents, a practice very common in the upper class.

Relations with "in-laws."—When a middle-class individual marries, he generally adopts his mate's kin as his own and follows almost the same pattern of behavior with them as with his own kin. This applies particularly to his spouse's immediate family. Parents-in-law are generally called by some modified parental term. Perhaps the most common of these is the use of a title such as "Mother Jones" or "Father Brown," although diminutives are often employed, especially if they are already in use by the mate. One middle-class woman called her husband's mother "other-mother." If one's own mother is living, it is generally agreed, among the middle class, that it is disrespectful to her to call another woman "Mother," for this is a relation which must be revered, and the term must apply only to one's actual mother. Should the mother be dead, however, one's "other-mother" may be called "Mother," and the whole pattern of the mother-child relation, in its entirety, may be projected to her. Middle-class individuals, especially wives, attempt to avoid the use of the term "mother-in-law," feeling that it is disrespectful and not intimate enough. One wife said emphatically that the husband's mother should not be introduced to friends as "mother-in-law" or as "husband's mother," but should be presented as "Mother Williams" (husband's surname). In their relations with their sons and daughters-in-law, parents show the same attitudes and patterns of behavior. Although the terms "son's wife," "daughter-in-law," "daughter's husband," and "son-in-law" are used more commonly than "parents-in-law" or "mate's parents," the usual terminology is simply "my daughter" or "my son." The surname is expected to explain the actual relationship.

An individual's relations with his mate's brothers and sisters and with his own brother's and sister's wife and husband have already been mentioned above. The terms "sister" and "brother" are applied to these relatives as frequently as the descriptive terms "sister-in-law" and "brother-in-law." Sisters-in-law usually exhibit an affectionate relation, participate together socially, visit one another, and include one another in their clique and club activities. Their relation resembles, superficially, the relationship of sisters but is, in fact, less intimate and less affectionate. Relationships between brothers-in-law seem to be very similar to those of sisters-in-law.

A person's relations with his spouse's more extended family follow the general outline of his relations with his own family. Relatives are treated in manner similar to behavior toward one's own kin of the same degree of relationship. Although, in speaking of them, an individual may differentiate between his own aunts and uncles, his own grandparents and those of his mate, his own nieces and nephews and those of his mate are generally all called "nephews" and "nieces" without any explanation of actual relationship.

Although, in almost all instances the mates of one's various kin are accepted into the extended family as kin, generally kinship is not claimed through them. An aunt's husband is one's uncle, a definite kin relation; but this uncle's parents, siblings, or more extended relatives are not kin, nor do they have any place in the kinship pattern. Similarly, a brother or sister's mate may even be called "sister" or "brother"; but his parents and other close relatives are not part of his extended family. In this particular relation, however, one may have some vague feeling of kinship, but even this is an indirect relationship through a brother or sister's mate.

CHAPTER VI

THE WHITE LOWER-CLASS FAMILY

IN THE lower class the immediate family is less frequently a permanent structure than within other class groups. Especially in the lower-lower class, the husband-wife relation is often a temporary one which can be broken easily by separation or by divorce. There is little compulsion upon a married couple, either from religious teachings or group pressure, to maintain the relationship throughout their lives. In fact, leaving or changing mates is the general rule in the lower-lower class and occurs often among upper lowers. Careful investigation indicated that very few lower-lower-class individuals over twenty-five years of age had maintained marital relations with the same mate over a period of years. What proportion of "marriages" were legal could not be determined, as the terms "marriage" and "divorce" were used loosely and did not necessarily refer to legal ceremonies. Illegal unions appeared to be common among lower-lower-class individuals and somewhat less frequent in the upper-lower class.

Conception of marital obligations.—Lower-class husbands and wives in Old City do not look upon child-bearing as the primary function of their relationship; and in the lower-lower class especially, sexual compatibility is considered the most important aspect of the marriage relationship. Economic security and physical comfort, however, are also regarded as important factors. As in other class groups, lower-class men are expected to support their wives; but in the event of illness or inability to do so, wives are not averse to earning a living for the family. Thus, through the combined efforts of husband and wife and by a division of labor between them, a greater degree of physical comfort in the home is achieved. Usually, the wife cares for the home and children, while the husband earns a living. This division of duties, however, is less strict than in higher-class groups, perhaps because the men are less regularly employed. Husbands assisting with child care, dishwashing, and sweeping were observed in many instances; and wives working outside the home were not uncommon.

Subordination of the wife.—Lower-class wives are subordinated to their husbands in most of their behavior. This subordination reaches its peak in the matter of economic behavior. Wives of men working for the Emergency Relief Administration, for instance, were almost never able to make any definite statement about the economic status of the family and almost never accepted any suggestions about economic behavior from the Emergency Relief Administration without first consulting their husbands. The reply to E.R.A. investigators was usually: "I don't rightly know. I couldn't say nothing 'till I talked to my old man." One wife explained: "You know how men is. Don't want their women-folk to be listening when they're talking business." Another said, when asked about her husband's wages: "I don't know. I can't tell you. My husband never tells me how much he makes at his work. He doesn't tell me those things. You'll have to ask him about it. I only know that it wasn't much of anything he made. He doesn't make much, I know that."

If a wife performs her household duties and cares for her children reasonably well, her social life during the day is free. She may visit with her neighbors for a bit of gossip without any objection from her husband. Extreme subordination of the wife is not accepted, either by the wife herself or by the lower-class group as a whole. Wife-beating and other forms of physical cruelty are generally condemned. Although in no case were neighbors known to interfere directly in husband-wife antagonisms, they usually sympathize with an extremely subordinated wife and condemn her husband for his behavior. One case was observed of a young couple living in one room of a tenement with two small children. The husband attempted to subordinate his wife completely in all her behavior. He forbade her to leave the room, censored all her relations with her neighbors, forbade her to talk with other women, and flew into a rage if she went out on the street with her children. He explained his behavior simply by saying: "She's a woman and she ain't got good sense."

After five years the wife took her two children and left him, going to live with her father and his second wife. She blamed her husband for the break:

He said I had to do everything just like he told me; he said he was the boss and I had to mind him! He said I had to mind everything he said and do just like he told me. Well, I ain't going to put up with being treated that way, like I didn't have no sense. I don't have to do everything like he says and I'm just going to show him. I ain't going to mind him and he ain't the boss of me. He wouldn't let me go nowheres—just made me stay in that one room with them kids. He had me cooped up there all the time. He didn't like for me even to go uptown nor nothing .... he's been that way even before Johnnie come, but he's just got worse. I said to myself, I said, I'd made my bed and I was just going to have to put up with it; and I stood it for five years, but I ain't going to no more. I been married to him five years and I kept thinking maybe if I was good to him he'd get better, but he ain't .... you ask any of the people there in the house. They'll tell you how bad he been acting, and they're ready to get him locked up in jail, he been carrying on so bad.

He don't want me to go nowhere. He says I ain't a good wife and I don't do like I ought to. Last night he started in and he hollered and called me all kind a things. It was when I come in from going down there to the Relief office here..... He called me a whore and a streetwalker. He said that's what I was and I wasn't no wife of his to be out walking the streets all the time, when I ought to be home in my own house where I belonged..... He don't even want me to talk to no women. He gets mad for me even to talk to the girls. And if I even so much as looks at a man, he goes crazy.

The neighbors who lived in the same tenement corroborated this woman's statements and condemned her husband for his treatment of her. One man said the husband not only treated his wife badly but "ran around" with other women:

Ain't nobody could get along with him. He's just that mean. He's the kind don't do nothing but run around with women all the time and then come home and treat her bad. I don't love to see no man treat a woman like he treats her. It ain't right to treat a woman that mean. She's had a hard time shut up there in that room with them two kids and she can't get out nowhere. He don't let her go no place. She's all right, but you just couldn't live with him he's so mean. . . . .

Yesterday morning he went off to work and she stayed around there till late in the afternoon. She was working around the place. She went in and washed out all the bathroom good, and then did her own wash. Then she sat down and did some sewing on some dress or something she got down there at the Relief. Then she took the kids and went on down to the Relief to take them things, whatever they was. Well, while she was gone, he come on home, and when she got home he started in on her, calling her all kinds of things, like I don't love to hear no man call no woman.

Another neighbor said:

I ain't had no words with her, only when I passed her in the hall. He don't like her to be talking to no one, so I don't bother them none, only if I see her somewheres you know. But I wouldn't want to make it no harder for her, with him carrying on at her the way he does. . . . . He don't do good by her, you can see by the way she looks so unhappy and all.

It ain't right for people to be fussing and carrying on like that when they get married. They ought to live good together and hadn't ought to be fighting all the time. It ain't right. . . . . He wouldn't let that poor little woman go nowheres, didn't want her to go out at all. He called her a streetwalker when she went out anywheres. Why, dearie, he wouldn't even let that girl go to church. You know that ain't right.

From these statements it is apparent that this man's effort to control all of his wife's behavior was not condoned by these other individuals of the lower class. Although wives are generally subordinated to the husband, this subordination exists only within their specific marital relationship and in their relations with their children. Subordination is not expected to extend to the wife's behavior outside the family, that is, to her relations with women neighbors and friends. In the thinking of the lower class, a husband should not attempt to control his wife's relations with other women as long as she fulfils her duties in caring for the house and children.

Care of home and children.—Lower-class husbands are not even subordinated to their wives in the care of the house, nor are they subordinated to the house itself, as sometimes happens within other class groups. In general, lower-class husbands make free with the house for their own purposes; they are not nagged about mud and ashes on the floor; they may demand their meals at whatever hours they wish; and they may bring friends home at any hour. The care of the house, however, is the woman's job.

Children are generally "raised" by the wife, but the husband (when he is the father) is looked upon as the final authority on their upbringing. If the father objects to the mother's treatment or discipline of their children, he is in a position to impose his authority. The wife herself, although she frequently punishes the children by whipping or beating them, often calls upon the father if her attempts at correction are unsuccessful. One mother indicated how strong the husband's authority in "child-raising" is when she told a neighbor to whip her children if they misbehaved, because: "Ain't nobody to mind if you do it. They ain't got no daddy to care if you whip them." Another woman explained that the wife is expected to care for the children but that her husband is an authority on this matter. She said:

> I told Jim I wanted to get me something to do just kind a to help out you know. It's awful for me here in this room here with them kids. But he didn't want me to do it. He said there wasn't nobody could look after them kids like me and he just didn't want me to go off working.
>
> I could get someone to come and stay with them. I thought I could get some Negro to come stay with them cheap. . . . . But Jim says ain't no nigger going to take care of his kids, ain't no nigger can look after them like me.

THE WHITE LOWER-CLASS FAMILY

Sexual behavior.—Although there is a great deal of so-called "divorce" and "remarriage," monogamy is a strictly observed rule in the lower class. An individual is expected to have sexual relations with only one man or one woman at any time. With little difficulty an individual may cease relations with one mate and start relations with another; but sexual promiscuity, the possession of more than one sexual partner at one time, is definitely condemned. One woman said that if she were "sick" of her husband she would

just go right to him and say to him, "I'm sick of you and I don't want to have nothing more to do with you no more. So you can just go on now. I am through with you and I got me another man." And then I'd give him his dee-vorce. It seems like that's the fair thing, so's he'd know what you was up to, and you wouldn't be sneaking around putting something over on him.

Another woman condemned the sexual behavior of her son's girl:

Right away they kind-a made up to each other and they said just as soon as she got well they was fixing to get married. Well, after a while she got so's she could be on her feet some and her sister come back and took her away. She said she was going to take Mary [the son's fiancee] somewhere to live with her. Well, she didn't do like she said she was going to; she took Mary and put her with another man. Of course, when John [the son] found that out, he was right upset and he went and told her it wasn't right her doing that way after her being promised to him. But he couldn't do nothing with her.

More details of the girl's infidelity followed, and the mother concluded:

I pleaded with him and begged him to forget her and all that. And I told him after her doing him that way he could see she wasn't the kind for him. And I just told him no girl like that was the one for him, and she wouldn't make him a good wife noway.

The lower-class marital relation is, thus, a reciprocal relationship in which each partner has certain definite obligations to the other. Should one partner consistently fail to fulfil his implicit obligations, as wage-earner, baby-tender, house-keeper, or exclusive sexual partner, the other partner usually feels that there is no longer any need to meet his own obligations. The offended partner leaves, and the marriage is dissolved. The extremely subordinated young wife discussed above complained of her husband that "he didn't do me right, and you know it. Like him going off to Atlanta. He didn't have no right to go off and leave me that way. . . . . He didn't send me no note nor nothing, just didn't come back. . . . . It seems like you got to eat just the same even if he don't come back. I got the children to feed and all." He had another woman as well, who had now forfeited her claim to the wife's friendship. "I'll tell you what it is though, just between ourselves. It's that girl! Emmie Riley, her name is. He's been playing around with her and that's what's the matter with him. I used to think she was a right sweet girl and I used to be friendly with her, but I ain't no more. I just ain't got no use for her at all no more." In view of this behavior the wife felt released from her obligation to "put up with him" any more.

Causes of separation and divorce.—Failure to fulfil the obligations of the marital relations—specifically, sexual infidelity, physical cruelty, and nonsupport—is a significant cause for separation and divorce. It is not, however, the only cause, nor perhaps the most important. Cruelty to children, real or supposed, lack of interest in the children, or being a "bad influence" on children were mentioned in many instances as reasons for separation. In all cases it was the woman who left her husband because of his attitude toward her children; in no case was a husband known to take the children and leave his wife. Apparently the presence of children in the family does not necessarily result in solidarity between the parents. It may as easily result in antagonism. Parents appear to separate as frequently when there are children as when there are not, and the children very rarely go with their father.

Transfer of children.—Stepchildren are a constant source of antagonism between husband and wife. In many instances, when the mother remarries, the children are given over to some other relative, usually to their maternal grandparents, occasionally to their mother's sister or brother. One woman who had taken in her husband's brother's child said: "His mother is dead, and his father got married again. And his stepmother wasn't good to him. So we took him here. It's nice for our little girls to have him." Another woman who had raised her granddaughter from babyhood stated: "When my daughter separated from her husband, why, of course, we took the baby. Then my daughter married again." Another who gave up her child and later remarried said that she had one grown daughter, but

she doesn't live with me. She lives with my sister, Mrs. McCoy. She's lived with her most of her life. It was when I separated from my first husband, she was just a little thing. I went into training for a nurse, and, of course, I couldn't keep her with me, so my sister took her. And I never did take her away from her. My sister never had any children of her own and she was so good to her, I just didn't like to take her away.

It is probable that a mother, after separation from the father, often gives away her children in order to leave herself free to earn her living and to establish a new marriage relationship with another man.

New husbands and the wive's children.—When they remarry, mothers frequently keep their children with them. In all such cases observed, the children were a source of antagonism between the husband and wife, and in many cases the stepchildren caused the dissolution of the second union. A stepfather usually resented the mother's preoccupation with her children, behavior in which he was not allowed to participate. Although, as we have stated earlier, the real fathers are the final authority in child-raising, stepfathers do not have this control and may not direct or criticize the mother in the socializing of her children. They resent the mother-child relationship in which they cannot, as stepparents, participate. A mother who keeps her children with her, on the other hand, is extremely jealous for her children, very sensitive of her husband's attitude toward the children, resentful of any attempt on his part to discipline them, and indignant if he does not profess to love them "like his own." The presence of stepchildren, then, produces a very awkward situation for the stepfather. He is not encouraged to adopt the whole pattern of the parent-child relation. He is expected to demonstrate parental affection but not to exercise parental authority. The children generally do not look upon him as a parent, and the mother makes no effort to have them do so. He is often referred to as "my mother's husband," generally called by his first name, and is superordinate only because he is older and not because of a family relationship.

Several instances were observed in which women left their husbands because they "wasn't good to the children" of a former marriage. In one case a man left his wife because he disliked his stepdaughter's behavior. A mother whose two grown sons lived with her and her third husband said that she "wouldn't stay with no man that wasn't good to my boys. I wouldn't stand for no man being mean to my children. You got to take care of your children. You can always get you another man." Another left her second husband and returned to her first because the former didn't "treat her good" and wouldn't feed her baby by her first husband. A third woman said that she remarried in order to have her children properly cared for but left her husband when he "wouldn't do right by them":

It was after my husband left me and I was right sickly, and this other man wanted to marry me. I didn't keer much about it, but I had the chance and I thought it would be a good way to get a home fer the children. The man he promised to take good care of the kids, so I married him. But no sooner than he had me in his power than he began to want to git rid of the children and he wouldn't do right by them. . . . . So I left that man and I ain't been back with him no more.

The same informant added:

THE WHITE LOWER-CLASS FAMILY

I had trouble with a man once before who wanted to marry me. I thought it might be a good thing if he would look after the children, as I was right sickly. I was with him as his housekeeper then, but I seen that he waren't going to be good to the children so I told him I wouldn't marry him. . . . .He kept after me quite a lot, but I just didn't want to get tied to him. The other man I was living with was too hard to get along with.

In another case a neighbor told of a separation over a stepchild:

Mrs. Conroy was married to an Eye-talian before she married to Louis, that was Mr. Conroy. She used to worry all the time about Louis. I don't see why she don't forget him. I used to tell her there wasn't no sense her worrying over him. I told her he's gone and she might just as well give him his dee-vorce and let him go. Then she's free of him. He just went off on account-a that child [Mrs. Conroy's child, his stepchild]. Mrs. Conroy told me that herself. She said he just couldn't get along with the child, she was so mean, and that was how he come to go off. That child just run him crazy and had him so worried he just up and left. And ain't going to come back with her there neither. She might just as well stop worrying over him and give him his dee-vorce and get her someone else.

"RAISING" A FAMILY

Attitudes toward having children.—In the lower class the birth of children is generally looked upon as an inevitable result of sexual relations. Married couples expect to have children; and, as far as can be ascertained, they make little effort to prevent conception. Contraceptive methods are little known and less used. In two of the cases studied, wives mentioned the possibility of contraception, but in neither instance was it employed. Apparently, continence is the general method of birth control when any control is considered, as in the case of a young wife who, having had five children in four years, said that she and her husband had ceased sexual relations in order to avoid having more children.

Pregnancy, and even birth itself, are accepted placidly by the women and their husbands. There is little ritual surrounding birth; and the woman's general pattern of behavior is seldom changed, except briefly at the time of birth. Attendance at birth varies from hospital confinement to unattended birth. Probably considerably less than half of the lower-class mothers go to the Charity Hospital—almost none to other hospitals. The great majority of lower-class babies are born at the home of their parents or grandparents. Frequently, if her mother lives in the same community or sufficiently near, a pregnant woman goes to her mother's house; less often the mother comes to her. In most cases expectant mothers are examined by a doctor at the Charity Clinic, where they are advised of the time of arrival. Births at home are attended by doctors, by Negro midwives, or by some older kinswoman. Doctors are most commonly called in by the upper-lower class; midwives or kin by the lower-lower class. In most instances the father of the new child has little concern about its birth. He is not allowed to assist in the delivery, nor are his suggestions concerning attendance and arrangements considered. When older kinswomen, most commonly the wife's mother, are present, they usually take complete charge of the new mother and her baby and exclude the father from all participation. For example, one young wife at the birth of her first child went to her mother's house and was attended by a Negro midwife, although the husband advised her to go the the Charity Hospital or at least to be attended by a doctor. The girl's mother, who took complete charge, speaking of the event, revealed her essentially folk attitudes:

Be two weeks old on Sunday and born right here in this room. Didn't have no doctor either, and got on just as good. We just had a woman in for her, and she was just as good to Laura [the new mother] as anyone could be. Ain't no doctor nor hospital nor nothing could-a been any better than that woman was. She didn't have a hard time at all. The baby come just as easy, and the woman done everything fine. She was a nigger. Maybe you know her, Clara, her name is. She sure was good. I wouldn't have no doctor for her. Jack [the baby's father] wanted her to have a doctor, and he got it all arranged; but, I talked him out of it, and we just had this woman. I always say, ain't no doctor can do for you like a woman can, when you're having children anyway. I wouldn't have no doctor around me. A woman can do just as good and better, I say. I had five of them and I never had no doctor in my house. That Clara was just as good, and she does everything just as easy. We didn't have her on account of it being cheaper either, because it wasn't no cheaper. She charged $15.00 for it. But I just think a woman is better.

When it was suggested to her that a hospital was a fine place to receive good care, she said: "Well, I reckon it is usually, if you ain't got none of your own people to look after you. .... I could look after her good though. I been through enough so I know how to do it."

Parents and children.—Once children are born, they are accepted as a not unpleasant possession. Babies and small children are viewed with pride by both parents and treated with affection. Their first words, first steps, and other evidences of progress are eagerly looked for and admired by father and mother alike. In the socialization and training of the young child the chief concern of the parents is that the child should not annoy adults, especially adult members of the household and, less particularly, adult neighbors. In a sense, there is no "child's world" in the lower class; children are expected to behave as adults at an early age. Fewer concessions are made to immaturity, and the child's pattern of behavior differs from the adult pattern less than in other class groups. Lower-class parents do not attempt to entertain their children, nor are they entertained by them except as babies. Parents and children seldom converse together except to exchange particular information or when parents give commands.

Lower-class children may be said to be almost completely subordinated to their parents. Exact obedience is demanded. The right to demand obedience is often extended to other adult kin and to adult neighbors with whom their parents are friendly. Insubordination—failure to obey or the voicing of objections—is generally punished by whipping or beating. This treatment is most often administered by the mother, although she may call upon the father for further punishment if she fails to subordinate the child. She may even give adult neighbors and adult kin permission to execute punishment.

A child who persists in insubordination—especially among the lower-lower class—is often threatened with a reform school and is occasionally sent to one. Extreme physical punishment is looked upon as the one means of forcing a child to obey, the general theory among lower-class parents being that children should be subordinated at an early age in order that they may be "managed" as they grow older. Children who are "unmanageable," who cannot be "handled," are regarded as a reflection upon their parents, especially upon the mother. One mother of three said:

I won't stand for no child talking back to me and saying he don't want to do a thing I tell him to. When I tell them to do a thing, they got to do it and no back talk. If you want to see me just take a child apart as if it was a rag doll, just watch me when one tells me he don't feel like doing something I tell him to do. I sure do lay it on hard.

Of her son, about seven, she remarked:

I been trying my damnedest to handle him. I beat him, and I don't mind telling anyone who want to know that I beat my children and beat them good. You have to do that. I beat Edward whenever he talks back, and I try to handle him. I sometimes push him just as far back under the bed as I can to make him behave, but it still don't seem to do him no good.

When a neighbor said to her, "There's more ways to handle a child than to just beat him half to death," she said:

No, there ain't much else to do when they don't mind you..... One thing I won't stand for and that is them running away from me. The first time one of them runs away just to get away from me, I swear I am going to put him in the reform school. Once they start that, they ain't worth a damn, because they never will mind you and they will just do it again no matter what you do. So the best thing is just to put them in the reform school where there won't be no other time.

Another mother advised a neighbor to whip her child if he annoyed her:

> Why don't you take a stick to him; that is the thing to do. Don't just bluff him. Just take a stick to him when he won't mind, and give him a good dusting. . . . . Just whip him good when he don't mind you and don't just try to skeer him.

Similar opinions were voiced by the mother of two boys in their teens:

> If they don't do like I tell them, I'll beat them today. I could do it too, those two grown-up boys. I brung them up that way. You got to raise kids right for them to be good when they get big. I raised my kids to know when I said for them to do something they had to do just like I said. You got to start that when they're just little if you want to be able to manage them when they get big. I raised my kids to know who's boss. If you don't, just as soon as they get big enough, they'll start getting sassy and bossing you and you won't be able to do nothing with them.

Lack of supervision outside the family.—Lower-class children, then, are to be seen and not heard, preferably not even seen in many cases. As long as they assist the mother in her household task to her satisfaction and are available for running errands, their whereabouts and occupation is not usually questioned. There are apparently few rules limiting the places children may go, whom they may play with, or how they may behave, except in their contact with their parents, adult neighbors, and adult kin. This is particularly true of lower-lower-class families. Upper-lower-class children are generally punished less severely, and their parents' supervision of their behavior more frequently extends beyond the child's contact with friendly adults. Upper-lower-class children may be said to be somewhat more "protected" than those of the lower-lower class. In both lower-class groups, however, children are expected to care for themselves at an earlier age than in higher social classes. At about five years of age, children—especially girls—start helping the mother with her duties. From about five to fifteen—when boys start earning money and girls marry—children assist with cooking, housekeeping, care of younger children, running errands, and so on. If the father has an independent occupation—such as farming, fishing, painting, plumbing—his sons may assist him instead of their mother. One painter and paper-hanger, for instance, was "teaching" his trade to his two small sons, aged three and four, and occasionally took them with him on an assignment!

Early training.—In both lower-class groups, children are taught to respect personal property and possessions, although this training goes much farther in the upper-lower class. In this group children may not put their feet on the furniture, are punished for defacing the walls of the house, are cautioned not to "track in" mud. In both class groups they are taught that possessions of others are forbidden to them. The rudiments of polite, ritualistic behavior are taught in both groups, more particularly in upper-lower class. Children are taught to respond to adult greetings as soon as they are able to speak, and are told to address adults as "Ma'am" and "Sir." This behavior, however, is not usually extended to their relations with their parents. Physical modesty is enforced, too, at a very early age. This occurs in spite of the fact that the mother frequently nurses her children in public. A public health nurse who recommended sun baths for many small children met with great opposition from lower-class mothers in their insistence upon physical modesty.

Life in the home.—One of the sharpest breaks between upper-lower class and lower-lower class may be found in the rituals surrounding eating and in the type of housing. In the lower-lower class, families seldom sit down around a table together for meals. Members eat when they come in, and, when food has not been saved for them, "forage" for themselves in the kitchen. The most common type of house is a two-room apartment; beds usually accommodate at least two people and often more.

In the upper-lower class, on the other hand, meals are more

formal. The family usually eats together. Although there is rarely a bedroom for each member of the family, three to five rooms are common on this level. A dining-room is almost as rare, however, as in the lower-lower class. In general, the physical conditions of life in the home on the lower-lower-class level are what all segments of the society would describe as "rough." In upper-lower class they approach more closely the middle-class norms of the white society.

FAMILY SOLIDARITIES

The mother-child relationship.—Lower-class children may be said to belong to the mother rather than to the parents jointly or to the father. As was mentioned earlier, the mother either takes the children with her or disposes of them among her kin in the event of separation from the father. Further evidence of this lies in the fact that the great burden of child-training falls upon the mother; and the mother-child relationship is the strongest and most enduring of all lower-class relations, especially in the lower-lower class. The fact that few children in this class group live with their own fathers throughout their childhood, although the majority of them do live continuously with their mothers, is, of course, a large part of the explanation for the greater strength of the mother-child relation.

In the behavior of adult and married children toward their kin the greater strength and permanence of the mother-child relation is also revealed. Although the mother-daughter relation appears to be more intimate than the mother-son relation, mothers and sons do have a greater and more permanent solidarity than fathers and sons. Married children, and adult children living outside the mother's home, still maintain a large part of their childhood behavior in relation to their mother. Absolute obedience is no longer required. Daughters are expected to transfer a large part of this obedience to their husbands; sons, as married men, are accepted by the mother as independent adults.

In periods of crises, however, adult and married children of the lower class turn to their mothers if the latter live in the same community and are able to assist them. Similarly, mothers seek aid from their married children when they are in trouble. In economic crises—continued unemployment and extreme poverty—a married couple turns most frequently to the husband's mother for aid, although they may go to the wife's mother if the former is unable to assist them. In sickness, childbirth, baby care, and so on, they turn to the wife's mother first. This differentiation in parental assistance seems logical in view of the general division of labor between husband and wife: In economic problems—the husband's sphere—assistance is sought through his kin; in domestic crises—the woman's problem—her kin are called upon. In the event that neither mother is able to help them, the married couple call next upon sisters of the wife when in domestic trouble and upon brothers of the husband when in economic difficulty.

Similarly, mothers turn to their married children in economic difficulties, apparently to their married daughters more frequently than to their sons. We found that mothers lived with their married daughters or received financial assistance from them more frequently than they received similar aid from married sons. Adult unmarried sons, however, supported their mothers more frequently than adult, unmarried daughters. In general, children and their mothers feel a mutual responsibility to assist one another in crises. A mother's home is a permanent refuge for her adult children, both sons and daughters; the homes of her married children, especially her daughters, are a permanent refuge for a mother. In no instances, however, were fathers found to be living with their married children; and in only one case observed did an adult child turn to a father in a marital crisis.[1] That fathers take refuge in the homes of their children less frequently than mothers can probably be explained in large part by the fact

[1] In this case the mother was dead. The adult daughter had no sisters and so could turn for aid only to a married brother or to her father.

that men are able to support themselves more easily than women. That children seldom turn to their fathers, however, is evidence that the father-child relation is neither so strong nor so permanent a tie as the mother-child relation.

Brothers and sisters.—The relations between brothers and sisters is often an intimate and affectionate one in the lower class, both as children and members of the same household and as married, independent adults. Among adults, sisters feel closer to each other than to brothers, and the brothers have a sense of solidarity between themselves. The explanation for this probably lies in the fact that lower-class social participation is almost entirely by males and females separately. Married sisters exchange domestic services, help to care for each other's children, and visit and gossip with each other during the day. Married brothers may loaf about together, visit in the evening, drink together, and so on. Possibilities for social contact between a married brother and married sister, however, are limited. Contact occurs chiefly through their respective spouses—that is, the sister and the brother's wife or the brother and the sister's husband.

As children, brothers and sisters participate together in some of their activities; but here, too, a sexual dichotomy exists. We have pointed out, for instance, that there is a division of labor between girls and boys, girls helping the mother primarily, while the boys help the father or stepfather. In their play activities there is also a division between boys and girls, although they do sometimes play together when very young.

Married brothers and sisters call upon each other in periods of crises, especially where the mothers are not available for help. In the lower-lower class, where moving is frequent and neighborhood relations are temporary and unstable, the mother-daughter relation, together with relations between sisters and, to a lesser extent, between sisters-in-law, is the primary basis for social activity. Sisters living in the same community call upon each other in the afternoons, take care of each other's children in case of necessity, gossip together, and sometimes assist one another in the event of illness. Whereas neighbors, who also fulfil these reciprocals, are continually changing, the relation with the sister remains the same whether they live in the same neighborhood or not. The same holds true for the social life of brothers. In the upper-lower class, where residence is more permanent and neighborhood relations are better established, such relations may be said to be secondary to proximity of neighborhood as a source of recreational activity. Such relations are still important, however, and last as long as brothers and sisters live in the same community. Unlike the mother-child relation, which very frequently is maintained in spite of geographic separation, brother-and-sister relations generally dissolve when the individuals live in very widely different localities. Whereas mothers living in different parts of the state sometimes correspond with their children, visit them and are visited by them, and maintain the mutual feeling of having a place of refuge, the children living far apart generally "lose track" of one another and seldom visit or call upon each other for aid.

The kinship structure.—The insecurity of the husband-wife relations and the strong feeling of solidarity between mother and child type the kinship structure of the lower class as predominantly matrilineal and matriarchal. As would be expected in such a system, grandmothers play a vital part and are symbolic of stability in a world of change and of affection in a somewhat "hard" world.

CHAPTER VII

SOCIAL CLIQUES IN THE WHITE SOCIETY

CLASS is no social anthropologist's abstraction to people in Old City, as we have seen. Sometimes they use the term "class." More often they do not. But they always act in terms of it. This is especially evident among the upper and middle classes with respect to their recreational activity. Such persons talk about "my crowd," "our set," "those people," etc. When pinned down to names and dates, they reveal that class is a reality, an ordering principle in their social relationships. For instance, the authors, who for some time had been accepting the hospitality of what seemed to be a small homogeneous group within the upper class of Old City, finally decided to pay off, at one stroke, both their social and scientific obligations by giving a large cocktail party preceding a public dance. Planning this party functioned as one concrete test of the class hypothesis, that *people have a range of social characteristics within which their friends and associates must fall; it is possible to describe this range, and for people in similar social positions it tends to be identical.* A summary from the authors' field notes indicates the nature of the "test":

We mentioned our plan to a few members of the group and explained that we wished to entertain their "crowd" and would like to know whom to invite. These members then prepared a list of about a dozen couples. We explained that we wanted a larger group, so they extended the list to about twenty couples, who, they said, represented *"all* of our crowd." In this larger list there were several couples whom we had not met or with whom we had only a very slight acquaintance, although we did know *of* them. Our informants insisted, however, that our lack of intimacy with these people was unimportant, that they knew who we were and would feel slighted if left out when we entertained, even though they had never met us formally. There were, also, a few other people whom we felt should be included since they were active in clubs with some of our friends or had appeared at one or two group affairs. These individuals were summarily dismissed by our informants with the following remarks: "She sometimes goes with our crowd, but she doesn't really belong. There is no reason why you should invite her." "He used to be in our crowd, but he dropped out and we seldom see him any more." "She would like to be in our crowd, but we can't stand her."

Careful analysis of this event indicated that these persons conceived of themselves as being members of a small, very intimate group—"our little crowd" (the *clique*)—to which, for certain types of affairs they were willing to add a few more couples to form "our large crowd" (the *extended clique*). Beyond these there was a somewhat wider circle of persons with whom they were willing to participate, who could not be ignored, and whose opinion mattered, but with whom they did not associate intimately. Any very large affair should include the entire extended clique, and to omit a member suggested discrimination. Members of the wider participation circle, however, might be deliberately excluded and there would be no ill-feeling, while beyond this latter group there were types of people who, under no conceivable conditions, could be invited to a social affair.

That this clique structure was no isolated phenomenon was subsequently verified by the identification of over sixty cliques, extended cliques, and *intermediate groups* (bridge clubs and special gatherings for the celebration of marriages). These groups comprised over seven hundred people, ranging from adolescence to old age, and were identified by observation, interviewing, and a careful analysis of the social columns of the daily newspaper over a period of two years. It was thus possible to describe the membership and typical behavior of cliques at various class levels, for, while all the members of any one clique may not be within the same social class, clique behavior is definitely "class-typed." The majority of the members of any one adult clique were usually of one social class, and the other members tended to be persons moving up in the social structure or otherwise somewhat loosely related to the clique.

UPPER-CLASS CLIQUES

A group of middle-aged married men and their wives might be used to illustrate a typical upper-class adult clique. In this group the upper-class members set the pattern, and a few upper-middle-class individuals participate with them. The most frequent type of participation, and the most important in the opinion of the group, is that of mixed evening gatherings, frequent and informal. During the summer months the clique meets almost every night at some one of their various homes or at the public dance pavilion, and during the winter they gather at least twice a week. Usually there is no invitation to these gatherings, and often not even a definite appointment. Wives sometimes plan to meet in the evening with their husbands, but more frequently couples drop in at one another's homes and then move about from house to house until they are all congregated together. One clique member explained the manner of "getting together" to the observers: "Just drive around past our houses any night about nine o'clock and see where the most cars are and then come in. That's the way we do. We don't invite people; we just all get together that way."

Behavior at these gatherings, on the part of both the women and the men is carefree. Each man brings his own whiskey which he deposits in the kitchen and from which he mixes drinks for himself and for the women. The host supplies glasses, ice, sugar, and water, and occasionally Coca Cola, the favorite mixer. Both men and women drink heartily, and all prefer to mix their own drinks. Early in the evening the group may sit in one room discussing personalities, group activities, and community affairs or making plans for future group participation. As the evening wears on, the conversation begins to pall; couples dance; the group spreads out into other rooms and the garden, and flirtatious activities begin. The men invite the women to assist them in fixing fresh drinks, and they may exchange kisses and embraces in the privacy of the halls and kitchen. Couples disappear into the garden for long periods; others sit intimately together holding hands, openly or furtively. Flirtations are the general rule and are often "high-pressure." Men sometimes have their particular "girls" over a period of months, and women their special "beaux." These affairs are recognized by the group and are expected of members, but are usually conducted surreptitiously and privately, in dark corners, in the garden, or in parked cars. For the most part, however, these flirtations are confined to group gatherings, and men do not generally have private or secret appointments with other men's wives.

The activities of this clique, then, and the behavior which members expect of each other center about three things: drinking, talking, and flirting. Both men and women are expected to drink continually but not to become violent or unconscious. Flirtations range from mere verbal flattery to prolonged "affairs"; and women may, and frequently do, take some initiative. Members must be able to participate in the conversations of the group spontaneously and without intellectual effort—conversations which deal principally with the "crowd" and its activities. The bulk of this conversation is apparently related to drinking and is a significant element in the clique behavior. In most of it there is little attempt to convey information or to discuss ideas. The clique members are not communicating but communing.

This mixed clique is, itself, composed of two other cliques— one male, the other female—each of which functions separately. The men gather during the day for coffee, and, after working hours, often get together in one of their offices for a few drinks. The women meet casually for soft drinks or highballs, shop together, drive aimlessly about town, and visit one another's homes. Sometimes the women join a group of the men at their offices, at a restaurant or drug store, or merely on the street corner. The men occasionally join the women's group in similar situations, but the mixed evening gathering is the most significant type of clique behavior.

Young uppers.—Among the younger people, solidarities between persons of the same sex tend to be stronger than among married couples. Thus, the eleven girls in one upper-class clique (which included a few upper-middle-class members) had associated with one another since early school days. At that time several small cliques, based on membership in the same high-school class, functioned as a large extended clique. When the older members of this group graduated from high school, about four years before this study began, the oldest clique broke up quite rapidly. Some members went away to college, while others married and dropped out of their clique activities. Those who remained in Old City and those who returned from college after a year or two participated with the younger group through the activities of the extended clique. Then, as the younger girls graduated from high school, they too began to disperse. Finally the remnants coalesced into the present clique, which is being described here.

The behavior of these girls when together is very informal and intimate. Although most of them are employed as secretaries, stenographers, and store clerks, they meet regularly during the day at a certain drug store for Coca Cola and often walk home together after work. They shop together, meet together for luncheons, play lotto at a local knitting shop, or call each other over the telephone for a chat. They are all single and living with their parents, and they frequently visit at one another's homes for meals or to spend the night. These overnight visits are not merely matters of convenience but serve to break the monotony of an evening at home without a "date." The hostess on these occasions, however, feels little or no obligation to entertain her guest. If her hostess has an engagement, the guest cheerfully stays alone, reading, playing the radio, or visiting with members of the hostess' family. When the hostess returns, they discuss her date together and talk about their other friends and more personal topics. The whole attitude and behavior in this situation is, in fact, very much like that of sisters.

While these girls themselves form a very intimate group, they are also a part of a larger mixed clique, which includes six or seven young, single men. Although this at first appeared to be an extended clique, that is, merely an extension of the girls' group, actually the behavior of these young men and women together has the intimacy and solidarity of a clique relation. The activities of this mixed clique are generally evening or week-end parties—casual, informal, and frequent. In many cases the girls and boys make their engagements as individual couples for particular times or events without regard for group activities. The girls may then decide casually to have their "dates" together, or a group of the boys may join forces. Not all of their social activities are in a group, of course, for a single couple often spends an evening alone together. But almost every evening, part or all of the group gathers together casually at some one's home, at a movie, at a dance pavilion, or some such rendezvous. If several couples appear at the same dance without prearrangement, they always congregate in a group; and most of their dancing, drinking, flirting, and general conversation is within their own group.

Not all of the activities of this mixed clique are in paired couples, however. The girls sometimes meet casually or at a formal party in the afternoon and decide to spend the evening together. Those who have evening engagements call their "dates" on the telephone and suggest that they all gather together for the evening. Apparently there is no feeling that each girl should have a definite beau at such gatherings, and the presence of extra girls apparently does not create difficulties. There is, on the whole, little open jealousy among members of the group; some have their special partners; others change about at random.

The behavior of this clique at either formal parties or casual get-togethers is quite uniform. Drinking is common. Each boy usually brings his own whiskey unless the host at an organized party states specifically that he is furnishing the drinks. Most gatherings are jokingly called "B.Y.O.L." (Bring your own liquor). Both boys and girls drink freely, usually the popular southern mixture of corn whiskey and Coca Cola. Everyone is expected to "carry" his liquor; and, in spite of the large quantities consumed, it is rare for anyone to "pass out" or to become violent, and such behavior is thoroughly condemned. At the casual gatherings in the homes of members, couples sit about one room, usually in twos, and discuss individuals or group activities. There may be dancing to the radio and an occasional game of lotto. Couples sometimes hold hands, but wandering into the garden or kissing in dark corners (as their elders do) is condemned. As the drinking progresses, the gaiety and activity of the evening increases. There is more dancing, a group sings together in a corner of the room, conversation becomes noisier, and no one pays much attention to what is said. Often the group decides to motor out to the public dance pavilion. This generally ends the group activity for the evening. Couples leave in separate cars, and some do not appear at the dance at all. Others go in for a dance or two and spend the rest of their time in the parked cars. The activity of the group ends here and that of separate couples begins.

The boys in this clique form a separate male group which meets together during the day for coffee or "cokes," plays lotto together, or occasionally has a stag poker party or hunting party. It differs, however, from the female clique in that the members did not begin their association in early high-school days. Apparently when the girls' clique formed, a number of these boys had just returned from a year or two at college. They began to "date" the girls in the clique, and the solidarity of this female clique brought the boys together in mixed activities. Gradually they became close friends and combined to form a male clique. Most of their social activities, however, are still with the mixed clique rather than with their male group alone.

Upper-class cliques generally do not have any systematic organization, and formal card clubs are rare. Group gatherings are very casual and informal, although these cliques do sometimes have "parties" to which members are definitely invited, and more formal kinds of gatherings are quite common among older women's groups. At clique gatherings, casual or formal, however, upper-class people are comparatively unrestrained in their behavior and do not limit themselves to a particular activity, such as dancing or playing cards.

MIDDLE-CLASS CLIQUES

In contrast to the upper-class behavior described above is that of a small group of married couples in the same age-range but middle class in social position. Most of the women in the group had been friends during their school days. After marriage their husbands became acquainted with each other. The behavior of this group is much more formal and restrained than that of the groups already described. They meet about once a week to play bridge at some member's home; and they participate together, periodically, in other activities, such as week-end parties and picnics. Neither the men nor the women have much other activity in common, although occasionally the women lunch together and play cards, and the men sometimes meet in town after working hours.

At the weekly bridge parties, although the hostess serves refreshments, alcoholic drinks and flirtations are absent. The mother of one of the women called the clique members "nice, quiet young people" who "get together and play bridge and just have a good time without all the drinking." She also revealed her middle-class ideology by describing the group as follows:

They aren't the four hundred by any means, but they are good clean young people. They don't drink and the girls don't smoke, at least most of them don't. Most of the girls knew each other in school and have just kept up their acquaintance since they were congenial and the same kind. Most of them are quite settled. They own their own homes and take a trip now and then. They don't have much money but they are comfortable.

Middle-class cliques in general are much more frequently characterized by formal organization into card clubs, by more restrained behavior, and by more definitely limited activity than among the upper class. In the middle class, mixed groups are not the rule, as they are among upper-class people; men have their groups and women have theirs, and informal activities in mixed groups are comparatively infrequent and are not considered the most important participations. Middle-class cliques, too, are less casual in their group relations. Members of a clique usually receive definite invitations to group gatherings. At these "parties" activity is generally prescribed and definitely limited to card-playing, sewing, informational conversations, and similar formalized behavior. Middle-class women, and men in mixed groups, generally "don't drink," although the men may have drinking parties among themselves, especially in the upper-middle class. Flirtations by married people are roundly condemned.

Often in their clique or club gatherings the women concern themselves with elaborate decorations and refreshments, vie with one another for the most unique appointments or the most unusual delicacies. This behavior is especially characteristic of the upper-middle class, where such embellishments are economically possible and where display of wealth has the greatest significance. This kind of preoccupation is almost entirely lacking in upper-class groups, where little effort is made to decorate the house as a setting for a gathering, where food refreshments are considered of only minor importance, and where a large quantity of corn whiskey is often the primary criterion for the "good party." (In several instances upper-class people expressed great indignation when they were served "fancy" mixed drinks rather than their customary "corn and Coca Cola"; they were annoyed when served elaborate refreshments, especially if early in the evening.)

LOWER-CLASS CLIQUES

Lower-class people generally do not participate in cliques, as that term has been defined. The most common type of informal social participation in the lower class is the casual neighborhood gossiping of the women when they meet on the street or chat "over the back fence." Neighbors may "mind" one another's children or help with the washing; and they sometimes call on one another, "just drop in," during the afternoon. Relatives, too, visit occasionally. None of these are group activities in the sense of upper-class and middle-class clique behavior.

Within the past few years a new basis of solidarity has developed among some lower-class women through relationships established by the Emergency Relief Administration. Although antagonisms arise over jobs and the amount of wages, people "on relief," in general, have a certain solidarity with one another and a feeling of unity which marks them off from others who are not receiving such aid. Among the men, employment on an E.R.A. project, especially when on the same kind of job, forms a basis for new friendships. For women, the E.R.A. sewing-room and mattress factory are an even more important means of social participation, since lower-class women have almost no other activity in groups. Working in the sewing-room, and, to a lesser extent, in the mattress factory, where the work is more confining and less leisurely, has real social significance for them. Although talking during work is not encouraged, recess periods are fairly frequent, and the lunch hour is a social time. Women gossip and express their friendship by sitting together or eating package-lunches together. They thus participate in a group which is their own, freely and without direction, in spite of the fact that their actual work is closely supervised.

Although there is some grumbling and complaining about

the work itself, the sociable part of a day in the sewing-room is generally looked upon as a pleasure; in some instances, wives who were not allowed to work there because their husbands had E.R.A. jobs felt definitely "left out." In a number of cases hot lunches are sent from home for the workers at the lunch hour, and carrying the lunch to the workroom is looked upon as a privilege. Although younger children generally carry lunches to men on the job, older girls or women of the family, or occasionally neighbors, assume the responsibility of taking food to the sewing-room, apparently for a few minutes of sociability. Women who worked in the sewing-room on Monday, Wednesday, and Friday sometimes appeared there at lunch hour on other days, ostensibly carrying some message or food to a worker.

Lower-class husbands and wives have little social participation *together* outside of the home. They do not often visit or entertain as a family group, except occasionally for kinspeople. Husbands tend to spend their time in the company of other men, talking, drinking, and sometimes gambling with them when they are at leisure during the day or after supper in the' evening. In one locality in Old City, an occasional dance and drinking party was held, to which young married men of the lower class sometimes escorted their wives. In general, however, there is little recreational activity in which husbands and wives participate together among lower-class couples.

CLIQUES AND SOCIAL STRATIFICATION

The identification of cliques.—Typical clique behavior at three social levels has been described in the previous section of this chapter, but in order to understand the relationships between cliques and the class system, it is necessary to examine clique structure and activities in detail. This is made doubly necessary by the fact that cliques are not necessarily composed solely of individuals from one class, although clique behavior is usually class-typed, and the majority of the members of adult cliques tend to fall within one class. Individuals, as

Names of Participants of Group I	Code Numbers and Dates of Social Events Reported in *Old City Herald*													
	(1) 6/27	(2) 3/2	(3) 4/12	(4) 9/26	(5) 2/25	(6) 5/19	(7) 3/15	(8) 9/16	(9) 4/8	(10) 6/10	(11) 2/23	(12) 4/7	(13) 11/21	(14) 8/3
1. Mrs. Evelyn Jefferson	X	X	X	X	X	X		X	X					
2. Miss Laura Mandeville	X	X	X		X	X	X	X						
3. Miss Theresa Anderson		X	X	X	X	X	X	X	X					
4. Miss Brenda Rogers	X		X	X	X	X	X	X						
5. Miss Charlotte McDowd			X	X	X		X							
6. Miss Frances Anderson			X		X	X		X						
7. Miss Eleanor Nye					X	X	X	X						
8. Miss Pearl Oglethorpe						X		X	X					
9. Miss Ruth DeSand					X		X	X	X					
10. Miss Verne Sanderson							X	X	X			X		
11. Miss Myra Liddell								X	X	X		X		
12. Miss Katherine Rogers								X	X	X		X	X	X
13. Mrs. Sylvia Avondale							X	X	X	X		X	X	X
14. Mrs. Nora Fayette						X	X		X	X	X	X	X	X
15. Mrs. Helen Lloyd							X	X		X	X	X		
16. Mrs. Dorothy Murchison								X	X					
17. Mrs. Olivia Carleton									X		X			
18. Mrs. Flora Price									X		X			

Fig. 3.—Frequency of interparticipation of a group of women in Old City, 1936—Group I.

has been pointed out in chapter iii, may be placed in the social hierarchy by the use of the interview method. Persons whose social position has thus been ascertained may then serve as points of departure for stratifying other persons, since, given an initial group of stratified persons, it is possible to identify and extend their cliques, thus determining with whom they actually associate and their attitudes toward these persons. The validity of the interview material is, in this way, checked by observation of the actual participants in informal group situations.

NAMES OF PARTICIPANTS OF GROUP II	CODE NUMBERS AND DATES OF SOCIAL EVENTS REPORTED IN *Old City Herald*								
	(1) 6/27	(2) 3/2	(3) 4/12	(4) 9/26	(5) 2/25	(6) 5/19	(7) 3/15	(8) 9/16	(9) 4/8
1a. Miss Thelma Johnson......	×	×	×	×	×	×	×	×	×
2a. Mrs. Sophia Harris.........	×	×	×	×	×	×	×	×	×
3a. Mrs. Kathleen Mills........	×	×	×	×	×	×	....	....	....
4a. Mrs. Ruth Turner.........	×	×	×	....	....	×	×	....	....
5a. Mrs. Alice Jones...........	×	×	....	....	....	×	....	....	....
6a. Mrs. Julia Smith...........	....	×	×	....	....	....	....	....	....

FIG. 4.—Frequency of interparticipation of a group of women in Old City, 1936—Group II.

By utilizing interviews, the records of participant-observers, guest lists, and the newspapers, it was possible to follow in detail the social participation of a large number of individuals and groups in Old City, including many of the persons who had been stratified in the original interview sample. Relationships of any one person who had been stratified to others in a group could be studied, as in the case of Mrs. Evelyn Jefferson, a part of whose participation is given in Figure 3. It will be noted that she participated six times with Miss Mandeville but only twice with Miss Liddell. Each of the women participated less frequently with some persons than with others. The women in Figure 4, although they frequently met on the same day as the women in Figure 3, were never, upon any occasion, at events with them.

From such participation records it was possible to determine, with precision, both the frequency and type of participation. Where it is evident that a group of people participate together in these informal activities consistently, it is obvious that a clique had been isolated. Interviewing can then be used to clarify the relationship. Those persons who participate to-

Type of Membership	Members	Events and Participations													
		1	2	3	4	5	6	7	8	9	10	11	12	13	14
Clique I:	1	C	C	C	C	C	C	–	C	C					
Core.......	2	C	C	C	–	C	C	C	C	–					
	3	–	C	C	C	C	C	C	C	C					
	4	C	–	C	C	C	C	C	–						
	5		P	P	P	–	P	–	–						
Primary...	6		P	–	P	P	–	P	–	–					
	7				P	P	P	P	–						
Secondary.	8				–	S	–	S	S						
Clique II:	9				S	–	S	S	S						
Secondary.	10						S	S	S	–	–	S			
Primary...	11						–	P	P	P	–	P			
	12						–	P	P	P	–	P	P	P	
	13						C	C	C	C	–	C	C	C	
Core......	14					C	C	–	C	C	C	C	C	C	
	15						C	C	–	C	C	C	C	C	
	16						S	S	S	–	S				
Secondary.	17								S	–	S				
	18								S	–	S				

Fig. 5.—Types of members of, and relationships between, two overlapping cliques.

gether most often and at the most intimate affairs are called *core members;* those who participate with core members upon some occasions but never as a group by themselves alone are called *primary members;* while individuals on the fringes, who participate only infrequently, constitute the *secondary members* of a clique. The analysis of the fourteen events in Figure 3 is presented in Figure 5 in such a manner as to indicate the types of membership which each of the 18 women has. It will be noted that they fall into two overlapping cliques, on the basis of frequency of participations. The "boundaries" of the cliques were ascertained by interviewing. Miss Ruth De Sand, for instance, was claimed by members of both cliques; but Miss Pearl Oglethorpe, by Clique I, though she was on the fringes. Miss Verne Sanderson was claimed by Clique II.

Social uniformities of clique members.—Once it has become clear, from a study of the frequency of participation coupled with interviewing, that a group of people form a clique, an extended clique, or an intermediate group, and the approximate social position of the group having been ascertained, the search for social uniformities can begin.[1] What kind of people tend to associate together? Are they of similar ages? Do they tend to be kinsmen? Do they pursue similar occupations? Do they have a similar standard of living? Do they attend similar churches and associations? Are there any generalizations about clique structure and behavior which emerge from the study?

Forty-three participation groups, representing a total of over 400 individuals, were analyzed intensively in order to seek answers to these and similar questions. The groups studied included a large proportion of all the informal groups which reported their activities to the *Old City Herald* during the period of the research. At the outset, two facts were obvious: (1) most of the newspaper items dealt with the activities of female or mixed male and female affairs; (2) lower-class adults were almost never mentioned in the social columns and among the personal items, although their children were sometimes mentioned in connection with school cliques. Since it is the women in Old City who tend to be most conscious of class lines, and since they "organize" the class behavior of the men, such data on female and mixed cliques is a definite index to

[1] The method by which social participation was recorded, and by which the interlocking and overlapping of .cliques was ascertained, is demonstrated in Figures 3, 4 and 5.

151

TABLE 1a

Social Characteristics of a Sample of 43 White Participation Groups in Old City: Clique Group I

Group	Type of Group*	Social Position of Group§		Age		Marital Status†	Sexual Composition‡	Church Membership	
		Average	Range‖	Average	Range			Average	Range
1a	EC	U1	UU–LU	65	50–80	m	F	Epis.	Epis.–Pres.
1b	Cl	LU	UU–M1	45	35–48	m	MF	Pres.	Epis.–Pres.
1c	EC	LU	UU–LU	35	28–48	m	MF	Epis.–Pres.	Prot.
1d	IG	M1	UU–UM	60	50–66	m	F	Epis.	Prot.
1e	Cl	M1	U1–UM	45	45–51	m	MF	Epis.	Epis.–Pres.
1f	EC	M1	LU–UM	40	35–47	m	MF	Prot.	Prot.–Jewish
1g	IG	M1	LU–UM	28	21–33	m	MF	Epis.–Pres.	Prot.–Cath.
1h	Cl	M1	UU–UM	27	24–42	ms	F	Epis.–Pres.	Prot.
1i	EC	M1	UU–UM	24	21–27	s	MF	Prot.	Prot.–Cath.
1j	Cl	M1	UU–M2	24	21–31	ms	F	Epis.	Prot.–Cath.
1k	IG	M1	LU–UM	20	20	s	F	Prot.	Prot.–Cath.
1l	IG	UM	U1–UM	27	23–31	m	F	Epis.	Prot.–Cath.
1m	IG	UM	M1–M2	21	19–22	s	F	Epis.	Prot.–Cath.
1n	Cl	UM	M1–M2	21	20–22	s	MF	Cath.	Cath.

Io.........	EC	UM	LU–M2	20	19–22	s	F	Prot.–Cath.	Prot.–Cath.
Ip.........	EC	UM	U1–LM	18	16–20	s	F	Prot.	Prot.–Cath.
Iq.........	EC	UM	LU–M2	16	15–18	s	F	Prot.	Prot.–Jewish
Ir.........	EC	M2	U1–LM	13	12–16	s	F	Prot.	{Prot.–Cath. Jewish}

* The types of participation groups represented are: Cl, cliques; EC, extended cliques; IG, intermediate groups (see pp. 158 to 161 for definitions of these types of participation groups).

† m, all members married; s, all members single; ms, both married and single members.

‡ F, female; M, male; MF, both male and female members.

§ See page 62 for method of ordinating groups.

‖ UU, upper-upper class; U1, upper-upper or upper-middle; LU, lower-upper; M1, lower-upper; UM, upper-middle; M2, upper-middle or lower-middle; LM, lower-middle; L1, lower-middle or upper-lower; UL, upper-lower; L2, upper-lower or lower-lower; LL, lower-lower class.

There were some persons who were obviously "mobile," that is, they had many of the characteristics of two subclasses. No attempt was made to assign these persons rigidly to one class or another. They were called "indeterminate" and are referred to as U1, M1, M2, and L1. Many of these persons will eventually become stabilized at some given class position. (Since there were no lower-class individuals in the sample, UL, L2, and LL have been omitted from the table.)

153

TABLE 1b

SOCIAL CHARACTERISTICS OF A SAMPLE OF 43 WHITE PARTICIPATION GROUPS IN OLD CITY: CLIQUE GROUP II

GROUP	TYPE OF GROUP*	SOCIAL POSITION OF GROUP§		AGE		MARITAL STATUS‡	SEXUAL COMPOSITION‡	CHURCH MEMBERSHIP	
		Average	Range‖	Average	Range			Average	Range
IIa	CI	UM	UM-M2	28	25-39	m	MF	Pres.	Pres.-Epis.
IIb	EC	UM	UM-M2	38	36-40	m	F	Cath.	Prot.-Cath.
IIc	EC	UM	UM-M2	40	31-57	m	MF	Meth.	Prot.
IId	EC	UM	UM-	40	28-45	ms	F	Epis.	Prot.
IIe	IG	M2	UM-L1	60	?-61	s	F	Prot.	Prot.-Cath.
IIf	CI	M2	UM-M2	18	16-19		F	Cath.	Cath.
IIg	IG	M2	M2-LM	27	22-32	m	F	{Prot. / Cath.}	Prot.-Cath.
IIh	EC	M2	UM-LM	27	22-31	m	F	Cath.	Jew
IIi	CI	M2	M2-LM	28	24-30	ms	F	Prot.	Cath.
IIj	IG	M2	UM-M2	29	22-35	m	MF	Cath.	{Prot.-Cath. / Prot.-Cath.}
IIk	EC	M2	M2-LM	40	27-50	m	MF	Jew	Jew
IIl	IG	M2	UM-M2	48	30-53	m	F	Cath.	Jew
IIm	EC	M2	UM-LM	32	30-45	m	F	Prot.	Cath.
IIn	IG	M2	UM-L1	50	33-70	s	F	{Prot. / Cath.}	Prot.-Cath.
IIo	EC	LM		14	12-16	s	MF	Cath.	Cath.

154

IIp	IG	LM	UM-L1	20	16-23	s	F	Cath.	Cath.
IIq	IG	LM	UM-LM	24	21-37	s	F	Cath.	Prot.-Cath.
IIr	IG	LM	M2-LM	27	21-40	m	F	Meth.	Meth.
IIs	IG	LM	LM	32	29-35	s	F	Cath.	Cath.
IIt	IG	LM	M2-LM	35	25-58	m	F	Cath.	Cath.
IIu	EC	LM	M2-LM	35	33-39	m	MF	?	Prot.-Cath.
IIv	Cl	LM	LM-L1	35	21-36	m	F	Cath.	Prot.-Cath.
IIw	EC	LM	M2-LM	40	25-58	m	F	Cath.	Prot.-Cath.
IIx	IG	LM	M2-LM	18	25-53	s	MF	Cath.	Prot.-Cath.
IIy	EC	L1	M2-L1		16-20			Cath.	Cath.

* For *, †, ‡, §, and ‖ see Table 1a.

155

class behavior, however. The absence of lower-class news items proves conclusively that there is a "social rift," which merits study, between the lower class and the rest of the white society.

Furthermore, comparisons between the core, primary, and secondary members of each clique and extended clique indicate that there is a certain limit to the amount of variation in social characteristics; that, in general, the uniformity in any one clique is such that it can be described as being of a certain age, class-behavior pattern, or educational level; that core and primary members are generally more uniform in these traits than secondary members; and that cliques are more uniform in social characteristics than extended cliques, especially with regard to class status of members.

Class and clique.—As has already been mentioned, cliques can be class-typed by the behavior pattern which the members exhibit. They may also be described in terms of the proportion of individuals within them belonging to a given class position. The social status of a clique may be stated either in terms of the class range of its members or in terms of a "modal average" of the class positions of its members. For instance, Clique Ic in Table 1, includes 13 persons, stratified as upper-upper and lower-upper class. It's average class position, however, is lower-upper. Each participation group studied has been designated according to its class range and class average and typed by its behavior pattern (see Table 1).

AGE, CLASS AND CLIQUE

Age uniformities.—As might be expected, there is a general tendency for people of the same age to associate together. An examination of the cliques listed in Table 1 indicated that age uniformities were more characteristic of core members than of primary and secondary members, and that cliques of young people tended to be more homogeneous with respect to age than older groups. This is due partly to the fact that young people tend to be age-graded by the school system but,

TABLE 2

ANALYSIS OF THE SOCIAL PARTICIPATION OF THE FEMALE MEMBERS OF 8 WHITE CLIQUES: AGE 20-29

Participation Groups*	Average Class Position	Average Age	Sex	Marital Status	Number of Females	Total Participations of Female Members			Extra-Clique Participations of Female Members			
						Total	Clique	Extra-Clique	With Groups Less than 10 Years Different		With Groups Less than 5 Years Different	
									No.	Percentage	No.	Percentage
Ig............	M1	28	MF	m	8	131	111	20	17	85.0	12	60.0
Ii............	M1	24	MF	s	11	293	234	59	54	91.5	40	67.8
Ih............	M1	27	F	ms	11	191	93	98	79	80.6	56	57.1
Il............	UM	27	F	m	9	140	88	52	44	86.7	39	76.9
IIa...........	UM	28	MF	m	5	32	25	7	6	85.7	4	57.0
IIi...........	M2	28	F	ms	13	119	75	44	44	100.0	34	77.3
IIj...........	M2	29	F	m	6	43	28	15	15	100.0	11	73.3
IIg...........	M2	27	F	m	9	55	35	20	17	85.0	10	50.0

* See Table 1 for description of each group.

157

upon leaving school, are no longer separated into more or less limited age groups and are thrown together, through employment and other relationships, with persons of wide age range. (Also, there are probably more people of the same general age group among young people, since, all other things being equal, as age increases, the actual number of individuals of a specific age decreases, and any participation at all on an extended scale must include younger people.) The participation of 72 young women in eight of the groups listed in Table 1 was studied in detail (See Table 2). It was noted that even when these women were associating with persons outside of their own cliques the bulk of their extra-clique participation was with persons less than ten years different in age. In general, the age range within cliques tends to increase as the median age of the clique increases.

Interclique participation.—It has already been demonstrated that individual cliques are associated with certain types of class behavior and that the range of social characteristics of the members of a clique is limited. The relationships between the members of different cliques is an even more revealing index since a person does not always participate within his own clique. A core member of one group may be a primary or secondary member of another clique or may, on some occasions, go to the affairs of cliques to which he does not belong. A study of the totality of overlapping cliques and of interparticipations between clique members reveals clearly the class structure of the society. It answers the question "With what kind of people does X, under no conditions, participate socially?" as well as "With what kind of people does X usually associate?"

All of the cliques and intermediate groups composing Clique Group I (Table 1a) were found by empirical analysis to be interlocking and overlapping; that is they formed a large

SOCIAL CLIQUES IN WHITE SOCIETY

interparticipating group.[2] The cliques and intermediate groups in Clique Group II (Table 1b) were similarly related to each other. The members of the 18 groups in Clique Group I, however, had virtually no social participation with the 25 in Clique Group II; they did not attend each others parties nor have other intimate relations.

That such a phenomenon—205 persons in old city who had virtually no intimate social contacts with 238 other persons— was associated with class factors was demonstrated by an analysis of the class position of all the individuals in the sample. Such a study revealed that while neither clique group contained any persons below the upper-lower class, Clique Group II contained no persons above the upper-middle class, and almost 40 per cent of its members were even below this class. In Clique Group I, on the other hand, over 20 per cent of the participants were in the upper class, none were as low as upper-lower class, and only 7 of the 205 individuals were below upper-middle class. (Table 3). These interrelationships between Clique Groups I and II are illustrated graphically in Figure 6.

It will be noticed that there are some persons in both Clique Groups I and II who fall within the range of upper-middle class and lower-middle class. This raises an immediate question: "Why do some middle class persons participate in a large clique-group containing uppers while others do not?" This is due, in the first instance, to an age differential, as can be seen from Table 4. Over 50 per cent of the middle-class

[2] The individuals were stratified by the method outlined in chapter iii, p. 62. Many of them were "placed" by persons whose social position had been worked out previously. Others were assigned a class position because their behavior and ideology conformed to that of the class configuration developed from interviews and observation. Secondary members of cliques which had been class-typed by behavior pattern were "placed" by interviews with core members. Thus, an upper-class woman, "old aristocracy," might state: "Mrs. X comes to our parties, but she's not 'old aristocracy'." The person referred to was, therefore, tentatively stratified as lower upper. If other interviews and an analysis of her family pattern confirmed the placement, she was definitely placed in that position.

159

DEEP SOUTH

TABLE 3
DISTRIBUTION OF 443 INDIVIDUALS IN CLIQUE GROUPS I AND II BY AGE GROUP AND SOCIAL CLASS

AGE GROUP	NUMBER OF GROUPS	NUMBER OF PERSONS	UU	U1	LU	M1	UM	M2	LM	L1	Unknown
Clique group I:											
Over 60	1	21	8	7	6	....	....	....	....	....	....
50–60	1	8	1	1	2	2	2	....	....	....	....
40–49	3	16	1	4	2	5	4	....	....	....	....
30–39	1	15	5	1	9	....	....	....	....	....	....
25–29	3	28	1	3	8	5	8	3	....	....	....
20–24	6	64	6	2	5	15	23	13	....	....	....
15–19	2	30	....	1	1	4	14	7	1	....	2
10–14	1	23	....	1	1	2	5	7	6	....	1
All	18	205	22	20	34	33	56	30	7	....	3
Clique group II:											
Over 60	0	....	....	....	....	....	....	....	....	....	....
50–60	2	15	....	....	....	....	6	7	2	....	....
40–49	5	49	....	....	....	....	19	23	6	....	1
30–39	7	67	....	....	....	....	6	27	30	2	2
25–29	6	54	....	....	....	....	8	32	11	1	2
20–24	2	25	....	....	....	....	2	11	10	1	1
15–19	2	20	....	....	....	....	1	8	3	7	1
10–14	1	8	....	....	....	....	1	2	1	3	1
All	25	238	....	....	....	....	43	110	63	14	8
Total for both clique groups	43	443	22	20	34	33	99	140	70	14	11

* UU, upper-upper class; U1, upper-upper or lower-upper; LU, lower-upper; M1, lower-upper or upper-middle; UM, upper-middle; M2, upper-middle or lower-middle; LM, lower-middle; L1, lower-middle or upper-lower; UL, upper-lower; L2, upper-lower or lower-lower; LL, lower-lower.

There were some persons who were obviously "mobile," that is, they had many of the characteristics of two subclasses. No attempt was made to assign these persons rigidly to one class or another. They were called "indeterminate" and are referred to as U1, M1, M2, L1, and L2. Many of these persons will eventually become stabilized at some given class position. (Since there were no lower-class individuals in the sample, UL, L2, and LL have been omitted from the table.)

160

persons in Clique Group II are over thirty years of age; less than 10 per cent of those in Clique Group I are within this age range. These younger middle-class people tend to partici- pate with persons above them in class. They are mobile people "on the way up." The middle-class people in Clique Group II are, on the whole, older; their status is more defi- nitely set; and they tend to participate almost exclusively

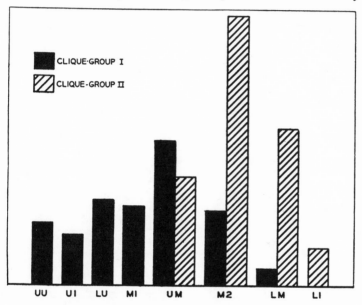

CLIQUE-GROUP I

CLIQUE-GROUP II

UU   UI   LU   MI   UM   M2   LM   LI

FIG. 6.—Distribution of 443 white clique members by social class.

within their own group and with persons immediately below them. The middle-class people, then, in Clique Group I, being younger and more mobile, are therefore found more often associating with upper-class persons than the members of Clique Group II, who are older and more stable and have fewer social contacts with persons above them on the social scale.

The participation line.—We have thus far dealt with two

factors that seem to be related to social participation in cliques and other informal groups—age and class. These relationships may be further clarified by an examination of Figure 7. Individual extended cliques are represented by rectangles arranged in age groups. The heavy diagonal line represents the basic division between Clique Groups I and II laid against age-class co-ordinates. (Figure 8 represents a more generalized conception of the "participation line.")

TABLE 4

AGE DISTRIBUTION OF THE UPPER-MIDDLE-CLASS AND LOWER-MIDDLE-CLASS MEMBERS OF CLIQUE GROUPS I AND II

AGE	CLIQUE GROUP I			CLIQUE GROUP II		
	Number	Percentage	Cumulative Percentage	Number	Percentage	Cumulative Percentage
Over 60......						
50–60........	2	2.1	2.1	15	6.9	6.9
40–49........	4	4.3	6.4	48	22.3	29.2
30–39........				63	29.3	58.5
25–29........	11	11.6	18.0	51	23.4	81.9
20–24........	36	38.6	56.6	23	10.8	92.7
15–19........	22	24.1	80.7	12	5.5	98.2
10–14........	18	19.3	100.0	4	1.8	100.0
Total....	93	100.0	100.0	216	100.0	100.0

The increasing width of the rectangles from the ten-fifteen year age range to the sixty-eighty year age range represents the fact that the age spread within cliques becomes greater as the average age of the cliques increases. The vertical arrows within the rectangles indicate that participation within any given age range has a limited class range. Participation between the extended cliques within a clique group is represented by diagonal arrows, so slanted as to indicate that extended cliques tend to link together individuals of at least two subclasses. The shaded area between lines a and b is indicative of the fact that in groups between ten and twenty-five years of age, some individuals who are classified as lower-

SOCIAL CLIQUES IN WHITE SOCIETY

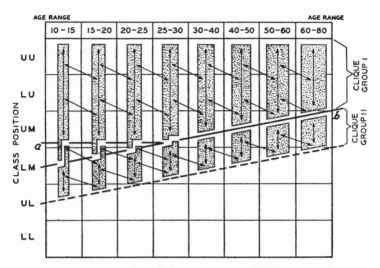

FIG. 7.—Interparticipation of clique groups I and II in an age-class configuration.

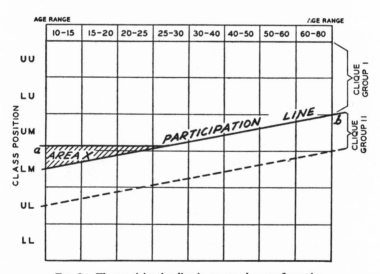

FIG. 8.—The participation line in an age-class configuration

163

middle class because of their parents' status belong to cliques composed largely of young people of a higher status. Conversely, some upper-middle-class young people belong to lower-middle-class cliques.

The heavy broken line is a second "participation line," dividing this entire newspaper sample from those persons who do not secure this type of publicity at all. Starting just below the upper-middle-class division in the higher age groups and dropping down to the top of the upper-lower class in the youngest age groups, it is the line of lowest status in Clique Group II—the "social rift," previously referred to. Below this line are the persons whose names never appear in the social columns, whose intimate affairs are not news, and who have little or no informal recreational activities with the persons above the line. Their pattern of clique behavior, too, differs radically from that of both Clique Groups I and II, a fact verified by interview and observation.

Further examination of Table 3 reveals that while cliques are linked together by interparticipation between the different cliques within a clique group and people sometimes participate across age lines, among the older age groups there generally is a narrower class range of participation. Thus, members of the oldest group in Clique Group I (over sixty) all fall in the upper class, while members of the youngest group (ten to fourteen) ranged from upper-upper to lower-middle class. The groups between these two extremes show a progressive decrease in range of social status with increase in age. We might conclude from this that *cliques with a predominantly young membership combine persons of a limited age range and a wide class range, while older groups tend to be limited in class range but have a wide age range.*

Significance of kinship.—Where people do participate outside of their age group, it is usually with people of their own class; and when this is not true, it is usually because of the fact that an individual has a close tie with some one person outside of his class-age group which relates him to another individual of that person's class. Thus, it is customary for a woman to have girls serve as "floating hostesses" at older clique affairs, and when this occurs, the younger person is usually in the same class, although one of the girl's clique members who might be in another class may serve, too. Occasionally, an older person gives a party for a younger girl in her class, or for one of her own relatives, to which some of the honored person's clique members below her in class may come. It is significant that, while kinship enters into less than 30 per cent of general interclique participations, 60 per cent of all participations in a wide age span but narrow class span involve kinspeople—daughters and mothers, aunts and nieces, or cousins.

THE LIMITS OF SOCIAL PARTICIPATION

The various "rules" of social behavior so far discussed are all general formulations and are, in no case, absolute. Exceptions may be found to the usual pattern of group composition and to the general schemes of intergroup behavior. There is, however, one kind of social participation which is so rare as to be almost nonexistent in Old City: participation *directly* "up and older" or "down and younger." That is, an individual seldom associates directly with others who are superordinate to him in both social position and age or who are both in a lower social position than he and much younger. When such participations do occur, they are *indirect*, through other specific individuals. For example, a lower-middle-class member of a predominantly upper-middle-class group of twenty-year-olds would not participate directly as a single individual in an activity of a twenty-five-year-old group which had a status above lower-middle class and which included no lower-middle-class members. She might, however, participate indirectly if some one upper-middle-class member of her clique were being entertained or used as hostess.

The scope of possible participations in terms of class and age, together with these "prohibited" participations, is represented in Figure 9. Here a theoretical individual of upper-middle-class status and thirty years of age is represented by a circle. The heavy arrows have been drawn to indicate in what directions she may participate. More specifically, a thirty-year-old woman of upper-middle-class status often participates as a member of an extended clique composed of individuals of about her own age and of a social position slightly above or

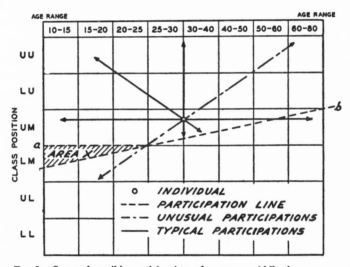

FIG. 9.—Scope of possible participations of an upper-middle-class woman

below her own. She may participate as a nonmember in the events of groups a little older or a little younger if they have a social position like her own. She may act as "floating hostess" for a member of a group much older than her own but of the same class position; or she may give a party for a girl much younger but of her own status. But she is almost never seen acting as "floating hostess" in a group of higher social position or giving a party for a group of lower status.

In the total study less than a dozen such participations, "against the rule," were observed. In each of these instances the ineligible individual participated indirectly, with and through another individual, who was eligible in terms of age and social position and with whom she had a strong individual relation. This situation is pictured in Figure 10, in which the upper circle represents an upper-class core member of Clique E, and the lower circle represents an upper-middle-class core member of the same clique. It will be observed that there

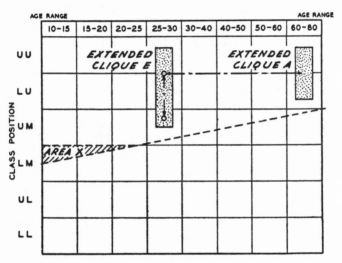

FIG. 10.—Social participation through an indirect relationship: "Up and Older"

is no arrow connecting the upper-middle-class individual directly with upperclass clique, A, but the arrows indicate that such an individual may be brought into contact with Clique A only through her relationship with the upper-class member of her own clique, E.

THE CLIQUE—A DYNAMIC UNIT OF SOCIETY

A clique is more than a statistical unit which makes convenient the study of social stratification. It is a dynamic unit of society, a group of people sharing a common pattern of life, changing through time. Cliques are small social systems within themselves, voluntary aggregations coming into being spontaneously, interacting, sometimes coalescing, occasionally disintegrating.

Each clique has a definite membership sharing a feeling of unity and solidarity and a common behavior pattern. The members, however, are not a socially significant group merely because of the uniformity in behavior or other characteristics, but rather because of the intimate interaction between them. The internal structure of each clique is a pattern of relationships, and this configuration of the relationships of each member to every other member is, in the ultimate analysis, the basis of the clique. The various parts of a clique are based on these relationships. Thus, a core member differs from a primary member because the sum total of his relationships is different. This configuration has considerable stability in time. Some changes do occur, but they are not rapid and do not include all members at one time. In spite of changes affecting the relations of some of the members, the general pattern of a clique persists over a period of time and sometimes lasts for years. Individuals often mention the duration of their cliques, saying, for example, "This has been our crowd since we were in school together," or "We have all run around together for years."

In spite of this stability of the total clique configuration there may also be a continual process of change apparent in the specific relations between individual members. Thus, strong one-to-one relationships between two core members will often disrupt a clique, particularly if the pair be a courting couple. The group is continually passing judgment upon its members' friends, accepting or rejecting them as associates. When quarrels arise between members, there is often a split on the basis of nonclique loyalties. Kinship ties seem to take precedence over clique ties in most situations of this type, although core members are less apt to break off from a clique because of such antagonisms than are secondary or primary members. There are frequent "falling-outs" and occasional reconciliations within the world of the cliques and extended cliques.

SUMMARY

While cliques exist at all class levels, such groups in Old City could be studied most easily on the upper- and middle-class levels, where newspaper accounts were available. It was possible to class-type cliques and to describe them and their members in terms of significant social characteristics. There were significant uniformities of social status and age among these groups and certain definite relationships between these factors.

To many an individual the clique is of tremendous emotional significance. Outside the family, it is often the only group to which one has a strong feeling of "belonging." It is a group to which an individual is bound by the strongest of ties. Clique mates are his "real friends," the ones to whom he turns in either pleasure or trouble. Since the clique is so important to its members, it exerts a powerful influence over their behavior. To be accepted, they must behave according to the standards of the group; and so the behavior of the members is "controlled," particularly in their relations with one another. As a result, each clique may be said to have definite behavior patterns which are fairly uniform for all members of the group and which follow rather closely the behavior patterns of the particular class level on which it functions.

The clique demonstrates, more clearly than any other group, the function of the class structure in determining the scope and context of an individual's social relationships. The class position of an individual determines, to a large extent, not only with what other individuals he may have frequent, intimate, and informal participation—that is, to what clique he may belong—but also with what members of other cliques he may have occasional informal and formal participation. The clique, furthermore, has a very important function for the class structure, since through the clique relations an individual develops his personal orientation to adult society, an orientation begun by his family but finished by "his crowd." If he is a member of a very stable group, his activities and associations may be restricted to a limited group throughout his life. The dynamic processes of change within his clique also establish new relationships for him and provide opportunity for him to change not only his clique status but his class status as well. Thus, by its effect upon its individual members the clique affects the entire class structure of the society.

It is evident, however, that the clique's acceptance or rejection of an outsider is not entirely explained by his social position. Rather, his relation to the group is dependent, first, upon his relations with one clique member and, second, upon the importance which that member has within the clique structure.

Under the censoring or approving eye of the clique the individual is constrained to abide by the class "rules." It is here, among his intimates, that social status is of supreme importance, that he becomes aware of social pressures. At the same time, the more subtle controls operate which make a person feel at ease with his "crowd" or ill-at-ease because he is out of place. The clique cements the individual to his class and also provides an opportunity for the mobile person to rise a notch in the social scale through his acceptance by those who are already slightly "above" him.

CHAPTER VIII

SOCIAL MOBILITY WITHIN THE WHITE CASTE

THE PROCESS OF SOCIAL MOBILITY

THE family, cliques, and associations in Old City constitute a social structure through which the various class standards find expression and which serve both to delimit and to tie together the social classes. Such groups as have been described, thus far, are the familiar "fixed points" by which people place and identify each other and through which they find individual expression and adjustment. These institutions and the sentiments associated with them form the matrix of existence. They also serve as mechanisms for social mobility, for permitting individuals to move up and down in the class system.

The preceding discussions of the characteristic behavior of the different social classes might suggest that class lines are rigid, that every member of the society fits absolutely and finally into a particular class position. Actually, however, there is a significant amount of social mobility, of movement from one class or subclass to another above or below. If this were not so, the groups would be castes, not classes. This process of mobility is, however, a gradual one, and the shift in individual positions is sufficiently infrequent and slow enough to preserve the class structure. The pace of mobility also permits analysis of class traits and definition of the general patterns of class behavior. That one's immediate family is the prime determinant of his social position and that an individual secures a class position at birth through his identification with his parents has already been pointed out. The extent of this identity alone, which varies in degree among the different classes and which reaches it peak in the time-conscious upper class, suggests that social mobility is not a simple process.

To become a member of a class other than the one into which he is born, an individual must learn to behave and to think like the class toward which he is moving, and he must come to participate intimately with members of that class. In other words, he must break his identity with the class of his birth and with his family; he must become identified with the class toward which he is moving. This process takes time. The actual amount of time involved in mobility and the various techniques employed, either consciously or unconsciously, differ, of course, for the various class groups, just as the patterns of class behavior differ. In general, mobility from one subclass to another within the same class is, on the whole, a simpler process than moving across a class line. To move from lower-middle to upper-middle class, for example, does not demand changes in the fundamentals of behavior and ideology, but rather requires a greater development of a pattern already held. Moving from upper-middle class to lower-upper class, on the other hand, is dependent upon a greater change in overt behavior and ideology. For this latter step one must abandon his criterion of wealth and adopt, rather, the upper-class reverence for time and the past. He must cease to concentrate upon giving the appearance of contemporary individual wealth and adopt, instead, a reverence for past wealth. He must pattern his behavior not upon contemporary group rules or religious teachings but after the old, traditional upper-class behavior.

Before attempting to analyze upward mobility between specific class groups, it should perhaps be noted that any social movement either up or down is usually a gradual and orderly progression. An individual born into lower-middle class, for example, may move upward into upper middle or downward into upper lower, but the probabilities are very slight that he would move directly into the upper class or into lower lower.

An occasional exception to this rule occurs in the marriage of individuals of widely different social positions. On the whole, however, an individual does not move directly into a class group more than one subclass socially distant from that of his birth. Even following the progressive class steps, an individual seldom moves more than one subclass within his lifetime; and sometimes a single step is not completed until the second or even third generation of a family. Unlike downward mobility, which will be discussed subsequently, upward mobility is usually a conscious movement, one which is desired and which assumes certain goals toward which an individual strives. In other words, while downward mobility usually occurs in spite of an individual's efforts or desires, upward movement is most often the direct result of a person's aspirations and efforts. A clearer understanding of upward mobility in Old City may be achieved by examining some of the techniques employed by mobile individuals in each of the five specific mobility steps from lower-lower class to upper-upper class.

FROM LOWER-LOWER CLASS TO UPPER-LOWER CLASS

"Making the grade."—Movement from the lower-lower class to the upper-lower class is a comparatively simple step, for differences in the behavior of these two groups are essentially differences in degree. Upper lowers are somewhat less insecure economically than lower lowers, more men in the former group being regularly employed. Reflecting this increase in economic security, upper-lower-class people take better care of their possessions, have more adequate housing, and emphasize neatness and cleanliness.

Several lower-lower-class individuals were observed in the process of moving into the upper-lower class, and in all cases their new adjustments were very similar. In all instances the men of the households had secured work under the Emergency Relief Administration program, and in most cases this represented greater economic security than they had ever achieved before. Although the wages were low—from $12.00 to $24.00

a month—the employment was regular and dependable. With this increased security, material possessions and interest in them increased. These mobile families moved out of lower-lower-class neighborhoods into areas predominantly upper-lower class. They usually secured larger houses. They began to take care of their homes and clothing, keeping them clean and in repair, at the same time condemning the uncleanliness and improvidence of the lower lowers. They also attempted to establish neighborhood relations and the exchange of services and social courtesies with upper-lower-class individuals in preference to their former associates. In two cases mobile women began to send their children to the Salvation Army Sunday school. In one instance a mobile woman became more and more disdainful of a married sister who made no effort to rise in the social scale. Although the behavior of all these mobile families was observed over a period of only a year, the families appeared to be on the way to acceptance into the upper-lower class. Neighbors of this status, with whom they were establishing relations, apparently did not resent these mobile newcomers or offer resistance to their social ascent.

Failure to rise.—In contrast to these successful cases, however, one lower-lower-class woman was observed who was very eager to "rise" but who did not. Mrs. McCarthy was the wife of a bricklayer who worked alternately for the Emergency Relief Administration and at small tasks of his own finding. The McCarthys had six children under eight years of age, five living. It is difficult to describe their housings or possessions, for they moved four times in less than nine months. They were continually buying furnishings on the instalment plan, items which quickly reverted to the store for defaulted payments. For one short period they owned a car, an old and inexpensive model. The following description of one of their many successive houses, as it was first seen by the observer, indicates the extreme to which lower-lower lack of concern with cleanliness may go:

SOCIAL MOBILITY WITHIN THE WHITE CASTE

The room which we entered from the porch was bare except for a litter of papers and dirty rags on the floor. The wall paper was hanging in shreds, and was filthy. The house was built with a long hall down one side and with small rooms opening off from it. As we went down the hall, I noticed a bathroom at the very end, with a tub which appeared to be full of dirty rags, papers, and other trash.

The room which we entered was a bedroom. It was furnished with one iron bed, a smaller iron crib, and one straight chair. The whole room was filthy. The floor was strewn with papers, rags, pieces of soggy bread, and other food too far gone to be identified. The closet door was open, and I noticed that it contained a collection of rubbish under which two dirty cotton blankets were buried. A baby was lying on each of the two beds. Each bed was covered with one dirty sheet, which had all the evidences that small babies were upon them. Each of the children was lying in a mess of excretion, apparent in spite of the fact that they were wearing diapers. Flies were very numerous about them. The older baby, perhaps ten months old, was asleep; it was caked with dirt on its arms and legs where it had evidently been playing in the mud. On a chair by the big bed, there were some dirty diapers and a mason jar half full of milk, around which the flies hovered.

Unlike the other mobile women of her class, already described, Mrs. McCarthy made no effort to improve either her housing or her housekeeping. Rather, she took an art course by mail and attempted to sell pictures, book-ends, doorstops, etc., of her own awkward and untidy creation. When she once sent her children to the Presbyterian Sunday school, rather than to the lower-class mission, she was roundly snubbed for her pains. Grieved that she was financially unable to buy a private lot in the city cemetery for her baby's grave, she tried to save money to buy an elaborate headstone for him. Dissatisfied with her lower-lower-class neighbors, she attempted to make social calls upon middle-class acquaintances whom she had known in her school days and who now lived in widely separated neighborhoods. She was hurt because her courtesies were not returned. Rather than trade at the small neighborhood grocery stores generally patronized by lower-class whites and Negroes, she went to the larger chain stores in the center of town, usually with several small children in tow, in the hope of contacting people above her social status.

That Mrs. McCarthy's efforts at mobility failed may be explained by several significant deficiencies in her behavior pattern. In the first place, she directed her efforts toward the middle class, a group too socially distant, and ignored the upper-lower class, the logical focus for her mobility. In other words, she was unaware that successful mobility, as we have already pointed out, tends to occur in an orderly fashion from one subclass to another immediately adjacent to it on the social scale. Mrs. McCarthy did employ a few conventional mobility techniques, however. She tried to develop a relation with those above her on the social scale; she endeavored to cultivate a talent; upon one occasion she asked the observer to teach her to play bridge; she attempted to give the appearance of wealth in a few isolated bits of behavior. All these efforts, however, were directed toward a middle-class goal. Furthermore, and even more significant to her failure, she completely ignored the high social value placed upon frugality, providence, and cleanliness in both the lower-middle and the upper-lower classes. In short, Mrs. McCarthy failed to move out of the lower-lower class not only because she focused her attention on a group too socially distant but also because she ignored some very significant social values held by all groups above her own and because she altered her lower-lower-class pattern of behavior in only a few isolated and relatively insignificant particulars.

From country to town.—With reference to mobility from the lower-lower to the upper-lower class in general, it should be pointed out that this movement occurs most frequently among rural families coming into the city to live. When this movement occurs, it is a comparatively easy step, often taking only a few years for completion. A farm family, usually young, moves into the city, where the male obtains odd-job employment. They live first in a tenement or shack in a lower-lower-class neighborhood. After a year or two, if the man's employment becomes more regular, the family moves again, this time into larger quarters and usually into an upper-lower class neighborhood. In another year or two they have established relations with these neighbors, and they are accepted as equals by the upper-lower class. Several examples of this rapid movement, geographic and social, were observed in the community.

All farm families who move into the city do not accomplish such mobility, however. Many of them move into lower-lower-class neighborhoods and never move again spatially or socially, although they may change houses frequently enough. Rural families who do accomplish this easy class mobility are those who, when they come to the city, already possess many upper-lower-class characteristics. They are those who already have ideas about the value and care of possessions and who are moderately provident, frugal, and clean. In a sense, then, their movement into the urban upper-lower class is not actually upward mobility, for they never did possess all of the lower-lower-class characteristics. Although data on the social hierarchy in the rural white society of Old County is comparatively incomplete, it may be said that a class structure and class characteristics similar to those in the city exist and that those farm families who move rapidly into urban upper-lower class are usually members of a rural upper-lower class.

FROM UPPER-LOWER CLASS TO LOWER-MIDDLE CLASS

Widening the social horizon.—Mobility from upper-lower class into lower-middle class is considerably more difficult and complex than movement within the lower class itself. It requires a pronounced change in the whole way of life, since it is a movement out of a comparatively unorganized and uncontrolled group into a highly organized, highly socialized, and rigidly controlled group. It is movement from a group in which relations and contacts are principally personal, family-to-family, individual-to-individual relationships into a class which is teeming with group relations and group participations. Upward mobility from upper-lower class involves, then, establishing relations not so much with single individuals as with groups of individuals.

Like mobility within the lower class, however, this movement is usually accompanied by increased economic security and by moving into a "better" neighborhood, where contact with individuals of higher status may be established. Successfully mobile upper-lower-class people begin to take an interest in politics; they are eager to canvass for office-seekers; and they seek small appointive offices, such as attendant at the polls. They begin to participate in associations, usually the larger national organizations and auxiliaries, which are primarily the domain of the lower-middle class. They become interested and active in churches, first in one of their own class churches, such as the Methodist Mission or the Salvation Army; later, perhaps, in a middle-class church in order to break their old class identity. In other words, mobile people of this class make an effort to integrate themselves into the complex middle-class associational world. They become interested in religious teachings, observe the laws of the community more closely, and become more sensitive to "what people will think." They thus adjust themselves to the more exacting social controls of the middle class.

This is the ideal-typical procedure for mobility into lower-middle class. Actually, the movement does not often occur in this orderly fashion. Like all members of the society, mobile or stable, lower-class individuals "on the way up" are not fully aware of the complex of social situations involved in class behavior, either within their own class group or within other classes of the society. As products of lower-class society, they are generally aware that middle-class behavior is different from their own; but they see only vaguely a few particulars in the complex pattern of behavior which constitutes this difference. Thus, two women in particular were observed attempting mobility from upper-lower into lower-middle class, each employing somewhat different techniques. In both instances the early processes are largely hearsay or speculation; the later processes were a matter of observation.

Struggling to "rise."—The first of these was Mrs. Green, wife of a mechanic and small garage owner, and the mother of a girl in her teens. The family had lived for about five years in a four-room house which they rented in an upper-lower-class neighborhood. During this time, Mr. Green's employment became increasingly regular and remunerative. The furnishings which they were buying on the installment plan, and which were a little more expensive and elaborate than those of their neighbors, were finally paid for. About the same time or earlier, Mrs. Green and her husband established political relations with an office-seeker, and Mrs. Green now began to canvass for the politician, to act as watcher at the polls, and to brag about, and enlarge upon, her relations with the politician. She, herself, taught Sunday school at the mission church, but sent her young daughter to the Methodist church. The girl attended high school, and she insisted that she continue with her schooling, although several other children in the neighborhood were obliged to drop out for lack of clothing and books. Mrs. Green next attempted to break her identity and to sever relations with her upper-lower-class neighbors. She ceased to exchange services with them, openly criticized their behavior when it differed from her own, and thus tried to demonstrate her superiority to them.

Subsequently, however, during the period of observation, Mr. Green had an accident and broke a leg. The family's income ceased, and they were obliged to apply to the Emergency Relief Administration for aid, behavior for which they had previously criticized their neighbors. The latter were delighted with this reversal of fortune and voiced their antagonism to the Green family for their assumed superiority. One woman said:

Mrs. Green on relief! I declare! And after the way she talked about me goin' down there!....

Yeah, she used to say to me how she wouldn't wash no man's dirty underwear. She didn't see how I would do it for my old man. She used to tell me I ought to get him to pay for the washing instead of me doing it. . . . . She was always carrying on like that. She was always saying she didn't see why I'd stand for it, washing out my old man's dirty underwear. But then they got in a bad way themselves. First thing I knew I saw her out there one day hanging up the wash. Well, I had to laugh. . . . . Yeah, I went out there and I had to laugh at her, and I just told her: "I ain't going to help you now after all you said to me. You can just go on and do it yourself now!"

Yeah, and that was another thing; Mrs. Green was always saying all about how it wasn't decent to let your men go without starch in their shirts. But my land! It don't make no difference! I ain't going to go to all that trouble!

In the face of this antagonism Mrs. Green found it impossible to maintain her superiority in this neighborhood; so she moved to a similar house in a neighborhood of lower-lower-class whites and Negroes, where she kept herself aloof, unidentified, and so seemingly superior. Explaining her attitude toward this new neighborhood, she expressed the middle-class ideal of equality by averring:

Of course, here on this street it isn't so nice as it is some places, but I manage. . . . . And I tell my daughter how it is. . . . . I just tell them we haven't got much money now, and we have to live this way; but I tell them they're just as good as anybody else, and there isn't any reason for them to feel bad about it.

I like it here all right. Well, there's two white families on one side of us, but they're carousing and drinking the whole night long. But I'll tell you how it is with me. The neighbors don't make no difference to me. Anywhere I am, I just don't pay no attention to who's living next to me. It's not the neighbors makes the difference to me. I can get along where-ever I am.

Observation of this family ended before the husband had reestablished his former earning capacity; so their subsequent progress is unknown.

Much of Mrs. Green's behavior may be seen as a successful mobility adjustment, such as her church and political activity, the interest in her daughter's schooling, the expression of middle-class ideals of "equality" and the appearances of wealth, together with the breaking of her upper-lower-class identity. On the other hand, she had failed to establish any relations of equivalence with middle-class people or to build up a middle-class identity. Her husband's temporary inability to support the family, furthermore, was a definite setback to her mobility aspirations. Ultimately, perhaps, through church, political, and school participations, she and her daughter might have established relations of equivalence with lower-middle-class people and so have become identified with that class group.

A neighborhood group "going up" together.—Another woman was also observed attempting to "rise" into the lower-middle class. The daughter of a saw-mill family and the mother of a nine-year-old boy, Mrs. Carey lived with her parents on the upper-lower-class Crowder Street, while her husband was employed as foreman on a levee gang. She was an active worker in the mission church in this locality. An analysis of her mobility behavior also involves some consideration of that locality and the church.

When this study began, the mission church, referred to previously, had been established about seven years, and its membership was very nearly coincident with the residents in the particular locality where it was situated. The church included as members almost everyone who lived on Crowder Street. These individuals formed a unified group, organized around their church activities, with their behavior controlled by religious and moral sanctions. Members of the church, and so of the locality, attended services regularly, participated in the several suborganizations, and attempted to follow literally the teachings of their denomination. This unity of outlook, formal organization, moral behavior, and group control suggests a middle-class pattern of behavior. It may, in fact, be interpreted as an indication of attempted group mobility into the lower-middle class. In other words, this church and neighborhood may be conceived of as a group of upper-lower-class individuals who are rising into the lower-middle class by patterning their behavior after that class configuration.

Before their church was established, there apparently had been no formal organization among these people. All group controls, furthermore, were apparently weak among them in this earlier period. Formerly, there had been several "unrestrained" and "immoral" residents of the neighborhood, but now all residents seemed equally obedient to the sanctions of the group. Before their own church was established, various individuals on Crowder Street had attempted to participate in activities of some of the larger churches in the community, seeking, as individuals, to rise into the middle class. Individually they failed to rise; and this failure, together with their existing neighborhood relations, gave them a common basis for establishing their own church. Subsequently, then, they organized a church of their own and patterned their behavior as a group after that of the class toward which they had unsuccessfully tried to move as individuals. By so doing, however, they isolated themselves from the established lower-middle class of the community and so had no intimate contacts with individuals in this class.

At first glance, one might wonder if these people were not actually of middle-class status rather than upper-lower, for they exhibit voluntarily organized group behavior and have a system of "rules" and methods for enforcing them. But the community as a whole and, in particular, the members of lower-middle and upper-lower classes see them as still part of the lower group. The bulk of their relations are with upper-lower-class individuals, and they have only subordinate relations with middle-class people. In spite of their high organization and group control, there are still many lower-class traits in the whole configuration of their behavior. Most noticeably, they are, as a group, economically insecure; they have inferior possessions; and they do not exhibit the middle-class emphasis upon display of "wealth." Their interest in education is elementary and does not include any consideration of education beyond secondary school or any uniform concept of the value of education in itself. They neither participate in any of the associational activities of the larger community nor take much part in politics. They may be seen, then, as a segment of the upper-lower class, a mobile group which has recently begun to remodel some of its behavior according to middle-class standards but which has not yet become identified with the middle class.

On the threshold of acceptance.—Mrs. Carey was a resident of this locality and an active worker in the church. Without ceasing to participate in this little group, without severing her relations with them, she was apparently attempting greater mobility than they. Unlike other members of the group, Mrs. Carey was trying to establish relations with individuals of higher social status. She placed great value upon higher education and attempted to develop a talent to exhibit her own superiority. The contacts and relations which she tried to maintain, however, were consistently with other individuals too socially distant from her, with the result that she was always subordinated. These individuals included, for example, an upper-middle-class woman who had been one of the sponsors of the neighborhood church and who was then acting as visitor for the Emergency Relief Administration. As a recipient of E.R.A. aid, Mrs. Carey was subordinated to this individual, who was on the "giving-end" of the relation. Another of Mrs. Carey's attempted contacts was with another upper-middle-class woman, who taught E.R.A. music classes in the neighborhood. As a student in the music class, she was again directly subordinated in a teacher-pupil relation. In both cases it was difficult to establish relations of equivalence. She had no social contact with lower-middle-class individuals, made no attempt to establish such relations, joined no associations outside of her own church, and took no part in community politics.

Mrs. Carey was very much interested in her son's schooling,

visited the schools frequently, discussed his progress with the teachers, and was very eager for the child to excel. She boasted continually about the child's progress and made every effort to exhibit her own interest in education. She herself attended the E.R.A. night school and looked forward to entering business school. Further than this, she tried to develop her musical talent and became a very enthusiastic and ardent piano student. She attended adult-education classes, practiced daily for hours on the church piano, and participated in small recitals sponsored by the church or music class. This interest in education and talent is a definite and often successful technique for mobility into the middle class.

It has already been pointed out that the middle class particularly values individual talent, being the group which organizes itself around "talent" and which sponsors unusual local individuals. Middle-class interest, however, is generally limited to educational talents—musical, artistic, dramatic, literary—all talents which require training and which are generally available only to those who have a certain amount of economic security or some wealth. The development of these particular talents is usually not possible for the lower class, a group which, on the whole, values and develops another kind of talent, not dependent on educational advantages— athletic ability. The upper class, on the other hand, is not wholly indifferent to the educational attainments of the middle class; but their recognition of these abilities is limited to individuals who have achieved excellence beyond the local community—that is, artists, musicians, and authors who have secured recognition from a larger community than Old City.

Mrs. Carey's preoccupation with the study of music and with education in general was oriented toward the middle class, the group which places the highest value upon these factors. This was, therefore, a useful technique for mobility into that class. Her religious attitudes and moral concepts, her church participation—all of which she shared with other members of the neighborhood and the small church—were also steps in the right direction.

That Mrs. Carey was apparently making no progress in her mobility and that she was in no way identified with the middle class as a group may be explained by several obvious deficiencies in her behavior pattern. In the first place, except for her interest in education, which may be looked upon in a sense as an evidence of wealth, she did not have the middle-class preoccupation with wealth *per se*. Nor could she display enough evidences of prosperity to meet their standards. Her husband was unable to support her, and she lived with her parents, who were supported by the Emergency Relief Administration. In the second place, she made no effort to sever relations with the upper-lower class. She apparently felt herself somewhat superior to them, as evidenced by occasional condescending remarks about her "less fortunate," less talented, less educated, and less moral neighbors. But she continued to participate with them intimately and so to maintain her identity with them. Finally, she failed to establish any new social identity, failed to secure and maintain any relations of equivalence with lower-middle-class individuals or groups of individuals. She contented herself with unequal relations with upper-middle-class people, in all of which she was subordinated not only indirectly by her lower social and economic status but also because in all these relations she was unable to reciprocate. She was "receiving"—education from her teachers, economic aid from the E.R.A. agents; in none of them was she able to "give." She was still on the threshold of acceptance.

LOWER-MIDDLE CLASS TO UPPER-MIDDLE CLASS

Acquiring wealth.—More than in any other case, movement from lower-middle class to upper-middle class is directly dependent upon increased economic security. There are, in the society, today, numerous individuals who were formerly lower-middle-class small merchants but who are now large merchants of upper-middle-class status or who have children of that status in the community. It cannot be assumed, however, that the acquisition of wealth alone will automatically change an individual's social position within the middle class. Mere increase in economic security from the simple ability to feed, clothe, and shelter one's self to the opportunity for luxurious and opulent living is not necessarily indicative of either increased social position or a desire for it. There are, in fact, several instances of wealthy individuals in the community who are stable members of the lower-middle class and who have apparently never attempted to increase their social status.

Frequently, however, an individual who achieves great economic security and wealth does attempt to modify his other behavior and so becomes mobile. Whether his attempt at mobility is inspired by his increased wealth or whether his increased wealth is inspired by his desire for mobility cannot, of course, be determined; but an individual is usually on the upgrade economically before he attempts to modify other kinds of behavior.

Entering the ranks of the "leaders."—It has been stated that the behavior patterns of the lower-middle and upper-middle classes are similar. Members of both class groups are active in the church, in associations, and in politics; both value wealth and concepts of equality; and both are highly controlled, respect the laws of the community and the teachings of the church. Lower-middle-class persons, however, may be said to be subordinated to the upper-middle class in almost every particular of behavior. In their organization and control, be it of churches, associations, politics, or the courts, upper-middle-class persons are the leaders, the organizers, the controllers; while lower-middle-class people are essentially the followers, the organized, the controlled. Middle-class ideology, too, reaches a much higher development in the upper group—is more complex, abstract, and intellectual than in the lower. Adjustment for mobility into the upper-middle class, then, is dependent not so much upon definite changes in specific types of behavior and ideology as upon a more complex development of behavior patterns already possessed. Such mobility consists in moving from a group in which most members are inconspicuous followers into a group whose members are, potentially, at least, leaders.

Exploiting "talent."—Given the requisite economic status, it is not surprising that use of education and individual talent excellence are the most noticeable and most significant mobility techniques of the mobile members of the lower-middle class. By exhibiting exceptional ability in a particular field, a member of the inconspicuous lower-middle-class group has an opportunity to be noticed by the group above and to demonstrate his superiority in one particular talent at least. By concerning himself with educational talent—artistic, dramatic, musical, etc.—a mobile lower-middle-class individual may expect to obtain the notice of the upper-middle class, since this class places high value upon such achievements, organizes its activity about them, and often sponsors talented individuals. An individual of lower-middle-class status, for example, who plays the piano well or who gives small recitals for her friends, will ultimately be noticed by the upper-middle class and will probably be invited to join the Music Club, an upper-middle-class association. A person who sings solos in her church choir may have the same experience. An individual who demonstrates dramatic ability in school plays or church pageants or who has attended a school of drama may be solicited for the Little Theater.

"Pushing" the children.—Quite frequently, parents who wish to move into the upper-middle class attempt to develop their children's talents through specialized study. One mother, for instance, forced her seven-year-old daughter to study and practice toe-dancing so continuously that she was condemned by the community for "ruining the child's life." The mother, however, who herself took art courses from an adult-education

class, extolled the child's ability and said that she was preparing to take her to Hollywood.

In another instance, an insurance agent and his wife, who themselves had had some success in their mobility into upper-middle class, had two daughters who showed some ability at the piano. They were encouraged, trained, and sent away to study. When they returned, their parents frequently invited groups of friends tó their home for small recitals. Gradually these gatherings were extended to include non-intimates and people of higher social status. The observer, for example, met the girls' father at the latter's place of business. At this first meeting, the father mentioned the girls' ability; and before the first interview was terminated, the observer had been invited to a home recital. Finally, the parents arranged a large public recital, and the girls were acclaimed as talented individuals. They were invited to join the Music Club and subsequently had conspicuous places on concert programs sponsored by various clubs and churches.

Seeking positions of authority.—Excellence in these particular talent fields is not the only means of mobility into the upper-middle class or the only adjustment required of even a talented individual. Acquiring positions of authority is equally rewarding. The great majority of lower-middle-class individuals have little opportunity to subordinate directly other individuals in the society. Most of their relations in the white society —occupational, political, associational, and so forth—are either relations of equivalence with other lower middles or relations in which they themselves are subordinated. That the direct subordination and "control" of the Negroes in Old City is primarily engaged in by members of this class group may be seen as closely related to their lack of high superordinate status within the white caste. Mobile members of the lower-middle class often seek positions of authority in their relations with other whites, positions in which they may directly subordinate other individuals and so demonstrate their own superiority. With an increase in their economic security, which is basic to their mobility, an individual may attain an occupational position of greater authority, may become an employer rather than an employee, or, through enlarging his business, may employ, and so subordinate, a greater number of individuals.

Occupations as positions of authority.—It is probable that the popularity of nursing and school-teaching as professions for mobile lower-middle-class girls is related to the fact that each of these professions carries with it a certain degree of authority. This authority is, perhaps, more readily seen in the case of teachers, who hold a position directly superordinate to children of all classes and thereby to parents of all classes in the specific school relation. Nurses, too, enjoy a certain amount of authority over people of all classes, although they are, in a sense, servants by the very fact of being employees. Like the doctor, the nurse is an "authority" in sickness. While a patient is ill, the nurse has almost complete control over the patient's behavior and over the family's behavior in reference to the patient.

It should be pointed out, however, that in both of these professions the economic factor is an equally important explanation of their popularity with mobile lower-middle-class individuals. In this community no fees are charged for nurses' training; a high-school education is the only prerequisite; and training is in the form of apprenticeship at one of the three local hospitals. There is here, then, an opportunity for a higher education of a kind, for those who are financially unable to obtain it otherwise. In teaching, also, the training is relatively inexpensive, consisting of two years of study at the state normal school. In recent years, however, this latter field as a means of mobility for local girls has been closed, as a ruling now prohibits the appointment of local teachers in the Old City schools.

Entrance into the professions—as, for instance, medicine, dentistry, or the law—as a means of mobility for lower-middle-class men is rare. Explanation of this probably lies in the fact that training for such careers, unlike professional training for nursing and teaching, requires the expenditure of more money than is available to most lower-middle-class individuals. Mobile men of this class more frequently find their occupational superordination as large merchants or other employers of many people rather than as professional men who function as superordinates to their clients in crisis situations.

Politics.—Positions of political authority are very much coveted by mobile members of the lower-middle class. Such positions as member of the Board of Aldermen, the Board of Supervisors, etc., are especially sought, and through this medium individuals may exhibit their superiority to the total community and, in some situations, subordinate all other individuals in the society. On the surface it might appear that positions of political authority would be equally sought by members of both the middle and the lower class. It is probable that such authority would be quite acceptable to the lower class, since such persons are consistently subordinated and have almost no authority over other individuals. Occupationally, lower-class persons rarely acquire the status of employer; and since they have little group participation, little associational, church, or political activity, these sources of superordination are closed to them. By and large, however, they have little opportunity to achieve important political positions, with the exception of one office, which is usually filled by mobile members of the upper-lower class, namely, that of policeman.

Associating with the "right people."—Most members of the lower-middle class have numerous contacts with upper-middle-class individuals, an essential preliminary to intimate participation with them. In their associational participations, church participations, political activity, occupations, and neighborhood, lower-middle-class members are continually in contact with upper-middle-class individuals in specialized roles. In most cases, however, these are not relations of equivalence but relations in which the lower-middle class is subordinated. By changing their associational and church affiliations or by becoming leaders in those of which they are already members, by acquiring more authoritative political positions, by becoming employers of many workers, mobile members of lower-middle class may become equivalent in their specific relations with upper-middle class, sometimes even superordinate. Furthermore, by thus modifying their behavior, these mobile individuals may establish relations with upper-middle-class groups rather than contacts limited to isolated upper-middle-class individuals. Participation in informal upper-middle class groups—that is, in extended cliques, bridge clubs, sewing circles—is often an easy step once the new pattern of specific relations of equality has been established. Moving into a new neighborhood is often an important basis for initiating this type of participation.

In the analysis of clique behavior it has been seen that an extended clique often includes both upper-middle-class and lower-middle-class individuals. It has also been suggested that this mixture is equally a result of the presence of socially mobile persons moving either up or down (see Fig. 6, p. 161, and Table 4). When a clique whose members are predominantly upper-middle class includes a few lower-middle class individuals, these latter are usually mobile individuals who already have relations of equivalence with individual upper-middle-class members of the clique but who are now joining groups. In general, this participation in informal upper-middle-class groups is one of the final steps in the mobility adjustment and is not achieved until many other types of lower-middle-class behavior have first been modified. Participation in these intimate groups may be said to represent successful mobility and to indicate that the mobile individual has become identified in large part with the higher-class group.

UPPER-MIDDLE CLASS TO LOWER-UPPER CLASS

Substituting the past for the present.—There are many cases in the community today of individuals and families who are attempting to rise from the upper-middle class into the lower-upper class. There are also many examples of those who have accomplished this type of mobility. Apparently, all members of the lower-upper class today have risen from the middle class, or their parents did so before them. As far as can be ascertained, there was no lower-upper class in this community two, or perhaps three, generations ago; at least, such a class did not have the family composition that it has today. The lower-upper class today cannot be said to have any behavior or any ideology apart from that of the upper-upper class but is a group apart chiefly because the upper-upper class thinks of it as separate. They have not been members of the upper class over a sufficiently long period of time to win recognition from the "old aristocracy." Since the existence of the lower-upper class has its foundation in the thinking of the upper-upper class, and since lower-upper-class behavior is patterned after that of the upper uppers, mobility from upper-middle class into lower-upper class is actually dependent upon social acceptance by upper uppers and upon the patterning of individual behavior after that of the upper-upper class.

More so than in any other step in the mobility process, mobility from upper-middle class to lower-upper class is dependent upon the alteration of a fundamental class ideology and upon the specific behavior which reflects this new ideology. Thus, mobility in this instance involves a definite change from valuing contemporary individual behavior to revering the past. It also entails a change from socially controlled "moral" behavior reflecting religious teachings to a behavior patterned after the traditionally extravagant living of the past—the drinking, entertaining, and flirtatious behavior of the old plantation days.

Acquisition of an "old home."—Among the several methods which may be used by mobile upper middles to demonstrate their reverence for the past, the one offering, perhaps, the greatest possibility for success is the acquisition of an old plantation mansion. Mere possession of such a relic, however, is not necessarily proof of reverence. Members of the upper-

upper class resent the purchase of an "old home" by a middle-class individual, and even resent, to some extent, such an acquisition by lower-upper-class persons; but they may be placated if every feature of the mansion, its merits and inconveniences alike, are preserved enthusiastically just as they stand. Such behavior is accepted as an indication that the new owner values the antiquity of his possession. Any changes in architecture, furnishings, or landscaping (even so-called "improvements") are loudly condemned. One middle-class owner of an "old home" offended the "old aristocracy" when he installed modern plumbing; he "ruined the floor plan" when he put in two bathrooms. On the other hand, "keeping up the mansion"—that is, caring for the grounds, reroofing, painting, reupholstering furniture, and so forth—is condoned if this upkeep is in character with the antiquity of the mansion. Brocaded chairs may not be recovered in any other material; gray or yellow paint would not be acceptable for a house that has traditionally been white; changing the position of the gardens or even the kind of plants would be condemned; and the carriage drive must not be straightened or widened to accommodate automobile traffic. In other words, a mansion may be "restored" but not "remodeled."

The acquisition of an "old home" may, then, be a very dangerous move for a mobile upper-middle-class person. Any implied lack of respect for his new possession may put an end to his chances for rising into the upper class. Although, in fact, less than half of the twenty-odd old mansions now standing are still owned by members of the original families or even by members of the "old aristocracy," upper-upper-class families, as a group, feel that they have a certain claim upon all of the "old homes." In a sense, the members of the upper-upper class cherish, collectively, all the "old homes" as symbols of their class past. This attitude is not surprising in view of the complex network of kinship which relates, either by blood or marriage, almost every upper upper with every other. An "outsider"—one who is not of the "old aristocracy" and not a part of this network of kin relations—when he buys an "old home," is attempting to become a member of this very extended family. He is assuming a position, as master of an "old home," which was formerly held only by a kinsman of all other "old-home" owners. To counteract this supposed presumption, this new owner must subordinate himself to his house. Symbolically, it is the house itself which is "kin" to the "old aristocracy"; not the new owner. The new owner is an "outsider," he is not within the kinship circle; and so he is subordinate to his house, which does have these "kin" relations with the upper-upper class.

Joining the Historical Club.—Another method of showing reverence for the past is to become a member of the local Historical Club. This association, composed of upper and upper-middle-class women, is primarily concerned with honoring the local past through an annual community celebration which is attended by a large number of tourists from all over the country. In this ceremony, "Historical Week," the Historical Club directs and supervises tours of the "old homes" and portrays in pageantry the life of the old plantation days. It is not surprising, then, that membership in the Historical Club is a primary goal of mobile upper-middle-class women who wish to demonstrate their interest in the past. Since its membership is limited, however, and since there is a long waiting-list from the upper class itself, the club is rather a hard nut for the upper-middle-class woman to crack. Lacking a chance to become members of the club, mobile members of the uppermiddle class therefore bend their efforts toward participating in the Historical Week in other ways. They offer themselves as guides for the tours, positions which the Historical Club must approve on the basis of an individual's attitude toward the local past and his knowledge of local relics. Another avenue of participation is through opening one's home as a rooming-house for visitors. Each home must be approved by the Historical Club. In several instances mobile members of upper-middle class, as well as several upper-class individuals, served meals (for a price) in their homes or gardens, where guests were served by Negro servants wearing the traditional antebellum servant costumes.

The Historical Week.—Perhaps the most sought-after positions in the Historical Week celebration for those who are neither "old home" owners nor club members is the role of assistant hostess in an "old home." Most of the owners of the mansions invite several other women, usually their intimate friends, to assist them in receiving the visitors while the tours are in progress. These assistants, usually dressed, like the hostess, in the hoop skirts of antebellum days, escort visitors through the home and discourse with some authority on the history and merits of various features of the dwelling. Occasionally, upper-middle-class women, if they have relations with upper-upper-class or even lower-upper-class home-owners, are invited to act as assistant hostesses. They then have an opportunity to claim the past as their own, temporarily; to dress as in the past; and to speak with authority and personal pride of the "old homes," remnants of the past.

For a similar reason, that is, because they may for a time claim the past as their own and look upon it not merely as something belonging exclusively to the upper class, roles in the old-fashioned pageants are sought by mobile upper-middle-class adolescents and by parents for their children. In these pageants, sponsored by the club and coached by its members, the actors dress and act the parts of historical characters who once appeared on the local scene. Here, again, is an opportunity to participate in a ceremonial showing reverence for the past, although the accident of birth into the middle class has excluded them from a proprietary interest in it.

Learning to be "immoral."—Demonstrating regard for the past, however, is not the whole story of mobility into the upper class. Perhaps the other most important adjustment is the change in recreational activity which is so necessary in order to participate with ease in the informal upper-class groups. Mobile members of upper-middle class must throw aside their aversions (inspired by religious teachings and maintained by the middle class as a whole) to drinking, dancing, smoking, gambling, flirting, etc., for these compose the major recreational activities of the upper class. Individuals who condemn this behavior may not participate in groups which indulge in it; they are excluded as "prigs" and "old sticks." Among older upper-class groups, it is true, all clique members are not expected to indulge individually in these types of behavior. They are, however, expected to condone such behavior among the younger groups and to participate occasionally at younger gatherings, without "spoiling the party."

Among the younger groups of the upper class, everyone is expected to conform and participate; everyone must drink a few cocktails, dance, accept a hug or kiss if offered, and be willing to gamble a few dollars at lotto. Numerous examples were cited by members of the upper-class cliques of otherwise eligible upper middles who were excluded from participation because of their "party behavior." They were said to be "stiff," or "sticks," or "prim," or just "no fun." Also, many examples were observed of mobile individuals who were trying to adopt this "loose" upper-class behavior: a man in his forties learning to dance; women in their thirties and forties trying to drink cocktails and be "good sports"; middle-aged men pinching women's arms in flirtatious attempts; and women trying to accept these advances coyly.

Changing churches.—These adjustments in recreational behavior, these shifts from a strict moral and religiously controlled behavior to a much less rigorously and differently controlled behavior, are sometimes accompanied by a change in church affiliation. Although changing church affiliation is not the general rule, it is probable that the greatest number of changes in church affiliation occur in the interest of mobility from upper-middle class to lower-upper class. With noticeable frequency, mobile individuals leave the Baptist and Methodist churches, which condemn upper-class recreations, and join instead the Presbyterian or Episcopal churches, which condone or ignore this behavior. Also, in the mobility process there is a general falling-off of participation in church associations. The upper class as a group is not sympathetic to such activity; it frequently ridicules individual concern for Sunday-school teachings, missionary-society activity, and similar semi-religious pursuits.

Except for the Historical Club, there are no upper-class associations toward which upper-middle-class individuals may aspire.[1] At one time the Roisterer's Club, an exclusive male recreational club, was a goal for mobile upper-middle-class males. It had been extinct, however, for ten or more years, when the study began. Mobile persons in upper-middle-class associations, in most cases, do not necessarily drop these activities in their efforts toward mobility. In some instances they continue as leaders of their associations; in others they gradually lose interest and cease to participate.

Turning business contacts into social relations.—Since upper-class individuals participate very little in associations and take no interest in church associations or politics, how, then, do mobile members of the upper-middle class establish contacts and equivalent relations with groups of the upper-class or even with individual members? There are two chief possibilities for such contacts, the only two avenues of contact which are used with sufficient frequency to be significant. The first of these is the occupational relations of the males; the second, and by far the more important, is the schools. In the clique analysis it was obvious that the greatest amount of informal recreational participation of the upper class, especially in the age brackets under fifty, is in mixed groups of men and women together. In the middle class, however, participation is primarily by the sexes separately. Therefore, in the upper class

---

[1] An organization of young women in their twenties, the Center Club, was organized in the last few months of observation. This association included a large percentage of upper-class girls. It was, however, too new an organization to demonstrate its function in the community or its possibilities for individual mobility.

more so than in the middle class, there is an opportunity for men to establish contacts for their wives, as well as for themselves, through their occupational relations. Similarly, though less frequently perhaps, wives may bring their husbands together through their neighborhood or school contacts. In other words, where participations are generally by men and women together, the chance of establishing contacts is doubled. One mixed clique in particular, composed of upper-class and mobile upper-middle-class husbands and wives, appears to have been established on the basis of just such a nexus of occupational, school, and neighborhood relations.

The primacy of school contacts.—It is a fact, however, that by far the greatest number of lasting upper-middle-class contacts with the upper class have been established in adolescence through the schools. The great majority of lower-upper-class individuals in the community today are people under fifty who established relations with upper-upper-class individuals in their school days. Similarly, the upper-middle-class individuals who are today moving most successfully toward lower upper-class status are those who are repeating this process. Mobility through school contacts is a continuing process, and old school ties are a significant factor in clique solidarity among adults in Old City.

Distinctions in social status among adolescents are less finely drawn than among adults, thus allowing friendships to form across class lines. School children of upper-middle-class and even of lower-middle-class social position have an opportunity to participate intimately with those of a higher social status. Some middle-class individuals do not continue to participate with upper-class individuals in adult life; others, as they become adults, continue this participation and at the same time pattern their behavior after that of the upper class, and so eventually become identified with the upper class. Such persons tend to be those with personality traits which makes readjustment relatively easy. They do not settle back into the conventional pattern of middle-class behavior in which their parents trained them. In school, they, as individuals, did not yet have a class status but were identified as children of particular middle-class parents. They were free to change, however, and did so.

It is not surprising, therefore, that the most successful mobility is that which starts in adolescence and continues into adult life. Similarly, it is not amazing that for adults, whose pattern of behavior has become fixed, whose identity with a particular class has been established, the mobility process is considerably more difficult. This difference between adolescent and adult mobility, discussed here with particular application to mobility from upper-middle class to lower-upper class is present in varying degrees in all mobility adjustments.

"Marrying up."—Marriage is, to some extent, a means of mobility on all class levels of the society. In moving into a group which places very high value upon kinship, it is particularly important. Throughout the society the great majority of marriages take place between individuals of the same social status, since the greatest opportunity for contact and for equivalent relations occurs within a class group. Consistently, too, throughout the society, the social position of a man and his wife become identical in the thinking of the community, with little regard for the differences in their antecedents. What, then, of marriages between individuals of different social status? How does the society determine the social position of a couple as a unit?

From our study it appears that the ultimate social position of a couple, originally of different social positions, is dependent upon the behavior adjustments which they make. An upper-middle-class individual who marries a member of the lower-upper class may acquire an upper-class position if he or she adopts the upper-class behavior pattern, thus gaining acceptance on an intimate level of participation. This means leaving behind the relations and participations with upper-middle class. On the other hand, if the upper-middle-class partner fails to make this adjustment, or if the lower-upper-class partner adjusts instead to the upper-middle-class pattern, then, as a couple, they have a social position of upper-middle class. This process of adjustment involves a certain amount of time before the couple acquires a fixed identity with a given social class.

In one instance, a male member of a mixed upper-class clique who was firmly established in the lower-upper class through kinship and clique relations married a middle-class girl of an old and stable middle-class family. At the time of this observation, eight years after their marriage, this couple was just becoming identified with the lower-upper class. They were just beginning to participate actively and intimately with members of the husband's lower-upper-class clique. After their marriage they had withdrawn from informal participation with either the upper or the middle class, with the exception of occasional participations in kinship groups. Eight years later, when the observer met and participated with this middle-class woman, there was no suggestion in her behavior of a middle-class pattern.

In another case, a young man of a stable upper-middle-class family began his mobility in an adolescent school clique. Finishing school, he continued to participate with the same group and patterned his behavior after that of his upper-class friends. At the age of thirty, he married a teacher in the local school, a newcomer in the community but one whose behavior and ideology was characteristic of the upper-middle class. After their marriage this couple participated only a few times with the man's upper-class clique and then was excluded. A member of that clique expressed the attitude toward the couple thus:

He married this Julia—somebody who came here and taught school. She just wasn't our kind of people, you know. Well, when he married her, we didn't ask her to our parties and we didn't see him for a long time. It wasn't that we didn't like her, you know; we just never thought of her because she wasn't our kind. We knew she wouldn't enjoy us, and we wouldn't have enjoyed her either.

The couple was relegated again to upper-middle class. Subsequently, they became members of a clique composed of mobile couples like themselves who were trying to pattern their behavior after that of upper-class cliques.

LOWER-UPPER CLASS TO UPPER-UPPER CLASS

The insuperable barrier of time.—It may be said that there is no mobility into the upper-upper class today. This group has its basis in time, and mobility into it is dependent upon the passage of time. Several attempts have been made by mobile persons to demonstrate to the upper uppers that they have the background necessary for acceptance through the device of tracing ancestry and compiling genealogies. Although this technique has had some success as regards mobility into lower-upper class, ancestry, of itself, is of no help in gaining admittance into the upper-upper stratum. The lineage must be strictly a local one. For example, a famous Virginian's descendants would be warmly received and elaborately entertained by the upper-upper class in this community, but they would still not be of the "old aristocracy" of Old City.

Becoming a member of the upper-upper class through marriage is very rare. Two instances were observed, however, of upper-upper-class status thus acquired. Both of these cases were of men over sixty years of age who had married into the community from outside forty or more years before. What their antecedents in their own communities were, or what length of time was required before they were accepted by the community as "old aristocracy," could not be determined. Among younger couples in the society today, there are several examples of marriage between upper-upper-class individuals and those of lower status. In none of these cases, however, has the partner of lower rank acquired upper-upper-class status. These partners of lower status have remained individuals unidentified with the social positions of their mates. In two cases upper-upper-class men married upper-middle-class girls. In both instances the latter became upper class, adopted upper-class behavior and attitudes, participated with upper-class groups, and broke away from their upper-middle-class antecedents except for limited participation with their immediate families. They became *lower*-upper-class, however, not "old aristocracy." They participated with upper uppers and behaved as they did, but both they and the "old aristocracy" were well aware that they just weren't "in."

The fact that members of the "old aristocracy" are not reproducing themselves, that many have left the community, and that they are marrying lower uppers with increasing frequency may ultimately lead to an increased mobility into the upper-upper class, perhaps in the next generation of adults. Members of lower-upper class, and even of upper-middle class, who have mated with upper uppers will achieve a certain degree of mobility through their children, since the children will have the status of "old aristocracy" by reason of their one upper-upper-class parent. It is possible, too, that, as adults, the children of two present lower-upper-class parents may become upper-upper class. This situation, however, presupposes a modification of the values of the "old aristocracy," for no amount of effort, nor the passage of time, can make such children into full-fledged descendants of the wealthy antebellum planters who were the ancestors of the present "old aristocracy."

DOWNWARD SOCIAL MOBILITY

The process of downward social mobility differs essentially from upward mobility in that it is not a consciously desired movement. It is not the result of any sustained drive toward new goals but is rather the result of failure to adjust to a given position. Individuals usually resist such movement. As in upward mobility, however, an individual does not usually fall very far down the social scale in one generation, although his children and grandchildren may continue the process. The rate of downward mobility varies for the different social classes, as does the rate of social ascent, being particularly slow in the case of upper-class individuals where time is an important factor. In general, it appears that social "descent" is slower than "ascent."

Loss of economic security.—Downward mobility is generally very closely associated with a decrease in economic security. It is not, however, a simple process in which the loss of economic security is inevitably and immediately followed by loss of social status. Rather, it is a complex process in which a decrease in economic power may influence many other types of behavior—one's possessions; political, church, and associational life; and clique activity. A decrease in economic security requires an individual to make new adjustments in all types of behavior so that he may continue to fulfil his part of the reciprocal relations which he, as a person of a specific social status, has established with other individuals. Failure to make this adjustment results in the loss of status.

This is an explanation of the results of individual economic loss, only, not of group economic failure. The economic depression which began shortly before the study, and similar local, regional, and national depressions in the past, have caused a decrease in economic security for many individuals. In the majority of cases, however, this decrease in security has either befallen a group of persons simultaneously or has been only a temporary setback for individuals. Thus, groups of individuals—classes and smaller social groups—have been able to maintain their relations with one another without much adjustment on the part of the individual. For example, the upper-upper class, the "old aristocracy," is no longer wealthy, although its superiority in the society is related to the erstwhile great wealth of its forebears. Loss of economic status, in their case, has been a gradual process in most instances, and one that affected almost all the group members simultaneously. Thus, their pattern of economic behavior changed gradually and for the group as a whole. In most cases they were compelled to make adjustments not as individuals but as members of a class. Throughout the process they were thus able to continue their reciprocal relations with one another. They all went down the economic scale together.

Other factors in loss of status.—There are other factors besides the economic ones which may result in loss of individual or family status. In the middle class particularly, failure to conform to the morally controlled pattern of behavior or continued unlawful behavior may result in downward mobility. In the lower class, such factors as extreme improvidence or contentment with unclean and unsanitary living conditions may result in downward movement from upper-lower to lower-lower class. In the lower-upper class, consistent failure to revere the past may send an individual back to upper-middle class.

Actual examples of downward mobility are not so easily observed in the community as are instances of upward mobility. There are several possible explanations of this situation. It is possible, in the first place, that downward mobility actually occurs much less frequently. It is more probable, however, that, since downward mobility is a slower process and an unconscious one, the society, as a whole, is largely unaware of such individual movement, and an outside observer cannot remain long enough to isolate the cases.

From upper upper—down.—All the examples of downward mobility which the observers were able to study in detail were cases of upper uppers. In these cases, two factors were of prime importance: first, withdrawal on the part of an individual from the typical pattern of upper-upper-class participation; second, participation with people below him in social status. Even in these cases, however, the process of "going down" extended through several generations, and there were cases in Old City of flagrant violation of upper-class standards which had not yet declassed the individual. Such persons' children, however, if they maintain the new parental behavior, will undoubtedly lose their status.

There were several cases of unmarried women who had withdrawn, or become "queer," as the uppers phrased it. Their plantations had fallen into decay; they were very poor; their clothing of tattered silk and yellowed lace which dated back to the turn of the century was adorned with five-and-ten-cent store beads and pins; they rode in old and shabby carriages drawn by almost equally old and emaciated horses. They lived in the past, sometimes serving sugarless and creamless coffee and very stale cookies to the rare guest who visited their mansions. But an upper-upper woman, referring to one of them who had exhibited peculiar behavior, said: "Poor Isabel, I do feel sorry for her. She isn't responsible . . . . , *but she's a lady.*" She was still "old aristocracy."

In several instances married people who were "queer" and had withdrawn, thus started their children on the road of social decline. Some of their daughters contracted unsuccessful marriages with men below them in status or with upper-class men from out of the city with whom they could not adjust.

One family of third-generation uppers, on the way "down," were trying to recoup their social position by inviting prominent visitors to their homes, giving tea parties and exhibiting similar behavior. Only middle-class persons were anxious to accept these favors, however, and the *declassé* uppers were unable to get any response from the class which had accepted their parents despite certain aberrations in their behavior. Upper-class persons, when questioned as to why they would not accept these children of uppers, referred to their unkempt personal appearance (which would not have barred them if all other things had been equal) and the fact that, if given a social inch, they took a mile. It was charged that they would accept one as a very intimate acquaintance on the basis of only a slight friendly advance. This fact seems more significant, perhaps, than the suggestion that the girls did not appreciate the importance of keeping themselves neatly dressed and well groomed, for they had lost the upper-class conception of the subtleties of social relations other than those of kinship. They attempted to behave in all their social contacts just as they had behaved toward their intimate kin. They had no conception of the obligations, reciprocals, and, above all, the limitations of friendly relations outside the immediate family. Thus, they offended upper-class people by attempting to behave in all their relations according to the pattern of behavior reserved only for kin relations within the family group. Although we have stated several times that individual peculiarities are not very significant to the upper-upper class, we have also pointed out that kinship is highly valued by this class. The extension of kin behavior into other social relations is, to the upper class, an almost blasphemous twisting of the accepted pattern of behavior.

Social participation with the lower social classes.—There were very few cases of upper uppers participating socially with persons far below them and in such permanent and intimate relationships as to lose status. The few examples known of this type of behavior were all men. One of these, a man in his sixties, was the son of a prominent upper-upper-class family. He received a college education, and studied medicine to please his mother, but against his own wishes. His mother and three sisters are living in the community today and participate as members of upper-upper class. The man, however, has never practiced medicine, and after finishing his studies, left them and went to live along the river front where he has been ever since. His intimates are fishermen and houseboat dwellers, all lower-class people. He is said to be a heavy drinker. Yet this man cannot be said to have acquired a lower-class social position, or any social position below that of upper-upper class.

Another son of an upper-upper-class family had a similar experience. As an adult he became a drunkard whose intimate associates were members of the lower class. He broke all contacts and relations with the upper class, and like the man discussed above, achieved a sort of sociological death. He had no home, and resorted to begging and to charity for his food. While still in his thirties he became a recognized public nuisance, appearing at public gatherings very drunk and disorderly. A group of acquaintances took up a collection to buy him sufficient clothing and to furnish transportation to send him to a sanitarium. The upper class took no notice of this and made no effort to assist. After a few months, however, he returned to the community, a reformed and respectable citizen. He had given up his drinking, dressed neatly, and conducted himself according to upper-class patterns of behavior. One of his cousins, of whom he had many in the community, offered him a home, and he went to live with his kinsman and family. Gradually, he re-established his contacts and relations with the upper class and was again accepted. In a sense, he had accomplished a sort of rebirth into the upper-class aristocracy. His temporary indiscretions were forgotten or ignored. It seems that persons who participate directly with those of lower social position but whose parents had not begun the social descent do not actually become identified with the class to which they fall. They are still "placed" by their upper-class families.

CHAPTER IX

SOCIAL CLIQUES IN THE COLORED SOCIETY

THE interrelationships between cliques, associations, and classes within the white caste have been described and analyzed in chapter iii. The colored society, too, has its structure of formal and informal associations integrated into a functional unity and related to the class system.

Records of Negro social participation demonstrate the existence of both small informal cliques possessing similar behavioral traits, and larger class groups whose members have approximately equal social status. It seems certain that the members of the colored society conceive of classes as groups of persons who can associate freely together; and in order to isolate the social classes, the first problem of the social scientist becomes one of identifying the members of various participation groups.

For this purpose, newspaper records of social affairs, lists of the members of churches and associations, and records kept by the field workers of clique activities are satisfactory evidence. Since the first two kinds of information were either unavailable or unsatisfactory for the lower caste, chief dependence was placed upon records of the daily group participations of individuals. As the field workers extended their interviewing or as newspaper records of social affairs accumulated, it soon became possible to identify relatively small participation groups. Where the records of an individual's participations revealed that he associated with two or more informal groups, he was considered a member of that clique or class with which he participated most frequently. A sample participation chart (Fig. 11) for a small clique is given herewith.

CLIQUE A

SEX: Female
MARITAL STATUS: Chiefly single

NUMBER: 5
AGE RANGE: 20–26

Key	Name	Sex	Age	Marital Status	Address	Oct. 3, 1934 Bridge at Miss A's (Bridge, Gossip, Eating)	Oct. 5 Dinner at Miss C's (Eating, Radio, General Talk)	Oct. 6 Movies (Auto Ride Afterward)	Oct. 8 Dance at Miss B's (Dancing, Eating, Jokes, Talk)	Oct. 11 Visiting Miss G (Gossip and Radio)
H_1	Miss A	F	21	S	32 Maple	X		X	X	
H_2	Miss B	F	25	S	126 Water	X		X	X	
H_3	Miss C	F	20	S	740 Jones		X			X
H_4	Miss D	F	26	S	826 Hill	X	X	X	X	X
H_5	Miss E	F	22	Div.	402 Hill		X		X	

FIG. 11.—Social-participation chart for the study of the Negro society

209

In spite of the limited staff engaged in the work and the lack of newspaper records, it was possible to identify 26 social cliques in the colored society, and in most of these cases to define their types of social activities, recreation and their other behavioral traits. In age they ranged from adolescent cliques to old-age cliques, and in rank from the bottom of the social ladder to the top.

The ranking of cliques.—The problems of discovering the social ordination of cliques in relation to each other and of identifying the classes into which they merged were met, respectively, by interviewing and by keeping records of attendance at large dances, charity affairs and concerts, and of club membership. Interviews showed, for instance, that the members of one middle-aged female art club and of one young-adult female bridge club were regarded as having the highest social rank in the lower caste. Their relative position was also indicated by the fact that they did not associate intimately with certain other cliques of their own age range. It was expressed also by the condescension and antagonism which they exhibited toward the women immediately "below" them and by the antagonism and gossip of these latter women directed toward the members of these two clubs.

Similarly, the ordination of large associational groups was demonstrated by expressions of condescension or of reciprocal antagonism. A hunting club of the upper cliques, for example, was severely criticized by cliques whose members were not admitted. Finally, as one member of these upper cliques said, "the rabble broke it up." On the other hand, the upper cliques expressed, both by nonparticipation and by contemptuous remarks, their superordination to such groups as the colored Veterans' Association and its parades. The most striking expressions of group status which came to the attention of the field workers revolved around the conflicts within one branch of the Colored Parent-Teachers Association, which was led by upper-class persons who received no cooperation from the parents, the great majority of whom were of the middle and lower classes. Over a period of eighteen months, only teachers and officers attended these meetings. The other branch, officered by middle-class persons, received the full co-operation of parents and was highly successful in all its efforts to raise money.

The relative social rank of cliques and of larger associational groups, therefore, is usually made clear to the field workers through verbal and overt expressions of antagonism, envy, or condescension. In other words, the members of the society not only group or "class" themselves by their choice of associates, but they also make clear the rank of these cliques and classes in a social hierarchy. Such groups are conscious of their status in relation to other groups and express their subordinate or superordinate position by their verbalizations, their manners, and their willingness or unwillingness to associate freely with the members of other groups.

Upon the basis of this evidence, the social stratification of cliques and of larger formal associations may be represented diagrammatically. In Figures 12 and 13 the ordination of a few of the most active cliques, for whom adequate data are available, has been shown. The second step, of relating this system of ordinated cliques to the larger system of classes, has been suggested by indicating class lines. Social space is pictured as having only two dimensions: (1) height, which represents the range of social status; and (2) width, which represents age range. A third dimension, depth, is not represented, for the relative size of classes is not considered. A diagram which represented the relative size of classes, as well as status and age, would require three dimensions and would be a truncated quadrangular pyramid, since class populations in the Negro become smaller as status increases.[1]

The fact that most of the cliques are represented by narrow, short ellipses, or by circles, signifies two general characteristics of cliques, viz., that both the age range and the

[1] In the white society of Old City the configuration would not be a pyramid, since the lower class is smaller than the middle class.

status range of these informal groups are narrow. The full significance of the clique ordination represented here will appear as the patterns of clique behavior are defined. The

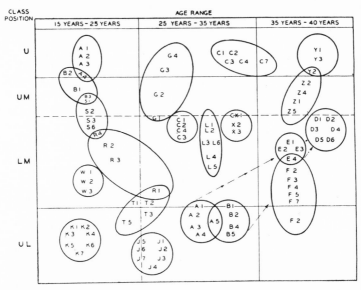

Fig. 12.—Social stratification of a group of colored cliques: ages 15–60

This diagram represents 20 age-graded cliques stratified on the basis of interview material and observed nonverbal behavior. Each clique is designated by a key letter, and each individual within it by a number. The long vertical ellipses represent cliques (F and L) which extend through a large range of social status; skewed ellipses represent cliques (C and R) with a wide age range. Where an individual participates with two cliques, overlapping occurs. This is more frequent in the younger age-ranges, where interlocking cliques extend from the upper to the upper-lower class. Cliques K and J are lower class with no mobile members. A and B (lower class) have mobile members, as indicated by arrows. The arrows represent the direction of social mobility of certain persons in Cliques A and B who are rising into the upper-middle classes through "caste leadership."

reader will then be helped by locating on Figure 12 the clique in question, using the key letter.

The second chart (Fig. 13) indicates the stratification of a

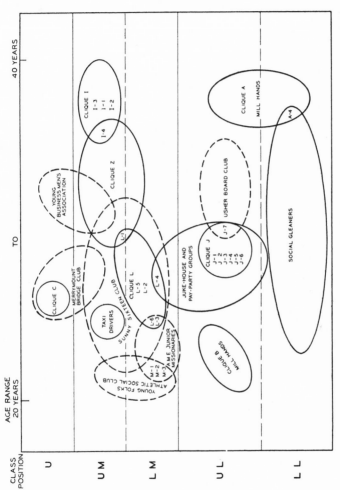

FIG. 13.—Social stratification of a group of colored cliques and associations, ages 20-40. Where overlapping occurs, at least one person is in both groups, and is of the social status and age-range indicated by the general area of overlapping. (Key: — — —, associations; ———, cliques.)

few of the more important cliques in relation to formal associations of the upper, middle, and lower classes. The age range represented here is narrower than in the clique chart; but the status range is greater, extending all the way from lower-lower class ("The Social Gleaners") to upper class ("Merrymount Bridge Club").

Clique traits.—Once cliques have been identified and their social rank has been discovered, the patterns of clique behavior may be analyzed and related both to class status and to the rank held by cliques within classes. The study of social stratification involves not only the definition of a series of ordinated groups; it also includes an effort to find the bases for this common association and for group differences in rank. The system of rank operates in two directions at the same time; it groups people upon the basis of their associates at the same time that it conditions them to accept the social dogmas, attitudes, language traits, and overt behavioral patterns of the group. To describe it in more individual terms, one may assume that persons accept other persons as their associates because they have similar social traits, and that these traits are maintained and their uniformity increased by this very group association.

In both this study and the study of a larger southern city which is now being made, it has been found that the following traits of individuals or families are the most important bases for clique and class associations in colored societies:

1. Status of the parental families
2. Economic traits
   a) Real and personal property
   b) Occupation
   c) Income of family head
3. Age
4. Education
5. Kinship
6. Color and hair-form
7. Friendship as schoolmates
8. Friendship of children

SOCIAL CLIQUES IN COLORED SOCIETY

9. Type of recreation
10. Church and associational membership
11. Talent
12. Manners and dress
13. Housing and furniture

Since all these traits, except color and hair-form, economic traits, and education are quite similar for parallel classes within the two castes, it is not advisable here to repeat the full documentation and analysis of clique behaviors which has been attempted in a previous chapter. In order to illustrate the behavioral patterns of colored cliques, it seems sufficient to analyze a few cases which the writers consider typical of each stratum.

HIGH-STATUS CLIQUES

Within the group of cliques having the highest status there was one extended clique (Merrymount Bridge Club, and Clique C within it, Fig. 13) composed of 13 single women and 3 married women which was the most active. All except 2 of the members of the clique were between twenty-five and thirty years of age, and all except 3 were engaged in schoolteaching or in other white-collar professions or had husbands so engaged. Of the 3 women who had lower occupational status, one was the wife of a barber but came from an upper-class family; one was a dressmaker whose manners, conversation, and party behavior were said by other clique members to account for her inclusion; the third was an office attendant whose collateral kin were upper class. Clique participations took the forms of gossiping, listening to radio programs, card-playing (contract bridge), cocktail parties, and of automobile and theater parties in smaller groups. There was little unorganized recreation, such as reading, painting, drawing, or playing a musical instrument. Analysis of the traits of these 16 women reveals a great similarity in their occupational level, their age, the economic traits of their parents, the length of their formal education, their church membership, and the types of recreation in which

215

they engaged. Ten of the 16 were white or yellow in skin color, 2 were light brown, 1 reddish brown, and only 3 were dark brown, a distribution which indicated color preference. This was an unusually large clique, however. Like all extended cliques, it was composed of smaller groups, which differed not only in respect to the frequency of their clique participations but also in their status within the extended clique. Clique C, the small group which had the highest status was composed of 4 unmarried women. Three of them were teachers (2 had been educated at a northern college which had high social rank); all of them were yellow or white in skin color, and all came from families of high economic status. Only 1 woman, however, came from a family which held or had held upper-class status. This woman, moreover, was the only one in the entire clique of 16 whose parental family had been members of the upper class. The "newness" of the members of the upper cliques was characteristic of the older age grades, also. An extremely high rate of upward mobility into these cliques had accompanied the large emigration of the children of upper-class families during the preceding thirty years. With rapid mobility, upper-class standards were greatly changed, as will appear later.

Another small group (not shown in Fig. 13) was found within the larger extended clique. It was composed of 3 unmarried women, who were the most frequent participants in clique affairs. In spite of their function as organizers of the clique, they were regarded by the other clique members as having lower status than the group of 4 women just mentioned. They were darker in skin color, had attended a college in Mississippi rather than in the North, came from families of lower economic and social status, and were regarded as being less observant of the sexual taboos. These finer distinctions in rank were typical of the gradations in status which existed not only within all classes but also *within all of the larger extended cliques* which were observed.

Our large upper clique of 16 women not only was composed

of smaller groups, but, as has been indicated above, some members participated much more frequently in clique gatherings than did others, and thus formed *a core*, composed of the 3 women last mentioned, and a *primary circle*, composed of the other members. A large number of less intimate friends also participated with the clique in large dances and parties and constituted the *secondary circle*. The line between this secondary circle and the primary circle is not an arbitrary one made by the field worker, for clique members regard the former almost as *nonmembers*. In general in the colored society it appears that the core (most active group) of a clique is composed not of those members who possess the highest status but of the most mobile ("climbing") and socially aggressive members. This characteristic of clique structure seems to hold for all classes and indicates that the mobile persons are the organizers of the society.

In addition to the uniformities of age, marital state, occupational level, types of recreation, economic traits, and of education which appeared in *all* the upper cliques, it was possible to isolate other characteristics which distinguish cliques from each other within the same class. For example, one clique seemed to emphasize light skin color, in addition to other uniformities; a second was organized around kinship; a third, composed of married couples, was held together chiefly by the fact that all the husbands were interested in hunting; and the members of a fourth female clique were brought together by their weak social position as the daughters of white fathers.

CLIQUES OF MIDDLE STATUS

The extent and importance of these interclique differences and the value of a knowledge of the origin of a clique will appear from the analysis of a large clique of 16 men and women (with a secondary circle of 30 participants) which held somewhat lower status than any of the cliques mentioned above. This clique, formally organized into the Sunny Sixteen Club (see Fig. 13), most of whose members were unmarried and between the ages of twenty and thirty, was also composed of persons of similar economic and educational traits. Its origin and its development into a dancing club, however, were the result of two other factors. Most of the female members had been friends in grade and in high school, and most of the men were working together as taxi-drivers. Since upper-class men were not available as mates for these women, they began to associate with the next highest occupational and social group of their own age level. These courting groups were then consolidated upon the basis of the close friendship of the women and the daily association of the men at their work. The result was a large male and female clique, which soon took on formal organization as a "pleasure club."

This group was regarded by the upper cliques of the same age grade as being below them; on the other hand, the lower cliques, which will be analyzed later, regarded the Sunny Sixteen Club as being far above them socially and economically. This self-subordination of the lower cliques seemed incongruous to the sister of one of the Sunny Sixteen members. She knew that most of the male members were taxi-drivers, and she regarded their occupational status from the point of view of the cliques above her rather than from that of the cliques below her. She said musingly:

It's funny how things can give you a place. Now just because my brother manages the taxi line, people [below her] think we're Big Negroes. "Yes," they'll say, "she's Dave Mott's sister. He manages the Elite Taxi Company!" And poor as we are, too! Yes, it's funny. If you run a little two-by-four business, they [people below her] think you're big!

The Sunny Sixteen may be regarded as occupying a middle position in the social strata, therefore, and as being near the top of this middle group of cliques. Six of its members were sometimes invited to affairs given by the upper cliques of the same age grade; 3 of these 6 were members of families which participated with the upper cliques. Although there was some overlapping between the membership of this clique and some of the upper cliques, the great majority of the 46 persons who participated with the Sunny Sixteen very seldom were invited to dances, card parties, or the smaller affairs of the upper cliques. On the other hand, the name of none appears on the participation records of the lower cliques of the same age grade.

This group had, on the average, less real property and slightly more personal property, in the form of cars and radios, than did the older age grades of the middle group of cliques. They had attained a much higher level of education than these older middle cliques but a lower level than the upper cliques of the same age. Their behavior was distinguished generally from that of white cliques of parallel status by the greater emphasis upon churchgoing, and associational activity in the comparable white middle cliques. The Sunny Sixteen members played cards regularly, like the white middle cliques; but they also danced regularly, drank freely, and "liked a good time." A few of them participated in church "programs," and most of the women were members of churches. A slightly larger proportion of them were Baptists than in the upper cliques. A few of these men and women were members of "civic" and "uplift" clubs, such as the Junior Missionary Society of the A.M.E. Church and the Young Business Men's Association. Almost none belonged to the sickness- and death-benefit societies, however, which were especially popular with the lower cliques.

Middle-status cliques of older individuals.—Cliques of middle-aged persons of the same social level were usually composed of active church members who avoided card-playing, dancing, or drinking except in the intimate groups of their fellow church members. Their social life was devoted almost entirely to the meetings of church clubs, welfare clubs, or benefit societies and to the visiting and money-raising which the service of these associations demanded. They strongly disapproved the dancing, drinking, and card-playing of the adolescent and young-adult cliques of the middle group. As these younger people married or came into their thirties, however, it seemed probable that they, too, would give up their "good-timing" and devote themselves to the work of organizing the churches and lodges. The life-histories of certain of the leading preachers, fraternal leaders, and church officers revealed, for example, that they had been the most enthusiastic dancers and "women-chasers" in their youth. Later they became the backbone of the middle class, organizing its churches and societies and exalting its taboos both by their teaching and their public example.

A field worker came to know intimately several of the leading middle 'cliques (Fig. 12, Cliques D and E) of this age grade. He lived in the home of one of the most active members of the group, and his observations of this woman, Mrs. Holdfast, will be especially helpful in illustrating behavior which proved to be typical of the middle cliques. She exhibited a certain mild antagonism to members of the upper group of cliques, but she also constantly expressed her admiration for their courtesy and "breadth of mind" (condescension). In her relations with these persons she was always deferential; to her own clique members she boasted of her acquaintance with two leaders of the upper cliques, Y2 and Y3.

These persons, as well as several members of the cliques at the top of the middle group, regarded her as below them in social rank, however. They objected to the occupation of her husband, a mill laborer, and to her ungrammatical speech, her manners, and her lack of advanced formal education.

Although Mrs. Holdfast recognized that these "big folks" were above her in social space, she was far more expressive of her superiority to those below her. She considered that her higher rank, as compared to these persons, was the result, first, of her larger accumulation of real estate; secondly, of her closer observance of the taboos of the church; thirdly, of her higher credit-standing with white merchants and bankers, and, finally, of her greater effort to advance in the world both economically and socially. She regarded most of the persons of the lower cliques as being immoral, dirty, and shiftless and felt that they were in an especially weak position because they could not secure credit from white persons.

To her intimate acquaintances, who wished to improve their place in the world, Mrs. Holdfast was constantly emphasizing the necessity for accumulating money and property and for increasing one's memberships in societies. To one admirer, she held up her own example, and prayer; "You got to have a gauge to yourself. So pray! Your mother may get on the pension roll. Look what us done done. I done payed for $200.00 sence I ben here. I doan draw no pension, but I eats, has good clo'es, an' look at the things I belongs tuh. You doan belong tuh nothin'!" The enlargement of her social prestige by increasing her associational memberships was Mrs. Holdfast's fundamental technique for social mobility. "Gottuh go ovuh tuh Hill Street tuh uh meetin! Gottuh go. Gottuh be with the people. You can't stay here an' not live with the people. I'm in the societies, an' I stays in 'em."

Her sentimental spot was her interest in her son, who, as she bragged to her husband, had always been sent to private schools so that he would not be a mill hand. She made it clear that she had hoped to remedy the sore spot of her husband's low occupational status by making her son at least a postal employee. For the time being, however, she had to be satisfied with the Pullman service, which the community regarded as a genteel vocation, as compared to mill labor.

CLIQUES OF LOW STATUS

The groups and individuals which Mrs. Holdfast considered inferior to her in social status are represented by Cliques A, B, E, and F, Fig. 12. These are typical of the lowest stratum which includes about three-fourths of the colored population. The traits of the lower caste are usually regarded by both colored and white inhabitants as typified in the traits of this lower class. The proportion of inhabitants in the lower class is much larger, of course, in colored than in white societies, because economic caste restricts most colored workers to domestic and common labor. Since the colored middle and upper classes are organized upon the basis of virtually the same traits as the white middle and upper classes, they will not accept common laborers, with little formal education and little money, as their associates. In most American colored societies the upper and middle classes together, therefore, do not include more than one-fourth of the population. Studies of white societies, such as that by Professor Carr-Saunders of England and Wales, and by Professor W. Lloyd Warner in New England, indicate that the upper and middle classes in Western urban industrial white societies constitute more than one-half of the population.

The fact that the overwhelming majority of colored persons are considered lower class, *according to the colored group's own standards*, seems to result from the conflict between the caste system and the class system. At the same time that the caste system subordinates most colored persons occupationally, the class system teaches them to compete for the occupational and social traits of the white group and to model their class sanctions after those of the white group.

To return to our lower group of cliques: the most common traits of their members were their relatively low incomes (about $1.00 per family per day), their low educational status (most of them had not completed a grammar-school course and were barely literate), and their low occupational status (unskilled laborers and domestic servants).

Occupation was extremely important. For example, the status of a group of novitiate preachers (Fig. 13, Clique A), whom we may take as representative of cliques near the top of the lower group, was below that of most preachers for the reason that they were also employed at common labor. The clique was composed of 7 men, 6 of whom were between the ages of twenty-six and thirty-five. Their average wage was $6.00 per week, but 3 of them owned their homes. They were often entirely without money, however. The core consisted of 3 men: "Smooth" Robinson, Henry Turner, and Jim

Pompous. At times, the clique members were unable to find enough money to buy gasoline for Henry's automobile, which carried them to their engagements. Upon these occasions they were unable to keep their appointments at distant rural churches.

This clique had had its origin in common work in the same department of the planing-mill. Ten of their other occasional associates were also mill workers. Until their interest in preaching had arisen, they had been a prominent "sinner" group, roistering and drinking on Saturday nights, gambling, playing baseball, and "chasing women." Jim Pompous had been responsible for 10 or 12 illegitimate children, according to "Smooth" Robinson, and "Smooth" himself had been especially fond of dancing and Sunday ball-playing. Since all these activities, except the producing of illegitimate children, were cardinal sins to church people, they were abandoned by the men as they became preachers and took upon themselves full adult status in the community. One of the primary members, a minister's son, was the first to be converted and to receive "the call" to preach. Then followed Jim Pompous and Henry Turner; "Smooth" was last. As each man became converted, he dropped his "sinner" friends; as the "sinners" were "called," they were then taken into the clique again. From that time on, their association consisted of discussions of the Bible, visits with one another, and club meetings. They sought increasingly to impress the adult members of the more highly organized lower-middle cliques with their new churchgoing and associational behavior. At the same time, they received a new deference from female members of cliques which were near them in social space. They were called "Reverend" or "Elder"; they were fed; and they exhibited, as the interviewer felt, "an authoritative 'wait-on-me-sister' air." Their new occupational rank was not firmly established, however, for the older women remembered their recent "sinning" and pointed out that they still joked too much and that none of them had a church.

Furthermore, since they all continued to work as mill laborers, they had little chance of being accepted by the middle cliques. Two of these men belonged to a small mutual-aid club, The Helping Hand. Their status was somewhat higher than that of most of The Helping Hand members, however. A study of the small group which organized and directed this society revealed, for example, that none of this group owned any real estate, that their furniture was of a cheaper quality than that of the novitiate preachers, their houses poorer, and the status of their parental families somewhat lower.

Slightly above this last group in status were 27 persons who participated in the Usher Board, the Pastor's Aid Club, and the Willing Worker's Club of the Marblehead Baptist Church (Fig. 13, Clique J and the Usher Board Club). The membership of these clubs was largely overlapping; the group really had the functions of an informal and intimate social clique, as the participation records show. In large part, the functions of the lower-class colored church are not those of religion but of associational and clique life. Of the 27 participants in these church clubs, for example, only 7 had no ties of family or friendship with another participant. Sixteen were related by kinship to at least one other person in the clique; 6 had been old school friends; 4 came from families which were friendly; and 6 had children who were friendly. The educational level was definitely lower than in the preacher clique. Five of the 27 members were illiterate, and 11 others had not completed more than four grades in grammar school.

The pattern of behavior for this lower clique differed from that of church cliques in the middle class in that it permitted the drinking of whiskey, the playing of dance music on a phonograph, and occasional dancing at club meetings. A large number of interviews and many visits to their meetings revealed that church groups in the lower class generally danced and drank more readily than did those in the middle class; they were also less anxious to conceal this type of behavior. Equally striking was the lack of emphasis upon age-grading in these lower cliques. In the Marblehead Church clique, for example, there were 4 women under twenty years of age, and 12 men and women over forty years of age. It seems likely that within the lower class age-grading is poorly defined after early adolescence, for the reason that most adolescents leave school, find work, and obtain sexual experience at a much earlier age than in middle class. They are therefore, also accepted as members of the adult society at an earlier age.

There was adequate evidence that these cliques within the lower class made distinctions of rank among themselves. Members of the Marblehead Church clique expressed antagonism to members of other cliques in the lower group, charging them with social ambition. "They're on the other side of the fence now," one Marblehead woman said of her former friends. She explained that they had joined another "bunch," composed of people who had more education. She felt that her own inability to rise had been due to her lack of education and her employment in the planing-mill. What she was saying was that her old friends had risen into the lower-middle class, while she still associated only with lower-class persons.

This same woman and her clique regarded certain other groups as below them in social rank, however. In general, these lowest cliques were composed of families supported by "the relief" (federal or local dole, and work relief) and of groups which attended "pay parties" or regularly frequented the "jook houses" (beer parlors where one might dance to an automatic phonograph or gamble).

As typical of the first group, the field worker selected the Social Gleaners (Fig. 13), a club of 16 persons which served as a credit union for its members. The age range was great, as in most of the large cliques on this level; it extended from fifteen to sixty. The core of the group, however, was composed of 2 men and 3 women whose ages ranged from fifteen to thirty. All of them lived in the same neighborhood, and 12 of the 16 were related by blood or marriage to some other member of the group. Most of them were illiterate; and even the secretary, who had been elected as a result of his "talent" in writing, kept records of the following kind:

Old City
Feb 7-1934

the Socil Gleanee club meet call to by the per. Reud the first chapah Sent Marth. Pray by brother curt. Sonng brother Winston Frather I Street my hand to the mothe made by bothe Winston Solce by Sister ————————— 25- will be loned to brother Gallimore.

Only 2 of 16 members came from families which owned houses. Eleven were Baptists, and the rest were "unsaved."

Although the Social Gleaners were primarily a credit union, they had established sanctions to govern the social behavior of members. At group discussions and "trials" members were rebuked for keeping late hours, for being seen drunk, and for cursing. The males in the group played cards, attended the theater, and at times could be found drinking or dancing. The women had formerly enjoyed quilting parties, but these had come to be considered old-fashioned. They were still remembered with relish, however.

Yes, they useta do quiltin'—all the wimmins in the club, right after ginnin' cotton. They git the cotton from the gin. The men come too, but they jus come to drink whiskey..... They all dance before they become Christuns an' some of 'em dance right on. We woulda had some dancin' too if it hadn' been for the old Christuns. Once I went to a party an' got drunk, an' I grabbed an ol' long gal an' such another dancin'!

The Social Gleaners and the church cliques spoke of the "jook house" groups as the "lowest" in the society, both in morals and in rank. The immorality of these groups which gathered at the beer parlors consisted in drinking in public, dancing regularly, and cursing. Their lowest social status seemed to be more the result of their failure to join the church and the associations, however, than of their frequenting "jook houses," inasmuch as persons of higher status also frequented "jook houses" and maintained their rank. (Note the wide class range of "jook house" participants in Figure 13. L–4 of the middle-class clique, L, was in this group.) Another distinction was developing. With the legalization of beer, adolescents and young unmarried persons were attending beer parlors increasingly. In the lower-middle and lower classes, the younger age grades did not lose status if they attended. Later in life most of these people will probably no longer attend the "jook houses"; they will join the church clubs or the "social and pleasure clubs" and will find their recreation in fish fries, barbecues, "trips around the world," or in church pageants, "programs," and meetings.

Some of the "jook-house" groups had a very low social position in the community, however. These were the groups which also attended "pay parties" in the section of Old City which was largely given over to prostitution. Analysis of a clique (J) of 7 women who attended such parties revealed that 5 of these persons were employed in domestic service or in the mills. All were casual prostitutes, and 3 had had illegitimate children. Professional prostitutes were regarded as being outside the class structure altogether.

The following chapter will discuss (1) the social classes which are formed in the colored society by the interlocking of cliques and (2) the sanctions which limit participation in these ranked groups.

CHAPTER X
THE CLASS SYSTEM OF THE COLORED CASTE

MEMBERS of the white superordinate caste in Old City are vaguely aware of the existence of social distinctions within the subordinate colored caste, and reference has been made in chapter II to some of the modifications in caste behavior incident to this awareness. Few, if any, of the white residents, however, are acquainted with the subtleties of these distinctions existing among the colored population in their midst or of the systematic nature of class controls within the colored society. The very nature of the caste system is such that white people must, perforce, view Negroes in terms of their relation to that system rather than in relation to the system of social classes. It is far more important to the preservation of white rank for whites to evaluate Negroes as "uppity," as contrasted with "good," rather than as "better class" or "common class" except when these class differences are felt to constitute a threat to "correct" Negro-white relations. Yet, to the Negro community the distinctions of social class determine thought and action to a high degree.[1]

[1] As has been stated in chapters i and iii, there exists within each caste a type of structure which ranks large groups of families and individuals within the castes. The colored people in Old City often refer to these groups as "classes," e.g., "higher class," "better class," "middle class," "low class," "common class"; and the members of one group are regarded as distinguished from those of another by characteristic "class" types of behavior. Within each caste, that is to say, individuals enjoy varying degrees of rank through the possession of superior or inferior social privileges, opportunities, and symbols; they also associate in small and large participation groups (cliques and classes) upon the basis of their similar rank. Such a system of social classes exists within each of the castes, although it is more fully developed within the upper caste. Since class is more fully developed in the white society, the full definition of class behaviors, together with a demonstration of an empirical method for defining classes, has been discussed in relation to white cliques and classes.

CLASS SYSTEM OF COLORED CASTE

THE DYNAMICS OF CLASS BEHAVIOR

Concealing class.—The first evidence of class which the newcomer to Old City's colored society meets will appear in the form of verbal expressions of class antagonism. As time passes, however, and he himself becomes a member of the class system, verbal expressions of class become increasingly rare and veiled. The practice of "hiding class" is general within each caste, for the democratic dogma that social privileges and the opportunity for social mobility shall be based upon merit alone is still a popular dogma. The fact that it is not effective in controlling overt behavior has not weakened its dogmatic prestige. In the same way, the Christian dogma has preserved its power as an ultimate logic for the white population, in spite of the fact that the caste system is a continuous and patent violation of the doctrine of the "brotherhood of man." It appears that widely accepted social dogmas such as these have a purely symbolic value for men, with little or no effectiveness as controls upon overt behavior and social relationships. On the other hand, it is possible to assume that one is observing a decline in the effectiveness of the Christian and democratic dogmas, a kind of vestigial stage in which only lip service remains, and that meanwhile the caste and class systems are evolving dogmas of their own which will be effective in controlling overt behavior. Such an assumption appears unnecessary, however, for the reason that the democratic and Christian dogmas have existed side by side with systems of class and of caste ever since the popularization of these dogmas.

As a symbolic or "ideal" system, then, the dogma of equalitarianism was still sufficiently popular within the lower caste in Old County to prevent free verbal expression concerning the system of rank which actually operates within the lower caste. For the most part, individuals did not refer to social "classes," nor did they verbalize their antagonism toward classes other than their own. Such expression as did occur was usually limited to gossip and to forms of censure which assumed the guise of individual criticism upon grounds of morality or etiquette. The fact that the individual whose behavior was censored possessed a social rank different from that of the speaker, himself, was generally expressed only by hints and innuendoes. It was clear, however, that this silence resulted merely from a taboo upon verbal expressions, and not from any failure to recognize that a system of social rank existed within the colored society.

The patterning of class antagonisms.—Not only did language and etiquette of either a deferential or a condescending type reveal these differences in rank, but in situations of emotional stress individuals from any of the classes were apt to express antagonisms toward other classes. Upper-class colored persons, when angered by the behavior of lower-class individuals, accused them of being black, boisterous, murderous, stupid, or sexually promiscuous, as a class. Middle-class persons were generally even more severe in their criticisms of the lowest social group, regarding shiftlessness, dirtiness, laziness, and religious infidelity as their chief characteristics. In the same fashion, lower-class people accused upper-class persons (the "big shots," the "Big Negroes") of snobbishness, color preference, extreme selfishness, disloyalty in caste leadership, ("sellin' out to white folks"), and economic exploitation of their patients and customers. They also accused middle-class persons, as a group, of sanctimoniousness, greed, miserliness, moral hypocrisy, and social pretentiousness. To complete these reciprocal compliments, the middle class regarded the upper class as sexually immoral, as practiced in lewd dancing, card-playing, drinking, and smoking, and as insincere in its religion; whereas the upper class accused the middle class of that crime which the middle class would most like to avoid, namely, of being "nice, respectable, honest—but nobody!"

The patterning of class antagonisms within the colored society appeared so involved and undemocratic to a lower-class preacher that he was led to cry out against them as a danger to the solidarity of the lower caste. He did not choose his own pulpit for this attack upon class, however; he was careful to speak in another minister's church where he could lose no members. There he was especially frank: "Some folks say educated Negroes doan lak ignorant Negroes, an' straight-haired Negroes doan lak nappy-haid Negroes, an' yelluh Negroes doan lak black Negroes. An' all dese things is true about *nigguhs*, dat's de wus' part of it!" His later remarks seemed to make it clear, however, the he himself was expressing his antagonism to a group of upper-class colored visitors who were present. He was a man who had traveled widely, had worked on jobs in Chicago, Baltimore, and Memphis, and had even been in foreign countries (with the navy). Probably it was for this reason that he always made an effort to impress his audiences with the fact that he was not "ignorant"—not lower class, that is. He attempted to associate with middle-class persons and even to obtain the symbols of upper-class status. For example, he bought an almost new automobile of a very expensive make (a make which no upper-class person in Old County would buy because it was considered pretentious); but he found no upper-class persons to ride with him. His lower-class congregation considered the car an evidence of his snobbishness.

Like other socially mobile persons, he displayed strong antagonisms both to the class which he was trying to enter and the class from which he was seeking to escape. By means of his constant disparagement of the colored "race" as a whole, for example, he succeeded in accusing his congregation of shiftlessness, ignorance, superstition, and sexual immorality, and thus of identifying them with the lower class, as represented in middle-class dogma. The lower-class members of the congregation did not like him, and they saw to it that he served as their minister for only a short period. The middle class did not accept him, and the upper class scarcely knew of his existence. It was understandable, therefore, that he should use the opportunity, in another minister's pulpit, to express in words his hostility toward the whole class system.

Upon occasion, upper-class persons spoke their thoughts about the lower class with equal frankness. As a rule, economic motives prevented them from expressing antagonisms to their patients or customers; but, when angry or disappointed, they were likely to reveal great class hostility. When angry with their children, parents accused them of talking or acting like "common alley-niggers"; church members who disliked revivalistic ritual spoke of the members of lower-class churches as being "ignorant as hogs," "wallowing in superstition," "just like African savages," or simply "black and dumb." A group of three upper-class adolescents, who had attended a very orderly and almost prim dance the night before, complained bitterly the following day against "the rough and common nigguhs" who were present. This latter group had been enabled to attend only because the dance was a pay affair, they said. What this upper-class adolescent clique wanted was to be able to give private dances for "decent people" who attended high school, as is indicated in the following colloquy:

HENRY MABRY: We ought to give invitation dances and keep those common nigguhs out of them! We could get the Catholic School Hall, and decorate it nicely—and don't let any of those common class of nigguhs in there.

JESSIE MABRY: Those nigguhs don't know how to act or talk at a decent dance. It was terrible the crowd they had last night. It makes you feel sick.

JOHN BOYER: The trouble is this town is too small for us to give a dance with just our group. Now in Martin City, you know, all that low and bad element of Negroes live on one side of the city, the west side, and all the better class of Negroes live on the other side of the city. Isn't that right?

HENRY MABRY: Yes. They are separate, mostly.

JOHN BOYER: Well down there, you can have a dance and that low element won't get across the city to it. But Old City is so small you can't do that. They all live together, here, and if you give a pay dance, you can't keep them out!

HENRY MABRY: Well we ought to get the Catholic Hall, and just invite people![2]

² At another dance an upper-class colored woman told a female interviewer that she hated to attend dances in Old City because the men she was compelled to dance with were so "awful." Fifteen years ago, she said, there had been a very exclusive social set in Old City, and there had been no "rabble" at the dances then.

CLASS SYSTEM OF COLORED CASTE

The socially "unclean."—The statement of the upper-class colored girl, quoted above, that association with lower-class people made her "feel sick" seems to represent a common experience of upper-class colored persons. They appear to regard lower-class colored persons as "unclean," as revolting physically, in spite of the fact that they may be no different in color, odor, hair-form, or other physical characteristics from these lower-class persons. One upper middle-class colored woman, a dental inspector, was averse to handling the colored school children and constantly washed her hands during inspections, to such an extent that a white public health officer regarded this woman as more "squeamish" over physical contact with colored lower-class persons than he himself was. This incident is especially striking for the reason that no question of association is involved. In general, white people in Old County testify to a feeling of sickness or nausea in regard to colored people only when social or sexual intimacy between white and colored persons is observed or imagined. When the relationship is in accord with the caste status of the individuals, however, the most intimate physical contact is acceptable, as in the cases of white adults who embrace and kiss their colored "mammies," or white patients who are bathed and attended by colored nurses. Between upper-class and lower-class members within the colored society, however, the most intimate of even these physical contacts are rigidly avoided, such as sexual intercourse or marriage with a black or lower-class woman. Colored people of the upper class and upper-middle class constantly express surprise at the ability of many white men not only to have sexual intercourse with "black and common" women but to love them.

In general, it appears that the objection of white people to colored persons as "unclean" is made usually in connection with violations of caste taboos to which the white individual has been accustomed since childhood. It is a ritualistic or social "uncleanliness," such as the idea or practice of incest arouses in most human societies, or marriage with a Gentile arouses in the orthodox Jew. Colored people of the upper and middle classes, however, constantly described lower-class persons as "dirty," "filthy," or "nasty," when referring to their bodies, clothes, and houses. Since physical uncleanliness was not a characteristic of lower-class persons or of their houses, as observed by interviewers, it seems certain that the sense of social "uncleanliness" of the kind indicated by the upper-class colored girl who "felt sick" because she had to dance among lower-class persons (not *with* them) is accompanied by an actual physical revulsion toward proximity with lower-class persons. If we were to hazard a guess with regard to psychological motivation, it might be assumed that blackness or darkness is identified with dirt as well as with social "commonness." "Common" or lower-class persons are almost always thought of, therefore, as being black and woolly-haired, even though many of them are not. It seems generally true that upper-class colored persons in large cities, for example, think of lower-class persons on State Street, Lenox Avenue, Rampart Street, or Seventh Street as black people. Relatively few of them are black, and a good proportion are light brown.

The influence of caste on class criteria.—In color, as in most other respects, the class sanctions of the lower caste are largely correlated with the traits of the upper caste, and the effort of colored upper- and middle-class individuals to maintain or to increase their class status appears to be equated psychologically with an attempt to acquire the traits of the white caste. The distinguishing traits of the white caste are skin color and hair type, so that it is to be expected that whiteness of skin and straightness of hair will have high value as class sanctions in the colored group. Those who possess these physical traits may even become members of the upper caste by migrating and "passing for white."

With the elaboration of class standards, however, other traits of the upper caste besides color and hair-form have become essential parts of the behavioral pattern of the colored upper and middle classes. High social status depends today not simply upon light skin color and "good" hair, therefore; it depends also upon a configuration of behavioral traits which include family status, length of formal education, manners, type of conversation, associational membership, dress, and economic traits as well. The configurational nature of class sanctions accounts for the fact that some colored persons with light skin color and straight hair are actually subordinated to lower-class status within the colored group.

This conflict within the colored group between the sanctions of caste status (whiteness of skin and straightness of hair) and the sanctions of class status accounts for much of the irrational behavior of colored persons. The traits of the upper caste must necessarily be the most precious; the operation of the society clearly demonstrates that the prestige of being white is infinitely more valuable than that of being middle- or upper-class colored. For this reason, whiteness and its associated physical traits are still the most important of upper-class criteria for high status. Other qualifications being nearly equal, colored persons having light skin and "white" types of hair will be accorded the highest station within the lower caste. This fact does not prevent the expression of strong antagonisms to light-skinned persons by the rest of the group. Such antagonism is an expression of the envy and humiliation of the darker individuals.

Since the system of classes operates within a caste system, the physical traits of the white caste must be accorded highest value; the darker individuals cannot but be conditioned to the all-important symbols of the upper caste, and so give them highest rank. The upper class, on the other hand, thinks of the lower class as black and woolly-haired, thus mentally associating the lowest social rank with the "lowest" physical traits. Whether the idea of their being also dirty is an association with blackness of skin or with lowness of economic and social rank is a problem for the clinical psychologist. The sociological fact is, as stated above, that many, and probably most, lower-class people in Old County are not uncleanly; they certainly are not black.[3]

Techniques for dissolving class-antagonisms.—In addition to statements made under the stress of anger, class antagonisms were likewise voiced by nonresidents of Old County and by several upper-class persons whose status was secure. (Both these groups of persons were withdrawn from the local competition for status and were not subject to the usual penalties upon expressions of an undemocratic nature.) For example, a church officer, who was a member of the upper class or upper-middle class in the city where he lived, explained to an interviewer his methods for overcoming the antagonisms of his lower-class rural audiences. As he rode with the interviewer to one of several rural churches which they visited, the church official said:

> You know, people like these out here are terribly sensitive. You've got to get out among them and know how to get along with them. You've got to keep them from thinking you feel you're above them. You've got to do it—of course you can feel it, and know it, but you can't let them see it.

It is interesting to notice here that the chief device employed by upper-class colored speakers for dissolving the antagonisms of a lower-class audience was to emphasize the *solidarity of the caste*, to invoke the ideals, that is, of "race pride" and "race loyalty." A device of middle-class preachers which had the same function was their continual use of dialect and of folk humor in their sermons to their lower-class congregations. Preachers whose social status was definitely above that of their congregation had to associate freely with their members, moreover, by visiting their homes, attending bazaars and church affairs, and fraternizing with members on the street. One minister in the upper-middle class who failed to employ

[3] Even in the alleys, there were surprisingly few black or "dark" women or children. In one sample of 34 women who lived in alleys, only 9, or a little more than one-fourth, were approximately black. More than half of these women were light brown, yellowish-brown, or yellow.

these conciliatory devices lost a large part of his congregation. His failure was explained by the president of a lodge in the upper class as follows:

Reverun' Meems is a good man; he's more intelligent than 90 per cent of the preachers here. He's too quiet, though. He should of made good for himself long ago, but he won't go among them, and mix with them. But you can't hold away from them, ef you want tuh be a powuh among Negroes. If you want to be powerful, you gottuh stay near the powuh-house!

CLASS CRITERIA—PAST AND PRESENT

Social classes and economic groups.—Social classes are conceived of in this work as differing in their traits from other crosscutting strata which have been called "economic groups."

In brief, an economic group has been thought of as a large informal group of persons (1) who exhibit similar attitudes and dogmas with regard to property and money and the distribution of these possessions among the members of the society, and (2) whose incomes, economic possessions, and economic functions usually fall within certain limited and characteristic ranges.

From this point of view, there are two major structural differences between an economic group and a social class. In the first place, the common behaviors of the members of an economic group are accompanied by a uniformity in only one kind of traits, namely, economic traits, those which relate to money, property, and occupation. The common behaviors of the members of a social class, on the other hand, are associated with a large number of structural traits, such as the social status of the parental families of the members, the length of their formal education, their church and associational ties, and their income and their economic possessions.

Besides this difference in the complexity of traits, there is a second structural difference between economic groups and social classes which relates to the extent and frequency of participation between the individuals within the group.

DEEP SOUTH

Although the members of an economic group share common economic dogmas and attitudes, they seldom participate with each other in group action. Social classes, on the other hand, are essentially participation groups.

The members of a social class themselves recognize that the fundamental test of their class status is their ability to participate regularly in the social life of certain other persons. In the colored society, for example, the expression "class *with*" is used to mean "able to go around with" (socially), and one middle-class person will say of another: "Joe can't class with the big folks [upper class]—he goes around with the people right here in Turnersville [middle-class neighborhood] just like the rest of us."

In the sense in which a social class is here conceived, therefore, its membership can be identified empirically upon the basis of either of two types of information: (1) by records of *common participation of individuals in noneconomic groups*, such as in churches, associations, and clubs and at large dances, teas, picnics, weddings and funerals; and (2) by the verbal expression by individuals of their *willingness to associate with other persons in these social relationships*.[4]

The same kinds of evidence will also identify smaller participation groups, of an informal nature, within each class. These smaller groups, including from 2 to as many as 30 participants who form an intimate circle of acquaintance, are the constituent parts of a class. They have been termed "social cliques" in this analysis. In the chapter dealing with class in the white society, it was possible to indicate that a

[4] The proportion of class membership defined by each of these types of information will vary with the size of the society. In large societies, for example, neither lower nor middle classes will ever participate as entire groups. Even in defining classes within small societies, verbal expressions concerning class status must be accepted, especially with regard to socially withdrawn persons or families, like those "old" upper-class families in Old County who have been reduced to poverty and have therefore ceased to participate with the upper class. Upper-class whites still regard these withdrawn families as members of their social group, however; they are therefore upper class, although they no longer participate with their class.

large number of cliques overlap in their social participation so as to form a class. It also appeared that the cliques within a given class are themselves ordinated in a series of social rank. No attempt will be made here to demonstrate that Negro cliques overlap so as to form the larger social strata which are called "classes," nor will the patterns of class behavior be analyzed with any effort at scientific completeness. The more highly developed class structure of the white society has offered a more adequate field for an intensive study of the relationship between cliques and social stratification.

If classes are participation groups, the first work of the social student in defining them is to identify their members. The next problem is to define the social and economic traits (behavioral patterns) of the members, and *to discover those traits or groups of traits which are shared by most of the members.* This analysis may show that several patterns of behavior are acceptable, that there is a range of behavioral patterns. If these patterns of behavior are the characteristics of a class, however, they will be found in only one class. The third step in the definition of social classes is a problem in social psychology, namely, to discover the sentiments, attitudes, and types of personality which are associated with the manifest behavior-patterns of each social class. The social anthropologist is primarily concerned with the first two steps in this analysis.

Relatively slight differentiation of Negro classes.—The most explicit and detailed expressions concerning class status were made by persons at the top of the colored class structure. These upper-class persons stated that there were three social classes. They knew and identified the members of the upper class and those individuals with highest rank in the middle class. They also stated their conception of the social traits and techniques by which these individuals had achieved high social status. All these upper-class informants emphasized the weakness, however, of class sanctions. They were especially dissatisfied with the traits of the upper class. Like the three adolescents and the upper-class woman quoted above, they felt that class lines were not drawn clearly enough, in church, at school, or even at private dances. Things had gone from bad to worse, they said. At present, upper-class standards were so "low" that "the best families are associating with bellhops and taxi-drivers," they complained.

While the disorganization of class sanctions seems to have resulted partly from (1) a very high rate of emigration among upper-class persons and (2) from the change in the value attached to miscegenation, there is no doubt that in this, as in most colored societies, the chief "weakness" of the class structure lies in the relative lack of economic stratification within the lower caste. As a direct result of caste taboos, for example, colored persons are excluded from all white-collar and professional occupations, except in the few colored businesses or educational institutions. Physicians, dentists, and lawyers, moreover, are relatively few in colored, as compared with white, societies in the South.

The caste system as represented by the southern state legislatures makes no provision for the education of colored physicians, dentists, or lawyers; and colored people are systematically excluded from white-collar work in business and government. The relative lack of economic or occupational differentiation within colored societies is fundamentally the result of educational and economic caste, therefore. Although the operation of the economic system permits a few colored persons to achieve high occupational status, it does not permit a sufficient spread of occupations to allow the development of an occupational hierarchy. In all modern Western class systems, on the other hand, occupational status and economic status are highly correlated with class status. Occupational and economic status may have been acquired from one's ancestors, or be largely honorific, as in the case of upper-class families who have lost their wealth but have preserved the reputation of wealth and of high occupational status in the past. In any historical view of class, however, there seems no doubt that economic stratification would prove the most constant factor.

Many of the social maladjustments within the colored group in Old County, and in America generally (such as the extremely severe conflicts over leadership, and the attendant disorganization), are attributable to the lack of economic opportunity for colored persons under the caste system. The relative lack of social ritual and associational development, which characterizes the colored upper class and upper-middle classes, appears to result from this lack of occupational differentiation. Psychologically, there seems no doubt, moreover, that many of the frustrations and compensatory mechanisms of upper-class colored people result from the fact that, while the white class system (their goal) is accompanied by economic and occupational stratification, theirs is not. They feel that it is lamentable, if one is a teacher or physician, to be rubbing shoulders at dances, at church—or even in college fraternities, of all places—with porters, waitresses, and jazz-band musicians.

The consequent frustrations and compensatory activities seem to divide the colored upper class into two groups: (1) a socially withdrawn and highly neurotic group which seems to be essentially fixated upon being white, and (2) a socially active group which seems to attempt to compensate for its not being white by being more free in its emotional and sensual expression than even the white upper class. In other words, this second group seems to be adopting the freer expression in language, dancing, and 'sensuality" which the society allows to a colored person. The first group within the upper class seems to be still the more numerous.

The type of frustrations over weakly defined class status which are experienced by upper-class and upper-middle-class colored persons in Old City has been indicated in the interviews quoted above. If the individual is to have any group participation, however, he must adjust himself to his situation; if he is a businessman or a physician, he dares not draw lines sharply in a group so small.

Since the system of economic caste finds its fullest development in "black" plantation counties such as Old County, occupational differentiation is extremely weak within the colored society there. Even at private dances of the upper class and upper-middle class, for example, female schoolteachers and the families of a few professional and businessmen constituted only a small proportion of those present. Most of the persons were from the families of store porters, drivers of delivery trucks, lottery-runners, barbers, and a few artisans. In general, the women were of higher status than the men, because most of the men of upper-class families had emigrated. At private dances given by unmarried upper-class women between the ages of twenty and thirty, the occupational status of the men was even lower. At one of the largest of these dances, only one man had professional or white-collar status. At the private dances given by upper-class adolescents, the general occupational level of the families represented was lower still.[5] This evidence concerning dancing groups is especially important, because class lines are stronger at dances than in any other group except cliques.

Economic motives were clearly important in weakening class sanctions. For example, the leading upper-class women's club in the city held a joint dinner and bazaar with rural middle and lower-class women in order to finance their club's activities. The leading upper-class professional man not only insisted that "all classes" should be invited to parties at his home but compelled his wife to visit his patients of the lower and middle classes and to attend their funerals.

The changing class standards.—The rapid changes which have occurred in the Negro class standards since the end of Reconstruction offer an excellent field for a study of the dynamics of class. The large emigration of colored people following the World War has especially accelerated the change

---

[5] At children's parties, however, the range of occupational and class status of the families represented was more narrow than in either the adolescent or the twenty-to-thirty age groups.

242

in standards of the upper class and upper-middle class. In order to obtain some insight into the development of class sanctions, therefore, it will be well to look more closely at the criteria of status in the colored upper and middle classes.

In older and more stable societies, even in the United States, a relatively long period of time is required to attain the family status requisite for membership in the upper class. Professor W. Lloyd Warner and his associates have found, in an old New England city, that an individual's family must have possessed economic, educational, and cultural traits of a high level for at least three generations if the individual is to be accepted as upper class. In colored societies, where the ancestry of most individuals can be traced for only seventy years before it leads into slavery, however, high status must be founded upon traits which may be obtained in a relatively short time, such as economic and educational attainments, or upon traits which are fortuitous, such as physical appearance.

There is no doubt, for example, that dress and the possession of light skin color and white hair-form are extremely important factors in upper-class status in colored societies. The greater emphasis placed upon their dress by colored people,[6] as compared with whites of the same economic level, has been evident to the writer in points as far distant as Liverpool and Mississippi. This emphasis seems to be a trait of groups with inferior caste status, for Mr. Cedric Dover[7] has remarked the same emphasis, amounting to extravagance, among Eurasian, half-caste communities. The purchase of expensive automobiles is certainly equally exaggerated among colored groups in this country as compared to white groups of similar income, and for the same purpose, namely, that these economic symbols have higher social value than in most white communities.

This emphasis upon dress and economic symbols is also

[6] See Paul K. Edwards, *The Southern Urban Negro as a Consumer* (New York: Prentice-Hall, 1932).

[7] See Cedric Dover, *Half-Caste* (London: Martin Secker and Warburg, Ltd., 1937).

related to the caste sanctions, however. Most of the symbols of status in our society are denied to colored persons. In the South and in most areas in the North, even those colored people who have the economic means are not allowed to share in most of the activities which serve as symbols of economic and social status for the parallel white groups. They appear to compensate psychologically for this deprivation by acquiring expensive clothes, furniture, and automobiles.

Color as a class mark.—The high social value placed upon light skin color and white hair-form is even more clearly related to the operation of caste sanctions. While it is not true that these physical traits alone assure a colored person an upper-class status, it is certain that, in most of even the older colored communities, social mobility proceeds at a faster pace for persons with these physical traits. It is commonly said by colored men of the upper and upper-middle classes today that they marry women for their "looks," while white men of parallel status marry for family status, money, and education.

The materials on the upper class in Old City seem especially clear on this point. The upper class of thirty years before had been organized chiefly around "white" physical appearance and certain types of occupations. Three informants who had been members of the upper class in 1900 agreed upon the main traits of 32 families of about 150 individuals who were members of the upper class in those days. In 1900, they said, there were a rural upper class and an urban upper class. The first was composed of rather large colored planters, all of whom were white skinned except for the members of one family, who were reddish brown in color but had white types of hair. Of the urban families, four were light brown or yellowish brown in color but had white types of hair, one was reddish brown with straight or wavy hair, and two were medium brown in color with white types of hair. All the others, amounting to more than three-fourths of the group, were olive, light yellow, or white in skin color, with white hair-forms. In occupation, they were chiefly proprietors of rather large stores catering to white trade, contractors, artisans, and teachers. One was a lawyer, and three held or had held governmental offices. There were a few of lower occupational status. Two were waiters and one a steward on river boats, one was a coachman for a wealthy white family, and one was a leader of a dance band. The great majority, however, were proprietors and artisans.

Most of the parental generation in this old upper class were the children of white persons. Some of them were the children of upper-class planters, and one was the son of a former mayor of Old City. Some of them had been sent away by their white parents to be educated in leading colored schools and colleges, and a smaller number had inherited considerable real estate from their white parents. Three of these colored families had been free for at least a generation before the Civil War, and members of two of them had fought with the Confederate Army.

Within both the rural and urban upper classes there were cliques all of whose members were white or light yellow in skin color. They constituted the so-called "blue-vein" society and possessed highest status in the colored group. In the rural areas the "blue-vein" group had consisted of six families, four of which were related by kinship. A member of the leading family in this group said in 1934 that "if a child turned out black or dark, it was just too bad for him." If "dark" children were born in these families, they were sent off to other cities to live with "dark" relatives. This group of rural families still held apart from the colored upper class in 1933–35; even the younger members insisted that they were not colored. They pointed out that until recently their families had *not* been treated "like colored people" by the white group but had constituted a caste of intermediate status, resembling that of the "colored" Creoles in Louisiana at about the same time.

In Old City the "blue-vein" clique was larger and even more

exclusive in its social participation. Even brown-skinned members of the upper class, who attended larger balls with this clique, were excluded from the smaller affairs. Like the rural group, the urban "blue veins" not only regarded themselves as a different "race" from the colored group but were so regarded by the white society. A dark member of the upper class in 1933–35 emphasized this intermediate caste status of the "blue-vein" group of a generation earlier which had excluded people of her color. She stated quite freely that they had regarded themselves as "better" than the rest of the colored group and had been so regarded and treated by the white group. At the present time, she said, "that attitude toward color is entirely gone here."

While she was not entirely accurate in this remark, she was certainly expressing the general tendency in the development of new class standards. Most of the members of the upper class today are brown in color, and very few of them have white types of hair. Membership in the learned professions has become a more powerful positive sanction than light color. Today, the questions tacitly asked about a person who is "pushing" into the upper class are these: (1) What has been his education? (2) Has he professional or semiprofessional status? (3) Are his language, manners, and dress "polished"? (4) Is he black? (5) In the case of women, have they had sexual relations with white men? The approved answer to these last two questions must be negative.

The gradual darkening of the upper class has been partly the result of the large emigration of the white-skinned group. Most of the lighter-skinned persons who have remained have not married. Very few of the brown upper-class women have married, probably for the reason that no men of high occupational or economic status have been available. The result has been that the upper class of today has been recruited largely from the middle-class families of a generation ago. Most of these middle-class families were darker than the upper-class families of 1900. Since they could not intermarry with the "blue veins," most of their children are also brown.

CLASS SYSTEM OF COLORED CASTE

With the rise of this brown middle-class group into the upper class, however, a color taboo has still been preserved against black people, notably against black women. For example, a large bridge party given by the agents of a colored insurance company, and attended by 26 men and 30 women of the upper and upper-middle classes, is a representative social event. Only 4 black men were present. They were all agents of the company. Two of them served the guests; the other 2 sat outside in the hall and did not participate in the party. There were only 7 dark-brown or black women present. Analysis of their status showed that all of them were relatives of men who were either light-skinned or had high occupational status.

The strongest and most general antagonism of upper-class persons was directed toward a well-to-do black man who was trying to rise socially. The most difficult step in upward social mobility in most urban colored societies appears to be that of a black woman attempting to move into the upper class.

One need no longer be olive, yellow, or white, however, or even brown with "good" hair, to be a member of the upper class. The upper class in Old City and elsewhere among Negroes today is largely a brown group, with Negroid types of hair. The emergence of this new upper class has been accompanied by an increase in caste solidarity, in "race pride," and in the development of segregated institutions. Although it is impossible, in our economic system, for the colored society to function successfully as a "solid" or highly organized group, it has been possible for it to develop at least a dogma of caste solidarity. The dogma and its related emotional patterns have been accompanied by the establishment of strong taboos against miscegenation. Whereas in Old County of a generation ago an individual's status was increased by his kinship to white persons of the middle or upper classes, today both miscegenation and illegitimacy are rather heavily tabooed in the colored upper and upper-middle classes.

The result is an ambivalent attitude toward color. The conflict between the standards of caste (color and hair) and those of class (legitimacy) leads colored people in Old County to admire and prefer the light-skinned illegitimate children of white men, at the same time that they condemn the violation of caste solidarity by colored women. As time goes on, the children of upper-class and middle-class white fathers will probably have to emigrate to other cities, where their parentage is not known, in order to obtain upper-class status in a colored society. While they are not, at present, subordinated by colored children of the upper and middle classes in the schools of Old City, their colored mothers are ostracized by the adults in the upper class.

The ambivalent nature of group attitudes toward color within the lower caste is also revealed by abundant evidence of color preference within the family itself. This subject has been treated in a recent volume by Dr. John Dollard and one of the authors, who collaborated in a study by the American Youth Commission of the effects of their caste status upon the personality development of colored adolescents.[8] Color preferences within the family in the cities studied were found to be important factors in the social conditioning of the child. One of the most dramatic evidences in Old City of the high value placed upon light skin color in the lower caste, and of the resultant conflict between this kind of evaluation and the complex standards of class, was afforded by the performance of a religious pageant in the leading colored church. In this representation of heaven, all of the "angels" and "saints" who had prominent positions on the stage were white or yellow in skin color. This prominence was not the result of any high social status, however, for upper-class persons stated that the angels were "nobody much," in social rank.

INTERDEPENDENCE OF THE CASTE AND CLASS SYSTEMS

The Negro class system and the color-caste system are mutually reinforcing. Although the increasing social differentia-

[8] Allison Davis and John Dollard, *Children of Bondage* (Washington, D. C.: American Council on Education, 1940).

tion within the colored caste may increase the types of caste relations it does not operate to sanction social mobility between the Negro and white groups. The Negro upper and middle social classes, for example, do not support any local associations or movements designed to disrupt the separate, endogamous system of organizing Negro-white relations.

In fact, the upper and middle classes secure status gains from their position within the Negro society; these gains in turn reinforce their lower-caste behavior. At certain crisis periods, this mechanism has been particularly evident, and Negro leaders of the upper and middle social classes have shown public disapproval of forces tending to disrupt the system. Such attitudes were expressed during post-war migrations, when they co-operated with white leaders in encouraging Negroes to remain in Old City. They were also manifested when certain younger, class-striving lower-middle-class—"radicals"—sought to organize a local branch of a national Negro organization attempting to modify the caste controls. One of these men (now managing a "jook house" in this era of his disillusionment) was particularly bitter against those "sane" leaders who restrained them. The projected branch of the association is now an innocuous men's club, still bearing a name symbolic of protest—the John Brown Club.

Lower-class leaders likewise are a conservative force in the society, especially lower-class ministers. It is true that a few lower-class individuals still maintain a rapidly dying branch of the Universal Negro Improvement Association and speak with nostalgia of Marcus Garvey. This organization is not conceived as a threat to the caste structure, however.

Only an occasional "bad nigger" openly defies the caste sanctions; the price for this defiance is either a severe beating, expulsion from the county, or, in exceptional cases, hanging. Negroes of all classes tend to identify vicariously with the "bad nigger" but accommodate themselves to the system, which is reinforced by punishment, the threat of punishment and by the minimum necessary rewards. It is not possible, however, within the confines of this volume to discuss in detail the operation of Negro associations and churches in maintaining the caste system.[9]

SUMMARY—PART I

The American caste-class system.—The first section of this volume has presented a detailed description of the American caste-class system as it exists in deep South. It is evident that the class structure, whether in the white or colored societies, lacks the definition and rigidity of the caste structure. There is movement from class to class; the class controls furthermore are dependent chiefly upon prestige motivation rather than upon physical violence or intimidation. Thus, the definition of social class structure, the position of individuals within the structure, and its effect upon their behavior, requires a greater refinement of technique and methodology than does the study of caste.

It is in terms of his position in the white or Negro class structure that an individual's social relations with other members of his caste are defined and delimited. Although there is not complete uniformity, there is a norm of behavior which differs from class to class. The adoption by a person of the behavior of a higher class than that into which he was born is frequently evidence of an attempt at upward mobility. Adoption of the behavior of a lower class is often symptomatic of extreme maladjustment both to one's own class and to the whole society. In fact, severe maladjustment of upper-class individuals results not in the adoption of middle-class behavior but rather in expression of the lower-lower-class irresponsibility and indifference to the formal social controls.

[9] The function of Negro churches and associations in maintaining both the caste and class structures in the deep South has been described fully by one of the authors, Allison Davis, in a research memorandum prepared for the Carnegie Foundation's study, "The Negro in America" (1940). For purposes of comparison, a similar analysis of Negro churches and associations in a northern urban community was made by J. G. St. Clair Drake.

CLASS SYSTEM OF COLORED CASTE

The class differences in behavior are accompanied by differences in ideology and values. The class structure is mirrored in these ideologies and dogmas just as the caste structure is expressed in caste dogmas. In fact, the same type of evaluation may often be applied to class differences as are used in describing caste differences. It thus appears that, in spite of the critical differences between class and caste, they are both hierarchies in which the lowest group symbolizes all the negative values, all the wrongs and sins, of the society. They differ, however, in that persons may sometimes be socially mobile in the class hierarchy; never in the caste hierarchy.

The second section of this study will be devoted (1) to a sociological analysis of the economic system, with which the systems of caste and class are integrated, and (2) the operation of the political system, the law, and the courts in maintaining the caste lines.

PART II

CHAPTER XI

GENERAL VIEW OF THE ECONOMIC SYSTEM

AN ECONOMY IN DECLINE

BEFORE the Civil War, Old City was a thriving trade center on the river route from the cotton country to the sea. Here, planters from the surrounding areas maintained fine homes and lived a life of leisure surrounded by their retinues of slaves. The Civil War was the first great crisis which disturbed this almost feudal way of life, and the landed upper-class still speaks with evident nostalgia of "The Past"—that far-off opulent era now enshrined in Old City's mythology. It was not the Civil War, alone, however, that shattered Old City's past, for the coming of the railroads diminished the importance of all the river towns. Old City could have been saved if her river-minded business men had foreseen the advantage of letting the mainline pass through their city. After their refusal, inland towns arose on the trunk lines in Old City's former trade area to serve as outlets for seacoast distributors. More recently, with the appearance of good roads, even the planters across the river on the rich delta lands have begun to turn their faces toward other wholesale centers, since the truck rates are cheaper than the ferry tolls to Old City.

Other factors, too, contributed to Old City's economic decline. In the early 1900's the boll weevil swept up from the Southwest and reduced the annual cotton crop from 14,000 to 2,000 bales. Old County has never recovered from this catastrophe to the plantation system. Debt-peonage was struck a body-blow. A steady decrease in Old County's rural population also has resulted from the weevil plague (see Fig. 14).

For the ten years preceding this study, the number of industrial workers likewise steadily declined; in 1929 the lone textile mill closed, throwing 500 persons out of work.[1] Myths have been elaborated to account for the failure of Old City to grow industrially, and in 1935 there was a general belief among workers in the city that the old planter-families, in order to "protect" their supply of agricultural labor, had prevented one of the largest oil refineries and one of the largest

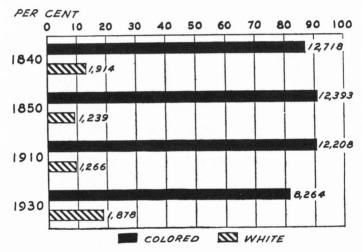

FIG. 14.—Rural population of Old County, by number and proportion for each color group: 1840, 1850, 1910, and 1930.

lumber companies in the United States from establishing important factories in the county. Such a situation actually occurred in the World War boom. In 1919 the opening of a factory, coupled with the migration to the North, created a labor shortage, and Old County landlords faced the prospect of a tenantry deserting them for Old City or for Chicago. At

[1] These workers are the segment of the white lower class referred to in chapter iii. They still think of themselves as textile workers, although most of them had been unemployed for nearly five years when this study was made.

this time they tried to prevent both the migration of the Negroes and the industrialization of the city.

The impact of the depression of 1929 upon the economy of Old County accelerated its decline. The period of this study coincided with a period of national deflation of the prices of agricultural products and farm lands[2] and of widespread failure among farmers in all parts of the United States. The cotton crop in 1932 was the second largest ever produced in the United States. With the domestic and foreign demand greatly reduced, the price of cotton declined more sharply than that of any other agricultural product. At the beginning of the season 1931–32 the price of cotton reached its lowest point since 1898, with no proportionate decline in the farmer's costs of production. The decline in the price of cattle and hogs also reduced the income of cotton-farmers from these sources. At the same time, values of farm land declined greatly, and the proportion of tenant-operated farms increased significantly.[3]

Such periods have been as common in the history of American agriculture as periods of good prices and of successful farming, however; indeed, cotton-farmers, like other farmers in the United States, had not recovered from the post-war deflation of 1920–21 when the deflation of 1929 occurred. Depressions are not exceptional in southern agriculture. With the exception of the period from 1900 to 1920, southern, as well as western, agriculture had suffered from overproduction and from deflation of prices. Old County has been responsive to all these forces.

[2] United States Department of Agriculture, *Yearbook of Agriculture, 1932, 1933*, (Washington, D. C.: Government Printing Office).

[3] In the general decline of prices in 1932 prices of agricultural products declined first and most severely; nor did the decline in farm expenses keep pace with the decline in the prices offered for farm products. Between August, 1929, and August, 1932, prices at the farm of all groups of farm commodities declined nearly 60 per cent, while nonagricultural prices at wholesale declined only 24 per cent.

DEEP SOUTH

THE PRIMACY OF AGRICULTURE

The fundamental class and caste structures which have been described in the first section of this book originated in the division of labor on the cotton plantation. They have persisted into the present, although the county has become in-

TABLE 5

LEADING FIELDS OF EMPLOYMENT IN OLD COUNTY, BY COLOR AND SEX OF EMPLOYEES: 1929*

FIELD OF EMPLOYMENT	WHITE				COLORED			
	Number		Percentage of All White Workers		Number		Percentage of All Colored Workers	
	Male	Fe-male	Male	Fe-male	Male	Fe-male	Male	Fe-male
1. Agriculture..................	285	32	11.8	4.1	2,072	823	49.9	27.4
Farmers (owners and tenants).	185	21	7.6	2.7	1,341	154	31.0	5.1
Farm-managers and foremen..	10	....	0.4	....	8	....	....	....
Farm laborers..............	90	11	3.7	....	722	668	16.7	22.3
Wage workers.............	67	5	2.8	....	325	170	....	....
Unpaid family workers.....	23	6	1.0	....	397	498	....	....
2. Wholesale and retail trade, except automobiles...........	460	213	19.0	27.3	266	35	6.1	....
3. All transportation and communication.....................	300	49	12.4	6.3	344	9	7.9	....
4. Professional and semi-professional service, except recreation and amusement........	120	185	4.9	23.7	78	109	1.8	3.6
5. Sawmills and planing-mills......	184	12	7.6	1.6	341	61	7.9	2.0
6. Building industry..............	162	1	6.7	....	133	....	3.1	....
7. Forestry.....................	122	2	5.1	....	173	16	4.0	....
8. Domestic and personal service, except in hotels, restaurants, and laundries..............	39	44	1.6	5.6	156	1,648	3.6	54.6

* U. S. Census, 1930.

dustrialized to such an extent that from 1929 through 1935 the planing-mill pay roll brought more money into the county than did the sale of the annual cotton crop. More of the county's workers (30.5 per cent) still are employed in agriculture, however (see Table 5), than in any other field; and most residents of Old County regard the cotton crop as the chief economic resource. More than 3,000 bales, valued at about one-quarter million dollars, were produced in 1934. Over $100,000 also came into the county under the Federal A.A.A. program. Old City itself is still primarily a wholesale center for a cotton county.

TABLE 6

LEADING FIELDS OF EMPLOYMENT IN RURAL COUNTY, BY COLOR AND SEX OF EMPLOYEES: 1929*

FIELD OF EMPLOYMENT	WHITE				COLORED			
	Number		Percentage of All White Workers		Number		Percentage of All Colored Workers	
	Male	Fe-male	Male	Fe-male	Male	Fe-male	Male	Fe-male
1. Agriculture..................	553	50	43.3	25.6	2,293	1,151	76.8	78.5
Farmers (owners and tenants).	375	35	29.4	17.9	1,423	167	47.7	11.4
Farm-managers and foremen..	9	1	0.7	0.5	2	....	0.1	....
Farm laborers..............	167	14	13.1	7.2	866	984	29.0	67.1
Wage workers.............	59	2	4.6	1.0	244	91	8.2	6.2
Unpaid family workers.....	108	12	8.5	6.2	622	893	20.8	60.9
2. Sawmills and planing-mills......	162	....	12.7	....	335	3	11.2	0.2
3. Wholesale and retail trade, except automobiles...........	133	44	10.4	22.6	53	1	1.8	....
4. All transportation and communication.....................	74	16	5.8	8.2	79	1	2.6	....
5. Forestry.....................	91	....	7.1	....	60	7	2.0	0.5
6. Domestic and personal service, except in hotels, restaurants, and laundries..............	10	11	0.8	5.6	37	240	1.2	16.4

* *U. S. Census, 1930*

Cotton, though still king, is not unchallenged. The acreage of corn, sweet potatoes, and pecans, always important supplementary sources of income, has increased under the stimulus of the federal cotton-control program.[4] The county still does

[4] This program, which was instituted in 1933, was designed to raise the price of farm products by controlling the supply. One of its features was a provision for subsidy payments to farmers for reduction of their crops by taking specified

not raise enough hay and oats for its animals, however. Small amounts of sugar cane and sorghum are grown, and a few farmers cultivate truck for the local market and Chicago. With the advent of the boll weevil in 1912 many farmers began to sell off their timber and to raise cattle, to obtain cash with which to meet mortgages, taxes, and operating expenses. The hilly land of Old County, however, has not made cattle-raising as profitable as in the neighboring Rural County,[5] where one of the largest planters, referring to the weevil invasion, stated that "timber and cattle pulled us through." In Old County, diversified farming is now weakly challenging the supremacy of cotton and is reinforced by the rise of industry.

THE DEVELOPMENT OF INDUSTRY

The lumber industry.—The saw and planing mills which were the chief manufacturing establishments in both counties encouraged this selling-off of the counties' timber. One of the largest stands of pine timber in the South and one of the largest sawmills were located in the eastern part of Rural County.

In 1929, 8.4 per cent of Rural County's workers were engaged in the saw- and planing-mills, and 2.7 per cent in forestry. In Old County 5.7 per cent of all workers were engaged in the saw- and planing-mills, and 3.0 per cent in forestry.[6] These were the only manufacturing establishments in the county[7] (see Tables 10 and 11). In 1933, 190 white

---

amounts of land out of production of the cash crop. Other crops could be planted, however.

[5] Rural County is an adjoining county in which there is no large town. References will appear to it frequently in this work, since it was used as a "control" situation.

[6] In Old County a large colored landowner sold $50 worth of timber a week throughout 1933 and 1934; another sold $5,000 worth of timber in 1930, and five years later again sold approximately $5,000 worth.

[7] In 1840, on the other hand, when a more local economy with less national division of labor had existed, there had been a large variety of manufacturing establishments in both counties. Old County had establishments which manu-

laborers and 510 colored workers shared the $290,000 in wages from the largest planing-mill; in fact, most of the colored people and poorer whites in Old City depended upon these planing-mills for their livelihood.[8]

Industry and the caste system.—Such industry as has developed has done so over the protest of landowners, who could not keep their farm laborers at $0.75 per day when the sawmill was paying cutters and loaders from $1.25 to $1.50. Since most of the available workers are colored and can be paid an even lower wage than can the "poor whites," any attempt to industralize the area must adjust itself to the caste system. When one of the planing-mills opened, it began to pay colored employees wages which were twice as large as those paid by the local employers. Old City's Chamber of Commerce insisted that the mills should reduce these wages, on the theory that otherwise they would make all the colored workers "discontented" with their jobs and help to undermine the caste system. The mill was quick to reduce wages by one-half. In 1934, colored persons in Old City still marveled at what they termed "the stupidity" of the white business leaders who had thus cut off a large yearly inflow of wages into a city whose economic resources were constantly shrinking.

Other industrial work.—In recent years other workers have depended largely upon the work furnished by the federal and local governments in the dredging of the river, the construction of new levees, and the building of roads. While the larger degree of federal aid available for such work since 1933

---

factured more than $30,000 worth each of (1) machinery, (2) bricks and lime, and (3) leather and leather goods. It also had establishments manufacturing metals, hats, sugar and chocolate, carriages and wagons, and furniture. The largest industrial field, however, was the construction of buildings, which had a value of $242,300 in the year of the census. The total capital invested in manufactures was $164,100 in Old County, as contrasted with only $42,800 in Rural County.

[8] Compared with other counties in the state, however, Old County ranked very low in the number of manufacturing establishments and in the average number of wage-earners per year.

has increased the number of these projects, the levee camps, the gravel-pit camps, the road camps, and the timber camps have long employed a large part of the nonagricultural population of both counties. Since 1933 various government relief projects have likewise furnished a minimum of work for this group of laborers.

Seasonal work for agricultural laborers.—During the late fall and winter months, when cotton does not require their attention, many farm-tenants and laborers also obtain work in the lumber camps, the saw- and planing-mills, and, in cases where their landlords have political influence, on the road-building projects. The most important types of seasonal work, however, are usually the government's construction projects on the river and cane-cutting in the south. Landlords and merchants in Rural County estimated that more than 1,000 agricultural workers left the county each October to cut sugar cane, returning after Christmas. Other types of seasonal work, existing in both counties, were the cutting of railroad ties, trapping opossums and raccoons, gathering of ginseng roots, and fishing. The leading fish-packing company in Old City sold over $250,000 worth of fish to northern and eastern markets in 1929, $60,000 worth in 1933, and about the same amount in 1934. An official of the company estimated that the total purchases of fish-packing companies in the county amounted to $100,000 in 1933, of which amount $50,000 were spent in Old County.

THE MECHANISMS OF DISTRIBUTION AND CREDIT

Wholesale and retail trade.—Since 1909 both counties have suffered a tremendous decline in wholesale and retail trade as a result of the reduction of their cotton crop by the boll weevil. The once powerful "advance merchant," who "supplied" everything and took a first lien on the crop, began to disappear with the advent of the weevil. A few advance merchants, charging as much as 8 per cent interest, are still active, however. About 10 per cent of the working population is connected in some way with retail merchandising.

GENERAL VIEW OF ECONOMIC SYSTEM

Credit agencies.—At one time the wholesaler was also the credit merchant, but the function of supplying credit later shifted to the banks. In an area which imports a large part of its food, all of its work-stock, practically all of its feed for this stock, as well as all of its clothes and equipment, banks will receive in deposit only a small part of the total income. Since the Civil War the overwhelming majority of the South's income from cotton has been paid out to other areas, which have supplied it with almost everything except cotton. In Old and Rural counties, as in most counties in the South, banks have been small and relatively weak; they have been compelled to accept mortgages not only on the farmer's property but also on cotton which has not yet been grown. They have been likely, therefore, to fail whenever cotton has failed over a period of years. With the financial collapse of 1929–35 and the fall of the price of cotton to as low as 6 cents per pound, one of Old County's banks was caught with many large outstanding loans to planters. After the closing of this bank and its subsequent reopening under a loan from the Reconstruction Finance Corporation, it was practically impossible to obtain credit in Old County between 1933 and 1935, except for commercial purposes on short-term paper. Those persons who wished to obtain loans on real estate, even for the purpose of making improvements on their property, were forced to resort to private individuals. The city would have been unable to conduct business at all during these years, no doubt, had it not been for the almost accidental facts that the two large planing-mills and the government river projects were operating there.

Credit agencies and the local government.—The banks and wholesale merchants of Old City control the financial structure of Old County and exert a considerable influence upon the functioning of the political structure. One of the banks was established, and for a long time was controlled, by a man who had risen to what was probably the strongest economic position in the county through the acquisition of real estate in the period just after the Civil War and through successful speculation on the stock market. He seems once to have controlled the dominant political ring in the city, both through his economic influence and through his leadership of the bloc of Catholic voters. His successor, a man of middle-class status, likewise maintained intimate relations with the dominant political ring. He appeared at their social gatherings and was in close touch with all of their political and governmental activities. One of the most important officers of the county government was heard to say that in many instances he submitted his problems to the president of this bank.

The other bank in Old County was formerly controlled by a large planter who was a member of the upper class. His bank was largely patronized by the planter-aristocracy. After the failure of this bank and its reorganization, a member of the middle class, who was socially mobile, was elected president. This individual had made his fortune in the lumber business and had married a woman of the lower-upper class who owned an old mansion. He was succeeded, in turn, by a successful business man of the upper-middle class. This bank has been less active than the first in the political organization of Old City, for the reason, probably, that it financed only a small number of the merchants, contractors, and businessmen in the city.

In Old County the cotton-buyers have had little control over the distribution of credit. As a rule, their activity has been limited simply to the buying of cotton. In Rural County, however, where there are no large towns, the functions of the buyer, the ginner, and the advance merchant have often been performed by one individual or firm. Such a merchant-ginner-buyer exerted a dominant economic control over the tenants and planters to whom he furnished credit.

The wholesale merchants in Old County who once rivaled the banks as credit agencies for planters were, with one exception, Jews. Most of them were socially of the middle class in Old City, but a few had risen into the upper class. The one gentile advance merchant controlled the sale of farm equipment and still did a considerable wholesale and credit business. He was a descendant of an old upper-class family of planters and owned two family mansions. He associated with the president of the more influential bank and, like him, was intimate with the dominant political ring.

The relationships between the political ring and the men and organizations which controlled the distribution of credit was made clear by an important lawsuit in 1935. A member of the family which owned the stronger of the two banks died, leaving a will which gave a rather large sum of money to the city. A city official, whose law firm had long been attorneys for the bank and the estate, fought the case for the family against the city to prevent the payment of this bequest.

EFFORTS TO INCREASE THE ECONOMIC RESOURCES OF OLD COUNTY

Most of the businessmen and planters of Old County have gradually accustomed themselves to a lower standard of living. They believe that most of their economic difficulties may be attributed to a passing depression of the market. They cherish memories of better days and continue to hope for the return of "good times" or even of a temporary "boom." Meanwhile, they have lost money on cattle-raising and are rapidly depleting their stocks of timber, the only thing that keeps the mills in the county. Government subsidies to farmers during the season of 1934–35 offered no opportunity for an increased income from cotton; and if they had, the competition of the Oklahoma and Texas prairies, as well as of the Egyptian and Indian cotton fields, would have made such a promise illusory.

Confronted by a shrinkage in the county's economic resources resulting from basic changes in agriculture and transportation, Old County's social and business leaders have made other efforts to remedy their situation. They have attempted to persuade textile and lumber companies to establish factories in Old County, emphasizing as the county's chief advantage its surplus of cheap, docile, and unorganized workers. They have also formed organizations to lobby in Congress for the establishment of a free ferry or a free bridge, in order to bring trade from across the river to Old City and to attract automobile tourists through the city.

Two factories which have been established, as well as the lumber industry and the river work, are only recent additions to the socio-economic structure, however. In proceeding to a detailed analysis of the society's control over its economic resources, therefore, it is advisable to begin with the most basic element in the economy, namely, the production of cotton.

GROWING COTTON—A GAMBLER'S GAME

Caste, class, and the cotton economy.—The production of cotton takes place under the control of a social system which has been less subject to change than the soil, itself, in which the cotton is grown. The social anthropologist is interested chiefly in the operation of this social system.[9] In the first place, he is interested in the caste and class structures which largely control the distribution of both land and profits. He is interested, in the second place, in the extended family structure of the large landowning families, which, as a result of the legal principle of the inheritance of property, concentrates the ownership of land within a relatively small group of families. Finally, he is interested in the integration of the colored patriarchal family, the colored church, and the colored lodge, into a Negro social system, which, together with the caste sanctions (notably the use of intimidation), keeps the colored tenantry on the plantation.

[9] The form which the economic organization assumes depends mainly upon the social patterns which control the behavior of the inhabitants in respect to kinship, age, sex, associations, church, color groups, social and economic groups, and so forth, all these structures, of course, being responsive to technological change. It seems useless, and it is certainly unscientific, to postulate that either the economic system or the social organization, per se, is a "first cause." The empirical study of human society in Old County reveals that each structure influences, and in turn is influenced, by the other.

GENERAL VIEW OF ECONOMIC SYSTEM

Old County is one of the fifty-four counties in the South where a majority of the farmers are colored; 87.4 per cent of all its farm-operators in 1930 were Negro. This numerical preponderance of colored people in the rural population has existed since the first establishment of the plantation system in Old County and was one of the basic reasons for the choice of the area for the present study. The authors felt that the caste system would be most fully developed in those southern communities where a relatively few white landlords controlled a relatively large number of colored tenants, rather than in those communities where the white inhabitants greatly outnumbered the colored. It seemed advisable to choose Old and Rural counties, as a field for the study of caste and class systems in the deep South because these two counties were the center of one of the oldest "black" plantation areas in the South. One would expect to find in Old and Rural counties, therefore, an elaborate development of these social structures.

Any community may be viewed in terms of several theoretical levels of adaptation of man to his natural and his human environment. Of these, the first adaptation is made by a technical system which is organized and controlled by an economic system. The second level of adaptation is effected by the social organization which relates the economic system to the family, age, sex, and other systems of social control. The third is a coherent set of beliefs and concepts—the social logics which explain and rationalize the other adaptations. A change at any one level affects each of the other levels. In the following analysis of the patterns of behavior involved in the production of cotton, it will sometimes happen that the effect of technological, economic, and social patterns of behavior will appear inextricably related, as they often are in human behavior. It is important, however, for our understanding of the factors involved in the social training of human beings in the cotton economy that we should distinguish the several systems of controls which govern this behavior (namely, [1] the technical system, [2] the economic system, and [3] the social system), and should view these systems in their relationship to the natural environment.[10]

THE NATURAL ENVIRONMENT

Cotton, America's most valuable export crop, demands a climate that will provide a 200-day season free of frost and an abundant rainfall concentrated in the winter, spring, and summer. Heavy rains in the autumn, when picking begins, are disastrous.

During the last thirty years the center of cotton cultivation in the American South has been gradually shifting from the South Atlantic Coast to the plains of Texas and Oklahoma in the Southwest. Old County and Rural County have been placed at a competitive disadvantage in relation to the prairies of the Southwest, for the hilly terrain of these counties makes it impossible to use certain types of labor-saving machinery. The amount of labor required for the cultivation of each acre of cotton in Old and Rural counties is also two to three times as high as that in the flat delta lands. Yet this area is second only to the Delta[11] in the quality and value of its staple and in its yield of cotton per acre.

Weather and the weevil.—Although Old City has a growing season of between 210 and 240 days, its windstorms, heavy rain, and sudden temperature changes are a constant menace to its cotton crop. For instance, wind and rain storms which occurred in the late spring of 1934 destroyed the early gardens and truck and greatly damaged the cotton crop. In February, 1935, after a month in which the summer-like weather had rotted the farmers' stores of fall sweet potatoes, a snowstorm destroyed the winter gardens. Two days before the snowstorm the temperature had been as high as 80 degrees.

[10] W. Lloyd Warner, *A Black Civilization*, (New York: Harper & Bros., 1937), pp. 10–12.

[11] The Delta, which will be mentioned frequently in Part II, refers to an area on the Mississippi River embracing portions of Louisiana, Arkansas, and Mississippi.

The boll weevil likewise is a constant menace. In 1934 and 1935, twenty-six years after the weevil had first reduced the cotton crop of Old County by almost 90 per cent, it was still a great handicap to production. The number of bales of cotton ginned in the county in 1932, the year before the first reduction plan of the government, was only one-fifth as great as the number ginned in the year before the weevil reached the county. In 1934 it was even less than the reduced number of bales allowed by the federal government. The customarily heavy rainfall favors the growth of the weevil, with the result that the greatest weevil damage occurs in those seasons when the damage caused by rain is likewise greatest. The season of 1934, when this study was being made, was such a period. Only a planned regimen of weevil control can combat the pest. Tenants are unable to pay for the poison to reduce weevil infestation, however; and landlords generally furnish it only when it appears that the crop will otherwise be insufficient to pay the rent.

Use of fertilizer.—The field evidence from both counties establishes the fact that the inability of both landlords and tenants to pay for the weevil poison and fertilizer is the chief reason for their failure to use them in any quantity.

Landlords, as a rule, blame the failure to use larger quantities of fertilizer upon the tenants. Even the agricultural agent in one of the counties spoke at great length on this point and seemed firmly convinced that the stupidity and dishonesty of the colored tenants had discouraged landlords from using fertilizer. It became clear, upon fuller investigation, however, that such opinions were merely expressions of social and economic antagonisms and that the basic reasons for the failure to use fertilizer were (1) that the landlords believed it was more profitable to them to plant without fertilizer than to buy sufficient quantities of it and (2) that both landlords and tenants had become accustomed to this method of cultivation. The bountiful supply of land and of cheap labor has encouraged landlords to increase cotton acreage rather than to use fertilizer; and both landlord and tenant have, in time, come to regard this method of cultivation as normal and inevitable.

AGRICULTURAL TECHNIQUES

Within broad limits the natural environment of Old County has determined not only what crops can be successfully grown but also what agricultural techniques can be successfully employed. Thus, the hilly terrain makes widespread use of machinery impracticable. This determination of techniques by the natural environment is exerted only within wide limits, however, and is constantly being modified by improvements and new inventions. The use of available techniques is restricted, furthermore, by social custom. In Old County, social custom selects only certain of the crops which the physical environment favors, and eliminates others which would grow equally well (and are grown in neighboring counties).

"Making a crop."—In Old and Rural counties the cultivation of the land usually begins in February or March, and the cotton is ordinarily planted in April or early in May. As soon as the cotton appears, the rows, which are from 1½ to 2 feet apart, must be carefully cultivated in order to keep out grass and weeds and to prevent the soil from drying and hardening. This operation is performed either by one-mule plows or by hand hoeing. When the cotton is about an inch tall, it is "chopped," i.e., thinned by hoeing, so that the stalks are not too close together, and the weeds and grass are eliminated. If the cotton is not cultivated and chopped at the proper time, the crop may be almost completely lost. By the end of July the condition of the soil and grass is such that no further cultivation or chopping is necessary, and the crop is then "laid by" until time to pick. Cotton-picking begins as soon as the bolls start to open, about the first part of September, and continues at its height until the end of October. In a mild season, when the cotton continues to produce bolls, picking may last until January. The cotton must be gathered as soon as possible after the bolls are fully open, for there is great danger of damage by rain or even by high wind at this period.

Once picked, the cotton is taken to the gin. There, by means of automatic machinery, the seeds are removed from the lint, and it is compressed into bales of approximately 500 pounds in weight, ready for sale and shipment. The cotton and seed are usually sold immediately after the ginning and compressing, and pass out of the hands of the producer. Usually, the crop is all gathered, ginned, and sold by the end of October.

From this description of the usual procedure, it is evident that the cultivation of cotton results in an annual cycle of farm activity. There is first a period of planting and cultivation during the spring and early summer. This is followed by a slack period in August, when the crop is "laid by." Then there is a period of great activity, "cotton-pickin' time," which is followed by another slack period during the winter months until the cycle begins again in February. So fundamental are these periods of farm work, that tenants date their social activities not by reference to the calendar but to "choppin' out time," "layin' by time," and "cotton-pickin' time."

The extremely long cotton season limits the number and kind of subsidiary crops which the farmer may plant. In the first place, no other crop can be produced on the same soil as cotton, because the period between the time when cotton is picked and the time when it is planted is not sufficiently long for a winter crop to mature. Furthermore, no subsidiary crop which demands attention at the time when the demand for cotton labor reaches its peak can be cultivated.

The most important of the subsidiary crops is corn, which is generally not considered a money crop but is raised largely for local consumption by livestock and farmers. Although corn is planted and cultivated at about the same time as cotton, it is worked entirely by plow. Cultivation, therefore, is comparatively rapid, since it does not include hand labor or "chopping." After the cotton has been "laid by," the corn may require a final plowing, but it then needs no further care until harvest time. It need not be harvested until after the cotton has been picked, since in normal seasons the ears may remain on the stalks until the winter rains begin, about the middle of November. At that time the ears are stripped from the stalks and stored in a crib for later use.

Sweet potatoes, next in importance to corn, may be planted early. They require little attention beyond an occasional plowing, and they may be gathered in the spring. A second crop may sometimes be planted in the summer and is ready to be gathered after the cotton has been picked. Thus the two potato crops seldom conflict with the cotton-labor requirements.

Other subsidiary crops are of minor importance, with the exception of sugar cane, the juice of which is boiled down for molasses. The cane requires little cultivation and is not harvested until November, just before the first frost is expected. Peas, oats, hay, and the other crops grown on the larger farms are not harvested until after the cotton is in.

Diversification of crops.—The most widely criticized aspect of the cotton-farmer's agriculture has been his failure, as a rule, to diversify his crops. The one-crop system which concentrates labor upon the cultivation of cotton and fails to grow food for the workers or feed for the stock has been regarded as typical of cotton-growing regions. The persistence of this one-crop system has been attributed chiefly to the cotton-farmer's "ignorance" and to his lack of technical skill. It is true, indeed, that the rate of diffusion of new techniques is slow among cotton-farmers, as it is among any agricultural group. The weight of custom in limiting the acceptance and development of new techniques and the great difficulty which human beings experience in changing manual habits are universal traits of human societies.

The rate of diffusion of technical knowledge among cotton-farmers in areas like Old County is especially slow because they work chiefly as individuals. The competitive nature of our economy and the lack of co-operative effort make it likely that the farmer will keep secret any superior technical knowledge which he may possess, so as to increase his personal economic and social status among his fellows. This was the case, for example, of a colored tenant in Old County who had been more successful than his neighbors in raising corn because he knew that the corn weevil was killed by frost. Whereas his neighbors pulled their corn before the first frost and lost much of it during the winter as a result, he did not harvest his until it had been exposed to a killing frost. "Ev'rybody doan know dat. You gottuh learn all such tricks as dat. Mos' people heah pull deir cawn even befo' dey picks cotton, but dey doan *know.*" He did not tell them either.

In the same way, a white landlord had learned that corn which was not planted until May was free of weevils, whereas that planted in February or in March was ruined by them. He had his own corn planted by day-laborers in May, but he let his tenants continue to use the incorrect method. Similarly, in the cultivation of cotton it was discovered that both tenants and landlords used advantageous methods of preparing the land and the seed for planting, devices of which, they boasted, their neighbors were ignorant.

The fundamental reason for lack of diversification of crops in the cotton regions, however, is economic. Cotton is a very profitable money crop, when the price is above 10–15 cents per pound. No other crop which it is possible to grow in most parts of the South, moreover, can compare with cotton as a source of cash income. As long as the price of cotton is high enough to afford landlords a profit and the yield is normal, crops are not diversified to any considerable extent in the cotton region.[12] Cotton is a money crop, and at times a "big-money" crop;[13] no other crop can compete with it in the cotton

[12] Cotton is the only crop in the United States (except flax) whose acreage increases significantly as the price of the product increases (correlation, .62) (Rupert B. Vance, *Human Factors in the Cotton Culture* [Chapel Hill: University of North Carolina Press, 1929], pp. 118–19).

[13] During the boom periods, several white planters in Rural County and in the Louisiana Delta made a profit of from $20,000 to $50,000 on their annual cotton crop. One colored planter in the Louisiana Delta had $80,000 worth of cotton in 1919, and another colored planter had $35,000 worth. Many tenants made a net profit for the year of from $800 to $1,000.

regions until the price falls so low that no profit can be made. The cotton-farmer gambles with the growing of cotton simply because he is gambling for large stakes, in proportion to his invested capital and his expenses. So long as he makes a satisfactory profit, he will continue to plant cotton on most of his cultivable land and to buy a large part of his food and feed. When the price drops severely or the yield fails, he will have the debt for a whole year's operation upon his shoulders. He will continue to plant cotton the next year or two, in the hope of recouping his losses in a short time. If the price stays low or the yield fails for a period of years, however, the cotton-farmer diversifies his crops, because he can no longer borrow money. At the height of the boll-weevil infestation[14] and during the period of low cotton prices from 1931 to 1933, cotton-farmers in most parts of the South diversified their crops. There was also some diversification incident to the depression of 1929. The census states that the number of cattle was larger by 62 per cent in 1935 than in 1930 and that the number of acres planted in corn, sugar cane, Irish potatoes, sweet potatoes, and forage crops was much larger in 1934 than in 1929.[15] During these years there was no lack of technical ability upon the part of the tenants to diversify their crops. A very large planter in Rural County said that most of his tenants had raised corn, beans, sweet potatoes, garden truck, hay, sugar cane or sorghum, and cowpeas. Most of them had hogs and chickens. A Negro tenant in the fall of 1934 said that he had planted only half of the 40 acres which he rented in cotton; the remainder he had planted in food and forage crops. "That's the way I'm makin' it, raisin' enough corn, and pigs, an' chickens, an' cabbage, an' potatoes to keep me all year, so I won't have to buy nuthin', an' that's the only way the rest of the farmers can make it!"

The evidence from the field indicated that there was a

[14] Vance, *op. cit.*, p. 101.
[15] Owing to rain and windstorms which occurred in 1934, however, the yield of corn and sweet potatoes was less than in 1929.

fairly widespread knowledge of the methods required for the cultivation of other crops besides cotton and that many farmers employed this knowledge when forced to do so by economic necessity. Others, including those who had not changed the improvident habits developed under the advance system, those who did not possess the necessary knowledge or equipment, and those who were on the poorer and more eroded soil, were reduced to virtual starvation. One colored man of sixty, who had grown cotton all his life and who enjoyed the reputation throughout Old County of being a highly skilful and "successful" farmer, summarized his life-experience with cotton—an experience which is typical:

By the first of June ev'rything on a farm is all laid by until time to gather, excep' cotton. That's what takes all your time an' stren'th, that dawg-gawn cotton. It's the devil! It works you to death, an' it ruins you. You got to plant it two or three times, or the fros' kills it, or the rain's too heavy, you know. That'll rot the seed in the groun', lak las' year. Oh, that cotton will work you to death an' then ruin you. Ev'rything else is "laid by," by June first, but you gottuh keep on hoein' an' foolin' with cotton all the summer. It's the hardes' an' dirties' work on the farm.

But despite the facts just cited, he felt that social custom was an almost insurmountable obstacle to diversification.

I'd jus' lak to give cotton up—let it go! I've tried to do it, but I jus' can't. My father raised cotton, an' his father raised cotton, an' I'm jus' bawn an' bred to it, I guess. You know? Can't break away from it! I wish I could! I wish I could. But all southerners, white an' black, are the same way! The South has been ruined by cotton, but they won't change! Jus' looks lak they can't git away from it. That cotton will ruin you! An' work you to death, too!

CHAPTER XII
CASTE, CLASS, AND THE CONTROL OF LAND

L IFE and labor in Old County, as well as power and prestige, are based on relationships to the land. Out of the land comes the cotton to the production of which the cycle of life is tied. The possession or nonpossession of land represents the margin between at least the minimum of security and stability and absolute insecurity. Yet, of the nearly 2,000 farm-operators in Old County, less than 400 owned any land in 1935. Of these 400, 36 persons owned or controlled practically half of all the land of the county and almost a third of the cultivable land. (Two of these 36 were Negroes.) Of these 36 persons, 7 owned or controlled 22.2 per cent of all the land, although they constituted but one-third of 1 per cent of all farm-operators. If we were to take, as the property-owning unit, the family and not the individual, we should probably find as much as three-fourths of all land in Old County owned by members of these 36 families.

Chief landowning families.—This concentration of the ownership of a large part of the farm land and almost all of the most desirable land within a relatively few families has been chiefly the result of certain patterns of social behavior. In the first place, it has been strengthened by extended kinship relations among the old planter-families and by frequent intermarriage between collateral lines in the same family. In an economic system where property can be inherited, these extended kinship groupings have operated so as to prevent the disintegration of large estates through the selling-off of land to economically mobile farmers and to newcomers. In the second place, the ownership of the large estates has tended to remain among a kinship group not only as a result of the size of the kinship group but also because land, once inherited, has been kept for its value in increasing the owner's social status. In Old County, and no doubt in most of the old plantation counties where cotton cultivation has remained profitable, the ownership of an old plantation, a large tract of land, or an old plantation mansion has been considered the most essential trait of a white person of the upper class. An analysis of the sanctions governing membership in upper-class white cliques in Old County has revealed the tendency of upper-class whites to identify the words "old planter-family" with the words "upper (or higher) class." As a result of this class sanction, a great many white persons whose farms are not large and whose ownership of land has not been of great duration have claimed descent from old planter-families, and practically everyone who could make such a claim legitimately has jealously kept his land. The inheritance of a small holding, or even of an unprofitable holding, was desirable, since it served as one's charter of membership in the "landed gentry." Once a member of a kinship group had inherited land, he was likely to keep the land; the large estates have, therefore, remained in a kinship group over a long period of years.

An analysis of the records of the Agricultural Adjustment Administration has furnished convincing evidence that, in the practical operation of farms, moreover, the concentration of family holdings is even greater than in ownership. Many of the largest cotton plantations in Old County are the pooled farms of a group of relatives, operated under the management of one relative; that is, land did not break up into small units of operation as the result of the extended kinship groupings but was kept in the form of large operator-units. This practice of operating, under one head, several farms owned by members of one kinship group increased the difficulties of the small operator who wished to buy good land, and also kept the rate of rental high for tenants who were faced by a virtual monopoly of the best land by a few families.[1]

[1] As a result of the boll-weevil infestation and the diversion of the river through the raising of the levees on the opposite shore, the amount of good

277

Six families controlled practically all of the most desirable land in Old County. Some colored workers of the lower class, who were not on plantations, expressed great bitterness against these families, many of whom had acquired land from the federal government or the railroads under the operation of the early land acts.

You go out heah an' you see wheah one man own all de lan' fuh seven miles, all 'long de road. Dat's all his. Hell, I know hundreds of dem all ovuh dis state and de nex'. All right. How'd dat ——— git all dat lan'? He ain' done nuthin' tuh git it. He got it from his fathuh, an' his fathuh got it from his'n. Cousins an' ev'ything gits it, an' aint nevuh done a lick of work on it. All right. Here's uh ol' ——— out here, Ewlan McIlroy, can't hardly read his own name, got mixed up in dat murder, you know all about him? Well, he got so much lan' he doan know wheah it en'!

All right, dere's Ol' Miss Twilton. She doan know nuthin' 'bout farm work, but she got so much lan' she can't tell wheah it en'. All right. Here's uh ol' wrinkle-neck ——— right outah town heah, got fifteen hundred acres! Fifteen hundred acres an' he's jus' one man! He come in heah ev'ry week tuh git a pint uh whiskey frum me.

All right. Here's all these ——— ol' worthless ——— wid all dis lan'. How'd dey git it? Dey gran'fathuhs come heah an' stole it from de Indjuns, an' den dey stole nigguhs to clean an' wuk it fuh dem. All right!

This colored worker was particularly incensed against a large white landowner who had forced a landless road worker to return a few limbs which he had broken from a fallen tree. "Dere wuz a ——— ol' rotten pine tree done fall down right by de road dere, an' dis felluh took awf a few daid lim's. He didn' cut no wood, mine you! He jus' took dese ol' broken

---

cotton land has been greatly reduced since 1908 by the taking from cultivation the fertile island and river land. These tracts were formerly the most profitable cotton areas in the county and were operated at a great profit by the leading bank and advance merchants in Old City. With cotton at 10 cents, the largest of the river tracts produced approximately $500,000 worth of cotton a year before the boll weevil. With the coming of the weevil, which thrives in wet soil, and with the later flooding of the lands by the river these areas were lost to the big planters. The supply of good land available for tenants was reduced, and the monopoly held by the leading planter-families was intensified.

lim's." His own plan for correcting these abuses was that the federal government should buy land and give every former landlord 100 acres of cultivable land and 50 acres of timber land, and every former tenant 40 or 30 acres of cultivable land and a smaller amount of timber land. He still adhered to the fundamental pattern of the economic system, however, for he planned to have the land descend through the male line in each family and to give "all dem people wi'ah tuh fence in deir lan', so *ev'ybody keep* his *own* lan' sep'rate."

Two prominent colored men attributed the poverty of the tenants to the fact that six families owned most of the good farm land. One of them claimed that this virtual monopoly of land had made the county "a wilderness," since there was no opportunity for enterprising groups of tenants and small owners to develop. He agreed with the colored worker quoted above that what was needed was a plan by which tenants could buy small tracts of land. Under the present system, he said, landlords generally will not sell to tenants; those who have pretended to "sell" have charged exorbitant prices and thus regained their land when the price of cotton had been low, or they have given colored "buyers" spurious titles or no titles at all.

Continuity of ownership.—This apparent monopoly of land raises the question of the extent to which the same individuals or families compose this group of the largest landowners over a long period of years. That is to say, what degree of economic and geographical mobility is there in this upper group of landowners? In an effort to answer this question, an analysis was made of the record of property acquisitions by 109 of the largest owners, for the twenty years between 1913 and 1932, inclusive. Only 12.8 per cent, or 14 owners, had lost or sold all of their land since 1913.[2] If we include the 5 owners who had made no change in their holdings, 76 per cent, or

[2] Of the remaining 95, 12 had decreased their holdings since 1913 and 5 had made no change; 78 of the leading landholders in 1913, therefore, had increased their landholdings from 1913 to 1932 or had willed their land, intact, to their families.

83 of the largest landholders in 1913, were themselves, or in the persons of their families, still among the largest landholders in 1932.[3] It appears, then, that approximately 87 per cent of the largest landholders in 1913 are still in Old County and that 76 per cent of them are still among the largest landholders and have increased their holdings. Only 15–20 per cent of them have been replaced by new landowners. It is clear, therefore, that the group of the largest landholders is a remarkably stable one, having been composed of the same individuals, or of their families, over a long period of years.

Position of leading landowners in the national economic hierarchy.—In order that we may keep Old County and its cotton economy in their national perspective, it is important to notice that the average yearly income of even the largest landlords in a good cotton year hardly exceeds $20,000. On the average, that is, the largest planters in Old County are what would be called, by comparison with a scale of nation-wide property (not farm) owners, "middle-class owners." Indeed, the average assessed value of property holdings of the 7 largest planters ($19,000) is not so great as that of many colored property-owners in southern cities. In Old Town itself, for example, there is a colored business man with real estate assessed at more than $30,000, and there is a colored landlord in a nearby city whose rents have totaled as high as $700 per month. Of course, when we compare the holdings of the largest planters in Old County and of their families with the holdings of American industrialists and of their families, we at once place the cotton-producer in his proper economic focus. Such a reflection offers little consolation, however, to a landless tenant in Old County.

CONTROL OF LAND AND THE DIVISION OF LABOR

The concentration of the ownership or control of approximately half the land in Old County in the hands of 36 cotton-

---

[3] Nineteen of the leading landholders in 1932, it is true, had purchased al[1] or most of their land since 1913. Eight of the 19 were absentee-owners. These new landlords are chiefly owners of extremely large holdings or are finance companies.

producers and the persistence of this concentration as a result of the operation of the legal principle of inheritance were responsible for a division of labor in which those who owned most of the land performed no agricultural labor and those who did most of the work owned no land. In 1930 approximately eighty per cent of all farm operators in Old County were tenants (Fig. 15). Although most of the cultivable land is owned in large tracts, very little of it is worked by day-labor under the supervision of the owner or his managers. The land is worked almost entirely under a tenant system, whereby

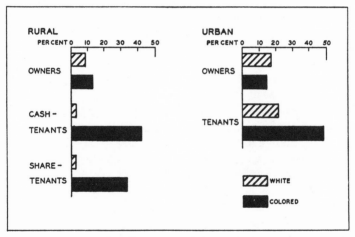

Fig. 15.—Relative size of white and Negro tenure groups in Old County: 1930 (stated as percentages of all farm-operators, and of all urban residents).

each farm-tenant-family works a definite tract under carefully stipulated conditions. Three forms of agreement between the tenants and the landowners are commonly recognized. Each of them carries certain definite obligations on the part of both tenant and landowner.

1. *Cash- and lint-rental.*—The commonest form of agreement is that known as "cash-rental" or "lint-rental." Under this form of agreement the tenant pays a fixed sum of money, or a fixed amount of lint-cotton, in exchange for the use of the land

and cabin. At the beginning of the season the cash-tenant and the landlord come to an agreement concerning the amount of money or of lint-cotton which the tenant must pay as land rent at the end of the season. The tenant furnishes his own teams and equipment; he may or may not be advanced supplies (food, clothing, etc.) by the landlord.

2. *Quarter-rental.*—The second type of agreement is known as "quarter-rental." Under this form of agreement the tenant agrees to pay the landlord one-fourth of the cotton raised that year, and usually one-third of the corn, in exchange for the use of the land and cabin. As in cash-rental, the tenant furnishes his own teams and equipment; in some cases he obtains supplies on credit from the landlord during three or four months of the year. The only difference between quarter-rental and cash- or lint-rental is that under the first type of agreement the rent, instead of being a fixed amount, varies with the success of the crop.

3. *Half-rental.*—Under the third type of agreement, known as "half-rental," the tenant pays the landlord one-half of the crop in exchange for the use of the land and cabin. The landlord furnishes the tenant with work-stock and equipment, and advances him supplies during part of the cotton season. The tenant furnishes his labor, in return for which he receives half of the cotton crop.

According to the census of 1930, cash-tenants amounted to 56.6 per cent of the 1,337 tenants in Old County; half-tenants, to 22.7 per cent; and other types, to 20.7 per cent. The records of the Agricultural Adjustment Administration show that this last group included not only 196 tenants who paid one-fourth of their cotton crop as rental but also 108 tenants who paid one-third of their crop and 51 tenants who paid three-fourths of their crop as rental. In addition to the three major forms of agreement, therefore, there also exist (1) a form intermediate between quarter-renting and half-renting, under which the tenant pays one-third of the crop, and (2) a form under which the tenant pays three-fourths of his crop. According to this latter agreement, the tenant is subordinated even farther than under the half-rental agreement.

In Rural County, third-tenants on the larger plantations received their work-stock and equipment. This form of agreement had been replacing cash-tenancy to a large degree because landlords had found that over a period of years they made a higher rate of profit by taking a third of the crop than by charging a cash-rent. The agreement represented an increased economic subordination of tenants, since tenants who owned their work-stock and equipment had formerly been allowed to rent for cash or for one-fourth of the cotton-crop.

The field evidence makes it clear that both the definition of the rental agreements and the form of agreement preferred by a landlord may be changed to accord with the economic interest of the landlord. The influence of economic considerations on the landlord group was clearly revealed at a meeting of farmers in the spring of 1934 for the purpose of discussing the proposed cotton-reduction plan of the federal government. The question of the tenants' right to a subsidy payment soon arose. Under the pressure of a liberal landlord's questioning, the county agricultural agent was forced to admit that cash-tenants were legally qualified to sign their own reduction contracts with the Agricultural Adjustment Administration and that their subsidy payment must be made directly to them. When the great majority of landlords asserted that they should be allowed to sign contracts for all of their tenants, because "all these people here" (even when they paid a cash-rental or a fixed lint-rental) secured some food or supplies from their landlords, the county agent agreed that such tenants were not cash-tenants and were not entitled to sign contracts under the Agricultural Adjustment Administration. The landlords agreed jubilantly. One of them shouted: "That would make all these people here share-croppers, wouldn't it?" The head of the Agricultural Adjustment Administration county board assured the landlord group: "I have always claimed that a tenant who gets food or provisions from the owner is really a share-cropper, even if he pays a cash-rental, or cotton. That's the rule I've been followin'." Such an interpretation would mean that no tenant who borrowed money from his landlord could be regarded as a cash-tenant, in spite of the fact that he paid a cash-rent. It was desirable from the landlords' point of view at this time, of course, because it enabled them to receive all the subsidy payments and tax-free certificates from the government.

During the same meeting, however, a landlord who owned more than 30,000 acres in Old County, alone, asserted that he would not agree to reduce any of his cotton acreage. The head of the Agricultural Adjustment Administration county board immediately suggested to him that, by calling most of his tenants "cash-tenants," he could claim that the land they cultivated was not under his control, and thus avoid reducing the cotton acreage on these tracts.

Two important facts concerning the rental agreements were revealed by this meeting of the largest landlords: (1) many tenants who paid a cash-rental or a fixed lint-rental also received advances from their landlords; (2) the privileges of a tenant, under the cash-rent form of agreement, were by no means fixed but were subject to change in accordance with the economic advantage of the landlord. A tenant who paid a cash-rental or a fixed lint-rental could thus be regarded as a share-tenant when the landlord wished to appropriate his subsidy payment, and as a cash-tenant when the landlord wished to maintain or increase his own cotton acreage.[4]

Variation in rental agreements.—The type of rental agreement which is dominant on any given plantation depends upon a number of factors. The correlation between these factors over a large area is not entirely clear. The relationships must be considered (1) for a given soil-area, at periods of (*a*) in-

---

[4] Although the census enumerated 757 cash-tenants in Old County in 1930, only 67 signed reduction contracts and only 266 received tax-free certificates directly from the Agricultural Adjustment Administration.

flated prices and (*b*) deflated prices, and (2) for different soil-areas and economic regions at the same period. The influence of fundamental differences in the soil and topography, and in the type of economy, upon the relative size of the tenant groups will be clarified by the second type of consideration, whereas the influence of the price of cotton will be revealed by the first.

With regard to the variation within a county at a given time, the field study in Old County indicated that the type of preferred rental agreement was dependent upon four main factors: (1) the degree of supervision exercised by the landlord; (2) the soil type and typography; (3) the amount of work-stock and equipment owned by the landlord; and (4) the average amount of work-stock and equipment owned by tenants. The correlations between these factors and the types of tenancy have only a statistical probability, however.

Landlords in Old County themselves accounted for the facts (1) that more than half (56.6 per cent) of the tenants in Old County were cash-tenants and (2) that cash-tenancy had been the chief form of agreement for more than twenty years, upon the basis of a high rate of absentee-landlordism in the county. In most parts of the state and of the cotton-growing regions cash-tenants amounted to only a small fraction of the total number of tenants.[5] In Old County, which has a city of over 10,000 inhabitants, and where most of the land is owned by descendants of old planter-families, one would expect to find a high rate of absentee-landlordism, and and therefore of cash-tenancy. The records of the Agriculture Adjustment Administration show that half of the county's 36 largest producers lived in Old City. One of the largest planters stated that most landlords rented for cash because they did not live on their farms and could not supervise the work of tenants. As a rule, those landlords who had chiefly half- and quarter-tenants lived "on their places and looked after them." One

[5] In the state, as a whole, they were only 10 per cent of all tenants (*United States Census, 1930*).

285

landlord said: "I farm that way out on my place, but I live there and look after the crop. But take fellows like Gregg, who has a place but who lives in town and has his business here. He just charges a fixed rent." It was the opinion of another planter that even most of those landlords who lived on their farms maintained little or no supervision of the actual work. Previously the authors had asked if there were many farmers who did their own work, and he said:

I only know of one farmer in the county who does any work. All the others either have tenants or hire Negro hands to do the work. If you want to see any of the farmers just hang around Crile's corner any day and you will usually see them loafing there all dressed up. Their families are all in town too; they go to the movies while the men loaf.

The unwillingness of most of the large landlords to supervise the labor on their farms accounted for the prevalence of the cash-rent agreement in Old County and the almost complete absence of day-laborers, according to another large planter: "Most of the planters in this country rent for lint-rent or cash as they don't want to manage the places themselves." When asked if any planters in this county worked their land with day-labor, he said:

No, none of them do that I know of. They don't want to work that hard as it takes a lot of work when you are using day-labor, as you have to look after everything yourself. If you try to have a manager, unless he is mighty good and reliable, it is a big risk, as it is too easy to pad a pay roll and steal from you.

Rental of land.—The rate of cash-rental on the best cotton land in Old County, which had a market price of not more than $50 per acre, was $10 per acre, or one-fifth of the market price of the land. On this best land tenants had no pasturage for cattle and no timber for firewood, since the land was all planted in cotton. For most of the land in the county, however, the market price, including the wasteland, which was always rented as an integral part of the farm, was only $7.50 per acre. The cash-rent charged tenants for this land, however, itself ranged from $6.00 to $9.00 per acre. It was quite true, therefore, as many tenants complained, that land in Old County could still be bought outright from the government for a smaller amount per acre than the landlords were charging as rent. Even swampland, which is the cheapest land in the county, rented for $5.00 and $6.00 per acre, although large tracts of this land had been purchased in the boom years for from $3.00 to $6.00 per acre. Interviews with tenants in all parts of the county with regard to the rents they paid before the "depression," established the facts (1) that most land rented for from $6.00 to $8.00 per acre; (2) that within the greater part of the county, owned by the leading six families of landholders, the rental did not vary according to the fertility or cultivability of the soil; and (3) that the exceptions to this rule were in the very good river land, which rented for $10.00 per acre, and the very undesirable swampland, which rented for $5.00 per acre.

The rates of rental given above prevailed among cash- ("fixed" or "whole") tenants in Old County during the two or three years immediately preceding 1932. Rent was paid in cash at these rates or in cotton whose value approximated the same rates of payment.[6] More than half of the tenants in Old County (57 per cent) paid such a cash- or fixed-rental.

Virtually the same rates of rental were paid by quarter-tenants, since landlords usually saw to it that quarter-tenants planted enough cotton to maintain the rate of cash-rental. With regard to the half-tenants, who amounted to only 24 per cent of all tenants, the rental paid included both the rental

---

[6] A landlord, when asked if most of the tenants paid a rent of so many pounds of lint, said: "All of them on this plantation have been renting that way for the last two or three years. Before, they paid a cash-rent; but when the price of cotton went down so low, this fellow came up and said he wanted to pay a lint-rent. We told him he could either pay $150 or pay 1,500 pounds; so he took the lint proposition. The first year we broke about even, but this year he gained by it; but maybe next year prices will be better and we will even up. If the prices go up to about 15 cents though, all these Negroes will be coming back and suggesting that they would rather pay a cash-rent. They keep a close watch on things like that."

for the use of the land and that for the use of work-stock and equipment. It is impossible, therefore, to calculate accurately the rate of land-rental for this group, but it is likely that the rate is usually higher than that paid by any other tenure group, since these tenants, in order to obtain the use of a mule, a plow, a wagon, and a cultivator, actually paid twice as much rental as quarter-tenants. They often had to share the use of this equipment with other half-tenants.

Therefore, when the price of cotton is "high" (more than 10 cents per pound), half-tenants pay a higher rate of land rental than any other tenure group. In years of deflated prices, however, when the value of the landlord's share of cotton decreases, the half-tenant becomes economically superordinate to the other tenure groups. In such periods tenants prefer to pay a share of the crop as rent, while landlords prefer that they should pay a cash- or fixed-rent. From 1932 to 1934, in a period of low cotton prices and low yields, the records in Old County show that the cash-renters paid approximately half of their total income from cotton as rental for land alone! During this period half-renters obtained for the same rental not only the use of the land but the use of work-stock and equipment as well. In fact, during the seasons of 1933 and 1934 the rate of rental paid by half-tenants and by quarter-tenants was reduced by half, so that it amounted to $3.00 or $4.00 per acre. On the other hand, cash-tenants and fixed-rent-tenants continued to pay from $6.00 to $10.00 per acre for the rental of land. The refusal of the large land-holders to reduce the rate of cash-rental, in spite of the subsidies they received from the Agricultural Adjustment Administration, was a source of great discontent to this group of tenants, who amounted to 57 per cent of all tenants in Old County.

Availability of pasture land.—The amount of free pasture land available to tenants in Old County has steadily decreased since the nineteenth century. While it is true that the hilly and eroded topography of a large part of the county prevents its use as pasturage and that the county has an average pasturage of less than 3 acres per cow, whereas most regions in the United States have an average pasturage of 5 acres per cow it is also true that the use of the available pasturage has been still further reduced by (1) the state laws which require the fencing of pasture land and (2) the institution of a one-crop system of agriculture by the families which owned the best land. Landlords who had lived in the county fifty or sixty years stated that until the enactment of the pasture law the use of pasture land was free to all tenants.

> Land was practically common property as far as cattle were concerned. If a Negro had 100 head of cattle, they could graze on the place of a white next to him, and nothing was ever thought of it. Every Negro had cattle, and when he needed money to buy food or a plough, he could sell two or three yearlings, and he didn't have to borrow from his landlord, or get credit from a merchant in town.[7]

After the enactment of the pasture laws, landlords were compelled to build fences. In order to pay the cost of these fences, they began to charge tenants pasture rent, a practice which is still followed in times of inflated prices. As a result, most of the tenants were compelled to stop raising herds of cattle and were thus deprived of their last aid to economic independence. As the power of the advance merchants and the concentration of the ownership of the best land within a few families increased, both advance merchants and landlords insisted that tenants should plant all their land in cotton.

Until the beginning of the present century, moreover, cowpeas and corn had been raised in large amounts by Old County farmers and exported; for many landlords they were more important crops than cotton. With the fastening of the quickmoney crop of cotton upon landlords and tenants by those who financed the system, however, these forage crops were no longer grown in sufficient quantities to supply even the local need.

[7] Howard W. Odum, *Southern Regions*, (Chapel Hill: University of North Carolina Press, 1936), p. 288, map.

While it is true that between 1933 and 1935 there were many landlords on the poorer and more eroded soil in both Old and Rural counties who allowed free pasturage to tenants or included pasture land in the land rented to them, those landlords who controlled most of the best land did not follow this practice. Since these largest landlord-families had no difficulty in securing tenants, they were not compelled to furnish pasture land. Those landlords who owned hilly and eroded land, on the other hand, offered part of their otherwise useless land to tenants for free pasturage, as an inducement to secure their services.

Contracts and liens.—Much of the behavior in the planter-tenant relation could be given legal sanction through the use of recognized forms of contracts and mortgages. The tenant could give a mortgage on his crop and teams; and, when properly recorded, this written agreement would become a binding contract. The amount of credit which the tenant is to receive in the form of supplies or cash and the amount of land rental the landlord is to receive could be stated in such written agreements. Actually, however, mortgages or other forms of contracts are very rarely signed and recorded in Old County except when security other than the crop is given.

Oral agreements with regard to the rental to be paid by the tenant and the amount of credit to be advanced by the landlord, of the type described by a large planter in Rural County, were found to be general in both counties. The authors asked if the landlords had a written contract with the Negroes, and this planter said:

> After they come back from the river, if they [the Negroes] want to make any changes, they come to see us; otherwise, they get out their plows and start work as usual. Some of them will come up to see about moving or about reducing the rent, but you bet they never talk about increasing their rent. We never have a contract; we both come to an agreement and they go to work.

A very large planter in Rural County was not accustomed to offer his tenants written contracts, but he allowed those on a plantation which he had just bought the privilege of choosing a written contract. Somewhat to his surprise, they accepted the offer.

I sent word to the tenants that I was coming out to see who I would keep on the next year; and when I got there, every Negro on the place was waiting there for me. I said to them: "Now, I don't know you, and you don't know me, so you all tell me how you want to rent. If you want a contract, say so, and we will sign one, although I'm not used to signing contracts with my tenants, as they all take my word for everything." They said they wanted to rent any way they could, and wanted contracts. I said: "All right, but I expect this will be the last time you will ask for a contract, as you will see that I will give you just what I promise."

The subordination of the lower caste by the operation of the courts, however, renders such written contracts worthless, since no colored tenant would dare sue a white landlord for any failure to abide by the rental contract. There was evidence, however, that some of the few white tenants in Old County were given written contracts by the landlords. On one of the extremely large plantations, colored tenants had only an oral agreement with the landlord, but a white tenant had a written rental contract for a five-year period. The landlord, the colored manager, and the white tenant each had a copy of the contract. The white tenant's contract was voided by the landlord, however, without legal procedure, because the white tenant was accused by the manager of having stolen cotton. When the landlord informed the tenant by letter that the latter had broken his contract and must leave the plantation, the white tenant had gone to the landlord to defend himself. The landlord had told him, according to the manager's report of the conference, that "he didn't want to discuss the matter with him, because he had already broken the contract so plainly, and there was no question about it!" Neither the white landlord nor the colored manager desired white tenants, and the tenant in question was compelled to move after his cabin had been twice burned to the ground by unknown parties. It seems clear, on the basis of this and other instances of the subordination of white tenants, that the subordination of colored tenants by the caste system is scarcely greater than the subordination of white tenants by the economic and legal systems.

In the making of an oral rental agreement between landlord and tenant the chief factors considered in the bargaining are the amount of credit which the tenant desires and the amount of security, in the form of work-stock and cattle, on which the landlord can obtain liens. These two factors were constantly mentioned by the landlords and tenants interviewed, and the actual bargaining was usually along the lines indicated by the following interview statement from a colored landlord:

> Now when they [prospective tenants] come to me, you know, the first thing they ask you is: "How much can you advance me this year, Mr. Naylor?"
>
> I tell them: "Well, that's a pretty hard question. What stock have you got."

Landlords who were unable or unwilling to make advances had great difficulty in obtaining tenants under any form of rental agreement. The amount of credit offered was one of the principal factors upon the basis of which landlords competed for tenants.

It is impossible to determine the exact state of crop and chattel mortgages, since the mortgages are not usually recorded in a legal manner when tenants give stock as security for advances. In 1933, however, there were recorded only 19 chattel mortgages given to private individuals or to banks, and in all cases except one these mortgages covered both crops and other securities. There were, besides, a number of government crop-production loans which were secured by straight crop mortgages. These mortgages involved fewer than 300 individuals out of the 1,850 cotton-producers (tenants and landowners, Agricultural Adjustment Administration census). It was certain, therefore, that written mortgage contracts were not regarded as necessary by the majority of the landlords.

CASTE, CLASS, AND CONTROL OF LAND

CASTE AND THE OWNERSHIP OF LAND

As Vance, Couch, and Raper[8] have pointed out, both the caste status and the occupational status of the colored tenant have made it extremely difficult for him to purchase farm land in the plantation areas. In general, landlords are unwilling to sell off their land in small tracts to anyone; they are especially unwilling to sell to tenants, for the occupational mobility of tenants becomes a menace to the tenant system and the labor surplus. In a plantation area, where nearly all tenants are colored, however, the caste system enables the white landlord to profit by "selling" land to colored tenants in boom times, without due process of law, taking the land back at the first opportunity in hard times. Evidence of a very large number of such "sales" by white landlords to colored tenants, with subsequent foreclosures, was discovered in the land records at the state capital in 1934 by an investigator for the Department of the Interior. The practice has been quite widespread in Old County in boom times, likewise. The authors talked with several colored tenants, and were told, on good authority, of many others who had attempted to buy second-grade land at $50 per acre in periods of inflation and had "lost" their farms during the period of deflation following 1929. The arrangement had had this result: The landlord had received a rental of $50 per acre instead of $6.00 to $9.00, and in addition had had his taxes paid over a period of several years. In at least two cases, landlords had "sold" to colored tenants land which they did not own.

While the process of reclaiming mortgaged real estate during periods of deflation is a universal one among owners of property, the caste system enables landlords to abuse their rights as mortgagees, since the colored mortgager can secure little or

[8] Rupert B. Vance, *The Negro Agricultural Worker* (mimeographed, 1934), p. 451; W. T. Couch, "The Negro in the South," in W. T. Couch (ed.), *Culture in the South* (Chapel Hill: University of North Carolina Press, 1935), p. 451; Arthur F. Raper, *Preface to Peasantry* (Chapel Hill: University of North Carolina Press, 1936), p. 30.

no protection of his legal rights in the courts. Even in the case of fraud by the landlord, the colored tenant was prevented by the caste system from prosecuting the white landlord. For example, a colored tenant and his wife, who were both more than fifty-five years old, agreed to buy 40 acres of land from a large white landholder for $50 per acre. According to an official in the assessor's office, the market price of the land did not amount to more than $20 or $30. The authors visited this farm. The land was badly eroded. The "40 acres" were actually not more than 30; of these, only about 10 acres were cultivable land, in spite of the fact that the former tenants were paying $50 per acre for all of it. Upon the death of their land-lord, after they had paid him a total of $1,100, in addition to the taxes, the colored buyers were told by the landlord's heirs that he had not owned the land. The old colored man and his wife, then over sixty years of age, began renting the farm again, for $100 a year. The landlord had succeeded in getting twice the rental from them over a six-year period, during which they had been trying to "buy" the farm.

This couple and the individual whose experience is to be related next were intelligent people. They and their families were regarded as leaders in their communities, and they both had children with higher and even professional education. In their cases it was not their illiteracy or stupidity which enabled their former landlords to cheat them but simply their unpro-tected position as members of the lower caste. The second individual had once been a very successful tenant, having rented 200 acres and having sublet it on shares to his own tenants. He had prospered and had sent his children away to college. He then began to buy a fairly large farm from his landlord.

I doan know why I got into it. I was mekin' money then, an' thought I could pay for it, if I kep' goin'. Yessir, they charged me $50 uh acre, an' I had to pay $75 uh acre for some of it. An' you know they [big landowners] buy all duh lan' they want all 'roun heah for $6.00 to $10.00 uh acre! But that's whut they charge you! I los' $3,000 tryin' tuh buy that lan'!

He had managed to save a small tract as a homestead; but he stated, in spite of his fear that the interviewer might "tell the white man on him," that the tract was less than 40 acres.

> I bought it for forty acres. That's what Mr. Holman tol' me, an' that's whut my contrack called for. [*Hesitating, and lifting his eyebrows.*] But ef you know enything about this part of the country, ef you knowed how things is done 'roun' heah—I doan guess you know much about this country, but ef you do [*eyeing me closely*] you know things ain't always the way you'd want them to be. I raly bought it for forty acres, but I doan think it's ovuh thirty. It may be thirty-five.

A prominent colored man, who knew this farmer, asserted that the large white landlord from whom he had tried to buy land had made a practice during the boom period of encouraging his colored tenants to "buy."

> In recent years, he has sold [*smiling*] some little pieces of land to Negroes at $50 an acre, knowing that they couldn't pay the price. Well, they lose the land as soon as a bad season comes, and he has made about ten times as much as if he had rented it to them for $5.00 an acre.

Another prominent colored man, who had lived in Old County all his life, attributed the poverty of the colored farmers to the concentration of land ownership within six families.

> Now if that land was divided up into 40-acre plots, and they'd really sell it to the Negroes, things would improve. But these men don't want to sell it to Negroes; they want to rent it to them. . . . . But if these big landowners would really sell little farms to Negroes, and when they paid for the land, it would be theirs, it would improve this country like everything. But these people will play a trick on Negroes. They'll get their money, and yet find ways to keep the title to the land. So Negroes have got wary, and won't try to buy land.

Since practically all (94 per cent) of the 1,337 tenants in Old County in 1930 were colored, it is not surprising to find that only 14.8 per cent of all colored farm-operators in Old County in 1930 owned their farms, whereas 59 per cent of all white farm-operators owned their farms. Since 87.4 per cent of all farm-operators (tenants and owners) were colored in 1930, it was also to be expected that there should have been more colored than white farm-owners (218 colored to 126 white). The important fact in connection with the distribution of land ownership in 1930, however, was that colored individuals owned just one-sixth of the farm land in Old County, although they constituted three-fifths (63 per cent) of the farm-owners. The proportion of farm land which colored farmers owned had been even smaller in 1925; it amounted then to little more than one-ninth.

In view of the difficulties which confront the colored farmer under a caste system when he attempts to purchase land, it is important that we should consider both the size of the holdings of colored farm-owners in Old County and the means by which they acquired their holdings.

Methods of acquiring land.—In 1934 there were 77 holdings in Old County, assessed at $900 or more, which were owned by colored individuals or families or were held as estates. Interview materials were obtained concerning the manner in which 65 of these holdings were purchased. Twenty-nine had been purchased during the period immediately following the Civil War by men who had formerly been slaves in Old County. Four other tracts had been purchased by the children of former Old County slaves. Fourteen of these 29 slaves who had bought land had purchased it from their former masters. Of these 14, no two had purchased from the same master. This evidence has several very important implications:

1. Half of these larger tracts owned by colored farmers had been purchased by former Old County slaves. This fact seems to indicate (*a*) that there was less opposition to a colored man's buying land from a white landlord in the period of social and economic disintegration following the Civil War than there has generally been in the half-century since 1875, and (*b*) that former slaves did not obtain their land by gift from their former masters but by purchase.

2. The facts (a) that half of the slaves who bought land

(14 out of 29) made the purchase from their former masters and (b) that no two of these bought their land from the same master seem to indicate that, even in the post-bellum society, white landlords would usually sell land only to their "favorite Negro," to one, that is, who meticulously observed the caste sanctions and who, therefore, would not seek to make other colored workers on the plantation dissatisfied with their landless condition.

3. The large proportion of former Old County slaves and of their children among these owners indicates that the colored farm population of Old County is, in large part, descended from those who had been slaves in the same county. The interview evidence from Rural County reveals that there, also, most of the colored tenants are descendants of former slaves in the same county and that many of them still rent from the same white family which owned their slave-ancestors. One would expect to find in these two counties, as a result of the occupational and social subordination of the tenant-family to the landlord-family over a period of several generations, that both the caste sanctions and the economic sanctions would be highly effective, as compared, for example, with those in the newer cotton areas of the Southwest and in those delta areas where there has been a high rate of immigration.

In view of the prevalence of miscegenation in Old County, both during and since slavery, it is surprising that only one family of colored people who were the descendants of white slaveholders had received land as gifts from their white relatives. Eight of the 65 holdings of colored owners which were assessed at $900 or more were held by members of this one extended family, however.[9] Two other holdings had been obtained as a direct result of miscegenation during more recent years, one having been given to a colored man by his white father, and another to a colored woman by her white common-law husband. The holdings which had been inherited

---

[9] Two other holdings had been bought by free colored individuals before the Civil War.

from white relatives, however, amounted to less than one-seventh of the total holdings; and all informants emphasized the fact that colored owners in Old County, with the exception of those in the one family mentioned, had not received their land as a gift from white parents or relatives but had "made it from the knucks," i.e., with the earnings of their hands. In Old City, on the other hand, there had been a surprising number of gifts of real estate made to colored paramours and common-law wives by white men.

The evidence definitely indicates that in the great majority of cases where real estate has been given to colored individuals by whites the relation from which the gift resulted was based not upon kinship but upon sexual partnership. Since the caste system ignores the sociological kinship between white parent and colored offspring but allows a definite place in the system for cohabitation of a white man with a colored woman, it is to be expected, perhaps, that white men should publicly admit the second relation by making gifts of property to colored women, but not the first. A gift of real estate to a colored paramour or common-law wife does not threaten the basic kinship and family system by which caste endogamy is maintained. The bequeathing of property to colored offspring, however, does threaten the caste line, because it is a public recognition of kinship and, to that extent, endangers the sociological and legal taboos upon intermarriage between the groups.

Methods of purchase.—About half (31) of the larger farm holdings of colored individuals had been bought with savings from money earned. Ten others had been purchased by colored veterans of the Civil War out of the pensions paid to them by the federal government.[10] Four had been purchased by Reconstruction politicians (chiefly overseers of the county criminal farm) out of their salaries. Other employment by which

[10] These pensions paid to veterans and the insurance and death benefits paid to their heirs by the federal government are extremely important in the economic structure of the colored community.

buyers were enabled to pay for their farms were: preaching
(2), teaching (1), working as a brakeman on the railroad (1),
bricklaying (1), and the selling of liquor (2).

Rate of upward economic mobility.—The evidence at hand
indicates that the opportunity for upward economic mobility
on the part of landless colored farm-workers was far greater
during the twenty years immediately following the Civil War
than it has been in the period since 1885. The evidence is
incomplete in that no record was available for those former
colored owners who had lost their farms prior to 1933. However, with regard to those who had been able to maintain
holdings, assessed at $900 or more, over a relatively long period
of years, it was true that about half of them (29) had risen from
the status of tenants during the twenty years between 1865
and 1885, whereas only about one-ninth (7) of them had risen
in the same manner in the forty-five years since 1885. Two
of these 7 individuals had made the money with which they
had bought their farms in Old County by working as tenants
in the Mississippi Delta, where the rate of upward economic
mobility among colored farm-workers seems to have been
much higher than in Old County.

CHAPTER XIII

ECONOMIC GROUPS AND THE CONTROL OF LAND

THE preceding chapter has dealt with the caste system as it affects the ownership and control of land. It was pointed out there that large holdings are concentrated in the hands of a group of 34 white and 2 Negro owners. The result of such concentration has been that the bulk of the Negroes in the county exist as tenants working white men's land. (Only 20 per cent of the Negroes own land, and these are predominantly small owners.) The very caste structure itself had its origin, historically, in the plantation economy.

It has been noted, further, that the white upper class in Old City is a "landed aristocracy" owning land in Old County. This has been a remarkably stable group, and its position of high status is still unchallenged. There are few white persons in the rural area, and they tend to be upper and upper-middle class.

The present chapter approaches the problem of the control of land from a different point of view, that of the economic groups into which cotton-producers fall. These groups, to some extent, cut across the line of caste and coincide but roughly with the lines of social class in the white community, except in the case of the upper economic group, which is also predominantly upper class. Economic groupings roughly coincide with social classes among Negroes in the rural areas of Old County, in that most of the lowest tenant group are also of the lowest social class. Some tenants, however, are middle class, as are some of the small owners.

These economic groups are based primarily on the degree of control of land which individuals and families possess. This control of land is most accurately reflected in incomes, as we shall see; and income, in turn, is based on the amount of cotton which a farmer produces annually. Cotton is a cash crop. The net returns from its sale represent effective income. It is important, therefore, to examine the relationship between ownership and/or control of land and the amount of cotton which the farmers produce.

PRODUCTION GROUPS

An agricultural economic system of the type described in chapter xii involves a division (1) of land, (2) of labor, and (3) of the resultant product among the individuals who live under the system. In an agricultural economy like that of Old County, where most of the labor is performed by tenants who own no land, and most of the capital and land is possessed by individuals who perform no agricultural labor, the share of the product obtained by each individual is likely to vary directly with the amount of land he owns and inversely with the amount of agricultural labor which he performs. The problem of analysis centers, therefore, upon the distribution of the product—cotton—among the members of the economic system. In the following pages, groups of farmers will be defined according to their relative production of cotton. All their economic traits, including their relative position as regards the possession of land, will then be considered in terms of these production groups.

For the purpose of this analysis the contractual agreements which 556 farmers in Old County made with the Agricultural Adjustment Administration in 1934 were used. A distribution table showing the average yearly production of lint-cotton[1] on the farms of these contract-signers for the five-year period from 1928 to 1932, inclusive, revealed that these individuals fell into three large groups of cotton producers:

A. A *lowest group*, with a yearly average lint production ranging from 1 to 4,000 pounds, inclusive. The average value

---

[1] Lint-cotton is cotton from which the seeds have been extracted in the process of ginning; it is practically equivalent to "baled cotton."

of the cotton produced on the farms of this group of signers was not more than $816 in 1928, when cotton sold for 20.4 cents per pound, and not more than $252 in 1932, when cotton sold for 6.3 cents per pound. This lowest group amounted to 76.6 per cent of all signers.

B. A *middle group*, with a yearly average lint production ranging from 4,001 to 20,000 pounds, inclusive. The average value of the cotton produced on the farms of this group of signers ranged from over $816 to $4,080 in 1929 and from over $252 to $1,260 in 1932. This middle group amounted to 16.7 per cent of all signers.

C. A *highest group*, with a yearly average lint production ranging from 20,001 pounds to over 80,000 pounds. The average value of the cotton produced on the farms of this group ranged from over $4,080 to over $16,320 in 1928 and from over $1,260 to over $5,040 in 1932. This highest group amounted to only 6.7 per cent of all signers.

There were additional concentrations within each of these larger groups, however. Each of the three larger groups split into three smaller groups of cotton-producers, as revealed in Table 7. The members of the lowest of these nine groups (Group I) had an average production of not more than 2 bales of cotton per year; they amounted to almost a third (31.1 per cent) of the autonomous producers of cotton. The value of the cotton which each raised, estimated upon the basis of their annual yearly production, was not more than $204 in 1928 and not more than $63 in 1932. The members of the highest of these nine groups (Group IX), on the other hand, had an average yearly production of more than 160 bales. The members of this highest group amounted to only 1.3 per cent of all autonomous cotton-producers. The value of the cotton raised on each of their plantations was over $16,320 in 1928 and over $5,040 in 1932.

Production groups and income groups.—The term "cotton-producer" is used here to designate an individual who contributes one or more of the necessary elements in the cultivation of cotton, i.e., labor, capital, land, work-stock, and farm equipment. Most of the "cotton-producers" in our highest groups, of course, performed no agricultural labor at all.

TABLE 7

PRODUCTION GROUPS, 1928-32, INCLUSIVE, IN A.A.A. SAMPLE OF 556
FARM-OPERATORS

| PRODUCTION GROUPS | | | LINT-POUNDS PRODUCED | BALES PRODUCED | INCOME | |
Group	Number of Producers	Percentage of Sample			1928 (@ 20.4 Cents per Pound)	1932 (@ 6.3 Cents per Pound)
Lowest......	426	76.6	1–4,000	0–8	$ 204.00–816.00	$ 63.00–252.00
I..........	(173)	(31.1)	1–1,000	Not over 2	204.00 and less	63.00 and less
II.........	(156)	(28.1)	1,001–2,100	Over 2–4	204.01–428.40	63.01–132.30
III........	(97)	(17.4)	2,101–4,000	Over 4–8	428.41–816.00	132.31–252.00
Middle......	93	16.7	4,001–20,000	Over 8–40	816.01–4,080.00	252.01–1,260.00
IV........	(57)	(10.3)	4,001–9,000	Over 8–18	816.01–1,836.00	252.01–567.00
V.........	(23)	(4.1)	9,001–14,000	Over 18–28	1,836.01–2,856.00	567.01–882.00
VI.......	(13)	(2.3)	14,001–20,000	Over 28–40	2,856.01–4,080.00	882.01–1,260.00
Highest.....	37	6.7	20,001–80,000	Over 40	4,080.01–16,320.00	1,260.01–5,040.00
VII........	(22)	(4.0)	20,001–50,000	Over 40–100	4,080.01–10,200.00	1,260.01–3,150.00
VIII.......	(8)	(1.4)	50,001–80,000	Over 100–160	10,201.00–16,320.00	3,150.01–5,040.00
IX........	(7)	(1.3)	80,001 and over	Over 160	Over 16,320.00	Over 5,040.00
All....	556	100.0	....	....	....	....

The groupings of these cotton-producers have been made upon the basis of the average yearly value of the cotton grown on the farms which they "operated." The only tenants who are regarded as "operating" a farm are the cash-tenants who signed their own contracts with the Agricultural Adjustment Administration. These production groups are not equivalent to "income groups," since they have not been based upon the total income of the producer, or even upon their net income from cotton, but upon their gross income from cotton. Since the larger part of the incomes of most farmers in Old County is still derived from cotton, however, our production groups are a fairly close approximation to income groups.[2]

Adequacy of the sample.—The cotton-producers concerning whom some data were available in the A.A.A. records amounted to only 30 per cent of the 1,911 farm-operators in Old County. They included 305 owners of cotton farms, 266 cash-tenants, and 17 half- and quarter-tenants. Only 35 per cent of all cash-tenants in the county and only 3 per cent of all half- and quarter-tenants were included; the remainder were prevented from signing contracts by landlords and by the administration of the law.

The sample includes practically all of those who ginned and sold their own cotton, but the most poverty-stricken and subordinated tenants are not included. Since 80 per cent of all farm-operators in 1935 were tenants, the proportion of individuals in the lowest groups would be much larger if our sample included all the tenants. The generalizations about the lowest groups will, therefore, apply to a much larger number of producers than those in the A.A.A. sample. With the foregoing definition of the production groups in mind, it is now possible to consider ownership of land in relation to these groups.

[2] In the case of the lower groups which are composed of cash-tenants and of small owners, the range of the values for the cotton raised by members of each group corresponds exactly to the range of their gross incomes from cotton. In the case of the higher groups of landlords, however, the group values must be cut at least in half to approximate the range of gross incomes from cotton, since the shares owed to the tenant have not been deducted. In a later section, dealing with the income of the landlords in the three highest groups (Groups VII, VIII, IX), the gross income from the cotton due to these landlords has been calculated.

ECONOMIC GROUPS AND CONTROL OF LAND

PRODUCTION GROUPS AND THE CONTROL OF LAND

Where a high rate of farm tenancy prevails, the ownership and control of land is the most important factor in the distribution of the product. In 1935, only 1 out of every 5 farm-operators in Old County owned farms, and 1 out of 4 in Rural County. It is obvious from an examination of Table 8 and Figure 16 that there is a high degree of association between the production groups and the ownership of land.

TABLE 8

NUMBER AND PERCENTAGE OF LANDLORDS IN EACH PRODUCTION GROUP: 1932

Production Groups	Number of Persons	Number of Landlords	Percentage Who Own Land
Lowest............	426	83	19.5
I................	173	17	9.8
II................	156	33	21.2
III................	97	33	34.0
Middle............	93	66	70.9
IV................	57	35	61.4
V................	23	21	91.3
VI................	13	10	76.9
Highest............	37	36	97.3
VII................	22	22	100.0
VIII............	8	8	100.0
IX................	7	6	85.7

The bars in Figure 16 indicate the increase in proportion of landlords to all producers from the lowest to the highest group. While only one-fifth of the 426 producers (83 out of 426) in the lowest group (Groups I, II, III) are owners of land, 36 of the 37 largest producers (Groups VII, VIII, IX) are landlords, and nearly three-fourths of those in the middle group are landlords (66 out of 93). In other words, those producers who grow over 40 bales of cotton are overwhelmingly owners of land. The 36 large landowners described in the previous chapter are all in the highest production group, and the 6 largest landlords constitute Subgroup IX.

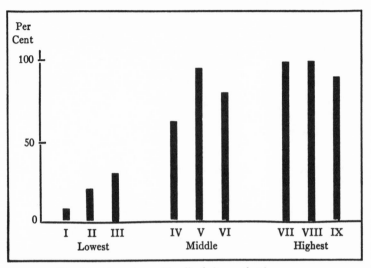

FIG. 16.—Percentage of landlords by production groups.

To appreciate fully the difference in the ownership of land, according to production groups, we must go outside the sample of cotton-producers who signed A.A.A. contracts and con- sider all farmers in the county. Of the 1,911 farm-operators who lived in Old County in 1935, only 18.7 per cent (356) owned any land; 81.3 per cent (1,555) of all those who oper- ated farms, rented. The 37 largest cotton-producers, however (Groups VII, VIII, IX), owned or controlled practically half (43 per cent) of all land in Old County, and they owned or controlled one-third (32.8 per cent) of all the cultivable land. Yet they were only 1.8 per cent of all farm-operators. Two of the 36 largest landowners were colored. Perhaps the group differences may be presented more forcibly if we consider only the 7 largest cotton-producers in Old County. These 7 individuals (Group IX) owned or controlled 22.2 per cent of all the land in Old County and 16.2 per cent of all the cul- tivable land. Yet they amounted to but one-third of 1 per cent (0.36 per cent) of all farm-operators (Fig. 17).

Fertility of the soil.—The control of land is of particular economic importance if the land is "good" land. A very pertinent question is: "Who owns the 'good' land and what is the relation between 'good' land and productivity of the farms in Old County?"

Old County is divided into eight areas, based upon variations in the soil type and topography. The four areas contiguous to the river (*A, B, C,* and *D* on Fig. 20) are considered the most desirable areas in the county, although there are

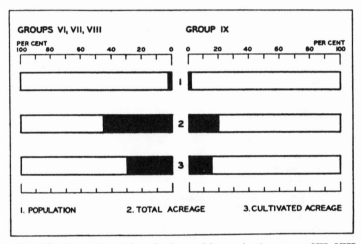

FIG. 17.—Proportion of farm land owned by production groups VII, VIII, and IX and by production group IX, compared with proportion which these groups constitute among all farm operators: 1934.

creek-bottoms in other areas which are also known as "good" land. In three of these four rich-soil areas practically all the farms are operated by large landowners using share-tenants. In the one remaining rich-soil area autonomous cash-tenants are numerous. In the poorest soil area there are no operators in Groups VII, VIII, or IX (largest owners) and only four in Groups V and VI. The "good" land in Old County is definitely monopolized by the larger owners and producers.

Control of land and value of farms.—A rough index of the

value of land is the assessed valuation of the farm. This evaluation, however, includes buildings and equipment, as well as land. One may first examine, however, the value of farms by production groups and then relate these findings to the yield per acre of the land—an index reflecting both the fertility of land and the efficiency of operation.

The average assessed value of land and buildings owned by cotton-producers in the lowest group (Group I) was only $555.[3]

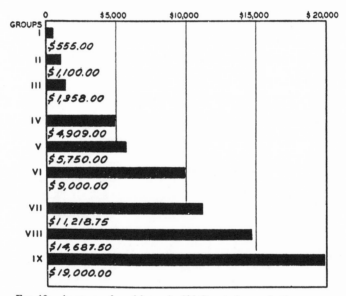

FIG. 18.—Average value of farms in Old County by production groups.

The average assessed value of the land and buildings owned by each of the other eight production groups is given in Figure

[3] It is necessary to remember, in connection with this figure, that it does not represent the average value of farm and buildings owned by *all* of those who produced 2 bales of cotton or less. It represents the average value of farm land and equipment owned by only those 25 out of 190-odd cotton-producers in Group I who signed reduction contracts. The great majority of cotton-producers in Old County, however, would fall into Group I if our sample were extended to include all cotton-producers in the county.

18. This chart substantiates the record of lint production in showing a great range between the lowest group and the highest. The average value of the farm land and buildings owned by the largest producers (Group IX) is more than thirty-four times as great as the average value of the farm land and buildings owned by the smallest producers (Group I). Figure 18 reveals, furthermore, that the division between the three lowest groups and the three middle groups is based upon a pronounced difference in the value of the real-property holdings of the three lower and the three middle groups. The average value of real property among individuals in the highest production group of the lowest bracket (Group III) is $1,358, while the value in Group IV, the lowest production group in the middle bracket, is more than three and one-half times as large. The production groups, therefore, correspond to quite distinct groups of property-owners.

Distribution of tenants among landlords.—Persons who control land in Old County also control people. Thus, the 6 owners in Group IX have an average of 51.8 tenants each; the 17 owners in Group I have only 1.6 tenants each; and Groups VII, VIII, and IX control two-thirds of all tenants in Old County (See Table 9).

The importance of the system of tenant-labor to planters in Old County is demonstrated by the fact that 60 per cent of owners of cotton farms had tenants. Almost half (44 per cent) of the landlords who had tenants were small producers, raising not more than 8 bales of cotton per year. When the distribution of tenants is considered, however, we learn that these 83 small farm-owners, who produced not more than 8 bales of cotton each, had only 10.4 per cent of the 1,300 tenants, while the 37 planters who each produced more than 40 bales of cotton had 66 per cent of all tenants. (It will be remembered that these 37 planters, who constituted the three highest production groups (VII, VIII, IX), also owned or controlled almost half (43 per cent) of the total acreage in Old County and 32.8 per cent of the cultivable acreage.)

The average number of tenants held by landlords ranged

from 1.3 in the lowest production group to 51.8 in the highest. The distribution as shown in Table 9 is very important, for it reveals that not only are the landlords in the three lowest production groups (I, II, III) small-scale farmers but that so also are those in the three middle production groups (IV, V, VI). Although the three lowest groups of landlords constitute almost half of all landlords, they control only one-tenth of the tenants and have an average of only 1.6 tenants each. The

TABLE 9

DISTRIBUTION OF TENANTS AMONG LANDLORDS, BY PRODUCTION GROUPS OF LANDLORDS: 1934

PRODUCTION GROUP	TENANTS, BY PRODUCTION GROUPS OF LANDLORDS			NUMBER OF LANDLORDS	AVERAGE NUMBER OF TENANTS PER LANDLORD
	Number	Percentage	Cumulative Percentage		
Lowest.........	135	10.4	10.4	83	1.6
I.............	22	1.7	1.7	17	1.3
II...........	40	3.1	4.8	33	1.2
III...........	73	5.6	10.4	33	2.2
Middle.........	307	23.6	34.0	66	4.7
IV...........	117	9.0	19.4	35	3.3
V............	95	7.3	26.7	21	4.5
VI...........	95	7.3	34.0	10	9.5
Highest.........	862	66.1	100.0	36	22.6
VII...........	298	22.9	56.9	22	13.5
VIII..........	253	19.4	76.3	8	28.1
IX...........	311	23.8	100.0	6	51.8
Total......	1,304	100.1	100.1	185	7.1

middle group of landlords (Groups IV, V, VI) controls less than one-fourth (23.6 per cent) of the tenants in Old County and has an average of 4.7 tenants each. The 37 planters in the three highest groups control two-thirds of all the tenants (66.1 per cent).

If we consider only the 15 largest producers of cotton, we find that they control 43.2 per cent, or almost half, of the 1,300 tenants in Old County. The 14 landlords in Groups

VIII and IX have an average of 37.6 tenants each; and the 6 landlords in Group IX who produced more than 160 bales of

TABLE 10

NUMBER OF TENANTS PER FARM, BY PRODUCTION GROUPS OF LANDLORDS

NUMBER OF TENANTS ON FARM	NUMBER OF LANDLORDS BY PRODUCTION GROUPS									TOTAL NUMBER OF LANDLORDS		
	I	II	III	IV	V	VI	VII	VIII	IX	Number	Percentage	Cumulative Percentage
1	15	27	10	8	0	0	0	0	0	60	32.3	32.3
2	1	5	16	8	4	0	0	0	0	34	18.3	50.6
3	0	1	3	8	5	0	0	0	0	17	9.1	59.7
4	0	0	3	4	3	0	0	0	0	10	5.4	65.1
5	1	0	0	3	2	1	0	0	0	7	3.8	68.9
6	0	0	0	1	3	3	0	0	0	7	3.8	72.7
7	0	0	0	1	2	1	1	0	0	5	2.7	75.4
8	0	0	0	0	0	0	1	0	0	1	0.5	75.9
9	0	0	0	0	2	0	1	0	0	3	1.6	77.5
10	0	0	1	0	0	0	3	0	0	4	2.2	79.7
11	0	0	0	1	0	1	2	0	0	4	2.2	81.9
12	0	0	0	0	0	1	3	0	0	4	2.2	84.1
13	0	0	0	0	0	1	2	0	0	3	1.6	85.7
14	0	0	0	1	0	1	0	0	0	2	1.1	86.8
15	0	0	0	0	0	1	1	0	0	2	1.1	87.9
16	0	0	0	0	0	0	2	0	1	3	1.6	89.5
17	0	0	0	0	0	0	1	0	0	1	0.5	90.0
18	0	0	0	0	0	0	2	1	0	3	1.6	91.6
19	0	0	0	0	0	0	0	1	0	1	0.5	92.1
20	0	0	0	0	0	0	3	0	0	3	1.6	93.7
22	0	0	0	0	0	0	0	1	0	1	0.5	94.2
24	0	0	0	0	0	0	0	1	0	1	0.5	94.7
25	0	0	0	0	0	0	0	1	0	1	0.5	95.2
27	0	0	0	0	0	0	0	1	0	1	0.5	95.7
31	0	0	0	0	0	0	0	1	0	1	0.5	96.2
43	0	0	0	0	0	0	0	1	0	1	0.5	96.7
44	0	0	0	0	0	0	0	0	2	2	1.6	98.3
62	0	0	0	0	0	0	0	0	1	1	0.5	98.8
68	0	0	0	0	0	0	0	0	1	1	0.5	99.3
77	0	0	0	0	0	0	0	0	1	1	0.5	99.8
Total	17	33	33	35	21	10	22	8	6	185	99.8	......

cotton a year have an average of 51.8 tenants each. If we abandon averages and look at the actual number of one-tenant farms, two-tenant farms, etc. (Table 10), we find that 60 landlords, or 32.2 per cent of all landlords, have only 1 tenant each, and that 128 landlords, or approximately 70 per cent of all landlords, have not more than 5 tenants each. Of the 6 largest owners, however, 2 have 44 tenants each, 1 has 62 tenants, 1 has 68 tenants, and the largest has 77 tenants. (The producer in Group IX who is not an owner controls 44 tenants.) These figures include only the tenants who are at the head of the squad or family occupying each rented farm, and do not include the family- and child-laborers on these farms. The actual number of workers available to a landlord, therefore, is several times as large as the figures indicate.

PRODUCTION GROUPS AND YIELD PER ACRE

Control of land and yield per acre.—The objective of cotton agriculture is to get the highest possible yield of cotton from each acre of land. In fact, the size of the yield of cotton per acre is second only to the amount of land owned by the producer as a determinant of his income from cotton. There is a wide range of yields in Old County, the maximum being about 400 lint-pounds. The amount of cotton which the farmer can produce from an acre is related to several factors, among which are the fertility of the soil, the adequacy of his equipment, and the organization of his labor. We have already shown that the largest producers have a "head start" from the standpoint of quality of soil and total value of the farm. The problem of yield per acre is a complex one, however.

In order to simplify the presentation of the results obtained from the study, only the lowest of the nine groups (I) and the five highest groups (V, VI, VII, VIII, IX) will be considered. The distribution of the yield per acre among these groups has been analyzed from two points of view: (1) The distribution of the yield per acre within the lowest production group and within the five highest groups has been calculated separately; (2) the yield per acre on each of the farms operated by producers within these six groups has been located on a soil map of the county. Before proceeding to a consideration of the results of these operations, it will be well to define again the particular groups of cotton-producers selected for this study of the yield per acre.

Group I consists of producers whose average yearly crop was not more than 2 bales and whose gross income from cotton

TABLE 11

YIELD PER ACRE BY PRODUCTION GROUPS: GROUP I

	OWNERS		CASH-TENANTS				ALL				
									Total		
LINT-POUNDS	Number of White	Number of Colored	Number of White	Number of Colored	Percentage	Cumulatiue Percentage	Number of White	Number of Colored	Number ber	Per- cent- age	Cum. Per- cent- age
Below 100.......	0	11	0	14	13.2	13.2	0	25	25	14.5	14.5
100–124.........	2	11	1	20	18.9	32.1	3	31	34	19.7	34.2
125–49..........	6	11	2	21	19.8	51.9	8	32	40	23.1	57.3
150–74..........	1	4	3	23	21.7	73.6	4	27	31	17.9	75.2
175–99..........	2	4	0	11	10.4	84.0	2	15	17	9.8	85.0
200–224.........	0	3	0	5	4.7	88.7	0	8	8	4.6	89.6
225–49..........	2	1	1	2	1.9	90.6	3	3	6	3.5	93.1
250–74..........	0	0	0	6	5.7	96.3	0	6	6	3.5	96.6
275–99..........	0	0	1	0	0.0	96.3	1	0	1	0.6	97.2
300–324.........	0	0	0	3	2.8	99.1	0	3	3	1.7	98.9
325–49..........	0	0	0	0	0.0	99.1	0	0	0	0.0	98.9
350–74..........	0	1	0	0	0.0	99.1	0	1	1	0.6	99.5
375 and up......	0	0	0	1	0.9	100.0	0	1	1	0.6	100.1
Total.......	13	46	8	106	100.0	100.0	21	152	173	100.1	100.1

was not more than $204 in 1928 and not more than $63 in 1932. In Figure 19 the yield per acre has been represented for the group as a unit, but in Table 11 the yield per acre has been considered separately for owners and cash-tenants in Group I.

Groups V and VI consist of producers whose average yearly crop was more than 18 bales and less than 41 and whose gross income from cotton range drom $1,836.01 to $4,080.00 in 1928 and from $567.01 to $1,260.00 in 1932. In Figure 19 and

313

Table 12 the yield per acre for these groups has been combined with that for the three highest groups.

Groups VII, VIII, and IX consist of producers whose average yield ranged from 40 to over 160 bales. The gross income from cotton of the members of these groups ranged from $4,080.01 to over $16,320.00 in 1928 and from $1,260.01 to over $5,040.00 in 1932.

The distribution of yields among the members of Group I and among the members of the five highest groups is summa-

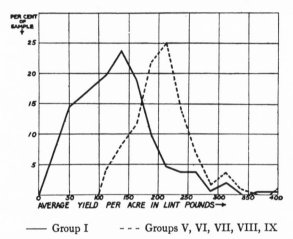

—— Group I   - - - Groups V, VI, VII, VIII, IX

FIG. 19.—Average yield per acre by production groups for five-year period, 1928–32

rized in Tables 11 and 12. These tables reveal that about one-third of the 173 cotton-producers in Group I secured a yield of less than 125 pounds of lint per acre, whereas only one-twenty-fifth of the 73 cotton-producers in the five highest groups secured a yield of less than 125 pounds. More than half of the producers in Group I secured a yield of less than 150 pounds per acre, as contrasted with less than one-eighth of those in the five highest groups. About six-sevenths (85 per cent) of the producers in Group I secured a yield of less

TABLE 12

YIELD PER ACRE BY PRODUCTION GROUPS: GROUPS V, VI, VII, VIII, AND IX

Lint-Pounds	Owners White Number	Owners White Percentage	Owners White Cumulative Percentage	Owners Colored Number	Cash-Tenants White Number	Cash-Tenants Colored Number	All White Number	All White Percentage	All White Cumulative Percentage	All Colored Number	All Total Number	All Total Percentage	All Total Cumulative Percentage
Below 100	0	0.0	0.0	0	0	0	0	0.0	0.0	0	0	0.0	0.0
100–124	2	3.0	3.0	0	0	1	2	3.0	3.0	1	3	4.0	4.0
125–49	5	8.0	11.0	1	0	0	5	8.0	11.0	1	6	8.0	12.0
150–74	8	13.0	24.0	1	0	0	8	13.0	24.0	1	9	12.0	24.0
175–99	15	25.0	49.0	0	0	1	15	23.0	47.0	1	16	22.0	46.0
200–224	15	25.0	74.0	3	1	0	15	23.0	70.0	3	18	25.0	71.0
225–49	8	13.0	87.0	0	1	1	9	14.0	84.0	1	10	14.0	85.0
250–74	4	7.0	94.0	0	1	0	5	8.0	92.0	0	5	7.0	92.0
275–99	0	0.0	94.0	0	0	0	1	2.0	94.0	0	1	1.0	93.0
300–324	3	5.0	99.0	1	0	0	3	5.0	99.0	0	3	4.0	97.0
325–49	0	0.0	99.0	0	0	0	0	0.0	99.0	1	1	1.0	98.0
350–74	0	0.0	99.0	0	0	0	0	0.0	99.0	0	0	0.0	98.0
375 and up	1	2.0	101.0	0	0	0	1	2.0	101.0	0	1	1.0	99.0
Total	61	101.0	101.0	6	3	3	64	101.0	101.0	9	73	99.0	99.0

315

than 200 pounds per acre, as contrasted with less than one-half of those in the five highest groups.

In Figure 19 the distribution of yields for Group I and for the five highest groups is shown in the form of two frequency polygons. The shift of the broken-line polygon to the right of the solid-line polygon reveals that the great bulk of the producers in the five highest groups obtained far higher yields than did the bulk of those in the lowest group.

Fertility of the Soil.—The second operation in the analysis is represented by a map, Figure 20. There the yield per acre of each farm has been marked on the location of the farm, for four groups of farm-operators:

1. Group I, cash-renters
2. Group I, owners
3. Group V and VI, owners (together)
4. Group VII, VIII, and IX, owners (together)

The county has been divided into eight areas, based upon variations in the soil types and topography. An analysis of the yield per acre among the production groups in these eight areas is summarized in Table 13, which reveals that, in seven of the eight areas, both the owners in Groups V and VI and those in Groups VII, VIII, and IX secured higher average yields than did the cash-tenants and owners in Group I. In five of the seven areas in which owners in Groups VII, VIII, and IX operated farms, they secured the highest average yields. On the other hand, owners in Group I secured the lowest average yields in six of the seven areas in which they operated farms.

With regard to soil types, the analysis revealed that the average yield for all producers was highest in areas *A*, *C*, *E*, and *H*, which were the only river-bottom and creek-bottom areas. It seems quite probable, therefore, that the natural fertility of the soil, as well as the better equipment and closer organization of labor which were correlated with it, was a factor in the higher yields in these areas. In three of these four rich soil-areas, practically all the farms were operated by large landowners using share-tenants.

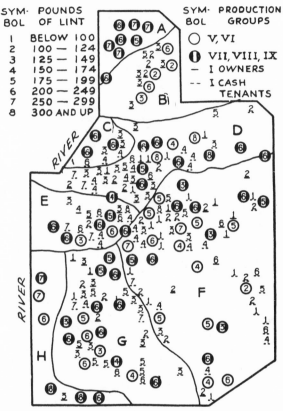

FIG. 20.—Variation in the yield of cotton per acre, according to soil-topography areas and production groups: 1928–32, inclusive (county boundaries generalized).

This map locates nearly all of the cotton farms, shows their yield per acre, and designates the production groups of their operators, by soil-topography areas. In Soil Area A at the top of the map, for example, all of the operators were in production groups VII, VIII, or IX, and the range of their average yields was from 175 to 299 pounds of lint per acre.

Efficiency of Operation.—Whereas the importance of soil types is indicated by the greater average yields secured on river- and creek-bottom lands, the influence of superior equipment and of large holdings is shown by an analysis of the yields secured by the various groups *within the same soil-area.* For this purpose the yields secured by members of the lowest group were compared to those secured by members of the highest groups on contiguous farm tracts. Although the range of yields within each production group was large in each area, it

TABLE 13

AVERAGE YIELD PER ACRE BY PRODUCTION GROUPS AND SOIL-AREAS
FOR 225 COTTON-PRODUCERS

SOIL-AREAS	RANGE OF YIELD PER ACRE IN POUNDS OF LINT	AVERAGE YIELD PER ACRE IN POUNDS OF LINT				
		All Producers	Groups VII, VIII, and IX (Owners)	Groups V and VI (Owners)	Group I (Cash-Tenants)	Group I (Owners)
River and creek-bottom Land:						
A	190–270	255	254	265	....	....
H	141–341	253	290	238	....	141
E	100–400	191	187	173	208	155
C	130–236	176	236	....	160	137
Other:						
D	71–350	169	233	244	143	147
G	72–250	166	191	189	163	121
F	68–300	147	187	189	129	122
B	101–222	142	....	148	142	132

was found, in six of the eight areas, that in any given cluster of contiguous farms the yields secured by producers in the upper groups were higher than those secured by producers in Group I. Since no important natural soil differential exists between contiguous farms in the same soil-area, the superiority of the yields in the upper groups was the result of the superior equipment (including seed) and superior techniques employed on their farms and of the fertility added to the soil by the rotation of crops and the use of fertilizer. These advantages were related to the greater economic resources which producers in the upper groups enjoyed.

ECONOMIC GROUPS AND CONTROL OF LAND

The only soil-areas where approximately the same yields were secured on the farms of producers in Group I and of producers in the higher groups were: (1) the single rich soil-area where autonomous cash-tenants were numerous, and (2) the poorest soil-areas, where the average yield was the lowest in the county. In the poorest soil-area, operators of all groups had poor equipment as well as poor soil. There were no operators in Groups VII, VIII, or IX in this area, (Figure 21, Soil Type B) and only four operators in Groups V or VI. It was an area of small owners whose tenants secured the lowest yields in the county.

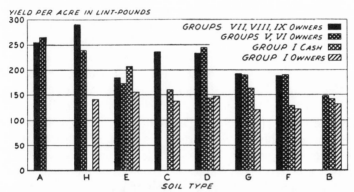

FIG. 21.—Variation in the yield of cotton per acre, according to soil-topography areas and production groups: 1928–32, inclusive.

In the one exceptional rich soil-area (E), cash-tenants in Group I secured even higher yields than did producers in the five highest groups. In this area, characterized by a high degree of absentee-ownership, cash-tenants rented a large part of the land and sublet it to share-tenants. The equipment, techniques, and organization of labor on the farms of cash-tenants in this area were more nearly equal to those on the farms of the larger producers than they were in any other area. Since the rate of rental in this area was the highest in the county and the competition for farms greatest, all except the most skilful and well-equipped tenant-farmers had been eliminated from the area. Field study showed that the most

319

prosperous cash-tenants and tenant-managers in Old County were concentrated in this area. Their standard of living (and that of colored farm-workers on the rich delta land across the river) was considerably higher than that of colored farmers in the hill-land of Old County. These colored cash-tenants sublet their rented tracts to share-tenants, financed the crop, advanced supplies, and controlled the sale of the cotton in much the same way as did the large white landowners. The work on their farms was as closely supervised as the work on the adjacent farms of producers in the highest groups. Both for them and for their tenants the desirability of the land acted, no doubt, as an incentive to harder and more efficient work. Their labor system was virtually the same as the system on the large adjacent plantations, where the work of half-tenants was closely supervised. Students of other cotton economies have agreed that the highest yields are secured under such a labor system, other factors remaining nearly equal. In the area under discussion colored cash-tenants occupied the place of landlords in this labor system and secured even higher yields than did large neighboring white producers.

In six of the eight soil-areas, however, it has been shown that the producers in the five highest groups secured higher average yields than those in the lowest group. These large producers also obtained higher yields than did small producers who operated farms contiguous to theirs. Differences in soil fertility, equipment, and organization of labor were chiefly responsible for these group differences in the yield per acre.

WORK-STOCK AND EQUIPMENT

The great economic advantage which larger producers had in the size of their holdings and the yield of cotton per acre was accompanied by a superiority in the amount and quality of their work-stock and equipment. In 1930 the average number of horses per farm-operator in Old County was 1.0, and of mules, 1.3; by 1935 the average number of horses had decreased to 0.8, and the average number of mules to 0.9. The price of a good mule was at least $150. The annual gross income from cotton of the majority of farmers in Old County was less than the price of a mule. Of the hundreds of these animals observed by the authors over a period of eighteen months, most were old and extremely emaciated. Small farmers and tenants were compelled to buy defective animals, which were undersized, sickly, partly blind, etc. During the winter and spring many of these farmers were unable to buy feed for their work-stock;[4] as a result, they lost their mules. Several cases were found where the cotton crop of a tenant or small owner had to be reduced or allowed to grow up in weeds as a result of the death of his mule. In some cases quarter-tenants' mules and equipment were of such inferior quality that the landlords insisted upon supplying their own and compelled the tenants to rent on a half-share basis.

The larger producers, on the other hand, each owned 20–50 mules of a superior quality. The quality of their work-stock undoubtedly contributed to the higher yields secured on the farms operated by these groups. There was a constant movement of mules from tenants to landlords, since the latter were enabled by the lien laws to confiscate a tenant's work-stock in lieu of payment of rents and debts. Such a tenant's entire capital was usually represented by his mule and a very few cows, it was these that the landlord seized in case of crop failure. A cash- or quarter-tenant, then, became a half-tenant or a wage-hand, or he began buying another mule, probably from his landlord. The operation of the lien laws over a long period of years thus increased the concentration of work-stock in the possession of the larger landlords.

[4] Although most tenants and small owners raised only enough corn to feed their work-stock during less than half of the year, the average expenditure for feed in 1929 on 458 cotton farms in Old County was only $42.48; and in Rural County, for 150 farms, only $38.38. These figures show that, even in good times, cotton farmers were unable to buy sufficient feed for their work-stock. In bad times, such as the period in which this field study was made, both men and work-animals virtually starve during January, February, March, July, and August, when landlords make no advances and harvests have been exhausted.

The same inadequacy existed with regard to tenants' farm equipment as with their work-stock. Plows and cultivators were old and inefficient; wagons were utterly decrepit. Even the less destitute tenants and small owners had wagons which were fifteen or more years old; they had been able to buy little or no equipment since 1918, when the average seasonal price of cotton had been 38.34 cents.

Caste-differentials.—The great advantage held by white farm-owners over colored owners and tenants is shown in Table 14. In Old County in 1930 the average value of the implements and machinery owned by white owners was $869,

TABLE 14

AVERAGE VALUE OF IMPLEMENTS AND MACHINERY OWNED, BY TENURE
GROUPS, AND COLOR: 1930

	OWNERS		CASH-TENANTS		HALF-TENANTS		OTHER TENANTS	
	No.	Average Value	No.	Average Value	No.	Average Value	No.	Average Value
Old County:								
White..........	126	$869.00	38	$428.00	18	$135.00	23	$217.00
Colored........	190	78.00	719	55.00	285	20.00	254	36.00
Rural County:								
White..........	312	305.00	39	106.00	26	99.00	54	129.00
Colored........	163	101.00	199	37.00	396	24.00	789	51.00

whereas among colored owners it was only $78. For colored cash-tenants the value was only $55; for half-tenants, $20; and for other colored tenants, $36. The few white tenants in Old County were chiefly capitalist-tenants, so that the average value of their implements and machinery was much higher, in every group, than that for colored tenants. In Rural County, values for colored tenants were equally low and were only from one-fourth to two-fifths as large as the average values among white tenants of the corresponding group. Since there was a large group of small white owners in the eastern hill-section of this county, however, the average values for white and colored owners were in the ratio of only 3 to 1, whereas in Old County they were in the ratio of 11 to 1.

With a knowledge of the differentials which existed among cotton-producers in Old County with regard to the amount of land owned and its productivity and the amount and quality of work-stock and equipment owned, we are now prepared to consider, in more detail, the division of labor by means of which the society organizes the use of the available land and equipment.

CHAPTER XIV

DIVISION OF LABOR IN THE COTTON ECONOMY

THE production of the annual cotton crop involves a complex division of labor which organizes the economic behavior of all of the farm inhabitants of Old County and many of the residents of Old City. Some persons supply credit, some supervision, and 90 per cent of the rural residents supply their physical labor under one or the other of the contract systems described in the previous chapter or as the owner-operators of small farms.

THE WORK-LOAD

It has been quite generally assumed and stated that the cotton-farmer works during only one-half of the year and that the labor required of him is both light and unskilled. This widely held belief is a myth whose foundation lies in the economic antagonism which exists in all rural cultures between landlord and tenant groups. In Old and Rural counties it receives increased emphasis because the occupational groups are largely equated with the caste groups; the myth, therefore, helps to support the dogma of caste. Like the myth which attributes the landlord's failure to use fertilizer to the "ignorance" of the colored tenant; the myth of the "lazy cotton tenant" has become popular because it has justified the superordinate position both of landlords and of white individuals. It has been generally agreed upon, even by "scholars," that the cotton-farmer does little or no work during almost half of the year. Landlords have expressed their antagonism to tenants and to farm laborers, as a group, and have justified the low income of these workers by asserting that they lead a lazy, carefree existence.

DIVISION OF LABOR IN COTTON ECONOMY

As a matter of fact, however, the growing season for cotton is longer than that of any other major crop in the United States, and its cultivation in the southeastern region demands more prolonged and intensive labor than does that of any other crop, with the possible exception of tobacco. An objective examination of the simplest facts of cotton cultivation immediately confirms this fact, but the myth of the lazy existence of the cotton-farmer persists.

In their franker moments, however, Old County landlords emphasized the fact that "making" a cotton crop is hard work. For instance, one large white landowner, speaking of the ability of his colored tenants to undergo periods of extremely severe labor, stated that in November, after they had picked $12,000 worth of cotton, they still had had a great deal more work. They had harvested 3,000 bales of hay for the landlord ("I never saw Negroes working so hard or fast as when we were baling hay"); slaughtered their own hogs, dug their potatoes, harvested their peas, cut and hauled enough firewood to last their families during the winter, and made their "settlements" and arrangements with the landlord for the following year. Then they went down the river to work on the levees until the time arrived for spring ploughing.

In addition to cultivating cotton, corn, peas, gardens, and caring for stock during the greater part of the year, many tenants and small owners also plough under their cotton and corn stubbles, clean ditches and bayous of undergrowth, clean out watering-holes, and repair fences during the "slack" months of December, January, and February. Some also cultivate winter gardens.

With regard to the severity of the work demanded by cotton cultivation at its height, both landlords and tenants are in agreement. The working-day is from "sun up to sun down." One very large white landowner in Rural County, boasting of the amount of work he was able to get from his half-tenants (in harvesting hay), stated: "We have to drive them hard, work them from 'can to can't.' At the first tap of the bell at daylight in the morning they rush to the barn for their mules and they work till dark. They don't mind hard work, and can sure do a lot, and we drive them."

A very prosperous colored landowner said that those of his tenants who had been unable to secure work in the sawmills or on the levees had little to do in mid-winter; but he added, unprompted:

.... they really need that rest. They need it! After they've worked on crops, from ploughing in February or March to picking it three times in the fall, they *need* a rest. Working from sunup to sundown every day. I don't see how they can stand it. And working cotton is not only hard work in this heat, but it's *skilled* work. It's really a skilled job. Don't you let anybody tell you that these Negroes are just dumb brute labor. Have you ever seen cotton hoed? Well, there'll be a little blade of cotton about the size of a knife blade, with grass or weeds all around it. And you'll see children, even, cut that grass away with those sharp hoes just as clean and never touch that blade of cotton! It's really beautiful to watch them.

Women and children all get out there and work all day, from light to dark. I never could see how these little children could stand it. A boy learns to hoe cotton when he's nine or ten years old! Some younger! And soon he's able to work out there all day, and keep up with them until it's laid by—You know, a boy begins plowing when he's no more than fourteen, and he's a man when he's sixteen or seventeen. He does all his growing in those two years between say fourteen and sixteen. At sixteen or seventeen he's a man, and a good one, too.

They *never* get too old to work! They can't! If they're weak or sick, they die off mostly, and the others [in the family] just go on renting and working—until they're seventy or eighty, if they live that long.

The hoeing out of the grass which endangers the growth of the young cotton plant is an arduous task which must be repeated every two weeks for a period of three months. One farmer, pointing out the grass, about a dozen blades to each cotton plant, said:

Ev'ry bit of that has to be chopped at least ev'ry two weeks. [It is a tremendous job for even 10 acres of cotton. Then there is the weed to be dealt with.] If you come across a weed growin' by yore cotton stand [plant], if the weed's higher than yore cotton stand, you don't pull up the weed! No! You figure the roots of the weed are bigger than the cotton's roots, an' you'll kill yore cotton, if you pull up the weed. So what you do is cut off the weed, an' leave it in the ground, you see? Then, the next time you come aroun' the cotton is taller than the weed, you see? So then you can pull up the weed, 'cuz yore stand of cotton is stronger than the weed.

The battle between the Weed, the Grass, and the Cotton is a death struggle, and the worker's job is a skilled and relentless one.

FEMALE AND CHILD LABOR

It is clear from the analysis presented in Chapters xii and xiii that the fundamental division of labor in Old and Rural counties is that between landlords who own most of the land and the tenants who work their farms. This division of labor is formalized by either of several types of rental agreements, involving varying degrees of subordination. While there are a few small farm-owners in these counties, the basic pattern is that of the plantation. Whatever the type of farm, however, the labor of women and children is essential to the "making" of the crop.

The hoeing of cotton, which must be repeated at intervals of two weeks during approximately three months of the growing season, and the picking, which may be repeated three or four times in a warm autumn, require a large amount of hand labor. Most of this labor is performed by the families of the tenants and small owners. In 1930 unpaid family workers amounted to 30 per cent of all agricultural workers in Old County and to 40 per cent in Rural County.[1] Since the cultivation of cotton under the present economy requires a large number of unpaid laborers, landlords are unwilling to rent to unmarried men and give preference to tenants who have a

---

[1]"The importance of women in the agriculture of the Black Belt is difficult to overestimate. One million Negro women are listed as unpaid family labor on the farm, while 11 per cent of all Negro farms are operated by women" (Rupert B. Vance, *Negro Agricultural Worker*, p. 43).

young or middle-aged wife and whose children are living with them.[2]

The value of a tenant to his landlord depends chiefly upon the size of the tenant's "squad," or household group, therefore. Both landlords and tenants bargain on the basis of this factor. A landlord considers that all the labor of a tenant's family should be used upon the cultivation of the rented tract during the growing season, and he exerts either physical or economic sanctions to compel the tenant to use this labor. Several landlords were heard to complain that the wives or children of some of their tenants were not working steadily in the fields. In such cases, the planter usually had only to reduce the tenant's credit for rations in order to compel him to use his whole family. In other cases, physical terrorization was used. Even the children might be intimidated by the planter. One landlord who was concerned about a tenant's crop at the height of the season ordered the little children of the tenant into the fields.

The interviewers were visiting a prominent planter, Mr. Curtis. As we were leaving, we met a little boy with a hoe, and a little girl carrying a baby. Curtis asked if they were the children of a tenant whose crop needed hoeing, and they said that they were. Curtis asked what they had been doing all day, and the girl said she was taking care of the baby. The boy said he hadn't been doing anything, and Curtis told him to get on out in the field and start chopping, as he had told his daddy that the cotton had to be cleaned out.

The authors met several colored tenants whose crops had been failures, they said, chiefly because their wives had been sick during the spring and summer. Among white tenants and small farmers, and among colored owners of the middle group, the sanctions of their caste or class status often prevented the use of women in the family as agricultural laborers, except in the garden or in the lighter work.

In addition to the tenants, wage-laborers, and unpaid family

[2] In Old County a man usually begins to rent a farm only after he had married; until that time, or later, he works on his parents' farm and usually receives his food, lodging, and clothes as wages from his parents.

workers, the only other aspects of the division of labor which require mention are communal labor and the supervision of labor. Several families, relatives or neighbors, usually join in the cutting, pressing, and boiling of their sugar cane and sorghum. There is a division of functions among the families—some hauling, some running the press, some tending the vats, and others pouring the syrup into cans. Each family group considers itself compensated for its labor by the labor which the other families have contributed to the total process and by the "party" or dance which usually follows the completion of the whole enterprise.

SUPERVISION OF AGRICULTURAL WORKERS

In an economy such as this one, the general pattern of the rental agreements which form the basis of the division of labor is accompanied by a general pattern of planter-tenant behavior. The actual cultivation of the cotton and subsidiary crops, the system of land tenure, and the economic requirements all influence the behavior of both the tenant and the landowner.

Although the landlord never tills the soil, plants, or plows, he may take part in the cultivation of cotton through supervision of his tenant-farmers. As we have seen, however, most of the landlords in Old County do not supervise the actual cultivation of cotton by their share-tenants, either because they are absentee-owners or because they are unwilling to perform this labor. The amount of supervision by the planter varies widely with the form of rental, size of the plantation, proximity of the landlord's residence, and other factors. One successful planter, who has 30 tenant-families on his 1,700 acres, retains a very close control over his plantation. Although he does not live on the plantation and although all the tenants are cash-renters, he advances supplies to the tenants and personally supervises the distribution of meat and groceries; he also handles all transactions and contracts with the government "for them." He makes frequent visits to each tenant, looks over his cotton, and gives him instructions if he

329

is not working the crop properly. When tenants are behind with their work, he puts day-labor in the fields and charges the wages for this labor to the account of the tenants. During the chopping period, before the crop is laid by, this planter lives on the plantation for several weeks in order to supervise the tenants more closely. When he is absent from the place, one of his colored tenants acts as foreman.

In Rural County, where there is a low rate of absentee-landlordism, planters generally spend a good deal of time during the growing season in riding over their tenant-tracts and in personally directing the work. The authors asked a landlord if it was necessary to keep after the tenants to see that they worked their crops properly, and he gave the following, typical reply:

> We always ride the fields just after they have planted to see that they put in enough acreage to make their rent. Then we ride the fields several times during the season to see that they are working the crops properly. If a tenant isn't working the crop right, we get after him and threaten to cut down on his ration-advances unless he gets busy. There are some that we don't really have to watch, as we know we can depend on them to make their crop just as well if we never see them.

The work of the half-tenants on this plantation was even more closely supervised. They worked by the bell, and their fields were ridden daily by the foreman or landlord. The organization of half-tenants and wage-laborers into gangs existed on a few plantations in Rural County and represented the highest degree of supervision. In Old County, gangs other than large family "squads" who hoed cotton together were found only at cotton-picking time. They were composed of wage-laborers, chiefly from Old City, and of tenants; and they worked under continuous supervision.

The system of land tenure, resulting in a lessor-lessee situation, carries with it certain limitations in the behavior of both planter and tenant. There is, however, a certain range of variation in this behavior which corresponds to some extent to the variations in the form of rental. Generally the tenant who works on half-shares is more directly controlled by the landlord than other tenants. Since the landlord supplies the teams and equipment, and since he receives a half of the tenant's crop, however large or small, it is to his advantage to see that the equipment is properly cared for and that the largest possible harvest is made from the crop. He therefore supervises the half-share tenants very closely, directs every stage of their cultivation, prescribes for the care of teams and equipment, and handles all legal transactions and governmental contracts pertaining to the crop. Some half-tenants, noticeably in Rural County, still "work by the bell"; that is, they are given signals to start and stop work by the plantation bell, which is rung at dawn, at noon, and at dusk. One planter said of his half-tenants: "We drive them hard, and work them by the bell from 'can to can't' [dawn until dark]."

Quarter-renters are generally not so closely supervised as are the half-renters. Since they own their stock and implements, the planter shows little interest in the care of their teams and equipment. They seldom work by the bell, and in many cases the landlord exercises only a nominal supervision of their crops, especially if he is not advancing rations for which they must pay.

Cash-tenants are generally less controlled and supervised by the landlord than any others. They pay a fixed sum of money or weight of lint as rent; they supply their own mules and implements; and often they finance themselves, so that the landlord is little concerned with their day-by-day movements. In some cases these cash-tenants are permitted to sign contracts regarding the use of the land or the production of crops without the written consent of the landowner. Under the governmental crop-control program there was some evidence of a cash-tenant's freedom in contracting with the government to reduce the acreage of his crops and in receiving rental and other subsidy payments. If the land was under the planter's close supervision, however, especially if his tenants were half- or quarter-renters, he signed the contract and listed the tenants as "interested parties." Of 1,597 heads of tenant-families in Old County in 1934, only 282 signed government contracts. Of those tenants who signed contracts, 265 were cash-tenants, while only 17 were share-renters. Since there were nearly 800 cash-tenants in the county in 1934, only about one-fourth of the total number of cash-renters were free to sign contracts. It is clear, therefore, that even the paying of a cash or fixed rent does not usually release the tenant from complete economic control by the landlord.

Tenant-managers.—Since most landlords in Old County do not personally supervise the work of their tenants, they empower an older tenant, as a straw boss, to perform this work, and usually compensate him by granting him a tract of land free of rental. The census of 1930 counted 18 farm-managers or foremen in Old County, of whom 8 were colored and 10 white; but it is certain that a great many additional colored tenants performed the work of managers without possessing the title.[3] The authors met 11 colored farm-managers and were told of others by landlords. Five of the colored managers for absentee-landlords were interviewed intensively and were found to exercise almost complete supervision over the plantations on which they lived. One of these men supervised the farms of the largest landholder in the county, made the rental agreements with tenants, hired the wage-laborers, dispossessed tenants, bought and advanced all supplies, and collected all rents. Another performed all this work and, in addition, sold the cotton and distributed the government rental and subsidy payments among the tenants. These managers for absentee-landlords actually performed all the functions of a landlord in relation to the tenants. Managers upon the plantations of resident or visiting landlords were in charge of the daily supervision of work which had been planned by the landlord, but had no control over "advancing," selling the cotton, or

[3] Across the river from Old County the use of colored farm-managers was almost universal, according to informants who had served as farm-managers there.

distributing the government subsidy payments. In other details their supervision of the labor was complete. Their landlords defined their powers in all cases, as did the planter who stated:

> That is the Negro I was telling you about who works on halves and looks after the place for me. I can depend on him to take care of everything when I am not there. Now I have him in charge of building a fence—I'm fencing off part where I can run my cattle and keep them off the rest of the place. He is looking after the work and keeps the time on the niggers working and sees that they do the job right. He has been with me about twenty-five years and acts like I belonged to him. You may have noticed how he was telling me what to do and how to do it. He plans things out and then tells me how he figures they should be done. He always speaks of the place as "ours"; and when anything is done, "we" did it.

In every case landlords stated that a complete solidarity of interest existed between them and their colored straw bosses, and emphasized the fact that the latter "knew their place" in the caste system and meticulously observed all the caste taboos.

The planter, or the foreman, seldom attempts to supervise the cultivation of any subsidiary crops except corn. Since he often receives a portion of the corn as part of the rent, he or his foreman keeps an eye on the corn crop as he makes his rounds over the fields. Other subsidiary crops, such as potatoes, peas, and cane, in the harvest of which he has no share, receive very little attention from the planter. When cotton prices are low, he may encourage his tenants to raise these food crops so that he need not advance them supplies. When the price of cotton is high, on the other hand, a landlord may discourage his tenants from planting other crops in an effort to concentrate all the land, time, and energy on the money crop. Generally, however, these subsidiary crops are the tenant's affair and have little or no place in the general planter-tenant reciprocals.

The nature of the controls which the landlord directly or indirectly exerts over his tenants will become clearer in our consideration of the systems of credit and of physical intimidation. The discipline maintained by a landlord or his foreman often reaches, in the case of half-tenants and wage-laborers, to the smallest details of the use and care of work-stock and to the actual cultivation of the crop. Landlords or foremen often demand that a definite amount of ploughing, hoeing, or picking shall be accomplished in a day, and that workers shall not smoke, gather in groups for rest periods, or devote time to the cultivation of a garden or the cutting of firewood in the midst of the cotton-growing season. Many cases of the use of physical intimidation or of economic sanctions to maintain such discipline were reported and will be cited later.

Supply of labor.—The interpretation of much of the behavior between landlords and tenants depends upon whether or not there is a surplus of agricultural labor. For this reason it is extremely important that we should determine the adequacy of the supply of labor in Old County. This question cannot be satisfactorily answered by the general testimony of planters that they had to compete for tenants. The attempt to measure the adequacy of the labor supply must be based upon the relation between the available labor supply and the amount of cultivable land in the county. There are other important considerations, such as the question of whether or not it would be profitable to use all the cultivable land and the deduction of land cultivated by wage-hands, but factors such as these cannot be defined.

The average tenant-family in Old County can cultivate only 10–15 acres of cotton. The average size of the farm (including land for other crops) which the landlord desires to rent is from 30 to 45 acres. The total number of families living on farms in Old County in 1930 was 1,984, and the total number of cultivable acres was 95,291. If all these farm-families actually cultivated the soil, there would have been available 48 acres of cultivable land per farm-family. The labor supply would then have been almost sufficient to cultivate the available land. At least a hundred of these farm-families were the families of owners who performed no agricultural labor, however.[4]

Analysis of the census figures reveals that in 1929 a cash-tenant and his family harvested, on the average, only 16 acres of land and that a share-tenant and his family harvested only 14 acres of land. It appears certain, since there were 48 acres of cultivable land available for every farm-family and 38 acres available for every family living in the rural area, that the labor supply was either barely adequate or inadequate for the landlord's desires.

During the years of low-priced cotton and reduced yields between 1933 and 1935, this shortage of labor did not become urgent. The fact that the number of tenants in the county increased by 205, however (an increase of 15.3 for every 100 tenants in 1930), during a period when many cotton counties experienced a decline in the number of tenants as a result of the government's crop-reduction system, indicated that the labor supply had been inadequate for the landlord's purposes. In the fall of 1936 incontrovertible evidence of the shortage of agricultural workers appeared. In that year, as a result of a large increase in the yield of cotton, planters in both Old and Rural counties experienced a severe shortage of labor in their attempt to harvest the crop and, according to the published reports of local county agents and planters, had to import workers in large numbers.[5] Our initial assumption (based

[4] If the labor supply is considered to be composed of (1) the families living within rural areas but not on farms (families classified under the heading "rural nonfarm" in the census) and (2) of those living on farms, the number of cultivable acres available per family was 38.

[5] It is interesting to note that Dr. John Dollard reported that his study in a Delta county, made between 1933 and the summer of 1936, had indicated that a shortage of labor existed and that this shortage probably accounted for the close "policing" of tenants by landlords. In the fall, after Dr. Dollard had left the county, the yield of cotton increased greatly in the Delta, and a serious shortage of agricultural workers arose. Planters and agricultural agents estimated that between ten and fifteen thousand additional pickers were needed in the Delta counties. Workers were imported in large numbers from Texas and Oklahoma, and law officers continued "to drag tramps from railroad boxcars, and hobo colonies, and *round up town vagrants for work in the fields*" (New Orleans *Times-Picayune*, September 23, 1936, p. 3).

upon the amount of cultivable land available per farm-family in 1930), that the supply of agricultural workers was barely adequate, has therefore been empirically confirmed, first, by the fact that there was a decided increase in the number of tenants between 1930 and 1935, although both the price of cotton and the yield were reduced, and, secondly, by the fact that a public demand for agricultural workers arose when the yield increased greatly in the fall of 1936.[6]

Competition for tenants.—With indubitable evidence of a labor shortage before us, it is possible to interpret the competition for tenants which exists between landlords and to understand the function of both the credit system and the system of physical intimidation in maintaining the supply of colored workers. It was typical of the difference between Old County, where there is an old and fairly large city, and Rural County, which has no city and only three small towns and villages, that the physical terrorization of agricultural workers should have been the accepted means of control in the latter county, whereas it was regarded by planters in Old County as a danger to the maintenance of their labor supply. A large planter in Old County, who supervised his colored tenants closely and often stopped their credit as a means of control, insisted that he had never hit one of them, for fear that he would be unable to keep enough workers. When asked if he ever had trouble and had to beat up any of his Negroes, he said: "I have never hit one. That will ruin you, because if you begin to get rough with them, the good tenants will quit you. They will tell each other, 'Better not work for him; he's li'ble to beat you up.'" Similarly, another white planter in Old County said, in the presence of the interviewer and a second planter, that he had been tempted to kill two colored tenants who, he

[6] The existence of this labor shortage, in spite of the great reduction in the size of the cotton crop since the coming of the weevil, is the result of two principal factors: (1) the large emigration of agricultural workers during the height of the boll-weevil infestation and during the period of the World War, and (2) the more intensive cultivation which has been necessary since the weevil infestation.

claimed, had deserted their crops, and also to beat two others who had overworked his stock, but that he had not done so because he was afraid he would lose his tenants. "I didn' wantuh get the reputation for bein' a bad felluh!"

In Rural County, however, as will be shown later, the beating, whipping, or shooting of agricultural workers, or the threat of such action, was constantly used to punish workers accused of stealing, deserting their crops, "impudence," or other violations of the laws of deference and to prevent the draining-off of labor. Even there, however, a tenant who had shot a white plantation-manager, who had hit him when the colored man had objected to the manager's living with his sister, had been allowed to return to the plantation by the landlord. The landlord wrote a social agency in the city to which this tenant had escaped, saying that, although the tenant and his family were "bad niggers always making trouble," they could return because he needed "hands for cotton-picking."

Other evidence of the competition for tenants in Rural County appeared in a large landlord's effort to have his brother made supervisor of labor, including his tenants, on a C.W.A. road-building project, so that his brother could "keep our tenants close to home and they wouldn't get to working on the other side of the county." Additional factors in landlord-tenant relations, which were based upon the competition for tenants, were (1) the landlords' practice of not allowing tenants to think they were short of money ("Never let your tenants think you are broke or they will quit"), (2) competing with other landlords in the amount of supplies furnished a tenant on credit, and (3) the practice of taking another landlord's tenant, in spite of the unwritten law among landlords that a tenant could not move to a new landlord's farm unless his present landlord gave his permission and the new landlord paid his debts.

There was also evidence that the landlord group had opposed the admission into Old County of factories and industrial establishments and that this opposition had increased as a result of the opening of the sawmills, which paid workers $1.25 and $1.50 per day, and had thus greatly reduced the supply of agricultural workers who are willing to work for a wage of $0.75 per day.

Agricultural labor supply and the migration of workers.—The fact that there has been a shortage of agricultural workers in Old and Rural counties in recent years, in spite of the great reduction of the cotton crop since the advent of the boll weevil in 1908, has been the result (1) of the emigration of large numbers of agricultural workers from the county since 1908 and (2) of the increased amount of labor required per acre for the cultivation of cotton since the weevil infestation. Before studying the operation of the cotton economy in periods when there has been a great emigration of workers from the counties, it will be necessary to consider the intracounty migration of workers from one plantation to another. Although data are not available to enable us to measure the rate of this migration, it appears certain that it is relatively high in Old County and relatively low in Rural County. The factors involved are closely related to the competition which has existed between landlords for tenants. Those landlords who have the reputation of furnishing more credit than their neighbors, of dealing more honestly in the settlement of accounts at the end of the season, and of avoiding the use of physical violence appeared to have little difficulty in keeping the same tenants over a long period of years. A very large landholder in Rural County attributed the low rate of migration among his tenants to the fact that he did not cheat them in the settlement of accounts.

We have comparatively little moving about of the tenants. I suppose we have about three squads move a year out of sixty on the plantation, and for every three who move we have a dozen others wanting to get on our places. We haven't enough cabins to use all who want to come on our places. If you treat Negroes right you don't have any trouble with them moving, but if you don't treat them fair they will know it, and will always be moving. You will find that is always true of them, and the places where they are cheated are the places where they never stay long, and give trouble.

According to a large planter in Old County, the landlords who dealt more justly with their tenants in settlements attracted the more efficient and stable workers, whereas those who had a reputation for stealing from tenants and "working them naked" experienced a high labor-turnover. ("They are always having to get new tenants, as the good ones won't stay long with them.") The same experience was reported by a very large planter in Rural County, who stated, with regard to the geographical mobility of his tenants: "They move about very little if you treat them right. The Negro loves his home and doesn't want to leave it." A very efficient colored plantation-manager, who was highly regarded by his tenants, both on account of his fair dealing and his high status in the local church and benefit society, likewise insisted that he had had no difficulty in keeping the same tenants over a period of years. "We doan have no trouble keepin' dem! Naw sah! They worry me to death to stay, an' people always comin' to me to ass me tuh let um rent from me!"

It has already been shown that a large proportion of the colored farm-owners in Old County are individuals who formerly were slaves in the same county or are the descendants of such individuals. There is agreement among landlords in both counties that there is also a large number of tenant-families which have been on one plantation for a long period of years.

A large colored landowner in Old County stated that there was a type of older colored tenant who had rented from one landlord all his life and who had the same permanent, semi-familial relationship with the landlord which the colored nurses and house servants often enjoyed. Such tenants stayed on one plantation as long as they could pay the rent, for they regarded it as their home. One of the largest white landowners in Rural County stated that he had a great many colored tenants of this type, who stayed upon his plantation because they regarded it as their home. There was never any question of their being released from the payment of rent, however, no matter how many years they remained; the payment of rent was as unquestioned a part of the economic relationship as were the patriarchal functions of the landlord and the necessity for raising cotton.

In Rural County, where there were no large towns and where the plantation system was more closely organized than in Old County, white landlords generally testified to the existence of a large number of colored tenants who seldom moved. A large white landlord in that county, who had owned his plantation before the Civil War, stated that the members of the same tenant-families had been on his plantation for generations. "They never leave the place, and new ones almost never come." White people in both counties—not all of them members of old landowning families—were fond of emphasizing the attachment of colored tenants to specific plantations; in many cases, no doubt, the statement was chiefly an expression of the patriarchal ideal of the loyalty of retainers and servants. The actual motivation of such tenants may often be economic, however. Several white individuals insisted, for example, that colored tenants had refused to leave the island plantations on which they had long been tenants, even when most of the land had been flooded over a period of several years. The white manager of the island plantations, who knew the situation at first hand, however, stated that his colored tenants had remained on the flooded islands "because they make fine crops when they do get a good year," and that they believed it profitable to remain there, working as timber-cutters and fishermen, until such a good cotton year came.

In spite of the existence of a more stable type of tenant, there was undoubtedly a large amount of interplantation movement in both Rural and Old counties. A somewhat cynical worker, who had lived in Old County for more than sixty years, explained this movement on the basis of the cheating of tenants by landlords: "Ev'ry year you see dem, whites too, packin' up on uh ol' wagon an' movin' somewhere else. Dis man done stole frum dem an' dey goin' tuh anuthuh ———— tuh let him steal frum dem! Dey ben doin' dat all dey lives!"

Many tenants moved to another plantation, no doubt, in order to rent more fertile land or to secure a better cabin or equipment; but one of the largest planters in Old County had observed the seemingly paradoxical fact that the colored tenants were most likely to move when they had enjoyed a profitable year.

> Yes, I think the Negroes move most when times are good and they are making money; they seem to feel that if they make money one year they must move on or the landlord will get it all back the next. We have had lots of them move off with hogs, cows, corn, and potatoes that they had accumulated in a good year, and then the next year they would come back to us with nothing left. Of course, a lot of our Negroes have been here for years and they have learned how that is, and when some Negro wants to move they tell him he had better stay here or he will come back with nothing.

The same fact has been remarked by students of other cotton counties and has been attributed by them to the colored individual's desire to assert his recently acquired right to geographical mobility. Although the explanation carries some weight in view (1) of the restriction placed upon such movement during the periods of chattel slavery, (2) of the operation of the Black Code which followed emancipation, and (3) of the widespread system of debt-peonage which existed up to the time of the weevil infestation, it is only a partial explanation. White tenants likewise frequently move after a profitable year. The planter last quoted stated that the turnover was relatively greater among his white tenants than among his colored and that "none of them won't settle any place long." It appears justifiable, therefore, to relate this behavior of tenants chiefly to their economic and occupational subordination to the landlord group: (1) to the operation of the lien laws and the system of debt-peonage which, until recent years, has bound the white, as well as the colored, tenant to one plantation over long periods, and (2) to the fear of the tenant that the landlord will actually find means to prevent the tenant's receiving a profit from his work in the following year. Among colored tenants this economic motivation may have been intensified by their knowledge of the historical processes leading to the abolition of the taboos formerly placed upon geographical mobility; but it is impossible to demonstrate such a motivation, since it involves a genetic process over a long period of years. One is unable to know, for example, whether the colored tenant who made the following statement was motivated by a revolt against the caste controls or against the economic peonage which has been basic in the tenant system or by a revolt against both. Mr. Rawls, who had rented here for eleven years, said:

> I don' lak to move. That's one thing I hates to do—move. An' I bin gettin' along pretty well here, so I ain't moved. A lot o' people won't stay on eny place mo'n one yeah. But I ain't nevah bin dat way. I don' b'lieve in movin' ev'ry yeah, lak a lot o' people. But if I tek a mine teh move, I tell you one thing—ain't nobody kin *stop* me! If I mek up my mine tuh move, I'm goin! Don't keer ef it's in de rain. I'll go in de rain; don' pay it no mine. Pull up er wagon, an' put ev'ry stick in heah in it, an' go!

The study of the social and economic systems operating at the time of our study indicates that migration, like most other types of behavior within the cotton economy, is characteristic of members of both castes. It seems clear, therefore, that explanations based upon caste status need be sought only when there is a widespread difference between the behavior of the two castes within the same economic group. It seems no more requisite to attribute the geographical mobility of colored farm-tenants chiefly to their caste condition than it does to attribute the wholesale moving of colored tenants in New Orleans and Chicago, at two definite periods in the year, to caste-conditioning. Since white tenants in these areas likewise often move, economic factors seem largely adequate to explain similar behavior of all tenants.

CHAPTER XV

FINANCING THE PRODUCTION OF COTTON

PRODUCING a cotton crop requires more than land and labor, supervision and equipment. It also demands either capital or credit. Like most businessmen, cotton-producers become largely dependent upon credit. Although the cost of producing cotton is spread over a period of eight or nine months, the income from it is generally received in one payment. As a result of the small income of the average cotton-farmer and the recurrence of years of deflated prices, most cotton-farmers in Old and Rural counties need to be financed over a period of from five to eight months in order to produce their crops. This credit has been furnished by means of a simple, but frequently abused, mechanism known as the "advance business." Any cotton-farmer who lacks the capital necessary to finance his crop can mortgage the ungrown crop and his livestock to a landowner or merchant. The landowner or merchant then advances to the farmer, from time to time, whatever food, seed, and other supplies are needed to support him and to "make" the crop. When the crop is sold, the mortgager is repaid his loans with interest, and the farmer receives the balance.

The advance business is therefore something of a gamble: advances are made against a nonexistent crop, and the mortgager risks a loss in case of crop failure or of a decline in the cotton market. For this reason, credit is usually kept down to a minimum until the season is far enough advanced to enable the mortgager to estimate the probable size of the crop and its value. Such a system of credit can exist only in an economy where there is a reasonable expectancy of producing the crop and of obtaining a market for it when produced.

Because almost all merchants have discontinued the furnishing of supplies to farmers on credit since the boll weevil, the landlords in both counties now are compelled to furnish credit to practically all their tenants. As the system now operates, it is regarded by both tenants and landlords as equivalent to the payment of wages by the landlord to the tenant over the period of four to five months, from March or April to July, when the planting and cultivating of cotton takes place. Legally, however, these payments are secured by the tenant's crop and livestock, and the landlord is entitled to collect his loans from the proceeds of the crop. Since the landlords sell the cotton raised by all tenants in Old and Rural counties, with the exception of a relatively small number among the cash-tenants, the landlord is certain to regain his money with interest unless he has advanced more than the crop is worth.

The tenant receives the loans in the form of food or in cash which he must spend for food. In order to understand the operation of the advance system, one must realize that most tenants earn only enough money from their year's work to enable them to live during one-half of the year. Each fall they are compelled to sell not only their cotton but also most of their food crops, in order to repay the loans which have enabled them to live while they were "making" a crop from March to September. What little money is left will enable them to live only until the late winter or early spring, when they again must begin to buy food on borrowed money. The agricultural system, furnishing an inadequate basis for the small farmer, operates in such a way that he is compelled to sell his food crops in the autumn, when the supply is greatest and the price lowest, and to buy food, with money borrowed at a high rate of interest, in the spring and summer, when the price is highest. As one tenant, referring to the sale of his cane syrup, peas, and corn, phrased it:

Now, they woan want tuh giv' me mo'n fifty cent a gallon fur dis here at de sto's. Den dey sells it fur a dollah latuh awn. Dey keeps it tell de spring, yuh see. An' ef yuh buys it awn allowance, dey doan charge no less den uh dollah an' a qua'tuh, nawsuh. Dat's right. Dat's whut yuh got tuh pay.

Now, yuh tek peas. Dey gives yuh only thirty-five cent uh bushel now; but w'en yuh buy dem back in de wintuh an' spring, dey charge yuh ovuh a dollah. Dat's de way dey do. Dey buys em up an' keeps dem, den dey sells um back to yuh fuh thruble de price. Same way wid cawn, same way! Yuh jus' gits forty cent uh bushel fuh cawn w'en yuh sells it now; but w'en yuh buys it back in de spring, dey charges yuh uh dollah 'n uh quahtuh or a dollah 'n uh ha'f a bushel.

Security for advances.—The small amount of livestock and farm equipment which the average tenant owns and which, together with his crop, is legal security for the loans made to him by the landlord or merchant is often seized by the landlord when the value of the tenant's crop is insufficient to pay his debts. Two colored landlords repeated, in detail, stories of how they had seized the livestock of colored tenants who had not been able to repay loans. One had seized all of a female tenant's cattle, eight head, on which he had bills of sale, and put them into his cattle lot; he stated that he had later returned two of the cows when the woman had pleaded that she and her children had been living chiefly on the milk from these cows. The other colored landlord related how he had seized a tenant's cow, without having a lien.

You know I advanced a man $200, and he didn't pay me back, and I didn't have eny bill uh sale on his stuff, either. He had just two cows, and I knew it would cost me more to get an attachment on them than the ol' cows were worth. I didn't know what to do. So I just took a chance, an' went up there an' got one of the cows when he wasn't there (*laughing*), an' took it home with me! I didn't know what he'd do, but I had him. He'd have to pay a lawyer to get it away from me, then. I had him where he'd had me. But you know that man came *runnin'* to me and said: "Oh, please don't take my other one!" (*laughing*).

It was typical of the losses which landlords sustained in making advances during the period of low prices from 1932 to 1934, however, that in all five of the cases of seizure related by these two planters the value of the seized cattle or mules was far less than the debt incurred by the tenant.

White landlords, who can invoke the caste sanctions of the courts and of physical violence, are usually thoroughly protected in the loans they make to colored tenants. One large white planter, speaking of the rental agreements made by another white planter with his colored cash-tenants, concluded: "He is perfectly safe, as they [tenants] have to pay the cash, or give him a mortgage." This same landlord, when asked if the mules used by his colored tenants belonged to them, answered: "The Negroes think they belong to them, but I have mortgages on them, and they are just the same as mine."

The function of the courts in securing the payment of debts of tenants to planters was explained by a justice of the peace in Old City. A merchant asked him how he could collect money owed him by two colored tenants, whose wives claimed all the mules and implements on their farms. The justice of the peace gave him a judgment against the colored tenants for the amounts he claimed, and then explained that he could collect it as soon as the tenants mortgaged their (wives') mules.

As soon as the Negroes started to make a crop of cotton, they would need credit and would give a mortgage on the mules. As soon as they signed a mortgage, that showed the mules werè theirs; then he could collect his money. Well, not long after, the merchant came in and said the Negroes had moved to Blanton's place and I told him I knew he would get his money as Blanton would demand a mortgage before he would let them have anything. I told the merchant to wait awhile and then go down and see if they hadn't given Blanton a mortgage, and sure 'nough that was what happened.

The planter paid the merchant's claims, with interest, and charged the sums against the crops of the two tenants.

The caste system facilitates the collection of loans made to colored tenants. The white landlord can employ threats of physical violence to force payment, or he can seize the colored tenant's property without fear of being sued by the tenant. Even in the operation of the federal government's plan of subsidy payments, the caste sanctions were invoked by a government official to aid landlords and merchants to collect their loans. This man stated that in one of the counties he had made a practice of turning over a colored farmer's payments to the landlord or merchant who held a lien on the farmer's crop, and that, even when no lien existed to justify such a procedure, he had told colored farmers that they must pay the landlord or merchant out of the government check. He took the initiative in establishing this system, by asking all those individuals who made advances to "look over the list of [government] contracts and mark the ones who owe them."

Advances by landlords.—Before the boll weevil, advances were usually made by merchants rather than by landlords. The plague of the weevil made the advance business unprofitable, however. With the withdrawal of merchants from the farm-credit business in Old County the landlords have had to assume the responsibility of furnishing credit to almost all of their tenants. Since the banks were unwilling to lend money to most landlords between 1932 and 1935, and since both the yield and price of cotton were low, landlords supplied only a minimum amount of food on credit to each tenant. They were compelled to furnish some credit, however, in order to obtain tenants, for one of the chief grounds of competition between landlords was the amount of credit which they were able to offer a tenant. In spite of the fact that during the years when our study was made the federal government assumed part of this burden by furnishing crop-production loans[1] to those tenants whose landlords would waive first claim to their crop, it was still necessary for landlords to furnish credit to practically all of their half-tenants and quarter-tenants and to most of their cash-tenants. The only landlords who did not supply credit to their cash-tenants were (1) those who owned the best land and (2) those whose plantations were close enough to Old City to allow their cash-tenants to peddle vegetables or to obtain seasonal work there.

[1] In 1933 approximately 200, or about 12.5 per cent of the farm-operators in Old County, received crop-production loans from the federal government.

There were three methods by which landlords in Old and Rural counties advanced food and other supplies to their tenants. Some plantations supported a plantation store, managed by a relative of the landlord or by a colored foreman, for which the planter bought food and clothing at wholesale. He then sold this stock to the tenants on credit at retail prices, with interest charges of 10 per cent or higher. This system was explained by a planter in Rural County, who with several brothers operated such a plantation store:

> The way we work it is this: Leonard [a brother] has his office and the Negroes come in to it. . . . . If they want stuff from the store, Leonard gives them an order and they take it to the store, and Jack hands out the goods. Then at night we get together, and Jack brings in all his orders and they all go over the books. We handle it just like a bank. In a lot of the business no money changes hands at all.

At times when there was no commissary, the planter bought food from a wholesale store and distributed it himself to the tenants once every week or two. As a third alternative, the planter could send the tenants to a store at which he had credit, with a written order for certain rations. In all cases the planter kept a close watch on the amount of advances to each tenant and refused to advance any tenant more than the crop appeared to be worth.

Advances were made to tenants only during the period of ploughing, planting, and cultivating, which lasted from March or April to July. During this period of about four months tenant-families on the larger plantations in Old County received credit ranging from $2.50 to $5.00 per week; the customary allowance on most plantations did not exceed $3.00 per week.[2] On the larger plantations in Rural County, on the other hand, tenant-families received credit to the extent of only $1.00 or $1.50 per week.

[2] Twenty large planters, or their managers, stated the amount of credit advanced to their tenants. A larger number stated the amount of food supplied; this evidence will be summarized in connection with our description of the standard of living of farmers.

FINANCING PRODUCTION OF COTTON

The total amount of credit allowed a tenant-family in Old County for the entire season was usually about $100; but in some areas, where the security offered by the tenant was exceptional, it amounted to as much as $200 per season. In Rural County most tenants on the larger plantations received credit to the amount of not more than $60 during the entire season.

The general practice in regard to the amount of credit furnished to tenants in Old County was summarized by the bookkeeper of a large truck-farmer, whose advances to tenants were several times as great as those of any cotton-farmer in the county. "We advance them for food from $2.50 to $5.00 per week, and allow extra for clothes when they need them. *Other planters usually only allow about a fourth as much as we do;* they can't advance more than that and get their money back." The greater bargaining-power of the white tenant was evidenced by the fact that the average amount of credit furnished to white tenants on this large truck farm, where most of the white tenants in the county were concentrated, was larger by more than one-third than the average allowance to colored tenants.

They [white tenants] are always wanting more than the Negroes. We advance them just the same for food. We base that on the size of the squad [family]. But the white tenants are always wanting silk stockings for their wives, and print-dresses, and things like that, and if you tell them you can't advance any more, they will probably just pick up and move out on you.

Decline in advances.—Every landlord and manager interviewed in both counties insisted that it was possible for the landlord to make a profit only if he "held the tenants down" in their demands for credit. During the years of low yield and low price from 1932 to 1935, many landlords claimed that they had been unable to collect a large proportion of the loans which they had furnished to their tenants and that they had therefore been compelled to reduce the amount of supplies advanced to an absolute minimum. The relief administrator of Old County repeated the testimony of many of the planters: "For several years now, the price of cotton has been so low that the tenants have all gotten deep in debt, and never have paid up. Now, with low prices [and yields] and a debt of several years' standing, the planters only advance bare subsistence rations." It was absolutely necessary, however, to keep the tenant and his family-laborers alive during the period of cultivation and to replace outworn machinery and implements and to buy mules. A large colored planter stated that he could not afford to make even the small advances he was allowing his tenants but that it was necessary to buy equipment for some of them, and that most of them were "so poor, and ragged, and hungry that it's hard to deny them something. If they ever make anything, you know you'll get it back."

Landlords' profits on advances.—Even during this period, however, it was established that the larger planters made a profit on the supplies furnished to tenants. An individual who was in an excellent position to know the credit operations of a large planter in Old County stated that he charged tenants exorbitant prices for goods supplied by his plantation store, in addition to interest at the rate of 10 per cent every four or five months. A large planter in Rural County stated that even "in the last few years" his brother had made a living from the plantation store. "We try to put the prices so as to cover losses from bad accounts."[3]

Cheating the tenant on advances.—Although landlords claimed that only a relatively small number of landlords cheated tenants in furnishing them supplies or in deducting the value of advances from the value of the tenant's share of the cotton, it appeared from certain evidence which came to light that such practises were extremely common in both of the counties studied.

[3] The statement was made generally by both planters and tenants that very large profits were made by landlords on credit furnished to tenants during relatively prosperous years and that landlords encouraged tenants to accept a large amount of credit and to buy silk dresses, automobiles, and even pianos at such times, so as to increase the landlord's profits on advances and to maintain their supply of workers by placing them in debt to the landlord.

FINANCING PRODUCTION OF COTTON

One large planter in Rural County attributed the existence of a large number of landlords who stole from their tenants to the difficulty of raising cotton profitably otherwise, under the present economy.

The only way a man can make money from farming is by stealing it from the Negroes, or by living close. Some people get ahead by living close and saving every cent, and then there are lots that steal from the Negroes. Some of them will take everything a Negro has, down to his last chicken and hog.

A businessman, in one of the counties, whose business furnished him with a close knowledge of the credit dealings of most landlords and tenants in the county, stated that "practically all landlords" cheated their tenants in "one way or another."

A colored man in Old County, who had had wide experience with the larger planters and with a great many tenants over a period of forty years, stated that the devices of overcharging tenants for supplies, and of charging them for supplies which they had not received, were still general on the rich-land plantations, as a means of keeping laborers in debt-peonage. He cited the cases of various very large planters who advanced the colored tenants money out of the tenants' proceeds from their own crop and then charged the tenants interest of 25 per cent on their own money.

Take————one of the biggest planters and one of the worst! Those tenants of his never have been out of debt in their lives. He just keeps them there year after year by debt-peonage. Here's what he did to a tenant whom I know—we'll call him John. John made 9 large bales of cotton. The planter takes it all and tells John he's holding it in his warehouse. That's a trick a lot of them use to beat the Negro out of all of his cotton. He told John he owed $200 for the year's advances. Now John's already given him 9 bales, but John never heard any more about those 9 bales. Well, about Christmas, or before, John tells him he'd like to get a little money to buy his wife and children some clothes and shoes. He tells John: "Why certainly you can have it. Nobody there has ever refused you any money when you asked for it, have they?" Well, John gets a little money then, and maybe a little more, once or twice afterward. You see John thinks this is his own money, part of what's coming to him from his 9 bales of cotton. And the planter let's him think that. But what does he find next time he asks the planter about his cotton money? He finds that he has the money down against him as an advance, and has charged him 25 cents on every dollar of it!

And there's nothing he can do. Even if he can read and write, as most of them can't, he knows he dare not dispute the planter or he'll get shot or beaten. He knows it's out of the question to go to court against him. And no other landlord will rent to him if this planter doesn't want him to leave. That's a universal rule among these planters. None of them will take a tenant unless the landlord he's been renting from is willing for him to go. Besides, John can't leave and nobody can move him away until his debt in the books is paid.

The advance system operates in such cases, in conjunction with the sanctions of caste, to maintain the landlord's supply of laborers and to extend his control over his tenants. It is only one aspect of the system of economic and social controls which helps maintain a supply of workers. It is important to examine this system of controls in greater detail.

ECONOMIC CONTROLS

Before and after the weevil.—There is incontrovertible evidence that before the arrival of the boll weevil the operation of the advance system, under a state law which provided that the tenant's crop and property were security for his debts, had reduced many tenants in both counties to a condition of debt-peonage.[4] The tenant, kept in debt by the honest or dishonest operation of the advance system, could move only

---

[4] A contributing factor was the passage of a state law compelling landowners to build fences around their pasture land. This law seems to have forced landlords to charge a pasture rent in order to pay for the fencing. At any rate, tenants were charged a pasture rent. Since most of them were unable to pay such a rent, they were compelled to stop raising cattle, which had formerly offered a means of obtaining ready cash. The effect of this law, therefore, was to compel the tenant to depend almost entirely upon advances from the merchant or landlord. The tightening of the economic controls upon the tenant at this period seems also to have led to a one-crop agriculture, for the merchant and landlord insisted upon the tenant's planting cotton as security for his debts. Before the passage of the law, according to informants, most farmers raised larger amounts of corn, cowpeas, and other food and feed crops than they did in the period which followed.

if a new landlord would pay his debts or if his stock, furniture, and machinery were sufficient to meet these obligations. In either case, he was immediately plunged into debt to the new landlord. The sanctions of physical violence and of legal subordination provided by the caste system bulwarked this structure of debt-peonage. Landlords in Rural County stated that they had "sold" colored tenants to planters in the Mississippi Delta between 1909 and 1911. A colored informant in Old County, who had seen the operation of the advance system before the arrival of the boll weevil, stated that debt-peonage had been widespread.

The control which the advance merchant exerted over the owners and tenants during the same period was almost equally stringent, it appears. A merchant-planter in a neighboring county stated that one firm of merchants, who still operated in several counties in the state, had "controlled all of the county" before the weevil came. The firm insisted upon taking a mortgage not only upon the farmer's crop but upon his real and personal property as well. "Nobody could sell uh thing, hardly do a thing, without them knowin' about it first."

Today, merchants exert little control over tenants in Old County with regard either to the tenant's management of his farm or his ability to move. In Rural County and in the Delta regions across the river, however, where merchants still furnish credit to a large number of farmers, they dictate the size of the acreage to be planted and control the sale of the crop.

The landlord's economic control of his tenants.—In both Old and Rural counties the economic control exercised by landlords over the tenants to whom they furnish credit is still well-nigh absolute.[5] It extends to the management of the

[5] The supervision by the planter of the tenants to whom he advances supplies has been incorporated in the local administration of the government crop loans. The agent for the government in Old County indicated the value of the caste sanctions in his supervision of the work of colored borrowers: "Yes, the loans are being paid up mighty well; they haven't lost anything yet in this county. I

tenant's work, the ability of the tenant to move, the food he eats, the clothes he wears, and often to the securing of a physician when some member of his family is ill and to the burial of those who die. In the case of all half-tenants and quarter-tenants, and of the majority of the cash-tenants, the landlord not only issues rations but also sells all the cotton. Even when the landlord deals honestly in settling accounts with his tenants, the basic income of most tenants is so small that they must continue to borrow from their landlords, season after season. A large white landlord's explanation of the continual economic dependence of the tenant upon his landlord had general validity. He stated that the average tenant-family received only about $50 clear of expenses at the end of the season and that by Christmas they were penniless.

I usually figure it costs about $10 to $12 a month to supply the average squad. Of course it depends on how many are in the family, but that is about the average for a squad of five or six. Now, that doesn't give them much except meal, lard, molasses, and salt meat. That means that by the time they get the crop out they owe me $80 to $100 for advances, and about $100 rent, which means that by the end of the season they owe me around $200. With 10-cent cotton, it takes about 4 bales to pay me off. If they make 5 bales, which is about average, it means they will end the season with about $50 cash.

When asked if that carried them until the next season started, he said: "They are usually broke in a week and are asking me for Christmas money. I don't know how they get along, as I don't advance any more until cultivating and planting starts again." The tenants on this plantation fared even better than most tenants, for the records of the Agricultural

---

am their agent in this county, and I keep my eye on things. Of course, I don't bother much with the white borrowers, but I keep right after the Negroes. I look over their places and see that they are working their crops, and keep right behind them, and they are all paying off in good shape. I can't do that with the whites, so I never bother with them unless the Riverdale office asks me to do something. You can't go and tell the whites what they have to do the way you can Negroes."

Adjustment Administration, covering the production of farmers from 1928 to 1932, inclusive, and the production allotments for 1933 reveal that the average income of tenants from cotton was little more than $100. It is clear, therefore, that most tenants not only had no net profit at the end of the season but were still in debt to their landlords.

The control exercised over his tenants by the white landlord, who could avail himself of the caste sanctions of the law and of physical violence to reinforce his economic control, was described by a colored landlord as it exists today.

I tell you these poor devils who are dependent on the white man around here are pitiable, pitiable! You can't know what they have to take. It's the Negroes who are renting from the white man or working for him, the ones who get credit from him, and are in debt to him all their lives— they're the ones whose lot is something you can't imagine. The white man will treat you and me all right, you see. They treat me and other Negroes here like me all right. They'll say we're fine, fine. That's because our dealings with them are in business, you see; and we go in and pay cash, and get what we like and come out, and the thing's over with. But the Negro who's down, and has to go to them for credit, those Negroes down there [*pointing to the floor*] are just the same as his slaves. The South won the war [Civil]. Before the war, they owned the Negro as a slave, and had to feed him and clothe him, and pay for medical attention for him, because a slave was worth money. Now, they have him still in economic slavery, and they don't have to feed him, or clothe him or pay a doctor when he's sick! Oh, I know what these Negroes go through around here, and it's terrible, I tell you!

The operation of such economic control by the planter was observed upon the plantation of a large white landowner. In the issuing of supplies to his tenants, this planter allowed rations for only one week to a tenant who had not used his family in his fields, whereas he furnished rations for two weeks to the other tenants. He warned the tenant in question that he would receive no more supplies until his crop was in satisfactory condition.

The use of the advance system by landlords so as to discipline tenants "through their stomachs" was most clearly explained by a large white planter in Old County.

My father taught me how to handle the Negroes. He knew just how to manage them; he was an overseer on a big plantation. He always told me to handle them through their stomachs. As long as they are poor they are all right, but as soon as they get some money they get uppity. When one starts getting smart on my place, I can just tell him to behave or get out. *If they won't act right, I can cut off the rations, and they quiet down.*

A colored landlord gave detailed evidence of cases of economic peonage in Old County. In one such case, which occurred in 1934, a white planter refused to allow the wife of a colored tenant to move, because he claimed that her deceased husband had owed him $300.

The woman is a good worker herself, but she has two sons on a place near there, and Billups [the white landlord] figured that by holding the mother, he could make these sons move on *his* place, and work out this $300. He knew they were good workers and he wanted them. But the two sons refused to move.

The interviewer then asked how it happened that a "good tenant," of whom the landlord had thought highly, and whose wife had been able to make a crop by herself (as had been stated by the informant), was $300 in debt at the end of the year.

They *were* good tenants. But that doesn't make any difference. You don't get any more by being a good tenant! Grosvenor still takes it all and charges them besides! If he [the tenant] makes 10 bales, give him 2; and if he makes 20 bales, you still give him 2! They all do it. I do it myself—some of these things. It's just the same everywhere. The tenant is helpless—so you know these landlords are going to take what they want. How can the tenant get his share? Most of them can't read or write. They can't sell their own cotton. They don't know what it brings. They can't dispute the landlord's word, if he's white, and they can't move if they owe him. Even if they don't owe him, another landlord won't take them unless the one they're renting from is willing for him to go.[6]

---

[6] The informant also related the case of three colored men from Old County who had recently worked as tenants in the Mississippi Delta. They had been refused a settlement of accounts by their white landlords, in spite of the fact that balances of several hundred dollars were owed each tenant. When they had tried to leave the plantations, their implements and furniture had been

The economic control exercised by the colored landlord over his tenants is less effective than that of the white landlord, for several reasons. He cannot employ the threat of physical violence to prevent his tenants from leaving; he is in an inferior bargaining position, as compared with the more wealthy and powerful white landlords in obtaining tenants; and he cannot be so certain as the white landlord of obtaining judgments in court against his tenants. Colored landlords stated that, although most of their tenants were constantly in debt to them, they moved to other plantations whenever they wished.

The effectiveness of the caste sanctions in establishing the economic control of the planter or merchant over colored farmers was indicated by the statement of a large merchant and cotton-buyer that colored farmers paid their debts much more readily than did white farmers.

> Negroes are the best people to do business with, much better than the poor-whites. White tenants will scheme every way possible to beat you out of anything they can get, and will never pay what they owe unless you force them. But Negroes will pay their debts every time if they have the money; they don't try to get away with things the way whites will do

When asked if the Negroes were more honest, or if it was just more possible to force them to pay, since they were afraid not to, he said: "Of course that may have something to do with it, but just the same, the Negroes are much better to deal with. My mother has a lot of small rental property in town, and when it is filled with Negroes it is just a gold mine!"

Keeping the tenant in debt.—In times when the income of tenants is relatively high, the advance system is used by landlords in such a way as to keep the tenant still in debt, and therefore unable to move. Statements to this effect were made by many landlords, merchants, and tenants. One of the largest

---

seized by the landlords. One tenant tried to bring suit through a white lawyer in Old City to obtain the money owed to him. Although the tenant possessed receipted bills for all advances made to him ($75) and gin receipts for 10 bales of cotton (over $500), the white lawyer had refused to take the case.

landlords in Old County explained the operation of the system of economic control most frankly.

> To tell you the truth, when prices are high and they are making good crops, we help them spend their money. When I see one is going to have a good crop, I will suggest that he get a new buggy or new furniture, and give him the cash to get them with. That way we sort of direct their spending so it isn't just wasted. Also, we might as well get it as anyone else, because they will spend it anyway.

Jim, the colored farm-manager, was called upon for corroboration.

> Jim, here, is a mighty good farmer. He took over that place of mine and worked it intensively, and the first year he made 40 bales at 25 cents a pound. He sure had plenty of money that year, and so did the tenants. We sold them lots of autos then, didn't we, Jim?
>
> "Yas, *suh*. Ev'ry one o' th' boys had uh car. There's still five sittin' roun' the place, but th' rest o' them we threw in the bayou when they wasn' no more good."

With the same motives, a large merchant in Rural County explained, he had allowed tenants to take a barrel of pork on credit before the weevil, because he wanted them to be in debt to him at the end of the season. "In this way," he pointed out, "we could manage them. *Now*, we don't like it, because if they get behind it's hard for them to pay out."

This practice of encouraging tenants to accept enough credit to keep them in debt to the landlord or merchant not only increased the profits of this group in times of high prices and good yields but also assured to them, under the operation of the lien laws, a permanent supply both of workers and of borrowers.

CHAPTER XVI

INCOME FROM COTTON

DISTRIBUTION OF INCOME

THE question of the income of cotton-producers has been treated less adequately by students of the cotton economy than has any other aspect of the system. Cotton-farmers themselves, as well as students of the question, undoubtedly tend to represent the average rate of net profit of both owners and tenants as being less than it actually is. This tendency results chiefly from the failure to consider two essential facts in computing the average rate of profit: (1) variation in the price and yield of cotton over a period of years, and (2) the ratio of the farmer's net profit to his total invested capital.

A study of incomes in Old County, taking these factors into account, revealed wide differentials incident to caste position and to control of land. These are clearly revealed by an examination of the income from cotton of the production groups defined in chapter xiv.[1]

[1] The variation in the gross income of farmers from cotton, within the five-year period for which we have records of production, will become clearer if we examine Table 12. In using the definitions of income given there, however, it is necessary to remember three important limitations:

1. The amounts of cotton and their value represent the gross production and income of farmers, within each of the nine groups. In the case of tenants, the value of the rental has not been deducted; in the case of landlords, the tenant's share of the crop has not been deducted. As we proceed with our effort to define "net incomes," these deductions will be made.

2. The gross income represented in the table is that for cotton only and does not include the gross value of other produce sold or consumed on the farm. In view of the facts (a) that cotton is the chief source of income for the great majority of farmers in Old County, (b) that the sample is composed entirely of farmers whose chief investment is in cotton, and (c) that the field evidence shows that neither landlords nor tenants in Old County receive any appreciable part of their cash income from the sale of cattle, truck, or forage crops, however,

Gross incomes by castes.—Nine-tenths of the colored farmers (90 per cent) fell in the lowest three groups (I, II, III), whereas less than one-half of the white farmers were in these groups. The maximum income for these groups was $204 in 1928 and $63 in 1932. On the other hand, one-fifth (20 per cent) of the white farmers were in the three highest groups, producing from over 40 bales to over 160 bales of cotton, resulting in a minimum income from cotton of $4,080 in 1928 and of $1,260 in 1932. Only two colored farmers (0.4 per cent) were in these three highest-income groups (VII, VIII, IX).

Gross income by tenure groups.—Nearly all (93.3 per cent) of the 248 cash-tenants in the sample fell in the three lowest groups (I, II, III), having a yearly average production of not more than 8 bales of cotton. Of the owners, 63.2 per cent fell in these three lowest groups, indicating that the bulk of the small owners had approximately the same income as the majority of the tenants. The distribution of owners and tenants in the groups is shown by Table 15.

Net incomes of landlords, 1928–32.—The rate of profit of landlords is the most controversial question which one has to face in a study of the agricultural cotton economy. Almost without exception, landlords and their families in both counties insisted that cotton-planting under the tenant system of labor was unprofitable to the landlord, that the landlord steadily lost money and eventually his land,[2] and that in most

---

these figures may be regarded as a close approximation of the limits of the gross cash income of the autonomous cotton-farmers.

3. The sample includes only those 556 owners and tenants who received subsidy payments and production allotments from the Agricultural Adjustment Administration. Some 1,100 tenants, amounting to two-thirds of the farm-operators in the County, did not receive contracts from the Agricultural Adjustment Administration, and therefore are excluded from this study of income groups. (Most of these 1,100 tenants, we are sure, received not more than $142.80, the maximum for Group I.)

[2] In Old County in 1930 the average amount of mortgage debt per farm was $2,396, or a little less than one-third (30.8 per cent) of the average value per farm of land and buildings ($7,770). In Rural County the average mortgage debt ($1,721) was a little more than one-fourth (26.6 per cent) of the average value of farms (*United States Census, 1930*).

INCOME FROM COTTON

years he is fortunate "if he makes enough to pay the taxes."
Almost universally they represented the tenants as "the only
ones who make anything out of cotton," and pointed out the
fact that the tenant was assured of food during at least that
part of the year when he received supplies on credit, whereas
the landlord had no such security but faced almost certain loss.

TABLE 15

DISTRIBUTION OF OWNERS AND CASH-TENANTS BY PRODUCTION GROUPS,
A.A.A. SAMPLE

PRODUCTION GROUPS AND INCOME RANGES, 1928 AND 1932	TENURE GROUPS			
	Owners		Cash-Tenants	
	Number	Percentage	Number	Percentage
Groups I, II, III: Income, 1928 $204.00–$816.00 Income, 1932 $63.00–$252.00	193	63.2	248	93.3
Groups IV, V, VI: Income, 1928 $816.01–$4,080.00 Income, 1932 $252.01–$1,260.00	76	25.0	17	6.4
Groups VII, VIII, IX: Income, 1928 $4,080.01–$16,320.00 Income, 1932 $1,260.01–$5,040.00	36	11.9	1	.4
Total..............	305	100.1	266	100.1

It is clear that at the basis of these statements is the failure
to take into account the great variation in net income which
results from wide fluctuations in the price and yield of cotton—
the failure, that is, to think in terms of average income over a
period of years. (Interviews have already been quoted, for
example, in which large landlords told of their great profits
in "good years.") In order to arrive at a close estimate of the

net incomes and rates of profit of the larger landlords, the record of the Agricultural Adjustment Administration with regard to the 30 largest landlord-planters in Old County were subjected to a further analysis.

It was necessary to assume that all tenants on any given plantation raised the same amount of cotton. In those cases where the average production of cotton reported by a landlord included cotton produced by cash-tenants as well as that produced by share-tenants, the rent of cash-tenants was translated into pounds of lint. It was then possible, since the number of each type of tenant was given by the records, to obtain the average number of pounds of cotton which the landlord obtained as his share.

The value of the landlord's average share was then calculated for the year 1928, when the average price had been 20.4 cents per pound, and for 1932, when the average price had been 6.3 cents per pound (the lowest in the preceding thirty-four years). Taxes on all land owned by the parties to each contract, plus interest on the assessed valuation at the rate of 6 per cent for a year, were then deducted from the value of the landlord's share. In Table 16, column 3 shows the amount of money, in addition to 6 per cent of the assessed value of his holdings, which each landlord made in 1928; and column 4 shows this figure for 1932. In 1928, when the average price of cotton was 20.4 cents, all except 3 of these 30 largest cotton planters in Old County had a profit equal to more than 6 per cent of the value of their holding. The 3 planters who did not make a profit of 6 per cent made some profit. In 1932, when the price of cotton was lower than it had been for thirty-four years, 11 (about one-third) of these 30 largest planters were still making a profit equal to more than 6 per cent of the value of their holdings, and only 3 failed to make some net profit.

The records show that most of the tenants of these landlords supplied their own mules and implements. If the average yearly expense of the landlord for mules and implements

INCOME FROM COTTON

TABLE 16
ESTIMATED PROFIT OF 30 LARGEST COTTON-PRODUCERS, 1928 AND 1932*
(Price of Cotton: 1928, 20.4 Cents; 1932, 6.3 Cents)

CASE NUMBER	PROFIT ABOVE TAXES		PROFIT ABOVE TAXES AND 6 PER CENT OF VALUE OF LAND AND BUILDINGS		RATE OF PROFIT ABOVE TAXES ON INVESTMENT IN LAND AND BUILDINGS (PER CENT)	
	1928 (1)	1932 (2)	1928 (3)	1932 (4)	1928 (5)	1932 (6)
1....	$1,099	$ 107	$ 180	$ −811	7.2	0.7
2....	3,123	847	2,661	385	40.6	11.0
3....	1,032	−56	−443	−1,531	−4.2	−0.2
4....	1,802	352	994	−455	13.4	2.6
5....	1,774	299	789	−685	10.8	1.8
6....	3,337	779	2,344	−214	20.2	4.7
7....	1,378	320	960	−97	19.8	4.6
8....	1,425	246	657	−522	11.1	1.9
9....	1,944	401	1,176	−366	14.8	3.1
10....	917	−173	−882	−1,972	−3.1	−0.6
11....	1,866	285	716	−863	9.7	1.5
12....	1,960	494	1,522	56	26.8	6.8
13....	1,589	260	677	−652	10.5	1.7
14....	2,421	246	441	−1,733	7.3	−0.7
15....	1,954	280	675	−998	9.2	1.3
16....	1,836	491	1,536	191	36.7	9.8
17....	3,111	778	2,391	58	25.9	6.5
18....	3,388	863	2,668	143	28.2	7.2
19....	5,159	1,403	4,409	653	41.3	11.2
20....	2,730	493	1,350	−886	11.9	2.1
21....	4,647	1,446	3,447	246	23.2	7.2
22....	5,328	1,396	4,344	412	32.5	8.5
23....	4,442	1,174	3,662	394	34.2	9.0
24....	4,948	1,425	4,539	1,016	72.8	21.0
25....	10,614	2,552	7,749	−313	22.2	5.3
26....	13,602	3,338	10,197	−67	24.0	5.9
27....	6,667	1,190	3,240	−2,235	11.7	2.1
28....	9,963	2,542	7,854	433	28.3	7.2
29....	7,682	140	−1,129	−8,671	−5.2	0.1
30....	3,406	280	360	−2,764	6.7	0.6

* In addition to the value of their cotton, the value of the cottonseed due these producers, above the cost of ginning, varied from about $175 (case No. 1) to about $1800 (case No. 26) in 1928. In 1932 the value of the seed barely equaled the cost of ginning.

furnished to half-tenants were known, therefore, this deduction would certainly make little change in the proportion of landlords who received a profit of more than 6 per cent. It must be remembered, furthermore, that the value of the cottonseed has not been included in the landlord's gross income; in most years this item would certainly balance the average cost of mules and implements furnished by any of these landlords to their half-tenants. In 1934, for example, the seed from 8 bales of cotton would pay for a mule, in addition to the cost of ginning. The net incomes given in Table 16, therefore, are probably not too high, and may be too low, since they are based upon the further assumption that each of these landlords took only his just share of the crop.

Columns 5 and 6 of Table 16 show the estimated rate of net profit of these 30 largest planters in 1928 and in 1932. In 1928 half of these planters had a net profit equal to more than 20 per cent of the value of their holdings.

Net incomes of landlords, 1933–34.—Further indication that some landlords make a profit, even when the price of cotton is low, is furnished by interviews gathered during the season of 1933–34. A detailed account of the income and expenses of an absentee-landlord was obtained from his colored manager for the year 1934. It showed a net profit for the landlord of $2,300 on land and buildings assessed at $5,500, or an annual rate of profit of 42 per cent. The landlord's subsidy payments from the Agricultural Adjustment Administration were included in this reckoning. At the same time, other landlords, whose accounts were not open to inspection, insisted that they were not making enough money from the operation of their plantations to pay their taxes.

A large landholder in Rural County stated that for the two seasons of 1932 and 1933, combined, when the price of cotton was at its lowest, he had made a net profit of $5,000.[3] It was typical of the confusion of landlords, in trying to state their profit from cotton, that the individual in question then stated that he had "to depend upon cattle for his profits."

[3] He stated that his greatest profit from cotton had been obtained in 1925, when the value of cotton raised on his plantations had been $125,000.

INCOME FROM COTTON

Gross income of cash-tenants, 1928–32.—During the five-year period[4] covered by the records of the Agricultural Adjustment Administration, almost half (43.6 per cent) of the 266 autonomous cash-tenants in Old County had an average yearly production of not more than 2 bales of cotton. Only 6.8 per cent of them had an average yearly production of more than 8 bales of cotton. In terms of gross cash income from cotton, these figures mean that almost half of the autonomous cash-tenants raised not more than $204 worth of cotton in 1928 and not more than $63 worth in 1932, and that more than nine-tenths of them (93.3 per cent) raised not more than $816 worth of cotton in 1928 and not more than $252 worth in 1932. In addition, there were 17 cash-tenants (6.4 per cent) in Groups IV, V, and VI who raised cotton worth between $816.01 and $4,080.00 in 1928 and between $252.01 and $1,260.00 in 1932.

Net income of cash-tenants, 1928–32.—If we deduct a rental of $100 (which has been the usual amount paid by cash-tenants in Old County, according to interviews with a large number of landlords and tenants) from the gross income calculated above, we arrive at an approximate figure for the limits of the net income[5] of tenants in each production group. Almost half (43.6 per cent) of the autonomous cash-tenants had a net income from cotton of not more than $104 in 1928 and had a deficit of not less than $41 in the season of 1932. The net income of more than nine-tenths of them (93.3 per cent) was not more than $716 in 1928 and not more than $152 in 1932. These figures do not allow for the average yearly cost of mules and farm machinery, which all cash-tenants had to supply. It must also be remembered that they are the incomes of families; in most cases, all members of the family did farm

[4] Production for any given year during the period 1928–32 did not vary significantly from the five-year average for these producers. Average price of cotton for the five-year period was 14.28 cents.

[5] The term "net income" is used with regard to tenants to designate income above and beyond rental; the term "net profit" is used to designate income above both rental and living expenses.

work and had to obtain their compensation out of the incomes estimated above.

Net income of share-tenants.—Analysis of the production-allotment records for the Agricultural Adjustment Administration for 1934 shows that the share-tenants on most of the plantations in Old County cleared, on the average, less than 1 bale of cotton for their year's work. Since only 17 of the 600 share-tenants received contracts from the Agricultural Adjustment Administration, and since the field evidence shows that most of them received nothing or merely a nominal payment from the landlord, out of the subsidy payment which came to him, it is certain that the overwhelming majority of these 600 share-tenants had a net income from cotton in 1934 of less than $74.75 (value of 1 bale, plus value of seed).

FIELD EVIDENCE CONCERNING INCOME OF TENANTS

Net incomes of tenants, 1933-34.—The definitions of income attempted in the preceding section by means of averages calculated from the records of the Agricultural Adjustment Administration are corroborated by the interview materials. The interviews show that most tenants and small owners made between 3 and 4 bales of cotton in 1933 and 1934. After rent had been paid, most tenants had less than $100 with which to pay their debts for food, clothes, and other supplies obtained during the season. A large white planter in Old County said that in 1933 and 1934 a tenant had to raise at least 5 bales of cotton in order to obtain $50 clear of rent and living expenses for the season. One of the most intelligent tenants in Old County, who had lived on a cotton farm for thirty-five years, said that a cash- or quarter-tenant had to raise at least 5 bales of cotton, with the price at 10 cents per pound, in order to pay rental and living expenses. Most tenants did not raise 5 bales of cotton, however. Some were in the position of one cash-tenant who raised only 1½ bales in 1933. The value of his cotton and seed was $25 less than the rental he had to pay. The general statement of tenants interviewed in 1933 and 1934 was that "cotton didn' hardly pay duh rent dis year."

366

If a tenant had no children to support, he could pay his expenses in 1934 with a crop of 3 bales. A large white landlord pointed out such a tenant to the interviewer. The tenant and his wife had raised 3 bales of cotton and had paid a rental of $100, with a profit of $50 on the season, which his landlord termed "a nice sum in the clear." A colored landlord who knew most of the cash- and quarter-tenants in his neighborhood stated that most of them had between $50 and $100 clear of rental in 1933 and 1934. This amount would scarcely pay for their food and clothing and would not enable them to replace mules or implements.

The manager for a white landlord showed the interviewer, by reference to his account books, that the tenants on this plantation in 1934 had an average of less than 1 bale of cotton per family after their rent had been paid. The proceeds from their cotton and from the seed, which was selling at the extraordinarily high price of $35 per ton, barely paid the debts incurred by the family for its living expenses during the season. "Dey didn' clear enything on their cotton, but dey paid up ev'rything dey owed. Dey don't owe nuthin' an' dat's good, to do dat in dese times, you know!" These tenants were more fortunate than most tenants in the county, in that they had all received some payment by the landlord from his government subsidy. They had still to find means of obtaining food, however, during the more than four months which remained before they could obtain credit from the landlord again. The manager, himself, had not made enough profit from his cotton during 1933 and 1934 to pay his living expenses but had been forced to depend largely upon his wages as manager.

Additional expenses of tenant.—In addition to the rental and the cost of supplies advanced him by the landlord, two other types of payment must be made by most tenants out of their gross income before any clear profit is secured for the tenant's immediate family. In the first place, a half- or quarter-tenant often has to pay the wages of day-laborers whom the landlord puts into his fields in order to secure a higher yield. In spite of the fact that the landlord himself benefits equally with half-tenants from the work of such day-laborers, it is the universal practice of landlords in Old County to compel the tenant to pay all the wages of this labor. This form of appropriation of the tenant's share was not concealed by landlords. In the second place, all tenants with whom large children or relatives were working had to pay these relatives a money wage at the end of the season. This fact was emphasized by several land-lords and managers, who pointed out that the desire to make enough money to meet their obligations to these grown rela-tives was one of the chief incentives of tenants.

Periodic variation in incomes of tenants.—For the season of 1932–33 the average price of cotton at New Orleans was 7.26 cents; for 1933–34, 10.92 cents; and for 1934–35, 12.44 cents. The last two prices compare favorably with the average price of 14.28 cents for the five-year period from 1928 to 1932, upon which the preceding statistical analysis of farmers' incomes was based. When the price of cotton has been un-usually high, the net profit of many tenants in Old County has undoubtedly been greater than that of most workers in the cities of the north. Many tenants have had a net profit in such years of from $800 to $1,000. When it is remembered that this sum is clear of all expenses for food and clothing, it will be seen that it is a considerable savings for one year. Such years occur very infrequently, for the average price of cotton has been above 20 cents per pound for only nine of the last fifty-eight years, but the hope of striking such a year is one of the chief reasons for the continued operation of cotton-farmers during the long periods of extremely low incomes.

The variation in the size of tenants' incomes, according to the price of cotton, was illustrated by a large white planter with the following history:

I had a good man on that farm who was a worker and he made 25 bales, and I sold it for a good price, 25 cents. When he came in to settle up at the end of the season, I deducted his rent and for the stuff I had advanced him, and the doctor's bill he owed, and a few other things he owed with the merchants, and in final settlement I paid him $1,250 in cash. He took the money and paid off his sons who had worked the place for him, and everyone of them came in town and bought automobiles.

That is one side of the picture; the other is this: Last year that same farm only made 17 bales, which sold for 6 cents. The result was that when it came time to settle up, the tenant didn't have a thing coming and even owed me money. After three years of this, he owes me several hundred dollars which I probably will never get, and yet he hardly has enough to live on.

The influence of variations in the yield of cotton, as well as of price, was illustrated by the case of a tenant in Rural County. In 1925, when the average price of cotton was 18.2 cents, this tenant and his large squad of family workers cleared about $1,800 on their cotton, above rental. In most years they raised between 15 and 20 bales of cotton. In 1933, when both the yield and price of cotton were low, this family raised less than 6 bales of cotton and cleared only $100 above the rental.

In years of high prices, other tenants received net incomes above rental of as much as $870, $800, and $1,100. One colored manager of a fertile river-bottom plantation had obtained a profit above rental of $8,000 in one year of high prices. In 1918 a colored tenant and his father sold over $2,000 worth of corn, and they received $425 for 3 bales of cotton, which would have been worth less than $90 in 1932. All these incomes were pointed out by the landlords or by managers as exceptional, however, even in times of high prices. It is likely that only tenants who had especially good equipment, fertile land, and/or large families obtained net incomes of as much as $800 in years of very high prices.[6]

Stealing by landlords and share-tenants.—All estimates of

[6] Upon the basis of a study by the Department of Agriculture of "the average return of the producer per acre of cotton," Rupert B. Vance has estimated that the gross income from cotton of the average tenant in the United States, cultivating 20 acres of cotton, would have varied between $215.60 and $1,212.40 from 1898 to 1919 (*Human Factors in the Cotton Culture,* pp. 124–26).

the incomes of share-tenants and of their landlords are subject to a rather high degree of error, because either or both parties may appropriate more than his due share of the crop. The danger of such an error does not exist in the estimates given above of the incomes of 266 autonomous cash-tenants, since all of these tenants sold their own cotton. It does exist in the estimates of the incomes of landlords, however, since all of the 30 largest landlords had some share-tenants from whom they may have stolen. In view of the field evidence of the widespread cheating of share-tenants by their landlords, it is certain that many of these 30 landlords had higher incomes than those shown in Table 21. The estimates of the incomes of share-tenants are also subject to error, both because the landlord may have stolen from the tenant and also because the tenant may have stolen from the landlord by not turning over his whole crop to the landlord to be sold. Both factors would affect the incomes of landlords also.

Selling the crop.—Landlords sell the cotton of all share-tenants in Old County and of a large number of the fixed-rental tenants. In most cases the tenant does not know either the exact weight of his cotton or the exact price per pound obtained for it. The authors observed the picking of cotton on a large plantation cultivated by share-tenants. As the cotton was brought from the fields by hired pickers, it was weighed by a white representative of the landlord. Neither the pickers nor the tenant whose cotton was being picked observed the weighing. At the end of the picking, the tenant was compelled to accept the landlord's report as to the total amount of cotton picked from his farm. One landlord stated that it was a maxim in Old County that the large white planters "make half and steal half." The landlord could then take either of two courses: (1) he could "pay off" the tenant on the basis of a weight of cotton which the landlord stated and at a price which he stated; have the cotton ginned, and hold it in anticipation of a rise in the price;[7] or (2) he could sell the cotton at once and give the tenant the buyer's check for "his share." This check often amounted to less than the tenant's due share, in which case the landlord either showed the tenant no bill of sale for the crop or showed him a spurious bill of sale. A large white cotton-buyer in Old County explained this method of stealing by landlords and stated that it was common.

> There are plenty of landlords who try to cheat their tenants. We have them come to us with cotton to sell and maybe I will make a price of 13.5 cents. He will then ask me to make out the bill of sale for 13 cents and give him a check for the difference. I will tell him I can't do that, as we don't do business that way, but what I will do is give him two checks. Of course, I know what he will do with them, but it isn't as if I had made out a bill of sale for less than it actually was. Then if he doesn't show the bill of sale to his tenants it is not my business. What he will do is just show the tenant the check, and show him that it figures out for 13 cents, and settle accordingly.

Since landlords signed contracts with the Agricultural Adjustment Administration for 65 per cent of the cash-tenants in Old County, it is clear that landlords sell the cotton of the majority of cash-tenants, as well as of all the share-tenants in the County. Landlords seek to justify the selling of the cotton of these cash-tenants on the grounds that they have furnished them with credit during the year.

Settlements.—Estimates of the income from cotton of share-tenants and of those cash-tenants who do not sell their own cotton are also subject to error, for the reason that some landlords still maintain the "pre-weevil" abuse of not settling accounts with share-tenants at the end of the season. A white planter in Old County stated that his share-tenants had become accustomed to this practice and did not ask for settlements. "I handle all the crop for them, and at the end of the

[7] Since tenants usually know the market price, within a half-cent variation, a landlord could not afford to put his price very far below the market price if he wanted to keep a supply of tenants. On the other hand, he could appropriate a fairly large sum of money by paying all his tenants just ½ cent less per pound than the market price demanded.

season I just take out what they owe me for rent and advances, and give them the balance. They never handle the cotton themselves, *and often never ask for a settlement.*" He pointed out one such tenant and his wife:

They do right well, too. He has several horses and cattle that he has raised, and he always has a little money coming from his crop. He never asks for a settlement, but every once in a while will ask if he has any money coming this year, as his wife wants to go to town to buy some things. I tell him of course he has something, and from the way he acts you would think he wanted a lot, and then she will come in, and maybe ask for ten or twelve dollars. She certainly does save it too; she will get a little money now, and still have some of it next spring.

One landlord stated that many share-tenants on the larger plantations did not receive their share of the crop because the landlord used the device of "holding the cotton for a rise in the price." Whenever a tenant asked for a settlement of accounts, he would be told that his cotton had not yet been sold. The cotton was held in the landlord's barn or in a warehouse in his name. "That's a trick a lot of them use to beat the Negro out of all of his cotton." A tenant who demands a settlement or who tries to keep an account book as a check upon his landlord's reckoning is regarded as a dangerous worker, as has already been indicated. He is usually beaten or forced to leave the plantation at once. Many cases of this kind were cited by colored landlords and tenants. One was the case of a well-known colored farmer who now lives in Old City. He had been a tenant on a large plantation where there were "200 nigguhs an' not one had evuh axed whut dey owed." He had been able to write and had kept his own account book, however. At the end of the season he had been dispossessed by the landlord. A colored tenant who knew of the case said:

It wuzn' on'y whut he wuz keepin' dem frum stealin' frum *him*, it wuz dat he wuz showin' de uthuh nigguhs de wrong idea, see? 'Cordin' to de white man, he wuz spoilin' his nigguhs!

So I know when Bernie Morris had made dat crop, dey paid him off an' let him go! He made a good crop an' wuz a fine worker, but dey didn' want him on deir place. Dey don't want no dealin's wid you ef you go behine yo' ear fuh dis [pencil] on dem! Dey tole Bernie, "Well, Bernie, you uh good farmer, but you got tuh fine yo'self a new place fuh nex' year. You got de wrong attitude. You bettuh go somewheah wheah you kin use yo' pencil!"

Dat's de way dey'll do you, ef you staht figguhing on dem. Dey wantuh keep de books, you know:

> "Nought to nought, an' figguh to figguh—
> All fuh de white man an' none fuh de nigguh!"

In addition to the appropriation of part of the tenant's cotton money by the landlord, other methods of stealing from tenants were attributed to landlords by merchants and physicians in Old City. One common method was for a landlord to agree to pay a tenant's bill with a store or physician and later to refuse to do so. The tenant, when questioned by the merchant or physician, stated that sufficient money to pay the debt had been taken from his cotton money by the landlord. Specific cases of this type were cited by informants, and records of the bills to the landlord were shown. Often the tenant did not know the amount of the bill, and the landlord had charged him more than was due. If the landlord did not pay the merchant's or physician's bill, the whole amount had been stolen from the tenant; if he did pay the bill, the overcharge had been stolen. Some industrial firms in the county had been guilty of the same practice.

Settlements and the boll weevil.—Colored landlords and tenants both agreed however, that the proportion of landlords who paid tenants the money for their cotton in 1933 and 1934 was much larger than before the boll weevil. They attributed this improvement (1) to the collapse of the system of debt-peonage at the time when the weevil had made the raising of cotton unprofitable, and (2) to the shooting of several landlords by colored tenants who could not obtain a settlement. It is probable, also, that the shortage of agricultural workers which followed the emigrations of 1915-22 compelled landlords to give some account of the year's money to most of their tenants. Evidence has already been cited to show, however, that many tenants still receive no such accounting.

Stealing of cotton by share-tenants.—Since the landlord sells the cotton, keeps the accounts, and makes all deductions for credit in the case of all share-tenants and most cash-tenants, and since, if he is white, his economic control of these tenants is rendered well-nigh absolute by the operation of the caste sanctions and the courts, it is likely that the total value of the cotton taken by landlords from tenants in both counties is greater than the value of the cotton stolen by tenants. The evidence at hand indicates that most of the stealing of cotton by tenants occurs on the plantations of absentee-landlords, which are managed by colored foremen, or on the plantations of colored landlords. In cases of the latter type, the tenant realizes that the sanctions of the caste system and of the courts cannot be invoked by the colored landlord; and in those of the former type, that they are greatly weakened by the absence of the white landholder.

Only one of the score of large white planters interviewed accused his tenants of stealing cotton. This individual, who lived in Old City but made frequent visits to his plantation, stated that he had had "some trouble" with his tenants on this account and that he had "caught up" with one such tenant in 1933 and had had him arrested. He believed that white gin-operators helped tenants sell cotton which they knew had been stolen.

A colored businessman, who had dealings with several of the more successful cash-tenants from the river-bottoms, boasted of the fact that "they never tell nobody what they make" and that they helped each other conceal the actual size of their crop from the landlords. These tenants were aided by white gin-operators and cotton-buyers, he added, in disposing of cotton which the latter knew had been stolen. The authors doubt the value of this testimony, however, for the reasons (1) that the informant was boasting at the time of the shrewdness of the local colored population, i.e., of their cleverness in hoodwinking white people; (2) that most of the tenants in the areas mentioned were cash-tenants who paid a fixed-rent, and therefore had no reason to steal part of their own crop; and (3) that colored farmers in Old County usually concealed the amount of their savings, out of a fear that they would attract the envy or disapproval of their white employers or neighbors.

A more detailed and credible account of cotton-stealing by tenants was given by a colored landlord in a conversation with the colored manager for a white landlord. They agreed that share-tenants diverted part of their crop to a key-tenant who had paid his rent, and that this tenant sold the stolen cotton for the group and divided the proceeds among them. It is difficult to see how this method could succeed, however, unless the key-tenant paid a cash- or fixed-rent. Otherwise, the landlord would supervise his crop and would know the approximate yield; he would also take his share of all cotton which he saw at the tenant's cabin. If the key-tenant paid a cash- or fixed-rent, however, or if the sharers in the pool had a place where the cotton could be hidden from the landlord, the method seems practicable.

The four individuals referred to above were the only ones who charged tenants with stealing cotton, although all of the landlords interviewed accused tenants of stealing stock or food. There are two very good reasons for believing that little cotton is stolen by tenants. In the first place, the landlord or his representative has complete charge of the weighing, ginning, and selling of the crop and can estimate, within narrow limits, what the yield will be. In the second place, baled cotton is very difficult to steal, even with the help of the gin-operator. Each bale of cotton ginned in the United States has a serial number; no bale of cotton can be sold without such a number. A white landlord can therefore check the bales ginned by his tenants by referring to records.[8] Even if a bale of stolen cotton has been sold, the legal owner can usually trace it and recover his property. Several instances of the recovery of bales of cotton which had been

[8] In Old County a colored landlord was refused this privilege.

stolen from planters in the Delta regions and sold in Old City occurred in 1933 and 1934.[9]

Unpaid labor.—In addition to the appropriation by the landlord of part of the tenant's income from cotton, there exists another type of appropriation by the landlord, which consists in his refusal to pay tenants for labor which is forced by the landlord or which accrues largely to his benefit. The chief form of this type of appropriation consists in the failure of the landlord to pay the tenant for clearing off tracts of land which have long been out of cultivation. The practice of many landlords is to promise to charge a smaller rate of rental for such farms but then to raise the rental when the tenant has cleared the land of overgrowth and tree stumps. Since the tenant has no written contract, and since the landlord has a legal right to take his rent out of the crop, the tenant is helpless in such a case. The clearing of land in the eroded hill-sections of Old County is very heavy work and requires the labor of the tenant's whole family. After the land has been put into shape for cultivation, however, it becomes attractive to other tenants, who offer the landlord a larger rental. The tenant who cleared the land is then compelled to pay the higher rental or to leave. The same type of appropriation by landlords takes place when a tenant voluntarily repairs a rented cabin, builds new fences, or is compelled to cultivate the landlord's garden. Tenants cite the danger of losing "a place," or having to pay an increased rent, as the chief reason for what the landlords call their "shiftlessness." The same explanation has been given by students of tenant systems in the Middle West and in Europe.

Wages of day-laborers.—It has not been possible to gather satisfactory records of the annual incomes of the agricultural day-laborers in Old and Rural counties. Such work was extremely casual under the operation of the government's reduction plans in 1933 and 1934, and the day-laborers who

[9] The court records for Old County in 1933 show no prosecutions on this count.

were interviewed were unable even to approximate their annual incomes. The prevailing wage for a day of ten hours on plantations and smaller farms in Old and Rural counties and in the Delta regions was 75 cents for all types of field work except cotton-picking. As has been stated previously, this wage was only half the daily wage paid by most sawmills in the county. The daily wages earned by cotton-pickers in 1933 and 1934, at the rate of from 40 to 60 cents per hundred pounds of seed-cotton picked, amounted to from 60 to 90 cents in most cases. Workers who picked more than 150 pounds, the usual amount picked by an adult per day in Old County, earned slightly more.[10]

Cash income from other produce.—The income of farmers from other crops is small, as has been indicated in chapter xii. Cotton-farmers are the great majority of all farmers, and only a few of these sell other crops or stock. At times, an exceptionally able tenant, who rents some cultivable land in addition to that required by his cotton and corn crops, makes more profit from the truck and poultry which he raises and sells than he does from his cotton.

Most farmers did not attempt to raise truck and other produce for market, however. Either they lacked the knowledge of techniques, or the land, or the money with which to buy fertilizer, or they had been discouraged by the experience of some who had tried. They raised cotton, a little corn, and a small garden, which, as we shall see in the next chapter, was not sufficient to prevent them from almost starving during a good part of the summer and late winter.

[10] The rate of pay for other types of work in which some tenants were engaged when the cotton season had ended will be given in the chapter dealing with industrial and domestic labor. About 100 of the more than 1,300 tenants in Old County obtained work in one of the planing-mills in 1933.

CHAPTER XVII

HOW THE NEGRO TENANT LIVES

THE estimates of average group incomes which have been given in the preceding section have little meaning until they have been translated into terms of the food, housing, clothing, and other necessities and comforts of living which they provide for these income groups. It appears certain that there exists for each social and economic group in most American societies a customary standard of living, defined by a limited range, which is regarded by members of the group as necessary for the maintenance of its social status and its physical needs.[1] With regard to the maintenance of the tenant system in Old County, one cannot fully understand the willingness of most colored tenants and small owners to remain within the system, in spite of the extreme social, economic, and at times physical subordination which they undergo, until he knows the standard of living to which they have been accustomed from their birth. It then becomes clear that most tenants have become accustomed to a standard of living which is so low in the scale of American standards that they leave the system only (1) during periods when they experience complete destitution, such as the early period of the boll-weevil infestation, or (2) during periods when higher wages become easily accessible for masses of tenants, and social conditions are generally disturbed, such as the period of the World War.

[1] Students of society have too often considered the standard of living of social and economic groups from the point of view of humanitarian criticism alone. Such an approach is likely to obscure the importance of the customary standard of living of these groups in maintaining the social and economic structures of the society as a whole.

378

FOOD

Seasonal fluctuations.—The amount of food which the average tenant-family eats varies according to the season of the year.[2] It is at its height (1) during the fall, when the tenant receives the money from the sale of his cotton and minor crops, and (2) from late March to July, when he receives credit from his landlord. During the other four to six months of the year, most tenant-families in Old County, between 1933 and 1935, lived in semistarvation. In years of low prices a tenant's money and his store of pork, meal, and sweet potatoes are usually exhausted by Christmas, or even before. He then faces a period of from two and one-half to three months (before advances begin in late March or April), when he has neither money, credit, nor stored food. A second period of destitution follows the stopping of advances in July, when he is again without money, credit, or stored food, and when the heat has withered the spring gardens. The months when most tenants have little or nothing to eat and no money, therefore, are the coldest months and the hottest months, namely, February, all or part of March, and all or part of July, August, and September. One of the landlords who defined these periods stated that, of the two, the summer was the period of more widespread destitution; practically all tenants were without money by July, whereas during the winter some few still had

[2] Owing to the high rate of illiteracy among tenants, it was impossible to obtain daily records of the food consumed by families, similar to the records obtained from lower-class and middle-class colored families in Old City. The following account will be based upon a large body of interview material, of which only a small part can be quoted within the limits set for this volume. The Old City analysis indicated that lowerclass families with any sort of steady income usually obtained sufficient food, but that most families experienced some periods of semi-starvation, for work in the planing mills and in the levee and timber camps was very irregular between 1932 and 1935. Begging of food from neighbors was common among families on the lowest income level and it was considered a duty in lowerclass neighborhoods to give food to destitute families. The researchers concluded, after a series of home visits that at least 250 families (about 12 per cent of all colored families) suffered from semi-starvation.

money from the sale of their cotton. In the summer, furthermore, pork and meal will not keep, the store of sweet potatoes has long since been exhausted, and gardens are withered.

Semistarvation during winter and summer.—In the hottest days of the year, therefore, when their physical resistance to malaria, pellagra, and other diseases is lowest, and in the coldest, most rainy months of the year, tenants are near starvation. The existence of widespread semistarvation among tenants during the winter and summer was confirmed by the statements of landlords and managers, themselves.[3] The consensus of statements by both landlords and tenants was the euphemism that tenants "have to get what they can to eat the best way they can" during these two periods. When pressed for a more detailed record of what tenants ate during these periods, landlords and managers invariably admitted that they had little or nothing to eat. The colored manager for a white owner, who had about one hundred members of tenant-families under his supervision and who liked to boast that his landlord treated his tenants more fairly than any other landlord in the county, reluctantly admitted that his tenants starved during these periods. The interview follows:

I asked him again in what months it was most difficult for the tenants to live.

"Well, frum January to March or April is about de hardes' time. Dey kin mek it after March pretty well, becuz advances begin."

"You mean that some people have used up their meal and potatoes and meat by January?"

"Yes indeed! A whole lot of dem have. An' some befo' January! A lot of dem have to git it de bes dey kin from January to March. But now my son, he knew he wuz goin' to git married, an' he prepared hisself fuh it. He raised enough potatoes an' cawn tuh last him tel nex' July."

---

[3] Landlords advised the field-workers that they could not rely upon statements of tenants concerning their consumption of food. With this warning in mind, the only evidence advanced here is that furnished by landlords and managers, although a great deal of evidence to the same effect was obtained from tenants.

"Does anybody raise enough potatoes and corn and meat to last after July?"

"Aftuh July? No suh. Not aftuh July."

"Well, what do they eat from July till October when they sell their cotton?" [*Gardens burnt up.*]

"Dey jus' have to do de bes' dey kin. Git whatever dey kin."

"Have they any corn for meal?"

"No suh."

"Any meat?"

"No suh."

"Any potatoes?"

"No suh. Dey ain't got none of dose, den. Dey jus' have to strap it."

"But what do they eat? Do they drink milk?"

"No suh. Dey jus' have to strap it, dat's all." [That is to say, they tighten their belts.]

This manager stated that during the winter there were periods when his tenants had no meat or potatoes but had to live on milk or bread, which they usually begged from him. At the end of the summer of 1934 a large colored landlord stated that his tenant-families were "so poor an' ragged an' hungry that it's hard to deny them advances." When asked what they had to eat, he replied:

A lot of times they haven't anything to eat. They starve for a few days then, really, until they can get a little money or meat. They don't have a hell of a lot to eat, now, I'm telling you for a fact. After Christmas, even befo' Christmas in a bad year like these last have been, most of them have no way of getting any money becuz there's no work nowadays. I really don't know how they live. They'll come to you for meat all winter, but this year an' last, I just couldn't give [advance] them meat. Of course in good years, we make money by furnishin' them meat. But they couldn't pay for it now.

When questioned as to what the people ate during these months he answered: "Nuthin' much excep' bread an' milk, if they have a cow, or kin borrow some milk."

Still another landlord complained that his tenants had no food as early as January, and a professional man in Old City complained bitterly that the tenant-family which had been keeping his hunting-dogs during the summer had itself been eating the food which he had sent to them for his dogs.[4]

> That's why you can't trust any of these people to care for your dogs. They won't give the food you buy to the dogs. They eat most of it, themselves.
> Phil Hayes brought his two dogs in, too. He'd been sending out meal and lots of meat for them, but this tenant was eating it.

Rations during periods of advances.—After the winter period of virtual starvation, when the tenant's cotton money and his store of meat, potatoes, and corn have been exhausted, there follows a period when he is furnished food on credit by his landlord. This period of advances begins in late March or early April and extends over four or four and one-half months. The amount of food consumed by tenants during this period of comparative "plenty," when the landlord assures them of enough food, since they must be able to work, varied slightly among plantations. The largest rations per person were probably issued by the landlord whose colored manager has been quoted in the preceding section. On his plantation the usual monthly rations for a family of eight were: (1) 190 pounds of cornmeal, (2) 95 pounds of flour, (3) 40 pounds of salt pork, (4) 25–30 pounds of lard, and (5) small quantities of sugar, coffee, and bicarbonate of soda.

It will be seen that these rations allowed $\frac{1}{6}$ pound of meat per day per person, $\frac{3}{4}$ pound of cornmeal, and about $\frac{3}{8}$ pound of flour. The manager stated that these rations were unusually large for plantations in Old County and that the rations furnished to most tenants on credit were "jes' uhnough tuh let dem live, an' dat's all."

The rations issued to most of his tenant-families by a large white planter, who supervised his tenants closely and worked

---

[4] A large merchant in Rural County stated: "I have often wondered how the Negroes get along; but if they haven't anything, they can tighten their belts and get by somehow. I have asked them what they have to eat, and they would tell me they have just had one meal a day, greens and corn bread, and maybe a squirrel or fish."

them hard, amounted to considerably less per person. A family of six or seven persons received per month: (1) 100 pounds of cornmeal, (2) 25 pounds of flour, (3) 2 pounds of coffee, (4) 12 pounds of sugar, (5) 18 pounds of shortening, (6) 2 gallons of molasses, (7) 22 pounds of salt pork, and (8) 2 boxes of salt. For a family of six, these rations provided only about $\frac{1}{10}$ pound of meat per day, $\frac{1}{2}$ pound of cornmeal, and $\frac{1}{7}$ pound of flour.[5] The meat and flour rations were so small that workers were compelled to live chiefly upon a diet of corn bread and molasses until they could obtain vegetables from their gardens in late May.

Investigations by the director of the federal relief projects in Old County likewise revealed the inadequacy of the rations furnished to tenants: "For several years now, with low prices [of cotton] and a debt of several years standing, the planters have advanced only bare subsistence rations."

Gardens.—During the late spring and early summer the supply of food of most tenants is increased by vegetables from their gardens. Although it is possible to raise turnips, collards, or cabbages during winters when the weather is continuously mild, years when killing frosts occur are so frequent that few tenants or owners actually cultivate winter gardens. Moreover, killing frosts frequently occur during the early spring, so that farmers who plant their gardens as early as March often suffer the loss of their entire stand. In spite of the high mean temperature of the area, therefore, early gardens are scarcely more practicable in many years than they are in the middle-western states. A former agricultural agent in the area stated that the season for most vegetables was short in either winter or early summer and that it was practically impossible to have vegetables of edible size in one's garden during more than half of the year. If the farmer was able to buy

[5] Just prior to the Civil War, Olmstead was told by a small farmer in Old County, who owned four slaves, that the usual meat ration for a slave was 3 pounds of "bacon" per week, or almost $\frac{1}{2}$ pound per day. This ration was several times as great as the meat rations cited above for 1933 and 1934 (Frank Law Olmstead, *The Cotton Kingdom* [New York: Mason Bros., 1862], Vol. II).

fertilizer and to use the most up-to-date scientific methods, it was possible, he asserted, to alternate crops of turnips, cabbages, mustard, and collards so as to have one green vegetable of edible sizè throughout most of the year.

The evidence gathered from landlords and tenants showed that most tenants had a 'full garden" of string beans, tomatoes, sweet potatoes, mustard, and cabbages only during May and June, however. A rather large number of tenants in Old County had no gardens even at this time. The failure of these tenants to cultivate gardens was attributed by informants to (1) the fact that they had become accustomed, through their restriction to a diet of fat pork, corn bread, and an occasional dish of purchased cabbage or "greens," to want nothing more; (2) the fact that vegetables could be purchased cheaply in Old City or at neighboring truck farms at the period when gardens matured; and (3) the fact that many tenants were unacquainted with the proper methods for cultivating vegetables. It was a fact, observed by residents in Old City, that tenants purchased vegetables there during the spring and early summer.

Since the authors' study of the consumption of food by lower-class and middle-class colored families in Old City revealed that a large proportion of those who had available space cultivated spring gardens, it seems probable to them that the factor of customary diet is perhaps the chief reason for the failure of many farm-tenants to cultivate gardens at any time of the year. Most families in the city have been accustomed to a more varied diet than have most rural families, and therefore place higher value upon the obtaining of a supply of fresh vegetables. Tenant-families, on the other hand, seem to have continued to live on a diet of corn bread, pork, and sweet potatoes even during the boom years from 1917 to 1920.

The refusal of landlords to allow their tenants sufficient land or time to cultivate gardens was not an important factor, between 1933 and 1935, in creating the group of tenants who had no gardens. In periods when the price of cotton has been relatively high, it seems to have been true that landlords have encouraged tenants to devote all their time to cotton and corn and to depend upon the credit furnished by the landlord for their food. During such periods tenants on the fertile river-bottom plantations have had too little land to enable them to plant gardens or to raise hogs. From 1933 to 1935, however, when the price of cotton was relatively low and when landlords reduced their cotton acreage in accordance with the government's subsidy plan, tenants were encouraged by landlords to plant gardens because the tenants were no longer good credit risks.

The store of sweet potatoes.—Although the majority of tenants and owners plant spring gardens, they store no vegetables for later use. The crop of sweet potatoes which is gathered in the fall is an exception. It is kept in a corncrib if the tenant is fortunate enough to have one; otherwise, it is stored under or inside his cabin. If the potatoes do not rot, they constitute the tenant's chief guaranty of security against starvation during the winter, and are regarded by tenants as exactly similar to the urban worker's store of wages—except that the potatoes are surer. At the time when sweet potatoes are dug, there is considerable rivalry among tenants with regard to the size of their crops, and great pride and happiness on the part of those who harvest a large crop. In a year of low incomes from cotton, such as 1934, tenants speak of their store of sweet potatoes in terms which make it clear that they regard this store as life itself. A man's sweet potatoes are his banked resources, his protection against starvation and destitution until advances begin in the spring.

It often happens, however, as a result of the lack of adequate storage facilities or knowledge of techniques, that a tenant loses his entire store of potatoes; he then faces starvation unless his pork and cornmeal are sufficient to feed his family until advances begin. In the winter of 1934, for example, the temperature was so variable that snow killed the winter gardens, although the weather previously had been so warm that it had rotted the sweet potatoes of most tenants.

Festive meals.—At its best, the diet of most tenants consists of corn bread (the meal ground at a cost of one peck out of every five), sweet potatoes, and fat or side pork. After April, sweet potatoes are exhausted, and none are supplied by landlords. The diet of tenants on the truck farms, who have a larger income than most of the other tenants in Old County, is added to, at times, by beef and goat flesh, purchased from the crossroads store. The most elaborate meals of the majority of tenants may be represented by those eaten by an interviewer (1) at the home of a rural preacher-tenant who was host to a high officer in the national hierarchy of his church, and (2) at a lodge celebration in a second, rural church. At the preacher's dinner for his superior officer, on a Sunday in December, 1933, the meal consisted of fish (baked and fried), sweet potatoes (baked and candied), egg salad, corn bread and wheat bread, coffee and water. At the lodge celebration, at the close of the harvest season in November, the food was more varied but coarser. No chicken, ham, or fresh vegetables were served. A pile of baker-made rolls, potato salad, fresh pork, beef, and hog-head cheese, three kinds of cake, and two kinds of pie were put on the table.

Even an industrious tenant, who was also acquainted with the necessary techniques for planting and storing vegetables, required money to buy groceries and lard, as well as clothes. During the period of this study, when landlords were insisting that tenants could live by planting gardens and raising hogs, tenants were handicapped not only by the weather, which killed all winter gardens and rotted the stored potatoes, but by the fact that their income from cotton had been too small to enable them to buy groceries after Christmas. A large colored landlord answered a second colored landlord, who insisted that tenants could raise enough vegetables and hogs to keep them alive, by pointing out this fact: "Yes, but they can't raise flour, and they can't make enough lard to last.

They have to buy coffee and tea and sugar and those things, and shoes and shirts! *They* take *money!"* Without money, tenants were compelled to barter their few chickens, eggs, or hogs with the rural storekeepers for lard, coffee, sugar, and even for meat. Not only were they at a great disadvantage in this barter, since the storekeeper set the ratios, but the price of meat, lard, and other necessities had increased tremendously under the government's agricultural reduction plans. The owner of the largest rural store in Old County, where the price of salt pork increased from 15 cents to 25 cents per pound between 1933 and the spring of 1935, had made large profits by bartering with tenants. Another rural storekeeper stated that he had made a large profit by exchanging groceries with tenants for hogs.

Water.—One of the farm-tenant's greatest difficulties in connection with diet is the securing of drinking-water. Landlords are unwilling to bear the expense of having wells dug or cisterns erected on most of their tenant-farms. As a result, tenants must depend upon a central well or cistern, which often supplied families within a radius of a mile. Cisterns, which form the chief source of drinking-water, are usually exhausted by even short periods of drought. Tenants then must find a well which they will be allowed to use.

SHELTER, CLOTHING, AND TRANSPORTATION

The usual tenant cabin consists of only one room and of a tiny lean-to, used as a kitchen and often as a bedroom. Its furnishings are limited to a few chairs and a kitchen table.[6]

---

[6] The interior of a better-than-average tenant cabin was described by an interviewer who visited a group of tenant cabins in February: "The inside of this tenant's cabin was bare except for two old wooden beds, one in each room, and a few rocking and straight chairs. (Yet he has been renting here for eleven years.) Parts of walls covered with one thickness of newspaper. Spaces of 1–2 inches between boards of wall and floor, through which wind blew and kept newspapers on the wall rattling. Temperature 30° at present—last night 24°—drop from 70° in last 12 hours. Little girl with cotton dress and thin ragged sweater, and little boy in overalls only, out on porch in freezing weather. One log in

The housing of tenants is similar to that of most lower-class individuals in Old City, and its influence upon familial and sexual behavior is the same as in the city where the high incidence of overcrowding leads to widespread commonlaw marriages among adolescents who find it physically impossible to remain in the parental home.

Clothing.—Whereas urban families of the lowest economic level are relatively better fed than they are housed and clothed, owing to the relatively high rents which they must pay, rural families of this group are relatively better clothed and housed than fed.[7] The fact that tenant-families are better clothed than urban families of the same economic level may be attributed to two main factors: (1) tenants receive the largest part of their annual income in one payment; (2) family-laborers are often paid by the tenant in clothes at the time of "settlement." A tenant who receives even $50 at the end of the cotton season has more money in hand than any urban worker is likely ever to have at one time. He is, therefore, able to pay for a suit of clothes or a dress for his wife, even if he is extravagant in so doing. With regard to the second factor, landlords reported that the ability to buy clothes for their families at the end of the season was a prime motive of tenants, and that unless they were able to do so, they lost "face" or "respectability".

Observations by the interviewers of the clothes worn by the families of tenants and small owners at churches, and the reports of individuals who lived in rural areas, indicated that colored tenant-families had better clothing than one would

---

fireplace in room where woman was ill with pleurisy and complication of diseases made little impression on cold, because there was no door to cut off cold air from next room. The walls of this second room and of lean-to kitchen behind it were filled with large spaces; one window space with no window in it."

[7] With the exception of preachers who were by far the best clothed men in the lower caste, lowerclass men in Old City wore only frayed and patched suits. Clothing was very inadequate for cold weather, overcoats and woolen clothes being very rare. Second-hand clothing was frequently purchased or secured in the form of gifts or wages from white employers.

have expected. A colored rural storekeeper commented in detail upon this fact:

> We were just discussing how well these country people around here dress, too. A white man who comes to our store said [*mimicking nasal drawl*]: "I ca-an't sa-ee ho-aw yore faowlk can fix themselves up la-ake they do. We ca-an't do things that they do!" Several of these white people around here have said the same thing. And it's really the truth. You see these poor farm people and tenants goin' by here to church, and the men have on good well-cared-for suits, and nice ties and shirts and hats, and the women will have on good dresses they buy in Old City, and shoes, you know, and they'll have their hair all fixed and curled! We were just discussing here last night how they can do it. They really look better and keep themselves much more decent-looking than the white people around here do! [Two colored men—one with new khaki trousers and clean khaki shirt, the other with clean, almost new overalls, in store, looked much better than two white men in old car, who had only nondescript soiled clothes. Also two colored women with baskets were dressed in clean cotton dresses.]
>
> Mrs. Brown [the storekeeper] told a story about Miss Millie West, leading church worker from Old City, who came down to a new colored church recently, near Harmon. Mrs. Brown saw Millie West dressed in old clothes, and said: "I guess Millie thinks she can dress like that because she's going to a country church, but she'll be fooled! Those people have hard-wood pews and ceilings in their church and expensive windows." Miss Millie West told her later that the women there were better dressed than most women in Old City, and that she'd never 'make *that* mistake again!' "

With regard to the clothing of tenant-families, exceptions must be noted, however. The clothing of children is entirely inadequate for the days of cold and even freezing weather which frequently occur in January and February,[8] and the work clothes of men are usually extremely old and worn. Observations of the following kind were frequent: "The tenant wore a pair of faded blue trousers with at least fifty small and large

[8] In such weather, heating is quite inadequate. Like water, fuel is difficult to obtain, since landlords object to the cutting of timber by tenants. Since cabins are not weather-boarded and always have open spaces in the sides and under the doors, stoves have little effect.

patches in them. Two other tenants on the place wore trousers which were practically all patches."

Between 1933 and 1935, the vast majority of tenants in Old County walked to church, and they came to the city in farm wagons which were from ten to fifteen years old. The personal-property tax lists did not separate farm workers from other inhabitants; but it was the observation of the interviewers, who attended a great many meetings and church services in the rural county over a period of eighteen months, that not more than six tenants operated automobiles, and four of these were tenant-managers. Saddle horses and buggies were rarely seen at rural churches.

MEDICAL CARE

During periods of low income, most tenants in the area are unable to pay for the services of a physician. Although the fee of $3.00 charged by physicians for a visit to a patient in Old City is equal to a week's wages for a domestic servant and to more than half of a week's wages for most workers in the planing-mills, the fee charged for a visit to rural patients (at the rate of $3.00 plus $1.00 for every mile the physician is compelled to travel beyond the city) is even farther beyond the ability of workers to pay. Patients who are able to sit up come into the city, where they can be treated for $2.00. The interviewers have observed members of tenant-families who had a fever of as high as 105° at the offices of physicians in the city. Their ride in a farm wagon or decrepit buggy to the city and back home often required the better part of a day. Others who were unable to sit up had bills as high as $18 and $24 for one visit by a physician. Physicians stated that many of those who were treated for malaria were unable to purchase the necessary medicine. The minority who belonged to sick-benefit societies were assured of medicine but received little treatment by a physician. Physicians generally regarded successful treatment of most tenant-families as impossible under the circumstances, since patients could obtain neither medicine nor the proper diet and were often suffering from undernourishment and even starvation.

ECONOMIC NEEDS

The charge of extravagance was constantly made against tenants by landlords and merchants when speaking of tenants' expenditures during the boom years. At the same time, landlords, merchants, and professional men boasted of the fact that they had made large profits during these years by encouraging tenants to buy automobiles, silk dresses, pianos, gold teeth, and other luxuries. The explanation for such expenditures by colored tenants is to be found in the facts (1) that they cannot buy land, (2) cannot improve rented cabins and fences without having other tenants seek to rent the improved property and thus lead the landlord to increase the rental charge, and (3) that they are conditioned by the whole plantation system not to give their children advanced education, which is the chief expense of the vast majority of people of the middle and upper economic levels in cities. A complex of economic and social factors, in other words, has prevented the rise of economic "needs" which have become basic among the middle economic groups in most parts of the United States. When a tenant has a net savings of from $800 to $1,000, as many had in the years of high-priced cotton, from 1916 to 1928, he is on the middle economic level. Yet he still has the economic goals and social place of the lowest economic group. The barriers of his caste position likewise restrict the use he can make of his money, for he cannot use it to buy many of the symbols of social status for which white individuals of the same economic level spend their money.

Neither the tenant nor the landlord is worried by the problem of what the tenant should do with his earnings during most years, however. It is only during years of unaccustomed prosperity that the tenant can buy an automobile, or even a gold tooth, as Old City's dentists often lamented.

CHAPTER XVIII

INTIMIDATION OF LABOR

IN AN area where most tenants are colored and most landlords white, the caste system is a powerful aid to landlords in enforcing economic sanctions upon their laborers.
When the deferential and obedient behavior which the caste
system demands of the colored tenant is not observed, the
landlord often resorts to the intimidation of the colored tenant,
either by beating or shooting him or by threatening to do so.
The use of threats for this purpose is universal among white
landlords. The actual beating or shooting of tenants is much
less common, chiefly for the reason that the frequent use of
such violent sanctions would increase the difficulty which
landlords already experience in maintaining a sufficient
number of tenants. The evidence which was presented on this
point, in the section dealing with the supply of labor, showed
that one of the bases of competition between landlords for
tenants was the landlord's reputation among tenants with
regard to his use of physical violence.[1] At the same time, the
field evidence reveals that the use of threats of violence by
white planters is one of the basic controls upon labor, just as
it has previously been demonstrated that intimidation is
fundamental in maintaining the restrictions of caste (cf.
chap. ii).

Before proceeding to the evidence of the control of workers
by intimidation, it is necessary to distinguish between the use
of intimidation by the planter and its use by gangs or mobs,

[1] According to the statement of an individual who had a large part in the
negotiations to prevent the lynching of a colored man in the Delta in 1935, a
lynching did not occur because the white planters did not wish colored tenants
to leave the area in the midst of the cotton-planting season.

usually from the towns, who have motives other than the planters', his need being the maintenance of a steady and adequate supply of workers. When the White Shirts were beating and killing colored individuals near the close of the period of Reconstruction in Rural County to prevent them from voting, white planters often protected their colored tenants. During this period, a white plantation-manager in Rural County killed six white men in a gang which was terrorizing and shooting his colored tenants. In the same county in 1933 white planters still refused to allow white gangs to beat their colored tenants, unless the planters themselves had decided upon the whipping as a means of enforcing their control. A member of a whipping-gang cited a case of a landlord protecting his colored tenant in 1933:

> You bet the whites look after their own niggers. I went out with a party just last June to whip a nigger. I thought then, and still think, he needed it; but just as we got to the place, the owner sent us word to leave the nigger alone, and that was the end of it. We just went home. We figured the owner of the place had to put up with the nigger, and it was his own lookout, and he could do what was necessary.

Intimidation and caste.—When we turn to the evidence concerning the use of intimidation by planters themselves, to perfect the economic and occupational control of their workers, we find that the caste system and the economic system constantly reinforce one another. Most cases of terrorization which occur in the rural areas of both counties arise from conflicts between landlords and tenants with regard to the management of the farm and stock or the settlement of accounts.[2] An analysis of a large body of interview materials gathered from both planters and tenants in both Old and Rural counties reveals that practically all cases of intimidation result either (1) from the landlord's charge that the tenant

[2] An officer of a relief agency of the federal government in a large neighboring city stated that most of their clients from the rural areas of Mississippi and Louisiana had fled as a result of conflicts with planters over these economic relations.

has stolen property, deserted his crop, hurt or killed stock, refused to perform work at the time when the landlord wished it done, or damaged plantation roads or (2) from the tenant's charge that the landlord has cheated him in the settling of accounts for the year. Some instances of the use of intimidation to enforce the taboos of caste do occur, however. Although the caste system usually insures deference to the landlord's every wish, on the part of the colored tenant, some colored tenants occasionally refuse to accord such deference to their white landlords. When such a tenant is "impudent" or "too smart," the use of intimidation helps oil the wheels of the caste system.[3] One white landlord in Old County stated that he had told his sons who were managing his plantation to shoot or hang such a tenant on a neighbor's plantation.[4]

There was one [colored tenant] out our way not long ago—he was on a place near ours—who was getting smart. I told my boys that if he didn't behave they ought to take him out for a ride, and tend to him, and tell him that if he didn't stop talking and acting so big, the next time it would be either a bullet or a rope. That is the way to manage them when they get too big—take them in hand before any real trouble starts.

Another large white planter in Rural County stated that he had beaten one of his tenants who "didn't do anything, but he had that insolent kind of manner about him. A very influential government official in Rural County felt that, "when a nigger gets ideas, the best thing to do is to get him under ground as quick as possible."

Economic control by intimidation.—In most cases of intimidation of tenants by landlords the purpose is not merely to enforce the caste taboos but also to maintain the economic system prevailing on the plantation. The wife of a large white

[3] A large planter in Rural County stated that he had made the fathers of colored children whip them for infractions of the rules of caste or of the plantation system. "It often makes good Negroes out of them."

[4] Although more than one hundred instances of the terrorization of colored workers by their white employers were cited by colored informants, all except three of the instances referred to in the following account were cited by white landlords themselves or by members of their families.

planter in Rural County who frequently whipped his colored tenants stated that whipping was the best method of controlling farm hands.

That [whipping] is the way they usually do with farm hands. It is the best way. They can't afford to send them to jail because they need them on the farms; so they just take them out and give them a good beating, and that teaches them. It is a good way. It frightens them and they are all right after that. If they just whip one, it frightens the others enough. The boys [whipping group] were at it again last night, but I don't think they got any one. A lot of the men from here went down to help them, Mr. Corliss and some others. That is the way they do, help each other that way.

For stealing.—The most common reason advanced by landlords in both counties for the use of intimidation was the punishment of tenants who had stolen the landlord's property. A white planter in Rural County said that he always whipped colored tenants who stole his hogs or chickens; he then gave a detailed account of the beating of a colored man who had stolen goods from the plantation store. It is the custom in Rural County, he stated, for the landlord whose property has been stolen to invite a group of his social equals to help him whip the suspected tenant. He insisted, as did several other landlords, that the poor-whites and town loafers were not invited to these whipping-parties.

Some planters whipped their tenants without the aid of a gang. A very large landholder in Rural County said that he did not allow whipping-parties on his plantations but that he himself whipped tenants who stole from him.

Tenants' attitudes toward stealing.—A large number of additional accounts of whippings of tenants charged with stealing are available, but it is not necessary to continue these descriptions. The fact that stealing is the charge upon which most beatings are justified is the result both of the fact that the ownership of property is the basic principle of the society and of the fact that stealing is the most frequent offense of tenants. Many colored tenants do not regard the taking of small amounts of stock or cotton from their landlords as stealing bur rather as a just compensation for the money stolen from them by their landlords in the reckoning of accounts or for the beatings administered to them by their landlords. Under the systems of economic control and intimidation exercised by the landlord, the colored tenant often justifies his thefts on the grounds that his only means of securing his fair share of the proceeds from his crop is by the use of stealth. This attitude was expressed by many colored workers both in Old City and on the farms. The fullest expression, however, came from two large colored landlords, who were interpreting the Negro tenants' behavior. One of these stated, in a conversation with another colored landlord, that a white planter once had asked him why colored tenants frequently stole from their landlords. He replied:

> The white man has beat him, and kicked him and shot him, and hurt him, and lynched him, and cheated him, and stolen from him for so long, that the Negro feels that anything he can steal or cheat the white man out of is no more'n what's been done to him! The white man has made him crooked and immoral.

The white planter then said: "You know, I believe you're right about that!"

In a conversation between two large colored planters and a colored manager for a white planter the talk centered upon recent thefts from the white planter by his colored tenants. One of the colored landlords, who had lived in the county for more than forty years, said:

> That's why you hear white people say the Negro's an inveterate liar and thief. But really, I can't blame him. You see that is his only protection. Of course *you* can't do anything with him. He isn't afraid of you. You're colored. But a white man will ride over his place with a Winchester across his saddle, and if they talk that way to him, he'll shoot them, and claim they started back here [*putting his hand toward his hip pocket*] on him. And that will be all to it, because they control the courts and everything else. Well, the Negro knows that, so he uses a different method. He doesn't consider he's stealing from the white man. He

considers that he's taking his part. He lies and flatters the white man as a way of getting around him.

The speaker then related the experience of a colored tenant who had recently shown his white landlord, by reference to his own account book, that the landlord had paid him $100 less than he owed him; the landlord had threatened to shoot him if he did not leave the plantation before nightfall.

So there was nothing for him to do but leave. Well, that's just an example to show you how the Negro has to work in order to live. He's got to get his by his wit, his cunning. I don't blame him. He isn't naturally a thief; it's the system he has to live under which makes him that way.

To make tenants work.—A second reason for the use of intimidation by white landlords is to force colored tenants to perform the specific work which the landlord wants done at the time when he wishes it done, or to punish them if they refuse. One white planter in Old County stated that he had forced a colored tenant to pick his cotton, even though the weevil and rain had reduced the yield to the point where the tenant would receive nothing for his year's work. The tenant was a "good, hard-working Negro." He had wanted to begin other work in Old City, but the landlord stated he had to "make the Negro pick the cotton" in order to get his rent.

Because he cut timber instead of pulling corn as he had been ordered, another colored tenant was shot by his white landlord in Old County. The tenant, fatally wounded, then shot the landlord, who also died. In a similar case, a white landlord told his colored tenant that he was going to kill him because he had not picked his cotton when he had been ordered to do so. The landlord went to the tenant's cabin with his shotgun, but the tenant shot first, killing the landlord. In a fourth case, corroborated by a relief agency, a white landlord severely beat a colored woman who had refused to continue work in the fields when her baby was about to be born.

DEEP SOUTH

For harming stock.—A third economic or property motive
for the intimidation of workers was to punish them for mal-
treatment of stock. Particularly frank and vivid accounts of
whippings on this score were furnished by a white planter in
Rural County. He stated that he had whipped one of his
colored tenants for beating mules which belonged to the landlord. "He started to run, but before he could get away, I hit
him so hard with the whip that the shock just stopped him in
his tracks. I then gave him a half a dozen good ones." The
same landlord also related how he had whipped another colored
worker for chasing calves instead of driving them in slowly,
and a third worker for an action which had really been committed by a relative of the landlord.

One day he [the relative] had gone to town in a wagon with a Negro,
and when they got back I noticed that the mule had a long whip-cut on
his back. I called the Negro up and told him I was going to whip him for
cutting the mule—he knew I wouldn't stand anything like that. I took a
piece of grass plow-line and thrashed him a bit with it. Afterward he
told me that my cousin had cut the mule. He should have told me that
before, and I wouldn't have hit him.

Over credit and settlements.—A fourth economic motive for
the intimidation of workers is to force them to pay for supplies
furnished by landlords and to accept the landlord's reckoning
of accounts in all matters pertaining to credit and the selling
of the crop. A Negro tenant who questions a white landlord's
reckoning is always regarded as a "bad Negro" and a danger
to the operation of the plantation system itself. He is usually
driven off the plantation before he can "spoil" the other
tenants. A large white landlord in Old County stated that,
when a colored tenant had refused to indorse his subsidy check
from the federal government in the landlord's favor, in payment for supplies furnished him, he had called the tenant up
before the other tenants, shown him a clasp knife, and told
him that he "was going to cut his throat from ear to ear"
unless he signed the check immediately. The tenant indorsed
the check in favor of the landlord. The landlord, who used a

knife in this case, said that he usually carried an automatic revolver when he rode his plantations.

Instances of the shooting of landlords by tenants who had objected to the landlords' reckoning of accounts were cited by colored informants.

Other reasons.—Intimidation was also used to preserve peace among tenants themselves. A planter in Rural County stated that he had forced two colored tenants, who often fought each other in "quarters," to fight for a whole hour and had allowed them to stop only when both had been severely beaten. In 1935 a use for intimidation which had not previously arisen, occurred in regard to the abortive efforts of colored tenants to organize a Huey P. Long Share-Our-Wealth Club. A large white planter said that he had told the wife of the colored tenant who was the leader of this group that he "would hate to have to help hang" her husband but that he would be forced to unless the man discontinued his efforts to organize the club. The tenant fled.

Whipping women.—The dogma of the caste system does not permit the extension of the code of chivalry to the women of the lower caste. Although colored women are usually allowed to escape unharmed when they have committed certain minor infractions of the taboos of caste (for which colored men would be beaten or shot), they also may be the victims of intimidation. Many colored women have been beaten, shot, or lynched by white individuals or mobs in the South—some of them in the area we are studying.

An instance of the beating of a pregnant tenant-woman by her landlord, when she refused to work, has already been cited. Other instances were described in detail by a white planter in Rural County. He related the story of his having beaten a colored woman for stealing, until "her head was all covered with blood." In a second case, he had whipped an old colored woman because she had insisted upon coming between the landlord and her son, whom he was trying to whip. "I didn't want to whip the old woman, but I finally had to. I just let her have it with the whip and gave her a good beating. Then I whipped the boy."[5]

Importance of "example."—The function of whippings and shootings such as these is to intimidate all colored farm workers in the area to the point where they will not object, either as individuals or as an organized group, to the economic and caste domination of the white landlords. One such incident is an effective warning to all colored tenants in the neighborhood. Interviews with colored workers show that an actual beating, shooting, or lynching serves as an "example" to most colored individuals in the area for years afterward. In most cases of conflict between a white landlord and a colored tenant, however, the landlord makes use only of threats. Threats are usually as effective as the use of violence because colored workers realize that the threats of white landlords are supported by the whole caste system, including the law officers and the courts.

[5] In the light of the above evidence of the widespread use of intimidation by planters in both counties, and of their entire willingness to describe beatings such as those cited in this account, it is necessary to attribute the following statement by a planter with regard to the treatment of colored workers in the past to an exaggerated form of the "Yankee hatred" which is still an extremely important factor in the politics, caste system, and myth of the South.

"I'm glad they've freed them [colored people] now, but the northerners all had the wrong idea about it. Of course, there were some hard masters, but most of the people were kind to their slaves and treated them just like members of the family. There were quite a number of what we call 'absent owners' here then, though. They owned the land, but they weren't here to manage it; so they had overseers to manage the Negroes for them. Those overseers were pretty cruel, a lot of them. But it was mostly northerners who were the absent owners, though. But most of the southern owners were kind to the slaves, and treated them like real members of the family."

CHAPTER XIX

THE PLANTATION IN ITS SOCIAL SETTING

THE primary sources of control in adapting the colored tenant to the plantation system lie outside the colored society. They are exercised through (1) the economic subordination and (2) the caste subordination of the tenant to his landlord. The major effects of these controls, as we have seen, are (1) that they keep the tenant dependent upon his landlord for food[1] and end by making such dependence a habit, and (2) that they accustom the colored tenant to the acceptance of the dominance of his white landlord through the systems (*a*) of intimidation and (*b*) of legal subordination. By far the most important relationship in maintaining the system, therefore, is the face-to-face relationship of landlord and tenant. These two are bound to each other by mutual economic interests, involving reciprocal duties and benefits. It is primarily from this relationship, organized by both economic and caste sanctions, that the great permanence of the plantation system in Old and Rural counties results. Before we examine the conservative functions of the colored family, church, and school in the caste system, it will be advisable, therefore, to consider the effect of the face-to-face relationship of white landlord and colored tenant in organizing the plantation system.

LANDLORD-TENANT RECIPROCAL

The generally accepted mutual duties and obligations of a landlord and tenant with regard to the production of cotton

[1] It is well to remember, also, that penniless groups cannot emigrate. Emigration requires an initial saving to enable the emigrant to travel to his new home and to live until he obtains work. The savings of tenants in Old County in most years are insufficient to furnish such a stake.

may be called the "economic pattern" of their behavior. This pattern requires that the landlord shall furnish land, supplies, and in many cases supervision, and that the tenant shall supply the necessary physical labor. As a result of this concert of interests, planter, tenant, land, capital, and product are organized into a system which supports the individuals within it, according to different standards of living, based principally upon a differential in the ownership of land. The pattern of this relationship is such that individuals of widely varying qualities, either of ability, experience, or financial status, may be fitted together into a functioning system, each with definite rights and duties. So long as each individual continues to perform his duties, the system continues to operate. To be more specific, a planter may hire a group of tenants whom he has never known before; but so long as he and they behave according to the recognized pattern, the system will continue unchanged. The existence of personal antagonisms, either toward the system or toward individuals within it, will not alter the situation so long as such attitudes do not prevent the proper functioning of the individual.

We have seen that the tenant is highly subordinated to the planter in the usual planter-tenant situation and that, furthermore, he is expected to behave in a manner indicative of this subordination. He must not only be obedient to the planter, but he must also be properly respectful and deferential in his manners and speech. The behavior of any tenant, white or colored, is, in fact, very much that expected of a colored individual in relation to a white. The tenant's deferential behavior not only is a matter of color but is partly a result of his occupational subordination to the landlord, for it is also found in relations between tenants and planters of the same color. For example, deference was observed in the case of a group of white tenants when a landlord entered a plantation store. One of the group immediately offered the landlord his chair near the stove. All of them greeted him deferentially and listened respectfully when he spoke.

PLANTATION IN ITS SOCIAL SETTING

White tenant in landlord-tenant reciprocal.—While the colored individual may fit into the planter-tenant situation with little change in his behavior, the white tenant's problem is more difficult. He is subordinated not because of the color of his skin but because of his low occupational and economic status. Neither obedience nor deference is demanded of him in those situations in which his behavior is merely that of one white individual to another; but when he enters a planter-tenant relation in a county like Old or Rural, where almost all tenants are colored, he must behave virtually as a colored tenant would, and must accept the same treatment. This situation gives rise to strong antagonisms between the planter and his white tenants, which result in insubordination by the white tenant, in demands which the planter considers excessive, in mutual suspicion, in attempts by the white tenant to cause trouble between the planter and other tenants, and in other violations of the customary relationship. As a result, the planters are generally antagonistic to white tenants and prefer the "properly" subordinated colored tenants.

Extension of relationship.—Frequently the relationships between planters and their colored tenants are not limited to the fundamental economic pattern which we have discussed, but extend to additional types of behavior and attitudes. In these cases, usually where the tenant is a favored worker, "a good nigger," or a member of a family which has worked for several generations for the planter's family, the solidarity between landlord and tenant is very strong, and the obligations and benefits of each party are increased. In time of trouble such a tenant turns to his landlord as his natural protector. In case of illness the planter sends a doctor. If the tenant is in jail, the planter pays his fine or hires a lawyer to defend him, and uses his influence to have the tenant released. One prosecuting attorney told of instances in which planters had made agreements with him by which the tenants would receive light sentences in return for a plea of guilty. In disputes among any of his tenants the planter may act as

403

arbitrator. Under the caste system the relationship is often extended farther, and the planter may punish his tenants himself, especially in cases such as we have noticed, in which tenants were accused of stealing or of being "uppity" (nondeferential).

Intercaste controls.—The superior power, status, and social prestige which the caste system affords white landlords, and the necessity which follows therefrom of the colored tenant's accommodating himself to this dominant position of his white landlord or employer, creates, as we have seen, strong antagonisms on the part of the colored tenant. On the other hand, the constant necessity of subordinating the colored worker, with regard both to his economic and caste behavior, likewise creates antagonisms on the part of the white landlord. A society of persons in such a relationship could not persist, however. In the absence of social mechanisms which served to control and organize these antagonisms, it would be destroyed either by open conflict or by the eventual emigration of the members of the subordinate group.

As a matter of fact, there do exist other structural relationships between landlord and tenant, the effect of which is to control the expression of their mutual antagonisms and so to preserve both the economic and the social systems. The existence of a strong solidarity between colored worker and white employer was frequently cited by colored informants of the middle and upper social classes and was constantly evidenced by the actions, although not by the verbal behavior, of tenants. The gist of this field evidence is summarized in the following statement of a middle-class colored man.

> I tell you one thing: You'll find that the Negroes here have been accustomed to lookin' up to the white man an' doin' what he tells them, an' it's a fact that these Negroes here will follow a white man sooner an' do what he tells them than they'll follow any colored man. It's becuz in slavery an' ever sence, down here, they've worked under the white man, an' done what he tol' them. They jus' believe the white man can lead them better than a colored man can.

The strength of the bond between white landlords and colored tenants was frequently testified to by white landlords in both counties, in their praise of "the good Negroes" on their plantations and in their assertions that almost all of them were of this type. Even in Rural County, where the beating and terrorization of tenants was admitted by many landlords, white landlords were constantly citing examples of intercaste solidarity. The most inverterate whipper of colored tenants in the county said that a former tenant of his who had returned from Cincinnati for a short visit had removed his hat when addressing his former landlord. The colored cook observing this scene, remarked: "He ain't forgot his manners yit. He done took off his hat, an' held it behine him all de time he wuz talkin' tuh de boss." The same landlord spoke in high praise of an industrious colored tenant whom he had helped buy a farm. All the members of the landlord's family were fond of this tenant. A second planter in the same county remarked on the friendly and courteous behavior of colored tenants there in general. "Country Negroes are very polite—much more than those in town. They always speak to me, and I always say hello or something. I call them all 'John.' "

The white planters, on their side of the reciprocal bond, professed a strong sense of responsibility for the welfare of their colored tenants. Although their actions did not confirm these professions in many cases, it was astonishing how firmly they believed them. Every large white landlord who was interviewed emphasized his feeling of responsibility for the physical welfare of his tenants and his obligation to deal fairly with them. A justice of the peace in one county, who advised landlords to whip their tenants for stealing rather than to have them arrested, nevertheless insisted that the local planters had a moral responsibility to deal honestly with their tenants. He was extremely indignant over the practice of landlords in another section of the state, where he had served as a plantation manager, of stealing from colored tenants and refusing to sell them land! "At least the people in *my* county are honest" (in their dealings with colored tenants), he had told the white landlord when he had quit the plantation. A large white planter said of his colored tenants "I look after them and handle them just as I would a bunch of children who need someone to take care of them." Although the planter's feeling of responsibility for his tenants is usually based upon his caste's dogma of the lack of intelligence and initiative of colored people, it is often associated with recognition of personal obligations to the colored tenant.

The grapevine.—One of the strongest bonds between colored tenants and white landlords is the "grapevine," or the practice of "tellin' the white folks." Although the grapevine is strongest between white and colored families which have been in a landlord-tenant relationship for a long period, the bond also exists between tenants and white landlords on neighboring plantations. A colored absentee-landlord in Old County stated, for example, that the tenants of neighboring white landlords constantly informed them of the activities of tenants on his plantation and that he learned of these activities from the white landlords.

Why there isn't a thing that goes on on that plantation of mine which I don't know by the next morning. Those white planters around there tell me. They get it from their Negroes..... Those tenants on my plantation can't understand how I know everything they do or don't do down there, when I'm miles away in town here. They tell Negroes on those white landlord's places, and those Negroes of course tell their white landlords just as soon as they learn.

Miscegenation.—Although, at the present time, kinship across caste lines is not recognized sociologically by white families in most respects, there was a period following the Civil War when it was recognized more fully. Many colored informants stated that, even as late as fifteen years ago, several white planters rode with their white and colored families in the same carriage, the colored family sitting on the coachman's seat, and the white family on the master's seat. In 1850 Old County was the center of the free colored population of the state, 27.7 per cent (258) of all free colored persons in the state having been in Old County and 23.0 per cent (213) in Old City. Almost three-fourths (70.3 per cent) of all the free colored persons who lived in cities in the state resided in Old City. Although the great preponderance of free colored persons in Old County lived in Old City, and although some of them had immigrated there from other areas, it is certain that many of them were the children of local planters, who sent them into the city to work as artisans and perhaps to escape the embarrassment of their presence on the plantation.

The chief form of recognition by a planter of a kinship tie with his colored offspring in the past, and the only form of recognition at the time of this study, was the giving of property by the white planter to his colored offspring. As we have seen, in 1933 only one extended colored family of this type owned farms valued at $900 or more. This family owned eight such tracts. Two other colored individuals in one of the counties had received farms of this value as a direct result of miscegenation in recent years; and a colored man in one county was said to have recently inherited a farm at the bequest of a white father. About one-seventh of the farms valued at $900 or more which were owned by colored people in 1933 in one of the counties, had been given to members of their families by white relatives; and there was undoubtedly a number of less valuable farms which had been inherited in the same way. Still others were known to have been inherited by colored persons from white relatives and then sold.

Although the bond of kinship seldom exists between white landlords and colored tenants today, there has admittedly been a time in the past when such a bond was more frequent. The effect of the high degree of miscegenation in both Old City and Old County in the past, and of the large number of free colored persons who migrated to the city before emancipation, has undoubtedly been to create strong intercaste solidarities. In the city the degree of miscegenation is still high. Both white and colored persons generally attribute the "good relations" which exist between the castes in Old City, and the lack of lynchings, to the relatively high rate of miscegenation in the past and in the present. The influence of the city upon the plantation system in this respect has undoubtedly been to control many of the antagonisms which exist between white planter and colored worker and to give rise to a relatively greater social tolerance than exists in the newer plantation areas of the South.

"Old servant-master" reciprocal.—A type of relationship which is a great deal more widespread, however, and therefore more important as a control upon the economic and caste antagonisms which exist between white landlords and colored tenants is the "old servant-master" relationship. The pattern of mutual obligations and benefits which both landlords and tenants who stand in this relationship recognize, above and beyond the ordinary services required by the rental agreement, was constantly emphasized by the white landlords interviewed. As has been pointed out in the account of land tenure, there is a large number of colored tenants in both Old and Rural counties whose families have rented from the same white family for generations. Many of these tenants are descendants of the former slaves of their present landlords; one-fourth of the largest farms which colored individuals in Old County own were bought by their slave-ancestors from their masters.

The evidence concerning the strength of this bond will be presented in detail when we consider the relationships of the domestic servant and the white family in Old City. Although it is certain that many local white families exaggerated the emotional attachment of the families of old tenants or servants to themselves and often lost sight of the importance of economic motives in conditioning such behavior, it is certainly true that, for a complex of reasons, the bond existed. The colored members of such a reciprocal called the white members, even to their faces, "my white folks." In return for increased services, courtesy, and intercaste loyalty on their part, such tenant-families expected and often recieved from the land-lord's family especial aid in times of destitution, sickness, or bereavement. The material furnished by members of white landlord-families concerning such relationships is not only too abundant to be quoted in detail but often suffers from the exaggeration demanded by the myth of the colonial mansion and the loyal and worshipful slave retinue. It is sufficient here to use only a few of the more sober and factual interview accounts.

Several landlords told stories of old colored tenants who had "refused" to be put off their plantations and whom they had finally permitted to stay. One white planter said that his colored foreman and family "act as if I were their father." He told several anecdotes illustrating not only their faithfulness in caring for him and his plantation but also his regard for them. A county agricultural agent said that many planters who wanted to change from cotton-farming to cattle production could not change the system because they had to take care of their colored tenants. "These plantation owners' grandfathers owned the ancestors of these Negroes, and they have to look out for them."

CONTROLS WITHIN THE LOWER CASTE

The secondary sources of control in adapting the Negro to the plantation system are the colored familial, age-grading, church, associational, educational, and class structures. In this chapter it will be possible only to indicate the mechanisms by which these institutions of the colored society aid in maintaining the economic system.

Family as an economic unit.—Since the cultivation of cotton in Old and Rural counties requires a great amount of hand labor, the tenant or small owner must have the aid of his wife and children in the fields. The success of his cotton crop depends chiefly upon the size of his family. This necessity for the operation of the whole family as a productive unit is an important factor in conserving the plantation system, for it results in the conditioning of children to farm labor and to the tenant system from their early years. A child begins to hoe and pick cotton when he is seven or eight years old, often earlier; when a boy is twelve he begins ploughing. Parents are anxious not only to have several children, to aid them in cultivating cotton, but also to keep the children on the farm, at least until they marry. By that time, the son usually has come to think of himself as a prospective cotton-farmer and tenant and is looking for a "place" to rent and a farm girl to marry.[2]

Extended kinship relation.—In this connection, it is interesting to notice the extension of the kinship bonds among rural families. Six of the largest colored rural families in Old County counted from forty to seventy-five members, most of them living in the county. Kinship by blood and by affinity was recognized as far as "third cousins" and "daughter-in-law's aunt." The most extended kinship relations not only were defined by terms but were recognized by the performance of services. One tenant-manager in Old County, for example, sold the cotton, paid the taxes, and performed many other services for extremely distant blood and collateral kin, who depended upon him for technical aid in such business matters. They, in turn, supported him in his management of church and lodge affairs. Illegitimate children, moreover, were included in the kinship pattern. A member of the largest extended family counted twenty-three children, many of whom were illegitimate. Although the extended family group seldom farms as a unit,[3] the organization of large kinship groups by visiting, performance of mutual services, and by church and

[2] Except for the sawmill and levee work, farming is the only occupation open to him. Old City offers an even smaller chance for making a living. His four or five months a year at the rural school have made him barely literate. They have given him no training which will encourage him to seek work in other fields in the large cities.

[3] In addition to the operation of some of the extended families of tenant-managers as a production unit, other extended families worked together in picking cotton and in making syrup from sugar cane and sorghum.

associational solidarity undoubtedly aids in keeping large numbers of tenants on the plantation.

Immediate family.—The immediate family of father, mother, and children, however, is a productive unit, and every effort is made to keep it intact by both tenant and landlord. A large colored landlord pointed out that the cultivation of cotton maintained the unity of the family in a manner that urban labor did not. He stated further that he had several very large families of tenants on his plantation, one tenant having twelve children at work.

References by white landlords in Rural County to the fact that their tenant-families remained on one tract of land for long periods have been quoted in the treatment of migration. Only the marriage of the children or the death of the head of the "squad" (family) succeeds in breaking up such family economic units, a large white planter stated. He had been unable to persuade his tenants to move onto a new and more fertile part of his plantation for this reason.

> They feel that those places are their homes and they love them; they feel like they were moving out of the state if they were to move over here [another part of the plantation]. What we have to do is to wait till one of them marries—maybe he marries a woman from over here and we can get him to move over. Or else the head of a squad [family] dies and the squad breaks up and we can move them. We couldn't just send the wagons over here and move one or ten of them over. They wouldn't stand for it and would always be a trouble to us.

The patriarchal family.—The best examples of the integrated and stable tenant-family, however, were those of tenant-managers. All of the eight colored managers who were interviewed had married sons working with them, or renting from them, on that part of the plantation which the manager himself rented. One of these extended families made from 20 to 30 bales of cotton a year between 1928 and 1932, five to eight times as many bales as the average tenant-family raised. Another tenant-manager had three married sons and their wives working with him. The communal division of labor extended even to the wives, each of whom had an established round of duties for each day in the week. A third tenant-manager had been able to buy a farm through the combined work of an extended family, including a nephew and a son-in-law, in addition to his own children. When they left him, he lost his farm.

The most highly organized tenant-family in Old County was that of a colored tenant-manager, his wife, his married sons, and their wives and children. As a result of the membership of his large immediate and extended families, this manager held the most important offices in the local church and benefit society. When he had undertaken the management of a plantation of approximately 1,000 acres, his first act had been "tuh git my fam'ly tuhgethuh," he said. He described the operation of his immediate family as a production unit in the following terms:

"What do you mean by your own place?"

"I plants 50 acres of cotton myse'f. Dat ain't so much, becuz I got 30 haid uh people jes' in my own fam'ly. I needs tuh plant dat much! I got my 2 sons, an' my daughtuh-in-laws, an' uh nephew, in houses wid deir fam'lies. Den I got 2 boys [unmarried sons] livin' wid me. I had 17 childrun settin' at my own table once!"

"All of your family together plant those 50 acres?"

"Yeahsuh. But I got about 90 haid uh people on de res' uh de place."

Matriarchal family.—One-seventh (14.1 per cent) of the autonomous cotton-farmers in Old County were women. Most of these were colored tenants. The solidarity of these matriarchal families as production units rivaled that of the patriarchal families cited above. A grown daughter in such a family explained that she had been unable to go to school because she had to work with her mother in the fields.

My mother had 13 haid of chillun, 'n' ez soon ez we ol' 'nough tuh work, she har [hired] us out or mek us work with huh in the fiel'. I wuzn' no where near ez big as dat chile [*pointing to white girl about ten years old*] w'en I left home tuh work. Seven of us harred out—'n' 5 work on de farm. Ef I coulduh gone tuh school, soon ez I git in school, hit time tuh come out 'n' git tuh work in de fiel's.

A daughter in a second matriarchal tenant-family stated that her mother, who had been deserted by her father, had managed the rented farm so well by using her eight children that she had chased her husband off the place when he had returned twelve years later.

Yas' ma'am, we's a big fambly—8 haid o' chillun 'n' me de oldes' girl, but dere be 2 boys older'n me. 'N' my ole man went away 'n' lef' my mamma when we be all small—twelve year ago th' twen'y third o' June; de younges' wuz a baby. 'N' my mamma raised us all by herself. She run de farm, an' raise us wid nobody to he'p. When my ole man comed back two year ago, seventeenth of October, she chase him awfuh de place —say she didn' want none o' him—'n' he want her to tek him back.

She say she don' nevah want no mo' husban'. She do bettuh by herse'f. She say long ez she kin make de good crops she git evah yeah, she'll git along wid out no mo' husbins. We makes 4½ to 5 bales o' cotton at dis place. Three years ago we makes 8. Dis earf *so* good. Cose all de chillun he'p.

The importance of the authoritarian family sanctions in maintaining the cotton economy of Old and Rural counties, therefore, lies in their continual pressure upon all members to participate in the raising of cotton. The strong central authority of the father or mother, reinforced by religious and moral sanctions, organizes all members of the family into a single productive unit, which often includes married sons or daughters and their families (and, in the case of aged tenants, children whom the tenant has adopted to help him on the farm after his own children have left him). The social authority of the family head, in turn, is greatly strengthened by his economic and technical power as head of the family's productive system. There is no doubt that on the larger and more fertile plantations, where the yield is sufficiently high to insure to all adult members of the "squad" some return for their labor, this type of authoritarian family has been effective in stabilizing the productive system.

Conservative functions of the church.—The analysis of the structure and functions of the rural colored church is too complex a study to be attempted within this treatment of the agricultural economy. The functions of the church organization in integrating the lower caste, in moderating violent antagonisms between the two castes, and in giving ultimate sanction to the caste and economic systems are so extensive, and the materials at hand so numerous, as to require a full-length study of the colored church. Only the most general functions of the church in stabilizing the agricultural system will be considered here.

Integrating the lower caste.—The contradiction between the Christian dogma of the brotherhood of man and the fatherhood of God and the caste dogma of the "natural" and social inferiority of colored people was pointed out by a former gravel- and levee-camp worker in extremely cynical terms. At the same time, he gave unwilling testimony to the strength of the church as an integrating association among the rural colored population.

> Nigguhs prayin' all deir lives an' goin' tuh church an' dey ain't yet got tuh wheah de white man give uh damn about dem! I seen women walk fo' miles to church, an' whut good it do them? I passed dem awn de road a hundred times at one o'clock at night—women walking home from church dat time uh night! Ben singin' an' shoutin' all night, an' got tuh walk fo'n five miles home an' git up at daybreak de nex' mornin', an' whut in Gawd's name good to it do dem? Whut good do it do dem? Dey out dere workin' fuh some white man an' he kin do enything in Gawd's earth he want to dem, an' yet dey got all de religion in de wurl!
>
> A whole fam'ly uh nigguhs now, all prayin' an' goin' tuh church all de time, an' dey make $300 worh uh cotton, an' de white man kin say dey owe him dat! De nigguhs all prayin' an' got so much religion, an'—pshaw—what in de hell good is it done him?

The rural colored church gains its strength not chiefly from the supernatural sanctions claimed for it by its dogma, however, but from the social bonds it establishes among its participants. Whereas the analysis of a great number of sermons by rural preachers reveals little dogmatic content, it shows great emphasis upon the necessity for effective organization and complete solidarity of the church as a social group. The highest development of this organization in integrating and stabilizing a local group of tenants was found in the community where the patriarch-tenant-manager, referred to above, was the leader. As a result of his control over both his large extended family and the other tenants on the plantation which he managed, this man had succeeded in building the most effective church and lodge organizations in Rural County. As treasurer of both organizations and head of his family and tenant group, he controlled the administration of both church and lodge, including the selection of officers. He had persuaded his landlord to make "advances" to tenants in cash rather than in supplies, so that tenants might be able to meet their financial obligations to the church and lodge. The "advancing" of from $12 to $15 every two weeks to a tenant-family provided a steady cash income for these organizations.

Yeahsuh. An' I has tuh give out de money to all dose people. I pay um in cash, too! Yeahsuh, I give dem cash money. Den, you see, dey kin buy whut dey needs. An' it he'ps de church an' de lodge, too. Ef I gives dem $12 on Sat'day, aftuh dey done bought deir meat an' flour an' lak dat, dey kin still have two or three dolluhs for de church an' de lodge. Dat keeps de church an' de lodge goin', yuh see. An' all but about thirty of dose people on my place belongs to dat church. All but 'bout thirty belongs!

The circulation of money from this man (1) to members of his family and to other tenants on the plantation, (2) thence to the church and lodge of which he was treasurer, and so (3) back into his hands is illustrated by Figure 22.

There was no doubt that the manager-patriarch-treasurer benefited financially from this centralization of power, for the church had paid almost twice as much for its building as the contractor had actually received.

Increasing intercaste solidarity.—The evidence of the operation of the dogma of the Negro rural church to strengthen the caste controls cannot be given in detail here. The fact that the dogma of caste has been incorporated into the symbols of the church, so as to give the powerful white individual (i.e., landlord) an ultimate and supernatural authority, is established by the fact that the "travels" or "visions" of all converts to the rural churches placed highest value upon whiteness. The "visions" of converts at four rural churches were heard, and seventeen of these accounts were recorded verbatim. In all of them the sinner had been convinced of the authenticity of his conversion and of his "state of grace" only when he had "seen" a white man, woman, or child, a white house, a white horse, or some other white object.

The analogy between the white landlord and the patriarchal Old Testament God was frequently used by rural ministers. The clearest expression of this part of the dogma occurred in the largest church. Following a prayer by an officer of the

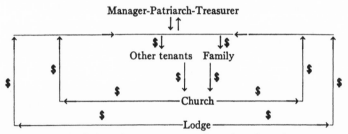

Fig. 22. Circulation of money on a plantation through a manager-patriarch-treasurer.

church, who said that when each man came up for his reward in the after-life, he would receive just what he merited, the preacher added: "Ef you worked hard, you know you due yo' pay, but ef you ain't, you know dere ain't no reward for you. *Ain't no use in goin' tuh de office unless you done made yo' crop.*"

Stabilizing the economic system.—That this analogy has a sociological basis in addition to its value as convenient imagery, is indicated by the general practice of landlords in encouraging tenants to build churches and in giving them financial aid for this purpose. The incorporation into the church doctrines of the dogma that not the agricultural economy but their own thriftlessness and sinfulness were responsible for the destitution of tenants at the time was constantly observed in the sermons of rural preachers between 1933 and 1935. No preacher in either the rural or urban county was ever heard to complain in his pulpit against the plantation system. The dogma concerning economic behavior was always that the members should be hard and faithful workers. Economic hardship was the result of their infringement of this divine sanction; as the preacher quoted above represented it:

> One thing you'll fine is that ouah people hates a man who preaches the true word of God. That's the reason times is so hard for us now. It ain't no depression. . . . . It ain't no depression that's causin' ouah trouble today. . . . . We talk about Roosevelt gonnuh do dis an' do dat! Roosevelt can't do *nuthin'!* Roosevelt mek plans, an' fas ez he meks them, *Gawd* changes them! The trouble wid us ain't no depression!

At the same time, he exhorted the members to be hard and persistent workers.

EDUCATION OF THE LOWER CASTE

In all of the southern states the democratic and general American principle that free and adequate facilities for education should be made available to all members of the society conflicts with the sanctions of the caste system. This conflict is most acute in those plantation areas where colored tenants are in the majority. Facilities for the education of colored children are markedly inferior to those for white children everywhere in the South, but they are most inferior in the "black" plantation counties.[4] In Old and Rural counties the term for the rural colored schools is from four to six months,

[4] Horace Mann Bond, in his *Education of the Negro in the American Social Order* (New York: Prentice-Hall, 1934), has made a well-rounded study of the political, social, and economic factors which control the public education of colored people in the South. Bond reveals, by a statistical demonstration, that in the "black counties," where colored people far outnumber whites, colored schools are most inferior to white because the diversion of funds from colored to white schools is highly profitable to the white schools. In "white" counties, on the other hand, colored people constitute so small a part of the total population that the diversion of funds to white schools would be of little or no value in improving those schools.

depending upon the amount of money made available by the white county school boards and upon the urgency of the need for cotton-pickers and choppers. Whereas most rural school buildings for white children were erected at the expense of the county governments, most of the schools for colored children in both counties were housed in colored church or lodge buildings or in other buildings provided by the members of the colored communities. The salary and training of colored teachers in the rural sections of the county were inferior to those of white teachers.[5] The counties furnished no transportation for colored rural children and seldom furnished blackboards, teaching materials, or stoves, but did furnish all these for white rural children.

The census of 1930 reported that 29.9 per cent of the colored people in Old County and 26.9 per cent of those in Rural County were illiterate. The figures had been practically the same ten years before (32.0 and 33.8 per cent). The authors' own field experience convinced them, however, that at least half of the rural colored population of Old County and a higher proportion in Rural County were illiterate and that most of the adults who were "literate" had only enough training to enable them to read their names and to calculate the value of their cotton.

Many landlords and some members of the county school boards were opposed to the development of more efficient schools for rural colored children. They expressed the fear that the providing of even a thorough grammar-school education for colored students would make them unwilling to remain on the plantation and would end by depleting the supply of workers.[6] Equally important in many cases was the belief that educated colored people were less amenable to the caste sanctions, less deferential, submissive, and dependent, and

[5] In at least one colored school in Old County the teacher's salary was paid by the colored community.

[6] The white superintendent of schools in Old County, speaking to a group of colored rural teachers in her office, gave these orders: "Now I want you all to teach these colored children not to be lazy. Make 'em work!"

418

therefore a danger to the efficient working of the caste system. Although the latter part of the theory was scarcely borne out by the authors' observations, the field evidence did support the former. Several instances of the refusal of a literate tenant to accept the landlord's settlement of his accounts and the subsequent dispossession of such a tenant have been cited in the foregoing analysis of income. The rate of emigration of those children of colored farmers who had received advanced education, furthermore, appeared to be much higher than for the similar group among whites. The educated children of six of the largest colored farm-owners in Old County emigrated between 1933 and 1935, and their parents were compelled to follow. Leaders in the colored community frequently spoke of the high rate of emigration among the educated children of colored farm-owners during the preceding thirty years. A leading colored business man, commenting on the emigration of all eleven children of a colored farmer who had once been very successful, agreed with the landlords that the education of colored people made them unwilling to stay in Old County. The interviewer asked: "Well, how do you account for the fact that T's children didn't stay? He has a fine farm, you say."

Yes, but T's children were all educated. He educated them all, and that made them unwilling to stay on the farm. They wanted to leave, as soon as he'd educated them. [*Bitterly*] This other man's sons aren't educated, you see. They are more or less ignorant. You know that's why these white people are against educating these Negroes. They say: "Educate a nigguh an' you ruin him for the farm!" And they're absolutely right, too! As soon as they get a little education, they're simply not going to stay on these farms. The white man knows that, and that's why he won't give these Negroes good schools!

Another colored businessman in Old County actually complained to the local white state senator that even the present system of rural education for colored people was causing too many of them to leave the plantations for the good of the county.

DEEP SOUTH

I told M. once, who was state senator from around here, that compulsory education was a dangerous thing, a dangerous thing. Because as soon as you take a country boy and teach him something about the world and give him new ideas, you ruin him for the farm. And you make a Negro dissatisfied with his position. As long as you keep him ignorant, he's satisfied to work for some white man on the plantation; but as soon as he learns to want other things, he comes to the city to try to get them. When he gets here, he finds the white man has everything, and he can't get the kind of work or job he wants, and he is dissatisfied. And then you have a dangerous situation.

A colored teacher from Old City, when addressing the colored members of a rural community at the opening of a school which they had built, insisted that education changed the tastes of rural students so that they were unwilling to adjust themselves to the plantation standard of living.

Once I was a great believer in Negro education—preached it all the time—but now I doubt whether it's good or not. You educate your children—then whatcha gonna do? You got any jobs for 'em? You got any business for 'em to go into? Well, if you haven't, do you think they gonna be content to come back and live in a li'l one-room house wid no 'lectric lights—wid no comforts? No! Education changed their tastes; they gotta have better things than you got—an' why? Jes' 'cause they got education and learned about things—got themselves usta things you don't even know about. Yeah, that's what education does!

So great has been the influence, even in the colored society of Old County, of the American faith in education as a means of economic and social mobility, however, that the speaker thereupon urged the audience to ask the county government for the establishment of a large "consolidated" school for colored people, such as the white citizens had, and further stated that the establishment of large businesses by colored people would furnish employment for the colored students educated in such schools.[7]

[7] As a matter of fact, it was impossible for graduates of the colored high school in Old City, during the period of this study, to obtain employment in either white or colored businesses, except as "runners" for the lottery houses. Colored businesses were limited to tiny grocery stores in which the owner was

Education is not a sufficient cause, by itself, however, to account for the emigration of those literate farm workers who go into Old City or leave the county altogether. The cultural level of the "educated" colored family and the relative strength of its bonds with the family of the white landlord or patron and of its organized relationships with the colored community through the church and associational structures are the chief factors which determine whether the educated children of a tenant or owner leave the farm. Nor is the educated tenant always a rebel against the system of caste and economic controls on the plantation. That the mere ability to read and to perform simple arithmetical operations is not necessarily a handicap to colored tenants in dealing with white landlords was proved by the success of the colored tenant-managers in Old County. Several of these men had complete supervision of the collecting of rents and the selling of cotton and handled large sums of money. At least two of them were able to familiarize themselves thoroughly with the involved regulations governing the various reduction plans of the Agricultural Adjustment Administration and to explain these regulations to other tenants.

As the efficiency of many of these more literate tenants was observed, on the one hand, and the confusion of the great mass of illiterate tenants on the other hand, it seemed clear that a thorough elementary education for colored rural children would greatly increase the chances of their modifying the caste and economic systems. As long as most tenants were illiterate, they could effect no important changes within these systems, nor could they benefit by the efforts of the federal government to modify the economic system.

---

the only clerk, small cafés, undertaking establishments, barber shops, and a branch office of a colored insurance company. There was no prospect, under the caste system, that colored businesses would absorb even a small number of the graduates of the colored high school.

CHAPTER XX

CASTE, CLASS, AND THE URBAN ECONOMY

O N THE plantation the occupational relationships between white and colored individuals are limited to the landlord-tenant relationships and the master-servant relationship. Since almost all tenants are colored and almost all farm-owners who have tenants are white, the study of the caste structure underlying these occupational relationships was greatly simplified. White and colored tenants do not work together in the fields or rent from the same landlord, so that the question of their occupational relationships does not arise. In Old City, on the other hand, there is a great diversity of occupations; and in some of these fields, such as the planing-mills or the levee camps, white and colored employees work on the same job. The economic relationship between the white and colored individual, that is, is not always that of a white employer to a colored employee, so that occupational superordination does not always coincide with caste superordination, as it does on the plantation.[1] The caste structure of occupational relationships varies according to the type of work involved. It is necessary, therefore, to distinguish clearly the types of urban occupational relationships between white and colored individuals and to consider separately the caste structure underlying each of these major types. Occupational relationships between white and colored individuals in Old City have, therefore, been grouped under the following types:

1. White factory worker ⟷ Colored factory worker
2. White employer ⟷ Colored artisan
3. White employer ⟷ Colored levee, timber, or road worker

[1] It is true, of course, that almost all colored workers in Old City are employed by white companies or individuals.

4. White levee, timber, or road worker ⟷ Colored levee,
   timber, or road worker
5. White employer ⟷ Colored store porter
6. White employer ⟷ Colored domestic servant

Although these types do not include all those nonfarm occupational relationships which exist between white and colored individuals, they include all the more frequent relationships.

In analyzing the relationship between white employer and colored employee, it is often difficult to distinguish the sanctions which are chiefly the result of the employer's occupational superordination from those which are chiefly the result of his caste superordination. The controls which the white employer in Old City exercises over his colored domestic servants, for example, are in many cases similar to those exercised by a white employer in Massachusetts or in England, or in any society where social classes are sharply defined, over his domestic servants. The same problem exists with regard to the sanctions governing the occupational relationship between white landlords and colored tenants. With regard to tenants, it can be answered satisfactorily when an empirical study has been made of the landlord-tenant relationships in a plantation area where most of the tenants are white. In Old County, as we have quoted evidence to show, the caste controls increase the economic subordination of colored tenants even beyond that of white tenants. The problem is more complex in Old City. Before attempting to define the variations of the caste structure in the various types of occupational relationships listed above, therefore, it will be well to indicate the kind of subordination of colored workers which may be attributed chiefly to the operation of caste sanctions.

Occupational caste taboos.—The most general occupational taboo in Old City's white establishments with regard to colored individuals is found in the fields of clerical or "white-collar" employment. The economic and political power of the white middle class and the taboo upon the social relationships which would exist between white and colored clerks in the same office or between a white employer and his colored stenographer operate to exclude colored individuals from employment as clerks, bookkeepers, or stenographers in white businesses.[2] Colored workers may be employed only as porters, messengers, janitors, or maids in white stores, offices, or banks.

In gasoline stations they are not allowed to receive and disburse money; and, although they frequently do the same work as white employees in such stations, they are paid a lower wage. In white automobile repair-shops, colored workers are not given the status of mechanics. In one instance where a colored man did such work, he was paid a lower wage than the white mechanics in the same shop and had additional menial duties. In levee construction, colored men are not generally employed as operators of tractors or trucks. Until the intervention of the federal government in recent years, all such work was reserved for white men.

In road-building work, in which the local government's authority is complete, the handling of machinery is still a function limited to white men. Similarly, in the handling of timber, only white men are employed as truck-drivers by white contractors. A colored man may serve occasionally as a "filler-in," but his status and wages are not those of a driver. In all work in forestry and in road and levee construction the position of foreman is held only by white men.

The local caste system, which reserves skilled and mechanical work for white individuals, has not been entirely successful in extending its operation to the large planing-mill, owned by a nonlocal corporation. In the planing-mill, where there is need for the supply of colored skilled workers, the company has given colored men such work but has paid

[2] Colored porters in white stores may act in the capacity of clerks in serving colored patrons, and a colored woman may serve as office girl for a white dentist. Neither of these functions involves social equality with white employees, however.

them a lower wage than white men who do the same work. In a few exceptional cases, colored "helpers" do skilled work for which the white man whom they are "helping" is paid. A colored worker in this position said of another:

> That felluh does about de hardes' job at de fact'ry. He grades all de lumber. 'Cose a white man, the foreman, is s'posed to be doin' it, jus' like a white man is s'posed to be doin' my work, but the white man is de foreman, you see, an' he knows this cullud man kin do de gradin' well as he kin, if not bettuh, so he got this [colored] man doin' his work for him. We call this [colored] felluh the "grader," but he ain't really. He does the work, but the foreman gits paid fuh it [cynically]. This [colored] felluh gits $13 a week, though.

The interviewer inquired as to the white man's wages.

> Ugh! He gits $50 a week. That's jus' lately. When times wuz bettuh, he got $75 and $80 uh week. But they ain't gonna pay no cullud man money like dat. They wouldn' think o' payin' a cullud man dat!

In the federal government's work-relief projects in the county the local caste sanctions with regard to skilled workers were similarly adapted. Colored men were at times given skilled work, but they were never given the status, or relief wage, of skilled workers.

With regard to unskilled or "common" labor, there was a decided change in the operation of the caste system during the period of widespread unemployment between 1930 and the time when this study ended in 1935. Until the "depression," unskilled labor was the province of colored men. The white society exerted strong social pressures to prevent white men from accepting such "Negro jobs." The result was that colored men found opportunity for such work in almost all industrial and construction fields, and colored women had a monopoly of the jobs for domestic servants. In 1915, colored informants stated, colored men did practically all the work in the cotton gins and compresses, oil mills, sawmills, brickyards, coal-yards, woodyards, wheelwright shops, and blacksmith shops. The existence of these "Negro jobs," sanctioned by the caste dogma of the division of labor, provided a basis of subsistence for the colored society and actually worked to the economic disadvantage of the white people in the lower occupational groups. A colored businessman, who had lived in the Middle West and North, criticized the practice in those regions of giving most of these unskilled industrial jobs to foreign immigrants and to poor-whites. He contrasted it with the local practice, which afforded employment for most colored people, stating that "the po' white in the South holds hisself above certain types of jobs, an' considers those fuh niggers—Negroes —and the Negro can git those jobs."

Weakening of caste in the occupational structure.—Between 1930 and 1935, however, the occupational dichotomy along caste lines was weakened by the entrance of a large number of whites into the field of "common" labor. Municipal jobs such as street-cleaners and garbage-collectors, which colored men had held, were given to white men, and the colored former employees were placed on federal relief. White men took jobs as common laborers on road- and street-construction projects and in the sawmills. Of forty men employed as unskilled workers on a road-building project in Old County in 1934, only three were colored. Local white men were digging with picks, pushing wheelbarrows filled with concrete, carrying water, and driving trucks. Caste sanctions existed, however, in the separation of the three colored workers from the rest of the group. The county-road foreman commented upon the entrance of white men into the field of manual labor, as follows:

Up until 1929 we never used white labor on the roads except for such jobs as tractor-drivers and things like that. I even used Negroes to operate the scrapers and to run trucks. Then times were good, and we paid common labor $2.00 and $2.50 a day. But since then, whites have begun to take work as laborers, and now they are glad to get anything.

Until recent years, when the federal government has supervised the operations of levee contractors more closely, colored workers preformed only the heavier, more unskilled labor in levee construction. The effort of white workers to maintain this caste line in the division of labor was described by a colored levee worker. A modified application of the local occupational caste structure resulted; colored tractor-drivers did not work on the same job at the same time as whites.

Well, dey said no nigguhs on top uh dose tractuhs. But de Guv'nuh says nigguhs and white both go awn de tractuhs. Wen de white git awf, nigguh git awn. De white, dey all come up to him, an' say nigguhs can't drive dose tractuhs, only de whites. He tol' um nigguhs goin' tuh drive um too; when de white git awf, uh nigguh git right up on it. Dey didn' lak dat, you know, but dey had duh do it. Dey wanted tuh keep de nigguh sep'rate from de whites awn ev'rything. Dat's whut dey'd ben doin' so dey could work de nigguhs longuh; dey worked 'em 10 an' 12 hours, tel de Guvnuh come, an' dey'd work de white 8 hours somewhere else. Now dey haf tuh work 'em bofe togethuh, an' dey all workin' 8 hours. Dey gittin' $2.50 and $3.50 uh day, 'stead uh $1.00 uh day whut dey use' tuh git.

White men have also taken work as common laborers on the levees in recent years, but they have not worked in gangs with colored men. Changes of this type in the caste occupational dichotomy have been common in Old County since 1929, but changes which involve the upward mobility of colored workers into the more skilled occupations have been limited to the levee work controlled directly by the federal government's engineers and to the planing-mills operated by nonlocal companies. They have not occurred within the locally controlled occupational system. In the area generally, the caste occupational dichotomy has been weakened by the downward movement of white workers who have taken "Negro jobs." The most acute expression of this conflict between white and colored workers over these "Negro jobs" occurred in 1932 in the effort of white railroad workers, chiefly white engineers who had lost their positions after 1929, to drive colored firemen from their jobs by organized intimidation.[3] Ten colored

[3] A detailed account of this organized effort on the part of white unemployed engineers to displace colored firemen was obtained from two colored firemen who remained on their jobs during this period and who, themselves, were warned to resign.

firemen were shot, of whom six died. One of the six was killed in Old City by two hired white "trigger men," after he had been warned several times to resign his position.[4] Since the colored firemen were members of a railroad union, and since other colored men were willing to take the places of those who had been killed or wounded, white men did not obtain these positions. Similar conflicts between white unemployed railroad workers and colored firemen and brakemen had occurred in previous times of general unemployment.

The preference of white employers for colored unskilled laborers was still general, and many white employers objected, as we shall see later, to the entrance of white workers into this field. The employers' statements of their reasons for preferring colored to white laborers, namely, (1) the fact that they could be struck or cursed, and (2) that they were more effective workers, indicated the application of the caste sanctions in this field. One white employer, for instance, said: "There is no labor better than the Negroes we have here. That is, if you know how to get along with them. They are good workers, and if they are lazy you just have to take a club to them, and they will work all right." One white man, a county-road foreman, said that colored men were better workers and that he thought it unfair to give white laborers preference over colored ones who had done the heavy labor in that region. The superintendent of the water plant pre-

---

[4] The following account of this shooting was obtained from two individuals who were on the scene a few minutes after it occurred and who there interviewed an eyewitness of the shooting.

"Well, the day this felluh was shot here, these white men drove down from Vicksburg an' waited for the train here. They shot at him once, right behine where you livin' now, Mr. Smith, jus' before he got to the yards. He jumped off an' ran, an' they musta cut through this little street below the power house, becuz they caught him, an' shot him right in front o' Miss Nettleton's house" (principal of colored high school).

At this point, Morse, a teacher in the high school, said: "Yeah, right by that telegraph post there. Right there on the main street! I heard the shots an' got up an' went down to see what had happened. He was lying right beside that post. His brains were blown all over the street. The man who shot him got off the car after he shot him the first time, an' went over an' put the barrel of his shot gun to his head, an' jus' blew his brains out. It wuz loaded with slugs."

ferred colored laborers, he said, because they were more able and willing to do heavy work. Both of these white employers objected to having colored and white laborers work in the same group, moreover. One said that the white laborers tried to boss the colored and expected them to do most of the work. The other complained that the white laborers refused to work as hard as the colored and that they stood around watching the colored men work, with the result that the latter also slowed down. Colored workers could be hit or cursed to speed their working, but white could not. "When you just have Negroes, you can make them work by cussing and cuffing them, not that you often cuff or kick them, but you can holler at them and sort of make them work. But with whites you can't do that. They all want to be boss."

THE MILL WORKERS

In turning to a detailed analysis of the caste structure of occupational relationships in Old County, it is convenient to begin with the occupation where the subordination of colored workers is least, namely, that of factory work, and to move to a consideration in the end of that occupation in which the colored worker is most subordinated, namely, domestic service. The planing-mills employ more colored workers than any other type of work, with domestic service second. The total annual wages which they pay to all their workers amount to more than the value of Old County's cotton crop. In 1933 the largest of these mills had an average daily force of 190 white workers and 510 colored workers, and it paid a total of $290,570 in wages (Table 17). A colored worker's statement that this largest mill was "the father of this town" did not exaggerate the importance of the mill in the urban economy: "That's the only thing that saves this town! That factory is the father of this town. If it wuz to close up [laughing], there wouldn' be anything left to Old City. You'd see most of these people here [storekeepers on main business street] closing up their doors an' leavin' here tomorrow!"

Although most of the white workers in this factory are

TABLE 17

ANALYSIS OF INCOME GROUPS OF WORKERS IN OLD CITY PLANING-MILL, BY COLOR OF WORKERS: 1933

INCOME GROUPS (YEARLY INCOME)	NUMBER OF WORKERS			AMOUNT		PERCENTAGE				
								In Entire Sample		
	White	Colored	All	White	Colored	In White Sample	In Colored Sample	White	Colored	All
$1,000.00 and over	20	0	20	$24,000.00	....	10.5	0.0	2.9	0.0	2.9
$750.00–$999.00	30	0	30	27,000.00	....	15.8	0.0	4.3	0.0	4.3
$500.00–$749.00	40	25	65	28,000.00	$15,000.00	21.0	4.9	5.7	3.6	9.3
Below $500.00	100	485	585	41,350.00	155,220.00	52.6	95.1	14.3	69.3	83.6
Total	190	510	700	$120,350.00	$170,220.00	99.9	100.0	27.2	72.9	100.1

430

engaged in the more skilled work and most of the colored in the less skilled work, there are some colored workers who have a higher status in the technical hierarchy than some white workers. In certain exceptional cases the work performed by colored employees is highly skilled. One colored worker, for example, had to check twelve widths of planks by sight on a rapidly moving belt and direct his aid in sorting them. Continual rapid calculation was necessary to determine wastage in sawing and the resultant size of the planks. The work not only required great skill and speed but involved a heavy responsibility. A colored "grader's" work was even more skilled. He had to determine, by sight, the several grades of lumber contained in each plank on the moving belt and to calculate the number of square feet of lumber of each type in each plank, making allowances for knots and other variations in each of the twelve widths of planks. In addition, he had to calculate the amount of lumber required to make a certain number of products with the least waste.

In a few instances, white and colored men work at the same jobs together. White and colored women generally work at the same tables; they eat their lunches at these tables, the white women sitting on one side of the table, and the colored women on the other.

No white worker was placed in the same work group with a colored worker of higher status, however; a colored machine-operator, for example, was never given a white helper.[5]

[5] The following note is an extract from the observer's notebook.

"I asked the office manager about the class of labor, and he explained that they use mostly Negro labor. I asked if the Negroes and whites worked together without trouble, and he said: 'We never have a bit of trouble with them; they work side by side. It isn't like it is in New Orleans, where the whites won't work with Negroes. The thing about it here is that there aren't enough white laborers here to run our plant without Negroes, so if any of them object they can just get off the job, and we can get plenty of others. On the whole I think the white labor is a little better than the Negro, but lots of the Negroes are just as good as one could ask. We have some of them on machines that are fine workers. Every once in a while you will find one that is intelligent and has a little education, and it is surprising how sensible they are. Some of the whites are

Several factors may be regarded as accounting for the weakening of the caste sanctions in this mill to the degree noted above. (1) The factory is owned by a nonlocal corporation. (2) It opened in 1919, during a period of labor shortage. (3) The variety of technical processes and the complex division of labor involved afforded an opportunity for some experienced colored workers to rise in the occupational hierarchy in the absence of a sufficient supply of white skilled workers. (4) Most important of all, however, has been the lack of a white union organization which might exclude colored workers from the more skilled work or close the factory to all colored workers except laborers and porters.

Caste structure of wage scale.—The possible modifications in the caste structure of occupational relationships, resulting from the fact that a nonlocal company employed most of the workers in Old City, was exemplified in the company's initial practice of paying colored workers double the wage paid them by local employers and by landlords.[6] The local white employers recognized at once the danger to the occupational caste structure which was inherent in this raising of the colored wage scale; the modification which they secured is indicative of the general compromise between the factory and the local caste system. A white man who had been a foreman at the mill at the time in question stated that the mill had reduced the wages as a result of the complaints of local businessmen and planters.[7]

There are six departments in the mill today, each with a

pretty poor and are just not good for much. It's just an individual thing. Some of both groups are not very good, and others are fine. Of course we never have a white man working under a Negro. We have Negroes working under whites though, in the same sort of job, and it is all right.' "

[6] When the factory opened, during the World War, it was making supplies for the government on a cost-plus basis, so that it was willing to pay unusually high wages.

[7] Later the mill itself joined with local businessmen in insisting that the government reduce wages of river workers, "since they were paying so much that when the quarter-boats would come here, they would take all the labor away."

different hourly wage for white and colored workers. In order to define the caste structure of these wage scales in 1933, the weekly pay rolls in each of the six departments of the mill were analyzed for the entire year. This extensive statistical operation was then summarized by graphs of (1) the average number of hours worked per week, (2) the total man-hours per week, and (3) the average wage per week for white and colored men and women, for every week in the year. It is possible to reproduce here only those graphs which summarize the variations in the average weekly wage paid to white and colored men in four departments. In reading these graphs (Figs. 23 and 24) it is necessary to remember that wages vary from week to week, according to the number of hours of work available and that after September 1, 1933, the National Recovery Act effected a reduction in the average number of hours worked, with a slight increase in some departments, and a decrease in others, in the average weekly wage.

In spite of the fact that some colored men received a higher wage and performed more skilled work than some white men, the analysis revealed a highly developed caste structure in the wage scale. Before the operation of the National Recovery Act the average wage per week for colored men varied from $5.00 to $8.00 in all six departments, whereas the average weekly wage of white men varied between $7.00 and $13.00 in four departments and between $16.00 and $26.00 in the departments where the work was most skilled. During the operation of the National Recovery Act the average weekly wage of colored men in two of the six departments showed little change; in the other four departments it rose to from $7.00 to $9.00. In none did it reach $10.00. During this period there was little change in the average weekly wage of white workers in four of the departments, because the average number of hours per worker was reduced. In those two departments where the work was most skilled, the average weekly wage of white workers declined.

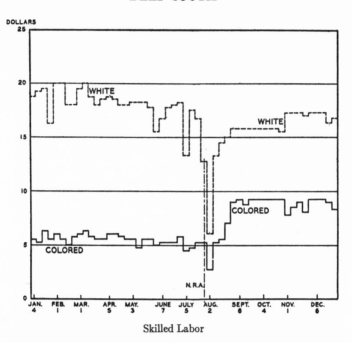

Skilled Labor

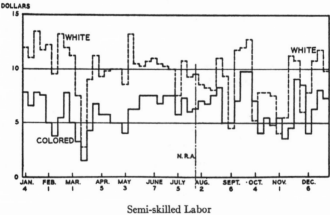

Semi-skilled Labor

FIG. 23.—Average wage per week of mill workers at Old City Planing mill: 1933.

434

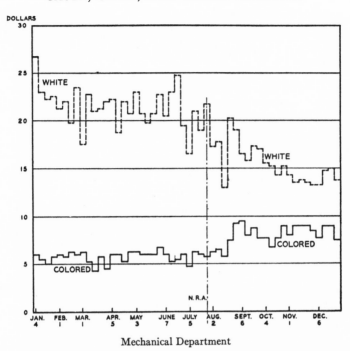

Mechanical Department

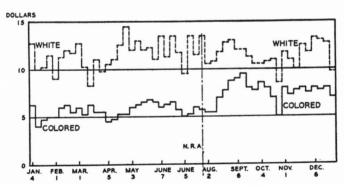

Fabrication Department

FIG. 24.—Average wage per week of mill workers at Old City Planing mill: 1933.

There was little difference in the average number of hours worked by white and colored men, except in the mechanical department, where white men had a slightly higher average before the operation of the National Recovery Act and colored men had a slightly higher average during its operation. The total number of man-hours worked by white men, however,

TABLE 18

HOURLY WAGE RATES IN OLD CITY PLANING-MILL, BY COLOR OF WORKERS: 1933

(Week Ending December 6, 1933)

WAGE RATE PER HOUR IN CENTS	WHITE			COLORED		
	Number	Percentage	Cumulative Percentage	Number	Percentage	Cumulative Percentage
0- 9.9.....	39	22.0	22.0	79	17.0	17.0
10.0–14.9.....	47	27.0	49.0	337	73.0	90.0
15.0–19.9.....	10	6.0	55.0	39	8.0	98.0
20.0–24.9.....	25	14.0	69.0	4	1.0	99.0
25.0–29.9.....	12	7.0	76.0	0	0.0	99.0
30.0–40.0.....	40	25.0	101.0	0	0.0	99.0
Total......	173	101.0	....	459	99.0	....

Average weekly wage:
For sample of 60 white workers........ $10.70
For sample of 68 colored workers........   6.80

was greater in all departments, except in those two where the work was least skilled.

The facts (1) that the average weekly wage of colored workers in every department was greatly inferior to that of white workers in any department (Table 18), and (2) that only 10 per cent of the colored workers were paid more than 15 cents an hour, whereas 51 per cent of the white workers were paid at this higher rate, demonstrate the thoroughgoing application of caste sanctions in the factory's wage scales at present. These sanctions were applied chiefly because the local white society placed a higher value upon maintaining the local caste structure of occupational relationships than upon increasing the total amount of money which the factory might bring into Old City. In spite of the caste distinction in wages, however, the caste structure of occupational relationships was relatively less rigid, i.e., the correlation between color and type of work less perfect, than in any other type of employment.

COLORED AND WHITE ARTISANS

The field of building construction was also characterized by a relatively weak development of the occuptional caste structure. Although colored and white artisans seldom worked together on the same building, there was a rather large group of colored bricklayers, carpenters, and plasterers in Old City who worked for white contractors on "all-colored" jobs. They constituted a distinct threat to the occupational caste system, which, in general, reserved skilled work for white men. Several of these colored artisans were themselves contractors, who maintained the existence of the group of colored artisans by furnishing them employment. In the boom years, a colored man had been the leading building contractor in the whole area, including the neighboring part of the Louisiana Delta, and had sometimes employed both colored and white artisans on the same job.

The three leading colored contractors were light colored men, as were most of the colored artisans. In order to understand the important position held by colored artisans in the building trades in Old County, and in many other southern cities as well, it is necessary to remember that colored artisans were trained on the plantations during slavery. Most of the skilled work involved in the building of the plantation mansions in Old County was done by colored artisans. Since many of these slave artisans were the children of white planters, and since Old City was a refuge for these children and for other free colored artisans in the state, a relatively large group of colored artisans has been concentrated in the city and has received the protection and patronage of leading white employers.[8] This group includes besides contractors, brick-layers, wheelwrights, blacksmiths, plasterers, etc., an important group of colored seamstresses. The colored upper social class in Old City has always been composed chiefly of the families of artisans. At the top of this group, until the rise of colored physicians and dentists in Old City, were the colored contractors, artisans, and proprietors. With the rise of a professional group composed of darker colored people and the emigration of a large number of light colored artisans and their families, the leading families of the artisan group have withdrawn from active participation with the present brown-skinned colored upperclass and maintain their light colored groups.

The influence of the relatively large number of colored artisans in weakening the caste structure of occupational relationships over a long period has been important, both because they compete with white skilled workers and because they receive a higher wage than white unskilled workers. Although few of them were employed for more than ten weeks of the year during the "depression" years of 1933 and 1934, they had been employed in preference to white artisans by white employers in many instances in the past and at times in 1933 and 1934.[9] The facts (1) that they could be paid a lower wage than white artisans and (2) that they could be more easily controlled as a result of the operation of the caste sanctions were the principal reasons for this preference. As a result of the technical superiority of their work, however, the supervision to which colored artisans were subjected, when employed by whites, was less constant than that to which

[8] Colored artisans constitute so large a proportion of artisans in the larger cities of some states in the deep South that they are included in labor unions with white artisans and sometimes hold offices in mixed unions.

[9] Colored seamstresses still had a monopoly of dressmaking and of curtain-making. The leading blacksmith and wheelwrighting shop had employed colored artisans for two generations.

colored laborers and unskilled workers were subject. When they worked for colored contractors or house-owners, they were entirely freed of the caste sanctions on the job, except those which governed wages.

LEVEE AND TIMBER WORKERS

Caste sanctions are much more thoroughly applied in the levee and timber gangs than they are in the planing-mills. Some two hundred colored men from Old City were employed in levee gangs at the height of the season in 1934, and almost an equal number in timber gangs, working at distances from 100 to over 500 miles from the city. Since the wage scales of levee workers were established by the federal government, their average earnings were greater than those of any other group of colored workers in Old County. Most river workers earned about $100 per month.

River workers usually lived in camps, but at times they were housed in quarter-boats. The subordination of this group of workers was still extreme, although the intervention of the federal government had reduced the power of contractors to hold workers in debt-peonage. Contractors still maintain a well-developed system of economic controls of levee workers, however, through the organization of extensive facilities for gambling and prostitution. This organization was described by several workers, including a gambler who had "run the games" in numberless camps for thirty years. This man had been employed by contractors to run dice and card games. All bets were made with the colored representative of the employer. Games were run every payday, from Saturday afternoon until Monday morning. Since the employer had enough money to benefit by the statistical laws underlying any game of chance, and since almost everyone in the camp gambled, the employer regained most of the wages paid out on Saturday noon by the end of the gambling on Monday morning. Between paydays the employers in camps and on boats lent money to workers to enable them to gamble or to pay a prostitute. The rate of interest on these loans was 50 per cent for two weeks. In camps such loans were deducted from wages. On government boats, however, they were not deducted from wages but were collected by the use of caste sanctions. The colored professional gambler, referred to above, reported:

De nigguhs wants money to gamble wid, an' dey charge um fo'-bits awn uh dolluh fuh de len'. Dat's whut dey do awn all dese rivuh boats. Dey have uh nigguh to run de game, an' mek de len' an' collec' it. Den w'en dey pays you, uh white man pay you awf, an' de Cap'n stan'in' right heah, lak, an' down at de do' dis nigguh stan' to 'duct de len' an' fo'-bits on de dolluh fuh int'res'. You gotta pay it right dere. You can't he'p pay it, becuz ef you don't, he sen' you right back up wheah dose white men is standin'.

Prostitution is similarly organized by some levee contractors and boat captains, although it is not so important a means of economic control as organized gambling. One boat captain charged each colored man who put up a tent, as a place of assignation for prostitutes, $20 for the concession. At other camps the contractor paid colored prostitutes a wage and allowed workers credit in this business, just as in gambling. White workers, as well as colored, patronized colored prostitutes. In timber camps in areas nearby, however, contractors did not allow women in camps; and although gambling was prevalent, it was not organized by the contractors.

Intimidation was another common means of subordinating colored workers. The use of physical violence by white contractors and foremen in "driving" colored levee workers was frequently reported by workers. One foreman made a practice of beating each new colored worker. The operation of caste sanctions with regard to the payment of wages was illustrated by the action of a white foreman on the opposite side of the river, who seriously injured a colored levee worker who asked for extra pay for extra work. Another colored worker on the opposite side was beaten to death by a white foreman in

1934 because he reported to the government officials the foreman's refusal to pay wages when due. This form of economic subordination of colored laborers was also practiced by white road-contractors on federal work-relief projects in Old County. A county-road foreman stated that he made relief workers, whose wage was set at 30 cents per hour by the federal relief agency, do three hours of work every one hour they were legally required to work.

They are supposed to be getting 30 cents an hour, but the supervisors refused to pay that much for that class of labor; they say it is competing with their regular labor which they hire for $1.00 a day, and so they won't use anyone that gets more than that. So when they present their work card, we tell them they will have to work three hours for every hour the card calls for. They griped some about this, but I won't sign the card until they have put in their time, so there is nothing they can do about it.

Until recent years the practice of withholding wages for a period of four, six, or even eight weeks so as to keep workers on the job was prevalent. All these devices for the economic control of workers existed to a modified degree in camps of white workers, also. There was increased subordination of colored workers, as compared with white, however, because the caste sanctions of physical violence and of the withdrawal of legal protection were continually operating.[10]

COLORED PORTERS AND WHITE EMPLOYERS

Next to professional men and artisans, store porters have the highest occupational status of colored workers in Old City, and their families are usually members of the upper-middle social class. Their wages vary from $8.00 to $15.00 per week, and most of them have held their jobs for a long period. Their relationships with their white employers are usually similar

[10] The difficulties of collecting damages from an employer for injuries received in the course of work were greatly increased in the case of colored workers. In timber camps workers were charged $1.00 per week for insurance against accident but were frequently unable to collect the benefit if they were injured.

to those between colored domestic servants and white employers. In stores or small business concerns, where a colored porter has been employed for a long period, this relation may become very strong and can be expressed by mutual obligations and services. One cotton-buyer, for instance, said that he "couldn't get along" without a colored porter who had been with him for almost thirty years. This porter often stayed around his place of business even on holidays. Another white merchant said of a former colored porter, who had worked for him for twenty-eight years, that he "could depend on him and he would do anything for me." He told of having aided the porter when he had been brought into court on a murder charge. The white employer had hired a lawyer and had finally persuaded the district attorney to agree to a light sentence. When the porter had returned from the penitentiary, the white employer had felt obliged to take care of him: "I can't let him starve after working for me so long." In another case, a former bank clerk expressed affection for a former colored porter in the bank: "Every once in a while he will stop me and ask me how the bond business is getting on and appears to take a great interest in how I am getting on. .... You can't help but have a feeling of affection for a coon like that." It is clear, therefore, that a white employer and his colored porter, in a small establishment, have a very close relationship, one which resembles in its sentiments and mutual obligations the family-servant relation.

COLORED DOMESTIC SERVANTS AND WHITE EMPLOYERS

Although a few colored women in Old City were employed in the planing-mills,[11] pecan-shelling factory, and steam

[11] In 1933 the average number of colored women employed in the planing-mills was 60; of white women, 12. The average weekly wage varied between $5.00 and $3.00 for white women and between $2.00 and $4.00 for colored women. Thirty colored girls, all of them under eighteen years of age and most of them under sixteen, were employed in the pecan-shelling factory in 1934. Their wages varied from $1.50 to $3.00 per week, with the mode at about $2.00. When

laundries, and a still smaller group as seamstresses for white and colored individuals, most colored women were employed as domestic servants for white families. The opportunities for colored women in this field of employment were the result of the fact that caste sanctions prevented white women from competing with colored women for these jobs. The census of occupations in Old County in 1930 counted 1,648 colored women and 156 colored men in domestic service with private families. Since all but two or three of the colored servants in Old City are employed by white families, the occupational relationships in this field are the most important of all occupational relationships for the study of both the caste system and the colored class system. The relationship between the white master and colored servant is as important in maintaining caste structure and behavior in the city as that between the white landlord and the colored tenant is on the plantation. Every white family down through the lower-middle class (and even some white families receiving federal relief between 1933 and 1935) has a colored domestic servant. This occupational relationship, therefore, is the most frequent form of intercaste relationship and receives greatest emphasis in the myth and in the symbolic controls developed by the caste system. The reciprocal relationship between the cook, the housekeeper, and the nurse or "mammy" and her white employer-family requires detailed study.

Types of servants.—Colored domestic servants fall into two general groups: first, servants with regular employment in the house of a particular white family; and, second, those who are employed occasionally or irregularly, such as washerwomen, extra servants for parties, and others.

The wage level for either group is low. A washerwoman

---

this factory was closed during the operation of the N.R.A. because it refused to increase wages, the employees petitioned to have the factory reopened on the same wage basis. It reopened on the same basis after two days. In the steam laundries which employed about 40 colored girls, the weekly wage varied between $4.00 and $5.00 for a sixty-hour week.

receives $0.75 to $1.00 for a family wash, and a cleaning woman or extra servant $0.50 to $0.60 a day. Weekly earnings depend upon the number of jobs obtained, but seldom exceed $2.00. The weekly wage for regular servants ranges from $1.25 to $5.00, with the mode falling between $2.00 and $3.00. Besides this cash payment, house servants receive their meals[12] and are usually allowed to take home scraps of surplus food and are given old clothes. They work seven days a week, coming in time to prepare the breakfast and staying until after the midday meal. In some instances they are expected to return to prepare the evening meal. At times casual workers found it impossible to collect their wages from white employers, as in the observed case of a colored gardener. An old colored washerwoman also complained to the interviewer that she had not been paid on time for her washing. The wages for regular servants, moreover, were extremely low, when it is realized that, in addition to their duties as cooks, nurses, and house-cleaners, they also had to wash and iron the family's clothing. One servant, who was employed by an upper-class white family at a wage of $3.00 per week, had 13 shirts in the family wash one week. She had to pay her cousin $0.25 for ironing these shirts, while she performed her other duties.

Duties of servants—Most white families employed only one servant, whose duties included cooking,[13] cleaning, washing, and nursing. When the family had several small children, two servants were sometimes employed. In such cases, one woman was primarily occupied with the house, and the other with

[12] It is a general practice among white employers to buy a poorer quality of food for their servants than for themselves. Ground meat, pig tails and feet, and cowpeas are usually given to servants. Colored domestics in Old City generally complained not only about the inferior quality of this food but also about the small amount furnished. One of many examples at hand is that of an upper-class white family of 3 members which had bought only 15 cents worth of tripe for their own dinner and that of 5 servants.

[13] Cooks keep their recipes as occupational secrets and guard them jealously. They often refuse to disclose them even to white people or to close friends.

the food; but the housemaid had to wait on the table, assist with the dishwashing, and even help prepare the food. Much more frequently the second servant was a nursemaid. Often a colored schoolgirl was engaged to play with the children in the afternoon and to give them their supper in the evening. Where a full-time nursemaid was employed, her duties extended to cleaning the children's rooms, washing their clothes, etc. The major division among servants was between nursemaids and other house servants.

Solidarity with white family.—The constant dependence of the members of the white family upon the colored servant for the daily and intimate services connected with the preparation of their food, cleaning of their houses, and care of their children and the reciprocal dependence of the colored servant upon the white employer-family for favor and patronage in economic and court crises are often expressed by a system of mutual services which are above and beyond those required by a purely occupational relationship. Colored domestics who have worked for upper-class white families for many years are often allowed not only a wide province of authority with regard to the house, the children, and the choice of foods but also a semifamilial relationship with their white employers. Caste taboos are relaxed within such relationships, especially with regard to colored nurses. Some colored nurses exert extensive authority over white children; often there is also a strong bond of mutual services between them and these white individuals in later years, and cases have been known where Negro servants left their meager property to these children when they died. Through her relationship with the white employer's children the colored nurse may also be released from certain caste taboos in her relation to adult members of the family; she may sit in a room with adults or discuss child care with neighbors.

Servants who have been with a family for a long time are often permitted great latitude in their behavior and conversation, gossiping with them about whites and Negroes and occasionally assisting them with their work. A certain amount of grumbling, arguing, and defiance is also permitted in old family servants, and the white family's attitude toward this behavior varies with the circumstances surrounding it. One white woman told of an old family servant who refused to be discharged. In another instance, although a colored servant was disagreeable and insolent, the white employer ignored her ill-humor. A planter said that his children's old colored nurse objected to his whipping them and sometimes would playfully strike him in return.

The grapevine.—The recognition by colored domestic servants of their solidarity with their white employer-families is best illustrated by their practice of reporting to these white families not only the church and associational activities of colored communities but also any expressions of dissatisfaction with the caste sanctions by colored people. In speaking of one such case, in which a colored man had been reported to the chief of police because he had told a group of Negroes that "white and colored folks sometimes eat together up North," a colored man complained to a group of lower-class men: "You know white people get [learn] everything you do from these cullud women who cook an' work for them. These ol' cullud women tell them everything that goes on in their church an' lodge, an' everything about white people you say to them."

Colored men were particularly antagonistic to this form of intercaste solidarity. Whereas they blamed miscegenation between colored female servants and white male employers on the white man, they blamed the grapevine upon the colored cook or nurse and regarded such communication as "treachery to the race," that is, as a violation of intracaste solidarity. It was well established, in the case of a colored school principal who had been charged by the city school board with diverting funds, that the charge was made as a result of protests by colored servants to their white employers. The generality of this gossip relationship between colored servants and white employers was also frequently remarked by white persons.

In the case of servants and nurses who have been employed by the same family for a long period, the gossip privilege enjoyed by the colored servant is often extended to include the circle of friends of the employer's family. One very well-known colored nurse and seamstress not only "visited" many upper-class white women to retail gossip about other white women but actually was heard by the interviewer giving information concerning white individuals to the society editor of the white newspaper. So important was this woman's function as a carrier of news in the white upper class that a group of white upper-class women called her aside on the main business street of Old City one day in 1933 and playfully rebuked her because she had not "visited" them recently. One white woman said: "Bessie, where on earth have you been? You must uv turned nigguh on us!"

A great deal of additional evidence of the recognition by old colored servants of their close bonds with their white employers could be given, but only a few more examples need be cited. At a meeting in a colored rural school an old servant yelled: "I sho luv my whut folks!" after her middle-class employer had addressed the group. In a limited sense, the colored servant does feel herself to be a part of the employer's family. Her relations within it are not limited to solidarities with specific individuals but extend to all the immediate family and often to relatives outside the home.

Return by employer—In many cases, upper and upper-middle-class white employers also perform services for colored servants above and beyond paying wages.[14] With old servants, especially, the white family often recognizes its obligation to perform these additional reciprocal services, and members of a family often speak with affection of both these servants and their children.

A servant relation with a white family may be of great value to a colored person, furthermore, in helping him avoid

[14] Although the general practice of giving food and old clothes to servants is considered by both employers and servants as a form of paying wages, some employers also furnished medical and dental care for old or favorite servants.

the caste sanctions of the courts. If the servant comes into conflict with the law, she always turns to her employer's family rather than to her own group. The white employer usually tries to protect her. He uses his influence to have the charges dropped; he may put up bail; and sometimes he even hires a lawyer to defend her. In some cases white people will even pay a Negro's fine and then let him work it out around the home.

At times the services of the white family do not end when the servant leaves their employment. One white woman said that she had called on her former cook, whose daughter had just died, to offer sympathy and help. She had formerly corresponded with this daughter concerning the old servant and had frequently exchanged gifts with her. The leading colored businessman of Old City during the first decade of the century had been enabled to start his business and to buy his property by the direct aid of white men whom he had served in the leading club of the city. Numerous instances of the attendance by white family groups at the funerals of former colored servants were observed by the interviewers. This service was recognized as a duty by most white families, even if the servant had not worked for them for many years. At the funeral of one such former servant, twelve white persons of three different families were present, and occupied the three front pews in the colored church.

Semifamilial status of servant.—The assertion that they regard an old colored servant as "a member of the family" is often made by white employers. What is referred to by this statement is usually the partial removal of the caste sanctions from colored nurses and "mammies," and the mutual services and demonstrations of affection, including kissing and embracing, which occur in later years between these servants and the white individuals they once nursed. At times, colored servants are also present as spectators at family ceremonies of their employers, and even former servants may also attend such ceremonies. One planter, telling of his daughter's wedding, said that all of the old family servants returned to the plantation to help with preparations, and all were present at the ceremony. Anqther woman said that all her servants attended her daughter's church wedding, sitting in the balcony of the church. There were also many instances of the presence of colored servants at white funerals. Tales are also told of white planters who asked to have their colored servants as pallbearers at their funerals.

Servants always participate in the Christmas festivities of the white family. They usually receive gifts from all members of the immediate family and often from relatives and close friends of the family.

For the most part, however, the semifamilial status of colored servants in the white household is limited to those employed by white families of the upper and upper-middle classes. In such families the master-servant relationship is likely to be governed by a paternalistic tradition, which is based upon the fact that the social rank of the white family is so high, and the social and economic distance between it and the colored servants so great, that the white family does not need to insist upon the rigid application of caste and occupational sanctions. In white families of lower social rank, caste distance is more jealously guarded. Even within white families of the upper and upper-middle class, in spite of the partial relaxing of the caste sanctions with regard to their colored servants, there is always a clear recognition in practice of the fact that the colored servant is not only a menial but also a member of the lower caste. Unless she is accompanying white children, she must always enter and leave the house by the rear door. She may never eat with the adult whites or in the dining-room. She appears among the white family and their guests only in the performance of her duties and not as a social equal. There is a limit, furthermore, to the extent of the nondeferential behavior permitted her. One white employer said, for example, that when a drunken colored servant of her friend had cursed her, there had been "nothing to do but fire her." The caste sanctions of physical violence may also be used. One white employer, a man, beat his cook severely for stealing; another white man beat his colored female servant for arguing with his wife.

When white employers say that a colored servant is a "part of the family," they never indicate that she is no longer considered as lower caste. They mean, rather, that she has a definite and very strong position as a servant in the family life, a position such that she has very intimate and emotional relations with the members of the family and with their home. She acts as a connecting link between members of the family and the care of the household, and she plays an important part in the preparations for activities within the home. An integral part of this situation is the nondeferential and affectionate behavior which is permitted. She may quarrel good-naturedly about her duties; she may be greeted and even embraced affectionately; and she may gossip and joke with the family. The fundamental caste structure of the relationships between her and her white adult employers remain, however.[15]

Failure of employer to return services.—In some cases which were observed by the interviewers, moreover, white employers failed to make the expected return of services to their old servants. This failure was observed not only in white families of the lower-middle and upper-lower social classes but in those of the upper class aswell. Cases were cited, by Negroes

[15] This fact is often commented upon by old colored servants, who contrast the intimate nature of their services to white families (i.e., in cooking their food, nursing, and often suckling their children, and caring for adults, male and female, in the sickbed) with the taboo of social uncleanliness which their employers recognize in their public relations with them. One of the most frequent remarks of this kind is directed toward miscegenation between colored female servants and white members of the employer-family. Three such cases were admitted by white employers in the present generation.

One old colored servant ridiculed the fact that her employer was active in supporting measures in the state legislature "to keep Negroes in their place," because she had always had complete charge of his children and often slept in the bed with them.

and upper-class white individuals, of the failure of upper-class white families to provide food or medical care for old servants and nurses who had been employed by the white family up to the time they had become ill. (But "they always went to their funerals," one colored man remarked bitterly.) It is impossible to say what proportion of white employers aided their incapacitated servants; complaints of this type demonstrate that the practice had been sufficiently general at some time to lead colored persons to expect white employers to follow it. It seems likely, on the basis of the observation of a large number of cases, however, that services by the employer-family to the colored servant have the following order of generality in white families of the upper and upper-middle classes:

Almost universal....
1. Relaxing caste sanctions
2. Intervening in court for servant and members of servant's family
3. Gossiping
Less general........ 4. Granting semifamilial relationship
Still less general..... 5. Caring for them when incapacitated

Disorganization of family of servant.—The children of domestic servants, at the time of this study, however, had none of the advantages which children of servants enjoyed during slavery and the two generations following emancipation. The loss of these advantages was associated with the change in residence of the servant from the employer's house or servant's quarters to a shanty in the colored community. As a result of this change, the children of the servant now have no contact with the family of their mother's employer and receive little care from their mother. Children are left with their maternal grandmother or aunt, or entirely alone, during the whole of the day. In cases of the former type the grandmother or aunt often "adopts" the children. In those of the latter type, children are under the care of the oldest child, who may be only five or six years old and is seldom more than fourteen, since at that

451

age a boy or girl finds a job and establishes a household himself. Servants place their children in school when they are four or five years old, so that they will be cared for during at least half of the day. In such cases, however, the child must often go to and from school unaccompanied, and usually receives no breakfast except a piece of cold corn bread and a cup of sweetened water. The interviewers visited 125 homes of colored families of the lowest economic group, and these visits confirmed the statement of a colored agent who entered more than 600 colored homes in Old County weekly:

> Mother and father are both away in mos' of them. On my roun's, I fine children six years ol' tekin' care of the house, an' mindin' the smaller children. [Interviewer found the same thing.] You'll see that often. The mother has to leave somebody at home, so one of the children stays away from school with the small ones. Often you'll fine that the mother leaves the baby an' little childrun with a frien' or neighbor to tek care of while she's at work.

The contrast between the neglect of her own children and the painstaking care of her white employer's children, which is typical of the colored nurse, is often bitterly commented upon by colored persons in Old City. The waiflike status of the child of the domestic servant, however, is not the result of the caste system chiefly but of the economic system which compels the mothers of these children to work outside their home, in order that they and their children may secure a living.

Status of servant in colored society.—Before the existence of a group of colored physicians, dentists, and teachers, those domestic servants who worked in white families of high social rank enjoyed higher status in the colored society than they now have. As a result of their intimate relationship with the most powerful members of the upper caste, they were able to obtain patronage for themselves and for their family and a knowledge of the white society and its manners which increased their status in the colored society.[16] However, with (1) the

---

[16] Colored people of the upper social class in Old City between 1933 and 1935 felt that colored domestic servants still believed that their social rank in

tremendous increase in the importance of formal education as a class sanction in the colored group, (2) the further elaboration of class sanctions as a result of the increasing complexity of the occupational system, and (3) the increasing development of economic differentials, colored servants have lost status because they are engaged in menial work, for low wages, and are "ignorant." The manners and the ability to read which many of them gained from their white employers, however, and the property which others received from employers who in some cases were their fathers have been factors in educating their children. Largely as a result of the patronage which their parents received from white employers, the offspring of domestic servants and of artisans of a former generation constitute the bulk of the family heads in the colored upper and upper-middle classes in Old City.

---

the colored group was increased by the fact that they worked for white families of the upper and upper-middle classes and that they felt that it would be greatly decreased if they worked for colored employers of any class. The belief was general among this class that colored servants were unwilling to work for colored families of any class. Several servants also claimed that colored domestics were generally unwilling to work for colored people, but disclaimed any such attitude themselves. Colored families who could afford servants, however, not only had been able to obtain them but had had no difficulty in keeping them over a long period. In all cases, it must be added, there were young women who had not had semifamilial relationships with white employer-families.

Within their own social class, servants often wash, iron, and sew for each other, on an exchange basis.

CHAPTER XXI

RELATION BETWEEN THE CASTE SYSTEM AND THE ECONOMIC SYSTEM

MODIFICATIONS OF CASTE SANCTIONS

THE extreme economic subordination of the majority of colored persons in Old County has been described in the preceding chapters. Yet, it remains true that economic relationships are less completely governed by caste than are intergroup relationships of any other type. Indeed, the only type of behavior by which the society allows a colored individual to express superiority to any white individual is economic behavior. This economic modification of the caste sanctions may be represented diagrammatically by the sloping position of a line symbolizing the economic subordination of the lower caste. In the familial, class, associational, church, legal, and political structures all colored persons are subordinated to all white persons, as indicated by the horizontal position of the caste line in Figure 25. In economic traits and possessions, however, some colored persons are superior to many white persons of the lower economic level. A few are actually superior, in their income and property ownership, to most white persons of the middle and upper economic levels. The sloping line in Figure 26 indicates this fact, namely, that some colored persons have an economic status parallel to that of some whites and superior to others.

For the reasons underlying this modification of the caste sanctions, one must look eventually (1) to the operation of solidarities and antagonisms between economic groups within the local society and (2) to the operation of the national economic system. First of all, however, it will be revealing to

454

examine the field evidence with regard to economic behavior which is in conflict with the caste dogma. Although the number of persons to whom the caste modifications apply is

STRUCTURE	DEGREE OF SUBORDINATION
Family structure ⎫ Class system ⎬ White Associations ⎬ ———— Churches ⎭ Colored	
Courts (inter- racial cases)	White ———— Colored
Politics	White ———— Colored

FIG. 25.—Relative status of Negroes and whites in non-economic structures of the society.

small, it is of theoretical significance that any exceptions at all are made.

The upper economic group in the lower caste.—The relatively higher economic position of some colored families to some white families could be shown for a variety of traits, such as value of real and personal property owned, value of automobiles

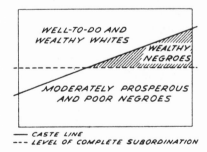

FIG. 26.—Relative status of Negroes and whites in economic structures of the society.

owned, size of income, etc., by counting the number in each color group whose property valuation, or income, falls within a defined range. It would then be possible to state the proportion of all colored families who were above a certain proportion of all white families at any point in the valuation scale.

A more dramatic method of emphasizing the anomalous position of some colored families, in relation to many white families, is to consider only those colored families in the highest economic groups. There are 20 colored individuals or families who were assessed on the city tax-rolls for real estate in Old City amounting to between $1,500 and $1,999, inclusive; 19 between $2,000 and $2,999; 8 between $3,000 and $3,999; 3 between $4,000 and $4,999; 4 between $5,000 and $10,000; and 1 whose property was assessed at $20,000. On the county tax-rolls the assessments for this same urban real estate were higher by approximately 50 per cent. For rural real estate, 12 colored individuals or families were assessed between $2,000 and $2,999, inclusive; 3 between $5,000 and $5,999; and 2 between $10,000 and $20,000. The combined assessed values for urban and rural real estate for each of two colored individuals was more than $20,000. In neighboring areas there were to be found a colored individual who owned a drug store valued at $10,000, a colored planter who obtained an average of 100 bales of cotton per year (worth about $5,000 in 1934), another planter who obtained an average yield of 200 bales (worth about $10,000), and a third colored man who recently left an estate of approximately $80,000, chiefly in cash. In Old County, itself, one colored man owned 3,000 acres of land, and one professional man had a yearly income which ranged from $25,000 to $8,000 between 1918 and 1934. Both his income and the value of his real estate were larger than those of all except 4 or 5 white residents in the county. Two colored contractors in Old County employed both white and colored workers and filled contracts for white firms which at times amounted to as much as $25,000. One of these colored men had been in charge of the construction of most of the store buildings in a neighboring city. The other had employed as many as 100 workers at a time. In general, this group of colored persons, whose economic status is higher than that of almost all white persons of the lowest economic group and many of those in the middle economic group, is composed of a few professional men, a few planters, a few storekeepers, contractors, artisans, and a few employees of the federal government, or of the heirs of men who held these positions. The existence of this group of colored families of relatively high economic status gives rise to certain modifications of the caste dogmas in their favor. Other modifications arise from the role of Negroes as laborers and consumers. The less drastic modifications will be discussed first, and the more fundamental modifications in the sections following.

Subordination of white salesmen to colored customers.— Observations of store behavior revealed that some subordination of white clerks to colored customers takes place. White clerks serve colored patrons with at least a semblance of courtesy, allowing them to examine the goods, making suggestions, and generally behaving much as they would toward a white customer. Clerks in the stores which have a large amount of colored trade do not openly discriminate between colored and white customers but serve them in turn, sometimes allowing white customers to wait until colored ones have been served. In some of the cheaper stores, white customers are often obliged to force their way through crowds of colored patrons or sight-seers, in order to receive any attention from clerks. This situation is especially common on Saturdays, when many colored tenants come into Old City from the rural districts. One white girl in Rural County said that the white people there did not attempt to shop on Saturdays, because the clerks were too busy with colored customers to take time for the white.

In the small county seat of Rural County, white cafés served colored patrons, although at a separate counter. A prominent white lawyer, who, like all other lawyers in the county, had a large number of colored clients, said that neither white lawyers nor white businessmen could succeed without colored patronage. As proof of this statement, he cited the fact that one white café which served both white and colored patrons was highly successful, whereas another which served only white customers was failing. In Old City a white female clerk in the most expensive women's store made a practice of being courteous and deferential to colored patrons, so as to induce most of them to ask for her, when they entered the store. The white proprietor of a grocery store located in the colored residential area made his children say "Yessir" and "Yesm'am" to all colored patrons. All the leading white stores in Old City allowed exhibits of the work done in home-economics and art courses by colored students to be displayed in their windows. In the municipal Charity Hospital white nurses waited upon colored patients (in two large southern hospitals in recent years, organized and militant efforts have been made by the white communities to prevent colored nurses from superseding white nurses in these jobs of caring for colored patients).

A most dramatic example of the power of the economic system to moderate the caste sanctions was offered by the successful boycott by colored patrons of the largest white theater in Old City. Colored patrons had formerly been allowed to sit in a section parallel to that occupied by white patrons in the balcony. As a result of protests by white organizations, they were later excluded from the balcony and were allowed to sit ony in the gallery, behind all white patrons. Colored persons in Old City began an undemonstrative but well-organized boycott of the theater which lasted for six years, in spite of the management's efforts to induce them to return. At the end of that period a section was again provided for colored patrons which was parallel with that for white patrons in the balcony.

Striking instances of the relaxation of caste taboos were also observed in the case of some white individuals, such as sales agents and insurance men. The head of one insurance company stated that collectors had "to put up with lots from the Negroes and you can't just bawl them out." Social distance was usually maintained, however, by refusing to remove one's hats in colored homes or to address colored policyholders as "Mr." and "Mrs." White store clerks, too, avoid these titles of respect even when making out bills. They also break the force of the subordination involved in "waiting on" Negroes by joking them about their purchases. When a few Jewish merchants in a Negro shopping area broke these caste rules, they were roundly condemned by other white merchants. It is evident, then, that the white group recognizes in the salesman-customer relationship an inversion of the usual colored-white relationship and is defensive about this behavior. So long as proper "social" distance is maintained, however, there is no open antagonism.

Colored employers and white employees.—A less frequent, but more fundamental, violation of the caste dogmas occurs when a colored proprietor or contractor employs and supervises white workmen. Several cases of this type occurred in Old County and in neighboring counties. A large colored contractor, although at first unwilling to speak on this subject, finally admitted that he employed white men and treated them in much the same fashion as he did his colored employees. Upon occasion, he was also forced to bargain and dispute with white businessmen.

A second large colored contractor had employed white and colored men on the same jobs over a long period. "I give them orders jes' like anybody else," he said; "Oh, things ain't as bad here as they try to make out." These three contractors all had the appearance of white men, a fact which indubitably contributed to their successful commercial relations with white people. All of them had lived in Old County for many years and were known to be colored, however. When another colored man, co-owner of a business with a white man in an adjoining county, discharged one of their white employees, white persons threatened to harm him, but nothing was actually done. In Old City a Negro man operated a taxicab business which competed so successfully with the white taxicab company that it forced the latter out of business. He estimated that three-fourths of his patrons were white. Later, when another white company began business, a "taxi war" ensued between the two companies; no pressure was brought against the colored company by the white community, however, and it continued to operate successfully.

Colored merchants and professional men and white customers. —In the relationships between colored professional men and their white clients, as well as between colored storekeepers and their white customers, even more striking inversions of status occurred. Members of the former group frequently remarked that white clients said "Yessir" and "Nosir" to them and were very "respectful." Several instances of such verbal deference were overheard by interviewers. Perhaps the most dramatic instances of this kind took place in the store of a brown-skinned colored owner, where white patrons were frequently observed. Most of these were poor-whites. In their begging of credit from the colored owner, the type of conflict which arises between the economic system and the caste system was forcibly expressed by the following incident. The interviewer asked Mr. Phillips, a colored storekeeper, if he had many white customers, and the storekeeper replied:

> I have quite a lot. I could have a lot more, but they want credit. I just tell them that I can't do it. They say: "You don't give credit?" I say: "Yes, I give credit, but I've got all I can take now. I can't stand any more." They look at me, and maybe say they just want it tel Sat'day, but I say: "I'm sorry. I can't give eny more."
> *Then some of them will send their wife back here.* Think I'll have to give it to a white *woman*. But I tell *them* the same thing.

ECONOMIC VIOLATIONS OF WHITE SOLIDARITY

Caste and a profit economy.—A more deliberate and basic infraction of the dogma of upper-caste solidarity occurs in the employing of colored workers, in preference to white, by white managers and planters themselves. In Old County the dogma of caste solidarity is usually ineffective in limiting the white employer's choice of a labor supply, except in the fields of merchandising and "white-collar" work, where the white labor supply can effectively use economic, political, or social caste sanctions upon the employers. The preference given the colored labor supply in other fields of employment is the result of the fact that the economic system and the caste dogmas are fundamentally at variance.

In the system of competitive industry, of which Old County's manufactures and agriculture are parts, industries operate so as to obtain the highest possible rate of profit. In Old County the caste dogma enables the white employer to increase his profits by paying colored workers a lower wage than he would be forced to pay white workers; that is, the caste system, by excluding white unemployed men and women from this work, actually subordinates them economically to these colored workers. Although white workers apply for these jobs and frequently appeal to white employers to hire them because they are members of the "upper" caste, Old County's white employers have consistently refused to do so. It is clear, then, that the dogma of caste is usually effective in economic behavior only so far as it is consistent with the interests of white employers. In an "ideal" caste society, according to the dogma, all members of the upper caste would be employers, and all members of the lower caste, employees. In Old County, however, the system of relatively free competition in industry has resulted in a certain amount of variance between economic status and caste status, as a result chiefly of the organization of industry so as to obtain the highest possible rate of profit.

One of the clearest examples of the difficulties which arise in the attempt to impose the caste system upon the economic system has been furnished by the efforts of the local white population to control the labor policies of the largest planing-mill. When this mill, controlled by nonlocal management, opened in 1918, it was faced by a shortage of both skilled and

461

unskilled white workers. It therefore employed chiefly colored workers. Two factors have prevented the replacing of most of these colored workers with white operatives during the next fifteen years: (1) The management has been unwilling to replace experienced workers with inexperienced workers. At the company's employment offices in 1934 and 1935 it was a common occurrence to see untrained white men refused work each morning, while experienced colored men were re-employed. (2) The success of the local Chamber of Commerce, in persuading the mill management to reduce the wage scales of colored workers, later proved a handicap to white workers, for the mill retained its low-waged colored employees in preference to white men, even after a sufficient supply of the latter became available. More than seven out of every ten workers were colored as late as 1935. For much the same reasons, colored workers were preferred to white by the manager of another large industrial firm; he employed them, he said, because they were "cheap and docile labor." He defended their ability both for heavy labor and for fast skilled labor, in which, he claimed, the "younger educated ones are just as active and capable as one could ask."

Other examples of the violation of caste solidarity as a result of the pressures of the economic system are too numerous to be analyzed in detail. Only a few other typical cases will be cited. When a group of white men organized a "burial association" to sell policies to colored patrons, several white insurance companies gave every possible aid to the colored undertakers in their fight against the white-owned "burial association." When the federal government asked for a poll of farmers to determine their attitude with regard to the continuance of the cotton subsidy, the landlords who favored the subsidy allowed all their colored tenants to vote, in spite of the fact that, except for the taboo upon intercaste sexual relations, the taboo upon the use of the ballot by colored persons is the strongest in the system.

While even the local white cotton-planters exert a blanket

exclusion upon white tenants, those industries which are not locally controlled go even farther in violating caste taboos when considerations of profit (the conventional economic behavior) so dictate. In addition to the case of the planing-mill, the following incidents may serve as examples of this conflict. When the local planters and industrial concerns were attempting to stop emigration of colored workers during the World War, the mayor of Old City requested the local ticket agents of the railroads to sell no more tickets to colored persons. The agents refused, on the grounds that it would be an interference with their business. Similarly, during the "depression" a railroad company provided only one coach to be used in common by white and colored patrons on a branch line. When white communities protested against this violation of the state law, they were told by the company that the branch line had been losing money steadily and that white people would have to ride in the same coach with colored or not at all. The arrangement continued.[1]

In a similar manner the economic depression of 1929-34 gave rise to other modifications of caste in economic relations. While the subordination of the unskilled colored laborer was increased, the superiority of the middle and upper economic groups of colored persons to the poor-whites was increased, and there was a marked increase in the deference with which white salesmen and merchants treated colored patrons. White gas-station attendants, for example, began the practice of tipping their caps to upper-class colored patrons. A colored leader remarked on this modification of caste in a public speech to a large colored audience: "You know, this depression has made the great [sarcastically] Anglo-Saxon easier to get along

---

[1] The converse of this type of situation occurred when a local white jury awarded a colored woman damages to the amount of $7,500 against a white man, insured by a white company, who had killed her son in an automobile accident. The mayor of Old City represented the colored woman in court. Both he and colored leaders explained the award on the grounds that a nonlocal insurance company, and not the local white man, would have to pay it, and that white merchants and lawyers would receive most of the $7,500.

with! He seems to feel more kindly toward us. He smiles and is very courteous at his gas stations and stores."

A second modification of caste during the "depression" consisted in the entrance of white workers into the field of "Negro jobs."[2] Although in a strictly economic sense this invasion resulted in the unemployment of many colored workers and thus increased the general subordination of colored families to white, from the point of view of the white workers it constituted an occupational degradation and a violation of their caste status. In addition, it increased the economic subordination of these white laborers to colored persons of the middle and upper economic levels. From the point of view of colored people of these groups, the upper caste lost much of its prestige by this occupational degradation of some of its members. A colored worker stressed this aspect of the new situation, in a conversation with a group of colored laborers who had complained that white men were doing pick-and-shovel work on a local federal relief project:

> Hell, I'm glad they swingin' those picks! They wouldn' do enything like that—that kine uh work wuz only fuh nigguhs [*sneering*]. The only reason they doin' it now is because they gottuh do it tuh live. I hear people talkin' 'bout takin' jobs away from cullud men', but I don't give uh damn how many uh *those* jobs they tek! Let um know how it feels tuh swing that pick! An' I jus' lak to walk by um in the mornin' with uh white shirt an' colluh on, an' my shoes all shined, an' let um know that I doan have to do that kine uh work [*laughing*]. I really enjoy it!

The greatest extension of such modifications of caste occurred (1) in the replacing of colored garbage-collectors by white men who collected garbage from colored homes, (2) in numerous observed cases of the borrowing of food by white families from colored families, and (3) in the organized effort of white women in another southern city to take jobs as cooks and waitresses on a federal relief project which fed only colored children.

[2] Evidence of the extent of this movement has been presented in the chapter on "Caste, Class and the Urban Economy," chap. xx.

CASTE AND THE ECONOMIC SYSTEM

In spite of the efforts of the upper and middle economic groups of white people in Old County to maintain the caste line between the white and colored relief groups by placing nearly all white clients on a higher dole, or wage, than any colored client,[3] it was clear, between 1933 and 1935, that the lower groups of white people were more concerned with economic than with caste loyalties. The best illustration of this tendency was the fact that the leading political candidate in the state in 1934 made his campaign speeches against "rich landowners" rather than against the efforts of the lower caste to achieve greater economic and social mobility. In Louisiana, at the same time, Huey Long was finding economic loyalties a surer basis than caste antagonism for appealing to the lower economic group of whites. The tendency toward a new alignment, as a result of the "depression" and the great increase in unemployment, was recognized by colored people generally. One colored urban worker expressed these ideas quite clearly:

Yeah, things is changing. A white boy who ain't got nuthin' now got a helluva chance of gittin' enything these days! Ef he's po', he gonnuh stay po' now! Ef he ain't got nuthin' tuh start wid, he can't git rich off de nigguh.

It use' tuh be:
> "Nought to nought, an' figguh to figguh
> All fuh de white man, an' none fuh de nigguh!"

Now, hit's:
> "Nought to nought, an' fo' tuh fo'
> All fuh de rich, an' none fuh de po'."

Caste in spite of economic superordination.—Before considering in detail the evidence with regard to fundamental antagonisms between economic groups, both within and across the caste lines, however, it is necessary to emphasize the fact that the conflicts dealt with above constitute only a modification, and by no means an abrogation, of caste as it applies to

[3] The median Federal relief payment to 105 colored families in 1934 was $5.14 per month; to 132 white families, $12.35. The modal payment was $5.40 for colored families and $18.00 for white families.

economic relationships. To use our diagrammatical imagery, the caste line still slants downward upon colored people, even if they are members of the upper economic group. For example, they cannot eat in white restaurants or live in houses in white neighborhoods of the same economic level as their own.[4] They cannot receive accommodations equal to those of even the poorer whites in theaters or trains. Well-to-do colored persons of the professional group cannot even wait inside white restaurants in Old City for sandwiches to be eaten outside. In some stores colored persons of the middle and lower groups are likely to be waited upon only after all white persons have been served, and colored women of even the upper group are called by their first names by most white saleswomen. Examples of the application of caste sanctions of this kind to prosperous colored men were frequently cited by informants. As usual, the most extreme cases were represented as happening only in other cities. In a neighboring Louisiana city, for instance, a colored man who rented some of his real estate to white persons had to follow the usual custom of going to the back door when he collected rent from his white tenants: "Now dat nigguh got to ack so humble an' meek! He goes 'roun' to de back do' of his *own* house, now, to ask de white people fuh his rent! Got his hat in his han', an' his back all bent! [*laughing*]. He's *bettuh* do like that, too; don't, dey'll run him 'way frum dere." The same behavior would have been required of a colored man in a similar position in Old City, however. A fairly prosperous colored man there remarked on the common practice among local colored people of concealing the amount of their savings from white people. He himself had kept his money in four banks, for this reason:

During the years when I was making money, I didn't put it all in one bank. I put it in *four* banks. I wasn't going to let them [white people] know what I had! .... If I made big money, I'd send it away from here, to the North, and keep it there. I never could see how these fools get run out of town with all their money in one bank.

---

[4] An upper-class colored man who bought a home in the middle-class white neighborhood in Old City was forced to move from it.

CASTE AND THE ECONOMIC SYSTEM

Therefore, it is clear that, were it not for considerations of space, facts such as these would be repeated as the dominant refrain throughout this discussion of the relationship between the economic and the caste systems. The object of this chapter, however, is to call attention to the elements of conflict which exist between the two systems and to point out that certain behavioral systems which usually have been attributed to caste are more properly attributable to the economic system.[5]

CASTE AND ECONOMIC GROUPS

Antagonisms between economic groups within upper caste.— Both the overt behavior of white landlords and proprietors and their verbally expressed attitudes with regard to the lower economic group of white people in Old and Rural counties testified to the existence of economic groups within the upper caste and to the occasional subordination of caste solidarity to the interests of the white upper economic group.

[5] The elimination of certain types of colored proprietors and artisans in Old County during the last thirty years, for example, has been largely the result of changes in the economic system. Between 1865 and 1900 there was a relatively large number of colored proprietors in Old City and a great variety of artisans. Some of these had been skilled workers on the plantations during slavery, and others had been free colored people. In 1900 this group included proprietors of a catering establishment, a restaurant, and a barber-shop (all of which served only white patrons) and a saddle and harness store, a drug store, a large wheelwrighting and blacksmith shop, a livery stable, a drygoods store, and two grocery stores, which were considerably larger than any now owned by colored proprietors. There were also colored contractors and artisans of all types who had virtually a monopoly of skilled labor. The disappearance of colored persons from most of these fields, however, has been the result of the tightening of competition in the more advanced stages of the economic system. Since white proprietors of the upper and middle economic groups have had more capital and credit than colored proprietors who sought to compete with them, they have forced most of these colored men from business. The elimination of many colored proprietors, contractors, and artisans, therefore, has been the result not of caste sanctions but of the fact that, in respect to capital, they were on the lower fringes of the businesses of their type. They have been forced out by the same basic factors in competition which have forced out many white "marginal" business men. On the other hand, those few colored proprietors and contractors who had a larger amount of capital and credit have been able to maintain their place in the economic system, as has been pointed out at the beginning of this chapter.

467

The evidence on this point is abundant. Only a relatively small part of it can be summarized here.

Exclusion of white tenants by white landlords.—In Old County and in many other plantation areas the solidarity of the upper caste is most seriously threatened by the general practice of white landlords in giving colored farm-tenants employment at the expense of poor and unemployed white men. In taking advantage of the caste system, which renders the colored workers more docile and less expensive, the economic system at the same time subordinates a large group of white families below even the lowest economic group of colored families.[6] The only landlords in Old County who made a practice of renting to white tenants or of hiring white day-laborers were two or three recently established truck-farmers, who used both white and colored workers. All the other leading white landlords in Old County, and most of those in Rural County, frankly told interviewers that it was their policy to accept no white tenants, and expressed strong antagonisms to the poor-white group as a whole. Their policy is summarized by the following statement of a large white planter in Old County:

> The white tenants can be pretty poor. I wouldn't want this generally known, but I wouldn't have one on my place. I am always having applicants, but I always tell them I am full up. White tenants will ruin you; they won't work, and they always stir up trouble. Those who are good farmers are liable to turn against you sooner or later, and cause trouble.[7]

One of the chief objections of white landlords to white tenants is based upon the ability of white tenants to resort to legal

[6] A second major conflict between the agricultural economy and the caste system has been dealt with in the chapter "The Division of Labor," chap. xiv, namely, the influence of the shortage of colored labor after 1918 in compelling white planters to restrict their use of terrorization and dishonest settlements.

[7] With regard to the Mississippi Delta, where white tenants have been trying to gain a foothold, Vance states: "Reports indicate that many planters are vexed by the demands and behavior of their new [white] tenants, and prefer to have their labor all Negro. . . . . It is a common saying that a white cropper 'ought to black his face, if he wants to get a good place' " (Vance, *The Negro Agricultural Worker* [mimeographed, 1934] pp. 44–45).

defense against dishonest settlement, terrorization, illegal eviction, or illegal seizure of livestock and personal property.[8] A colored plantation-manager in Old County also advanced this reason for the exclusion of white tenants and added that the practice had been common in his father's time, when "these rich white people here wouldn't have poor-whites on their farms at all."

A second reason advanced by white landlords for their exclusion of white tenants, especially during the years of low income, was that white tenants demanded more credit than colored tenants. The landlord who hired more white workers than any one else in Old County emphasized both of the above objections:

> The reason most planters don't like white tenants is because they want more advances and you can't hold them down the way you can a Negro. If you tell a Negro he can't have any more, he will go back to work, but a white will grumble and won't work, and will even move out on you. I have seen the time when you even had to advance them enough to buy a car, if you wanted them to work. Then they always think you have beat them out of something. They go around telling everybody that you cheated them, and they hold a grudge against you, and tell everybody that you are crooked.

A third complaint made by white landlords against white tenants was that they tried to "boss all the Negroes" and thus interfered with the landlord's control of both groups.

Merchants and bankers had similar policies with regard to allowing credit to white tenants. The president of one of the banks expressed extreme antagonism to poor-whites and stated that white tenants "never" had a bank account and seldom were granted loans. One of the leading merchants in Rural County said he never allowed credit to a white tenant

[8] This reason for excluding white tenants was also given by a colored plantation-manager in the Delta regions across the river from Old County. Colored laborers were preferred to white because (1) they spent their wages more freely in the plantation store and (2) they were more easily controlled than white tenants, "who will try to get up with the other white man."

if he could avoid doing so; the other merchant claimed that poor-whites would not pay their bills and that therefore he would not allow them credit.

In Rural County a prominent government official told an interviewer: "White tenants are no good, and nobody wants them. The Negroes are better people than the poor-whites." He was especially hostile to a political organization of the poorer white people, which he derisively called "The Woodpeckers' Taxpayers League." Another county official objected to the immigration of white sawmill workers, who, he claimed, were "a detriment" to the county. The leading white landlords in Rural County were unanimous in accusing white sawmill workers of being "lower than the Negroes" and in preferring colored workers to them.[9]

A large white planter in Old County, who refused to accept white tenants, said that there was a concerted movement by white planters to force the poorer whites to leave the county. "They are a bad lot, worse even than Negroes." A justice of the peace in Old City, who claimed to have shot six white men of a group which sought to terrorize his colored farm labor in 1872, angrily insisted to the interviewer that white tenants were "a worthless, shiftless, no-count lot"; that in Old City itself there existed "the most low-down poor whites—that never do a thing but drink and carouse around"; and that the white planing-mill workers were "just the most worthless sort" who worked "a little" during the day but drank and caroused all night and every week-end.

White storekeepers, cotton-buyers, and insurance agents expressed similar antagonisms to white persons of the lower economic group. A large cotton-buyer and credit merchant preferred colored to white tenants, he said, because the latter usually paid their debts, while the former were "always scheming to beat" him. The local head of a white insurance com-

[9] One type of criticism of sawmill whites was that they violated caste taboos, however. "They are the kind who drink and gamble with the Negroes, and sleep with their women, and then if anything happens they want to kill all the Negroes."

pany likewise felt that the poorer whites were "pretty bad," and just as dishonest as colored patrons. The white fisherman who "squatted" along the river banks were regarded as the most "worthless" of the poorer whites by both landlords and merchants, and even by officials of the local fish-packing company.

The reasons advanced by white individuals of the upper economic group to justify their disapproval of poor-whites seem to be group dogmas. It seems probable that the conflicting interests of these economic groups—together with the class sanctions which operate between individuals who are members of different social classes as well as of different economic groups—account both for the subordination of the poorer whites and for the "reasons" offered as an explanation of this subordination. Two especially clear examples of the conjunction of social and economic group antagonisms were offered by (1) the eviction of a group of white tenants by a white landlord and (2) the behavior of upper-class white people toward white visitors of the middle economic group during Historical Week. In the first instance, a large white landlord who had been prevailed upon to accept twelve white tenants evicted all of them after one week because their wives paid a formal social call upon his wife. "The very first Sunday they were there, the women got all dressed up in their church clothes, you know, an' all went up to see Mrs. Curtis [the landlord's wife]!" The landlord's wife met them outside of her house, gave them each a flower, and sent them home. Later in the week, her husband evicted all his white tenants, and thereafter rented only to colored families.

In the second instance, a white woman of the upper social class, who served dinner to visitors at her mansion during Historical Week, charged them $2.00 a plate. She explained her motive in charging what was relatively a very high price: "This $2.00 isn't to pay for the food—it's to keep all the damned poor-white trash out—and I know it will. I don't want one of 'em to come here—walking over my house."

Antagonisms between economic groups within the lower caste.— The existence of economic groups within the lower caste likewise was indicated by abundant evidence of the same kind. To subordinate colored tenants, colored landlords used the same legal and customary techniques (except for caste sanctions) that white landlords employed; and their attitudes, as well as those of their children, were equally antagonistic to the tenant group. Finer gradations within economic groups also existed, for the more prosperous cash-tenants looked down upon the half-tenants and attributed the economic disabilities of these half-tenants to their inveterate "shiftlessness." In Old City, unemployed colored men were strongly antagonistic to the colored professional men. One of them angrily told a group of thirteen others:

> An' de Negro who got somethin' is jus' as bad! Those Negroes up on Water Street [colored business section], an' dose doctuhs don't keer uh goddam about *eny* of you! All dey keer about is yo' money! When my mothuh or my sistuh gits sick, dey ask me ef I've got money to pay them befo' they'll come. An' if I ain't got the money, them — — — will let her die, first. They jus' as bad as them pecks [white people]![10]

Similar economic group antagonisms were expressed by the lower group toward colored business men. The leader of a colored secret society and insurance company, which had failed two years previously, made several speeches in Old City in 1934 in which he attempted to dissolve antagonisms toward his new business by invoking "race pride" and "race business." His speeches were received coldly, and his new organization was boycotted by the lower economic group.

Other evidence seems to show that economic behavior conflicts with caste solidarity (race loyalty) among the colored group just as it does among the white group.[11] The resultant

[10] This charge could justifiably be made against only one of the four colored physicians in Old City. An audit of the books of the leading colored physician in 1934 showed that he had collected fees for less than one-half his calls.

[11] Like members of all other groups in the society, the members of the colored upper economic group were inconsistent in their attitudes and overt behavior. For example, a colored timber-contractor, who enthusiastically approved of

antagonisms are perpetuated for long periods. For example, the mass of colored people in Old County boycotted the stores of a group of colored businessmen because joint-stock enterprises organized by the parents of these men had failed a generation earlier. When the children of these former promoters opened businesses in Old City, most of the colored people refused to patronize them. This type of "silent" boycott had been repeated against three different stores. According to an upper-class colored businessman who had not been a member of the boycotted group, the boycotts had been an organized expression of antagonism toward these proprietors by the lower economic group of colored people: "They froze them out! They let them die in their tracks. They don't forget!" One of these former owners, a man who had never been accused of dishonesty, mentioned the boycott of his shoe store in a speech at a colored church where an interviewer was present. Even when he had decided to close his store and had offered shoes for half the price which a white proprietor was asking for identical shoes, he said, colored people had refused to buy them: "Why I stood right in my door and heard two rural Negroes talking. One of them said: 'Dose is nice shoes dey got in dat winduh!' The other one said: 'Dey sho' is.' But the first one said: 'Yeah, damn if they don't rot, befo' I'd buy eny of dem!'" As the story was told, there was embarrassed laughter by the audience in the church, and nodding of heads.

Economic solidarity across caste lines.—It is necessary to define the extent to which individuals of similar economic status may be said to constitute a "group." Evidence of concerted action and of the consolidation of attitudes by the passing of dogmas from parents to children, such as has been cited above, indicates that "economic groups" do exist in Old County. Although the interaction between members of these

---

"race loyalty" in conversation with a group of friends, a few minutes later boasted of the fact that he had bought both land and timber from an illiterate group of colored people "for what the timber alone is worth."

groups is by no means so frequent or intimate as that between members of social classes, as a rule, the evidence from Old and Rural counties indicates that sufficient interaction and solidarity do exist between individuals to enable them to function as a group in some economic and political situations.

The caste system organizes the relationships between these economic groups into configurations which differ according to the economic status of the groups involved. In general it appears that in Old County the caste system operates so as to create a concert of interest between the upper white and colored economic groups and to place the lower white and colored groups in direct competition in many occupational fields. At any rate, the evidence at hand leaves no doubt that a strong solidarity exists between the leading white and colored business and professional men with regard to the manipulation of the caste sanctions.

There is less uniformity in the organization of relationships between the lower white and colored economic groups. While some members of these groups both on the farms and in Old City expressed friendly attitudes toward one another, denied caste antagonisms of any kind, and even participated in a modified type of neighborly relationship, others exhibited strong caste antagonisms both in their speech and in their actions.[12] The "reason" usually given by such informants for their antagonisms to members of the lower economic group of the opposite caste was that the occupational and economic systems gave preference to the latter. White rural persons of

[12] For example, white tenants were known to have intimidated colored tenants and forced them to leave a plantation in Rural County. Colored tenants, on the other hand, twice burned a white tenant's cabin in Old County and thus forced the landlord to adopt a policy of excluding white tenants. On the levees unskilled white workers sought to displace colored workers by force and then by political manipulation. Similar antagonisms were expressed by white people of middle economic groups toward colored people of higher economic status. The wife of a white mail-carrier, seeing the well-dressed child of a colored professional man enter a store, said loudly to another white woman: "It's a shame how these nigguhs can dress their children all up. They fix them up better than we can afford to fix ours!"

this type, for example, said they were antagonistic to colored tenants because the latter were preferred by landlords, whereas the colored tenants objected to the white tenants because they were economic competitors. The same basis for caste antagonisms appeared in interviews with white and colored former workers in the planing-mills and with applicants for federal relief work, namely, that members of the opposite caste were competing successfully with them for jobs.

A certain amount of co-operation exists, however, between parallel economic groups, across caste lines. This intercaste solidarity is especially strong between the two upper economic groups. Reference has already been made to the co-operation of colored and white planters in preventing geographic mobility of colored tenants between plantations,[13] and to the point-to-point similarity of the behavior and attitudes of white and colored landlords with regard to the tenant group. Other examples of economic solidarities across caste lines are available for the urban society. A rather typical instance was the case of a white man of the upper economic level who sold a lot to a colored man of the same level and then protected the colored man from the encroachment of a poor-white family living behind the property.

In spite of the lack of ties based upon miscegenation between the present upper economic groups, the traditional solidarity between well-to-do colored people and the "rich white people" is maintained. This co-operative relationship between the two upper economic groups consists not only of economic co-operation during critical periods of the local economy[14] but also of co-operation in organizing the caste system. The relationship appears to be a conscious use of techniques by

[13] The white Chamber of Commerce, moreover, co-operated vigorously with the local Colored Business Men's Association to persuade colored farmers not to emigrate during the post-war years.

[14] Co-operative effort of these two groups to preserve the labor supply during the post-war years has been cited. In 1936 and 1937, furthermore, members of the colored upper economic group subscribed heavily to bond issues to establish several factories in Old County.

both groups for subordinating the lower caste. By its exhibitions of patronage and protection toward the colored upper economic group, the white upper economic group both (1) dramatizes the patriarchal dogma of caste and (2) restricts the intercaste relationships to the minimum of co-operation necessary between caste "leaders," i.e., to face-to-face relationships of patronage with only that group in the lower caste which has economic interests similar to its own. Such exhibitions are rather frequent, and the habitual and open granting of favor and protection to their "leaders" is certainly an important technique for controlling the antagonisms of the colored inhabitants.

In general, the protection extended to the colored upper economic group exempts it from the caste sanctions of the white courts and of the mob. Patronage, on the other hand, is extended to the lower caste as a whole, although it is distributed through members of the colored upper economic group. In this community, as in other stratified societies, charity appears to be essentially a form of organized subordination of the receiving group and operates to maintain the society by furnishing subsistence to the lower group, by dissolving its antagonisms to the upper group, by preserving its segregated institutions, or by combining all three of these functions. In the caste system of Old County's society, patronage is notably effective in minimizing caste antagonism, not because the gifts have any great monetary value, but because they are regarded by both castes as symbols of the paternalistic relationships of the upper caste to the lower. A third type of relationship, based upon patronage extended by the white upper group but verging upon a quasi-class relationship, occurs when the white upper group attends entertainments or concerts in the church of the colored upper group, or when the colored group seeks to reciprocate by attending church funerals of members of the white upper group, even though they are segregated in the gallery.

Evidence of the existence of these three types of relationships is too abundant to be cited in detail. Perhaps the following examples will serve to illustrate the usual behavior, however. The protective relationship of the white upper group toward the colored was typified in the minds of the latter group by the experiences of two leading colored professional men who became involved in caste crises. A white woman of the lower economic group accused one of these colored men of striking her as a result of a disagreement over a property line; actually, the colored man had knocked from her hand a pistol which she was leveling at him. In spite of the fact that she ran down the main business streets of Old City, screaming "That nigger struck me!" and later had the colored man arrested, her charge was thrown out of court by the upper-class white judge who heard the case. An even clearer example of this relationship was afforded by the experience of another colored professional man, who drove his automobile into a drunken white man of the lower class and killed him. Not only did local white bankers offer to lend this colored man money with which to defend himself, but a group of upper-class white women called upon him at his place of business to assure him that they considered him a "great influence for good in the community" and that they intended to see that no harm came to him. He was not arrested.

A great many examples of the extension of charity to the lower caste by the white upper group, using the colored upper group as an intermediary, are available. Such gifts are made not only for the benefit of the colored lower economic group, as in the case of gifts for the Colored Poor Children's Christmas Fund, but also to churches which are patronized chiefly by the upper colored group. The obligation is extended to the point where white upper-class women secure from their white friends contributions for church "rallies" conducted by colored upper-class women!

Quasi-class relationships between white and colored members of the upper groups occur chiefly at entertainments and concerts held in the church of the colored upper group, and especially during the programs of plantation songs by which this church celebrates Easter. At this annual entertainment and also at periodic concerts by colored singers, upper-class colored women receive the congratulations of white upper-class sponsors who are present, and in some cases are addressed as "Mrs." by these white persons.

SUMMARY

The foregoing analysis of the modifications of color caste in the field of economic behavior seems to possess the following major implications. In certain fields, notably in storekeeping, contracting, farming, and professional service to colored persons, the economic system is still sufficiently "free" in competition to prevent the rigid application of caste taboos. Although a large proportion of colored proprietors and contractors have been unable to compete successfully, owing to their lack of adequate capital, the operation of the economic system has maintained a small group of colored persons of relatively high economic status. It has thus prevented the full extension of caste, i.e., a development in which all members of the lower caste are legally, or by virtue of unbreakable custom, below all members of the upper caste in wages, occupational status, and in the value of property owned. In so far as the system has prevented this full extension of the caste principle, it appears to have been operating upon two principles: (1) the principle of the sacredness of private property, and (2) the principle of free competition.[15]

This latter aspect of the national economic and legal structures gives rise to the presence in Old County of nonlocal factories and sawmills. These manufacturing firms hire labor as cheaply as they can get it, with the result that in

[15] In the field of personal service to colored people, such as in colored schools, restaurants, barber-shops, and burial establishments, the caste system, rather than the larger economic system, has been chiefly responsible for the existence of a group of economically superordinated colored persons. In the field of medical and dental service, white men still compete with colored men for colored business.

industries where white workers have not been able to establish caste taboos, colored workers are employed to do much the same type of labor as whites. They may even be preferred to white workers, because they can be hired for a lower wage.

Not only do these nonlocal industries tend to disrupt caste in labor, but they put into the hands of colored workers money which the local white storekeepers are extremely anxious to obtain. Since money has the highest value in the economic system, it causes white middle-class and lower-class storekeepers to wait upon colored patrons deferentially. It thereby increases the difficulties of adjusting caste, which seems to be essentially a structure of pastoral and agricultural societies, to manufacturing and commercial economies. This money economy likewise leads the group of entrepreneurs and middlemen to whom it has given rise—the most powerful group in the production of cotton because they control credit and therefore production—to be unmindful whether they buy cotton from a colored or white farmer, whether they sell food, automobiles, and clothes to one or the other, whether they allow nonlocal industries to subordinate the lower economic group of whites to the lower group of colored workers; they care principally about increasing their money. Even the local white farm owners prefer colored tenants to white, because they can obtain higher profits from the former. From the point of view of the white lower group, such behavior is a violation of caste. It indicates a fundamental conflict between the economic system and the caste dogma.

In the second place, the principle of the sacredness of private property has generally operated to prevent the expropriation of colored owners. Even during the period of slavery, free, colored persons were allowed to own property in Old City and in the state generally. This right was not taken from them during the twenty years immediately preceding the Civil War, when the legislature severely restricted their behavior in other respects. At the close of the Civil War the same reactionary legislature which passed the so-called "Black Code" in this state, providing for the virtual restoration of slavery by the use of vagrancy and "apprentice" laws, granted to freedmen the right to own property in incorporated towns and cities. Since that time, colored owners have not been expropriated, except in isolated cases of terrorization. To expropriate colored property-owners would be to violate the most fundamental principle of the economic system and to establish a precedent for the expropriation of other subordinated groups, such as the lower economic group of white people, Jews, Italians, and "foreign" ethnic groups of all kinds.[16]

It is necessary to point out, however, that the modification of the caste system in the interests of the profits of the upper and middle economic groups of white people by no means amounts to an abrogation of caste in economic relationships. The economic interests of these groups would also demand that cheaper colored labor should be employed in the "white collar" jobs in business offices, governmental offices, stores, and banks. In this field, however, the interests of the employer group conflict not only with those of the lower economic group of whites but also with those of the more literate and aggressive middle group of whites. A white store which employed colored clerks, for example, would be boycotted by both these groups. The taboo upon the employment of colored workers in such fields is the result of the political power and the purchasing-power of the white middle and lower groups. As a result of these taboos in the field of "white-collar" work, the educated colored person occupies a well-nigh hopeless position in Old County.

The political power of the middle and lower groups of white

[16] In South Africa, in most parts of which the right to own real property is denied the natives, the basic economic situation was different. The South African natives owned land communally; the principle of private property was not challenged, therefore. The wholesale expropriation of South African tribes, like that of American Indian tribes, is justified by imperialistic colonial policy upon the basis, usually, that the natives have no ideas of land tenure and that therefore the right of property ownership is not violated, especially if the chief is told that he owns the land and is "persuaded" to accept a payment for it.

people—that is to say, the disfranchisement of the colored population—has enabled these groups to establish a caste barrier to the employment of colored clerical workers in municipal, state, and federal governmental offices. The inability of these groups to extend caste taboos so as to prevent colored persons from owning real estate and from competing with white skilled and unskilled labor may be attributed to the fact that the rights of private property and of a free labor market for the planter and the manufacturer are still sacred, legal rights in Old County.

A more detailed knowledge of the caste system, as it exists in economic settings which differ from the old-plantation economy of Old County, would enable one to define the degree of subordination of the lower caste, according to the type of economy. A tentative hypothesis might be advanced that the physical terrorization of colored people is most common in those areas where their general economic status is highest. In the "newer" agricultural, oil-producing, and manufacturing sections of the South, where relatively large groups of colored people are superordinated economically to relatively large groups of white people, open racial conflict and terrorization seem to be at their height. Such conflict results from the fact that in many economic symbols, such as clothes, automobiles, and houses, a relatively large number of colored people are superior to many of the poorer whites. The white society, as a whole, often resorts to terrorization to reassert the dogma of caste and to indicate that in physical and legal power over life and limb of colored people, at least, the caste sanctions are effective.

In the Delta areas of the state, where white and colored tenants are competing at an increasing rate, or in a mill-town society, a sawmill society, or an oil-mining society, where similar competition exists, most of the white men *work* for a living (as contrasted with the white planters in Old County), and work in daily contact with colored men, even though they may be termed "supervisors." In such a society, where most white men, dressed in overalls or work clothes, are almost as poor as the colored workers and occupy approximately the same occupational level, it is most difficult to maintain the caste lines with the rigidity and authority which the dogma of caste demands. In such a community, therefore, the white population must resort to terrorization continually in order to impress the colored group with the fact that economic equality or superordination on the part of the latter is not real equality or superordination—in other words, that caste exists all along the line, as the myth demands, and that actually any white man, no matter how poor or illiterate, is superordinate to any colored man and must be treated with the appropriate deference.

In the old plantation areas, on the other hand, where almost all of the colored people are families of poverty-stricken tenants and almost all of the white people are families of owners or large landlords, caste is almost "perfect" economically and socially, and there is relatively little terrorization of the lower caste. In fine, where caste is most fully extended, there is little need for violence, because the colored people are thoroughly subordinated economically, occupationally, and socially. When the castes are in economic competition, as laborers and tenants, however, violence and conflict seem to be at their height.

CHAPTER XXII

CASTE, CLASS, AND LOCAL GOVERNMENT: WHITE POWER

THE POLITICAL SYSTEM

OLD CITY does not exist in isolation from the larger world of the state and nation. In fact, it is heir to the whole democratic tradition of America; its legal codes state that political power "originates with the people, is founded in their will only, and is instituted solely for the good of the whole." "Power is vested in and derived from the people." The governmental structure represents the highest authority, the supreme power, the collective will. All men are "equal in the eyes of the law"; they are even *born* "free and equal." Such a tradition, however, exists side by side with certain other dogmas and practices which contradict it, as we have already suggested in our study of caste, class, and economic groupings. In the actual operation of the governmental system certain groups are excluded entirely from participation, while others are limited drastically.

The basic form of political differentiation in Old County is directed toward separating the residents into two groups: those who control the governmental structure by voting and holding office, and those who exercise no control. To belong to the control group, one must have resided in the state and election district for a certain period and must have paid all of his taxes. He is then theoretically eligible for registration, the initiation ceremony which will admit him to the ranks of the politically active. But there are some for whom there is no admittance to the circle of control.

The society legally excludes certain groups from political participation. Thus, all persons under twenty-one are barred from active political participation on the basis of age; and all idiots, insane persons, criminals, and Indians are excluded by law from voting and holding office. (Prior to 1920 women, too, were not allowed to vote and seldom held office.) The operation of the caste system functions effectively (albeit illegally) to exclude most of the Negroes from political participation and equal protection before the law.

Certain other groups within the white society are excluded from decisive political participation by the operation of informal social controls. Thus, the bulk of the white population, although allowed to vote, is excluded from the small political ring which wields political power. This ring, in relation to decisive issues and in ideology, represents the interests of the upper-middle class, although it must be responsive to pressures from above and below it in the class structure. The circle of power is thereby narrowed still more.

The political system thus operates to exclude progressively some groups from control and to limit the participation of others. It exists in contradiction to the basic myths and dogmas of political democracy. The remaining portion of this chapter will describe these processes of progressive limitation of power in detail.

CASTE AND POLITICS

Exclusion of Negroes.—Negroes in Old City are effectively excluded from political participation.[1] There were only two

---

[1] The present structuralization of political activity along caste lines has been the outcome of a gradual process. Before the Civil War, Negroes were slaves without any legal claim to participation. During the Reconstruction era, however, Negroes actually controlled the government for a short time. The caste-class structures were re-established in a modified form during the first decade of Reconstruction, and by 1895 the white caste was able to exclude Negroes from political participation entirely. This was accomplished with little or no obvious violence in Old County, although in Rural County a large number of Negroes were murdered in order to re-establish caste lines in politics after Reconstruction. An "old-timer" discussed Old County's "Compromise Plan" as follows:

"It was a plan which the Democrats in this county offered to the Republicans. By it the Republicans were to be given certain offices—the circuit clerk,

Negroes registered as city voters in 1934, and six as county voters. Not one voted in any election during the two-year period of the study. Exclusion from the polls and from holding office is accomplished by certain informal methods, since caste differentiations are not legally recognized.

This is accomplished, however, with the aid of certain convenient laws. For instance, the requirement that all voters must have paid, in full, all taxes—poll and property—for two years preceding tends to eliminate the majority of the Negro group because of their poverty. The ritual of registration can also act as a complete barrier to the Negroes, because of the legally sanctioned literacy clause. This clause requires that the voter be able to read and interpret the state constitution. What constitutes an adequate interpretation is left entirely to the judgment of the registrar. Thus the Negro comes before a white official, who functions in a dual role as a representative of both the government and the white caste, identifies himself, and is asked to interpret a passage from the constitution. When he gives an interpretation, the official states that it is wrong and refuses to register him. If the Negro argues, he is breaking the caste rules, and may be silenced by force. If he

---

the county treasurer, and a representative to the state legislature, provided their candidates were first approved by the Democratic committee. This was in '78, and the Republicans saw the handwriting on the wall and took this compromise rather than lose everything. The Republican party was mostly Negro with a few whites; one was a very fine man of good family. This plan continued in effect until '95, several years after the new state constitution which, in effect disfranchised the Negroes.

"What happened was that the political ring perpetuated the 'plan' for their own benefit, and for that length of time they controlled the elections and had a group of perpetual officeholders, who were always re-elected. There was a Negro circuit clerk. In '91, a year after the new constitution was in force, there was an election in which the political leaders were afraid the Negro circuit clerk would be defeated. In some manner the county was flooded with sample ballots, and the Negroes were taught to count down so many names and mark the name of the Negro circuit clerk. In that way the political ring remained in power. There was never any violent feeling against the Negroes here, as there was in other parts of the state, and the local politicians made use of the situation."

takes the matter to the local or state court, he faces the white caste, intent on subordinating him, and he loses. The case is closed, and he has no recourse.

An election official recounted an incident in 1923 when some Negroes attempted to register and vote. He stated that he was on the committee at one of the polling places when he heard that some of the Negroes were getting ready to vote.

We got a bunch of men together and put them in two cars across from the polls. I walked up to one of the Negroes and asked him if he was looking for something, and he said that one of the candidates had insisted that they come up and vote. I said: "Now, you have the reputation of being a good citizen and everyone likes you; but if you insist on this, you will lose your reputation and cause a lot of trouble."

He said he agreed with me, but the candidate had insisted that he vote. I told him to go back and tell the candidate that we just wouldn't allow that, and it would be much better if they just went home and did nothing. He left, and that was the end of it; but we had decided that if they insisted we would take care of them right then.

This was a hotly contested election, and a white candidate had had the temerity to ask Negroes to support him. When the interviewer asked what the registrar would do if some Negroes were to come in to register now, the informant smiled and said, "If a few were to come, I suppose he would let them register; but if a large number began to register, I suppose there will be a card on their door some morning telling them to stop."

It should not be thought that this is the invariable procedure, however, for a few Negroes were registered; and during the study the registration of another was observed. A Negro came into the office of the circuit clerk. He was roughly dressed and looked and talked like a laborer. The circuit clerk asked what he wanted, and the man asked, after some hesitation, if a person who had paid his poll tax could register as a voter. The clerk said, "That's right," and the Negro said that he had paid his poll tax for about six years and would like to register. The clerk, without hesitation, brought out the register and asked the Negro's name and address. The street address given was indefinite, and the clerk questioned him carefully to get the correct address. He then read the oath to the Negro but did not ask him to raise his right hand and swear to it, merely asking if he would swear to it. He then had the Negro sign the register, and the registration was complete. Throughout the affair the Negro appeared ill at ease, although the clerk treated him in a matter-of-fact, almost indifferent, manner. The Negro was apparently surprised and relieved at the simplicity of the proceedings. After the Negro left, another official said:

> We only have a few who register. I don't know why one of this sort would want to register, although I can understand why some of the more educated and better-class Negroes would. They can vote in the presidental elections; they are all Republicans and like to vote for the president. I think there is only one who gets any patronage, and he goes to the Republican conventions.

The whites frankly admit, however, that any great increase in Negro registrations would result in a tightening of the control; an attempt by a large number of Negroes to become voters would be interpreted as an attack upon white dominance in the government. In practice, the procedure of registration is in itself a strong deterrent, since the Negro is drawn forth from the anonymity of his caste into full view of the whites. He no longer is merely another Negro but is a specific ,Negro suspected of attacking the barriers of caste, an open enemy of the whites. He exposes himself to white attack either by open force or, more subtly, through the economic structure. Although the few Negro voters exist without molestation and even with the high regard of the whites, the political situation, nevertheless, is fraught with the ever present possibility of hostilities, as both Negroes and whites are well aware.

The state primary system is also effective in barring the

Negro from participation in elections. Under this system, the various party candidates for state or county offices are selected by vote of the party members at a primary election. The Democratic party rigidly draws the caste-line and will admit no Negro to membership even though he be a qualified voter. Since all the local white voters are Democrats, any attempt by the Negroes to participate in the selection of candidates can be carried out only by organizing a separate Negro group or by attaching themselves to the Republican party. Either method immediately accentuates the caste situation and arrays the Negroes against the whites. So long as the whites maintain their strong superordinate position, no such attempt will be permitted to succeed or even to start.

Under these conditions the few Negro voters are able to vote only in the national elections. In their alignment against the southern whites or Democrats, however, they are the only local Republicans, and as such they receive scraps of patronage when the Republicans are in power. The Negro chairman of the local Republican committee enjoyed a certain amount of prestige from his connections and received occasional trips to Republican conventions as patronage. As he once jokingly remarked: "I raly have missed them pickin's sense these Democrats have ben in. I know I don' get nuthin' but the crumbs, but oh-h man, them crumbs is so good."

Caste in political campaigns.—The caste system operates to exclude Negroes from political participation, despite the fact that at one time they were allowed some participation in a modified caste relationship. There have also been occasions when the violations of caste taboos on the part of white people in nonpolitical relationships have been used to discredit an aspirant for office.

For example, occasionally office-holders or candidates were accused of living with Negro women. Some people opposed them on moral grounds for this reason; others claimed, on practical grounds, that it tended to weaken their control over the Negroes and was therefore a threat to the caste system.

One individual said: "The officials are all nigger-lovers so you have to expect the niggers to get smart. They are always living with them and you can't expect them to do anything about them."

An upper-class white woman, protesting against the relations between a candidate and Negro women said:

I voted against two of those who won in the local election. I never would vote for Johnson: I never could stand him. You know he lives with Negro women, and that is one thing I can't stand for. That is one thing a Southerner won't put up with. They talk about how he controls the Negroes and how they are afraid of him, but it isn't so. They certainly aren't afraid of him.

The supporters of the candidate ignored the charges that he was a "nigger-lover" and claimed that his immoral behavior had no effect upon his fitness for office. One said: "People object to Johnson on moral grounds. He is very immoral. But I think that is his own business as long as he does his job. He is a good official and had a wonderful reputation in his work."

The ability to subordinate Negroes is for some positions a prime requisite, and such a reputation a political asset. Mintaining the caste system intact, "keeping the niggers in their place," is extremely important to the whites and is part of the informal obligation which the officials assume. The caste element is particularly important in the case of law-enforcement officers such as the sheriff and chief of police. A candidate for these offices may be supported because he can "control the Negroes," "keep them in their place." His supporters may tell lurid tales of what would happen if "Negroes got out of hand" and revolted against the caste restrictions. In one campaign the chief of police was accused of protecting a Negro who had insulted a white girl by asking her for a date. This aroused antagonism to the chief until he and his supporters managed to stop the rumor. Under proper conditions, charges of this nature will serve to unite the white group in defense of the caste system and in support of the candidate who will best defend it. Special emphasis may be placed upon the idea that without firm control the Negroes would attack the strongest caste taboo, the taboo upon white women. As one politician said with startling sophistication:

> Gilmore is elected chief of police on the idea that he can control the Negroes. When election comes around his friends get out and talk about how he controls the Negroes and how bad it would be if he were not elected. That goes with these old maids, who feel that if it wasn't for him they would be in danger. It is a big talking-point, and people get all excited over what would happen if he wasn't there to protect the whites.

The interplay between voter and candidate results in a body of elected and appointed officials charged with the duty of making, enforcing, and interpreting the law in conformity with the preservation of white supremacy. While they have the routine duties of civic officials anywhere in America, they have the added task in Old City of maintaining the caste system.

THE SEAT OF POWER

"*The ring.*"—The caste system and the political structures of the society reinforce each other through the virtual exclusion of Negroes from political activity. "White power," however, is not evenly distributed throughout the superordinate caste; and although all adult white persons possess the franchise, effective political control is vested in the "ring," a large political clique.[2] The ring serves to exclude a large segment of the politically active residents of the county.

There is an observable natural history of political rings. As time passes, a ring tends to become more and more ex-

---

[2] The operation of economic status in the selection of voters is revealed by the distribution of voters according to the production groups defined in chapter xiii, Table 7. Whereas only 11 per cent of the smallest producers (Group I) were registered and only 16 per cent of the three lowest groups, more than 79 per cent of the three highest groups (VII, VIII, and IX) were voters.

clusive, drawing the line between itself and the electorate tighter and tighter. The people on the outside become restive; they begin to doubt whether the ring is really representing their interests, and from this discontent may emerge a "reform" movement. The combined pressure from the outside and the very exclusiveness of the ring itself serve to shatter and disperse it. A new one is formed, its integration starts again, and the whole process is repeated. It is this life-history of the ring which will emerge from the following brief discussion of the political ring in Old City.

Most of the elective officials, especially those in the higher positions, together with a number of lawyers and businessmen, constitute this ring, and the leading members of it are usually socially mobile individuals of the upper-middle class. With these individuals, a political career appears frequently to have been an important factor in their mobility, both economically and in enabling them to relate themselves to the social values of the middle class.

Since political control is vested in the upper-middle class of the white caste, it is not surprising that there is a close connection between political power and the control of the economic system, which is also in the hands of this class. A number of prominent businessmen either are active in the ring (though they may have no political position) or have close relations with it through professional and business ties, as e.g., a bank president whose attorneys were prominent politicians. Such relationships further integrate the political and economic controls.

The principal ring members are well known to the community and they have a high degree of solidarity among themselves, which involves extensive social participation—week-end parties with eating, drinking, and gambling, for instance—as well as political affairs. The solidarity of the ring is further heightened by its sponsorship of the annual poor children's Christmas tree. Funds are collected, and the day before Christmas all the poor white children of the community gather at a local theater, where Santa Claus gives each one a bag of toys. Before this takes place, Santa Claus and an escort of about a dozen men ride about the city, blowing horns, ringing bells, and stopping at various houses for refreshments. On one occasion, while the distribution of gifts took place, the escort gathered in a near-by court clerk's office, where drinks and sandwiches were served. Most of the group were either ring members or closely related to them. After the distribution of gifts, the entire group went to the various orphanages, distributing gifts and money to the orphans and stopping after each visit at the homes of various members for more food and drink. This continued all day, and the final orphanage visit was not completed until late in the afternoon, by which time all participants were nearly exhausted. The whole affair, in the hands of the ring and its extensions, was marked throughout by a considerable amount of "kidding" about politics. This affair was held every year, and the same group had run it for years, their favorite anecdotes being about previous parties.

This internal solidarity makes the ring a close-knit self-perpetuating group which has a definite advantage in elections. A citizen of Old City, speaking of a nonring candidate, said: "I can't see that he has a chance. These fellows don't have a chance against men like Morris, who has all the big politicians supporting him." The ring sometimes defeats independent candidates through backing third candidates to split the opposition's votes; by "buying off" strong opponents with the offer of appointive offices; or by controlling the election committee, which has the right to strike off from the register all the persons whose taxes are delinquent. The scratching of eligible voters antagonistic to the ring is not unknown. As one official told the interviewers: "Of course, if they had their tax receipts, they had to let them vote. The idea was that, if they came to the polls without the receipts, many would not go to the trouble of going home to get them or wouldn't be able to find such papers on a moment's notice." The solidarity of the ring is further illustrated by the fact that, of the last four sheriffs (who by law may hold that office only one term), the three ring sheriffs have been provided with other policital jobs, while the one nonring sheriff has been unable to obtain another position.

Activities of the ring.—One of the primary functions of the ring is to establish informal relationships between city, county, and state governmental officials. Thus, when the county wishes to obtain state or federal funds for various projects, such as road construction, public health, etc., the mayor, the president of the board of supervisors, state representatives, and others will make trips to the state capital or to Washington and handle the matter informally. The ring thus tends to organize the relationships of the two local governments toward each other and toward the federal government.

It was frequently asserted that the ring controlled the government of Old City and Old County, and through this control offered its members considerable opportunity for graft. According to some accounts, this came in the form of excessive fees for those offices which are on a fee basis; "rake-offs" such as on the feeding of prisoners for whose welfare the county allots fifty cents each per day; and in the form of "protection money." In the case of the latter, it was said that bootleggers, gamblers, and prostitutes usually paid off to the policemen on duty, although in some cases the "deal" was made directly through City Hall. And it was often said that protection not only afforded immunity against arrest by policemen, but that even when the federal agent arrived to check bootlegging, the local authorities warned the protected people to "lay low."

Arrests for bootlegging were virtually unknown in Old City, except for one or two Negro distillers. Yet, it was no secret that the proprietor of a small restaurant, popular with the police, took orders for gallon lots of corn whiskey and made delivery anywhere in the city within thirty minutes. Another retailer, noted for the quality of his corn whiskey, kept his stock near the offices of the Federal Relief Administration. If he was not around, orders could be left with his friends at a near-by filling station. When the federal officers brought a warrant for his arrest, the sheriff said he'd "never heard of" the individual.

When nonring officials begin to uncover evidences of graft, the ring acts to protect its members by preventing the gathering of evidence, seeing that charges are dropped, and "fixing" juries. The greatest danger to illegal ring activities is the grand jury, and some control must be maintained over it. With the sheriff, chancery clerk, circuit clerk, and board of supervisors working closely together, a very close control over the selection of the twenty grand jurors is made possible, and any "suspicious" persons who might insist on probing ring activities can easily be excluded. One politician stated that, in compiling the list from which the jurors were selected, the above-named officials eliminated "trouble-makers," "stubborn people," and those "who don't like to serve."

Despite the widespread taking of graft, ring members do not show many signs of permanent economic gains. It was definitely ascertained that certain sheriffs, police chiefs, and supervisors who participated somewhat heavily in the "take" did not retire as wealthy men. In a small city the individual "protection" items are never very large, and they have to be distributed among a wide circle. If too much is exacted, there will be no more geese to lay the golden eggs. A more important factor, however, is the necessity for maintaining good relationships with the electorate. This means gifts to churches and associations, contributions to "worthy causes," loans to indigent machine members, payments to deputies, and campaign expenses. In some cases, the graft was actually paid directly to subordinate officials *outside* the ring, as in the following case, mentioned by an official.

This is not exactly graft. At places like the Inn, where they have gambling and drinking, the sheriff may tell them that he is going to keep two deputies on duty there, and they must pay them so much a night. The sheriff doesn't make anything . . . . there is no reason why he should pay deputies out of his own pocket to police illegal places.

Disintegration of a ring.—A given ring, despite its control of elections and patronage, does not last forever, although *some* ring is usually present. One factor which serves to break up a ring is the increasing concentration of the rewards of office in the hands of the ring, with the consequent dimunition of patronage. Reform movements may then secure a mass base and oust the incumbent ring.

A typical defeat occurred during the period of widespread Ku Klux Klan activities in the 1920's, when a Klan sheriff was elected. The ring at that time had been controlled by a Catholic group which had organized a powerful nucleus. The opposition voters had finally organized around the Klan, an anti-Catholic organization, and defeated the ring candidate for sheriff. Several factors were operative in the Klan's overthrow of the ring. There was, to begin with, the usual antagonism between Catholics and Protestants. In Old City the political subordination of the great mass of Protestants by the Catholic ring had sharpened this antagonism. Finally, the ring was accused of violating the code of "decent government" by refusing to oust members who had been flagrantly accepting graft. These conditions gave rise to the formation of an anti-Catholic, anti-ring opposition, led by middle-class Protestants.

The new sheriff set out to "clean up the town," and at one time people were afraid to be caught "with even a pint." He went so far, however, that he began to lose his following; and when his bondsmen, fearful of lawsuits, tried to desert him, he had to appeal to a ring lawyer for support. This lawyer stated: "He has a big following among the lower class and the Baptists, who are so against drinking and vice. . . . .

He finally came to me and we talked things over and since then have been close friends."

The one case of an internal split within a ring occurred in a contest for the office of sheriff between several ring candidates and several outsiders, one of whom was very strong. The apparent reason for so much competition for the office was the economic situation during the "depression," when political offices became economically more alluring than ever. Many of the ring members were hard pressed financially, and the available patronage was not sufficient to take care of all of them, with the result that they competed among themselves for the very lucrative position of sheriff. Not only was there an unusual amount of competition for that office, but there was also considerable competition from nonring members for other offices, so that almost every ring candidate had strong competition. Under these conditions no ring candidate dared give active support to other members for fear of endangering his own chances. The result was a run-off election between a ring candidate and an outsider, who, by then, had so well established himself with the voters that the last-minute efforts of the ring to support their man was ineffective.

The rewards of office.—In view of the struggle for the various offices during the "depression," it might be well to consider their significance in the economic sense. All the city officials and most of the county officials receive salaries which are not large but which are fair middle-class incomes. The mayor is paid $250 a month, the largest salary, but actually spends only part of his time in official duties, so that he is free to carry on other activities. The chief of police is paid $175, and the city clerk $200, a month; they spend all their time on official duties. The county supervisors receive $100 a month, for which they give part of their time. All the other salaried officials receive salaries within this range. The sheriff is on a fee basis. According to a ring member, the sheriff should clear as much as $15,000 a year legitimately, which explains, somewhat, the intense competition for the office. The chancery clerk is also on a fee basis and should net about $4,000 a year, a relatively high income for the community.

The rewards of office are not, by any means, entirely economic, however, for there are also status gains. Political leaders are persons who wield power, who enjoy prestige in the eyes of the total society, and who have relations with similar officials throughout the United States. It is an "honor" to sit in a seat of power, as well as remunerative.

Summary.—Political power in Old City is exercised largely by the ring, which in turn is dependent for its support upon the rank and file of middle-class and lower-class voters. These voters are manipulated both by the ring and by individuals and blocs in the community which wish, for one reason or another, to oust a given ring or to attack ring politics. The determining factor in the functioning of the political system is not the general class structure but the specific pattern of relations between voter and politician and between politicians themselves. These patterns do not follow class lines but cut across them in all directions. The leading officials, however, and also the leading ring members, are usually mobile middle-class persons with the ultimate control in the hands of upper-middle-class members.

The upper classes, on the other hand, are much less active in politics and are apt to be ineffectual when they do become active. Frequently they seem unable to lessen the social distance between themselves and the voters enough to obtain the wholehearted support of the lower class. In spite of their lack of political power, however, their superordinate class position is clearly recognized by the officials. They are free from many of the minor legal restrictions, are almost never arrested for drunkenness or for minor traffic violations, are seldom called for jury duty, and usually receive any favors they request.

The ultimate seat of power in Old City is in the upper-middle class, for it is members of this stratum who normally dominate the ring, manipulate the symbols of the society, dispense patronage, and, for all practical purposes, control elections. They delegate the "dirty work," however, to the law-enforcement officers, drawn from the lower-middle and upper-lower classes. Upon them devolves the day-by-day administration of the "law," which will be discussed in the second section of this chapter.

DAY-BY-DAY LAW ENFORCEMENT

The lower courts.—There are two groups of officials in Old County concerned with the routine of day-by-day administration of the law—the police force in the city, and the sheriff, deputies, and constable in the rural areas. Police cases are handled in the police court, while the sheriff's cases are handled in the justice-of-the-peace courts. Although both sets of courts are similar, the judge of the police court has had some formal legal training, while the justices have had no such training, are usually poorly educated, and are reputed to use only "common sense" in settling cases. They have little knowledge of the legal rules regarding evidence or the interpretation of the law, nor are they bound by technicalities. As a result, there is considerable individual variation among these courts. It is frequently asserted, for instance, that one particular justice could always be depended upon to find the defendant guilty, regardless of the law. In dealing with Negro cases, especially, this man often overstepped his legal limitations and acted in cases where he had no legal jurisdiction. The city police found him very co-operative whenever they had a case in which the legal evidence was weak. The fact that these justices are on a fee basis rather than on a salary, as is the police judge, gives them a direct pecuniary interest in convicting the defendants. Probably the only type of case in which both groups of lower courts show any uniformity of treatment is that in which a Negro is accused of a crime against a white person. In such a case, both types of lower courts are unanimous in proclaiming the Negro a rebel against the superior caste.

Caste, Class, and Crime.—In spite of the many stories of Negro stealing, fighting, or drinking, it was found that, in proportion to the number of individuals in the lower class (the class within both castes which provides the largest number of arrests), more whites than Negroes were arrested by the police. While the population of Old City is approximately half Negro and half white, the majority of the Negroes are in the lower class, whereas not more than a third of the whites belong to that social stratum. In other words, although the Negro lower-class group outnumbers the white lower-class group about three to one, police arrests during a period of twenty-two months were only 60 per cent Negro and 40 per cent white.

This is partly due to the fact that the police, like the whites in general, believe that fighting, drinking, and gambling among Negroes are not crimes so long as they are strictly limited to the Negro group and are kept somewhat under cover. It is only when this behavior is brought out into the open and thrust upon the attention of the whites that it becomes a crime for which arrests are made. As one upper-middle-class white woman expressed it:

> We have very little crime. Of course, Negroes knife each other occasionally, but there is little *real* crime. I mean Negroes against whites or whites against each other. Negroes will stab each other. There was quite a stir a while ago. A Negro man chased his wife out on the street and stabbed her to death in front of some white woman looking on. But there isn't much of that, even.

A white doctor and several police officers also commented on the number of fights and cuttings among Negroes in which the police take no action unless someone is killed. One policeman summed up the conversation by saying, "They don't often put them in jail or do anything to them for fighting among themselves unless they get *too* bad."

DEEP SOUTH

Treatment of Negroes arrested by the police.—Although frequency of arrests among Negroes is not high, the treatment of those arrested is in complete accord with their inferior status. If they resist arrest, they are beaten and maltreated by the police as well as given a jail sentence. If they act "uppity" or surly, if they complain about their treatment, refuse to obey orders, or attempt to escape, they risk direct but unofficial punishment. In one instance, a Negro resisted arrest and inflicted a severe scalp wound upon a policeman. When he was finally taken into custody, the police beat him severely with clubs and fists, claiming it was essential in making the arrest. In another case, a Negro prisoner ran out of the courtroom when he was brought in for trial, an event described by a city official as follows:

I was sitting here about four o'clock when I heard someone running and somebody shouted to catch the nigger. I looked out the door just as the darky ran by and started down the steps. I grabbed my gun and ran to the window to try and get a shot at him; but as he ran out, a girl was coming up the steps, and I couldn't get a shot at him. He ran down the street, and a taxi-driver jumped in his cab and ran him down and brought him back. They took him in the police station, and then was when the fun started.

Darrell hit him over the head with a club a few times and then the lawyer who was there blew up and called it an outrage and cussed the cops. Darrell got mad and told him it was none of his business; he had no right to bawl them out, and he wouldn't stand for it. Next day the lawyer told me he was sorry he had lost his temper and felt he was in the wrong. I told him that I thought so too; he had never been a police officer and didn't know what they had to put up with, with some of these Negroes. I think I would have done just the same if I had been a cop there.

In another case a Negro woman arrested for shoplifting "talked back." An official related the story:

She sat there and told the cop that if a Negro man insulted a white woman the way the white men insulted Negro women there would be some killings. He tried to quiet her, but she got nosier and nosier. He

500

hollered at her to be quiet, but still she wouldn't shut up, talking real smart. Finally the judge said to let her talk; it would calm her down to get it off her chest. Later they took her back in the cells. I heard a couple of cracks and she hollered, and I knew the cop had hit her at least twice.

A policeman spoke of another beating with perfect candor: "We had that fellow in one time and sure 'worked him over.' He is the hardest-headed Negro I ever saw. We raised lumps on his head that he still has on him."

There is some indirect evidence which suggests that Negro prisoners are given the "third degree"; the police were frequently praised by whites for their ability in handling Negroes and in getting information from them. One policeman spoke of another policeman with professional admiration: "We pick up anyone who acts suspicious and turn them over to Joe, who questions them. He certainly knows how to find out what they know, and by the time he gets through, they tell everything they know." There is, however, no direct evidence that the police beat Negroes in order to obtain information or confessions, although it is reasonable to suppose, in view of the extent of violent treatment of Negroes, that this does sometimes occur.

Unofficial punishment by police.—In general, it appears that the police beat Negroes as a form of punishment. The Negro who resists their authority in any way is "bad" and subject to direct punishment by the police themselves. Also, when, in the judgment of the police, the courts fail to punish Negro offenders properly, the police take it upon themselves to judge and punish criminals. One policeman commented on a Negro who had been arrested for fighting with his wife. She had refused to prosecute, and the case had been dismissed. He said: "The next time he raises hell down there again I am not going to arrest him but just 'work him over' myself. That is the only way we can handle some of these troublemakers because, if we don't see the fighting or trouble ourselves, the others will never prosecute."

When too many of "these boys" get off "without a lesson," the policemen sometimes use a leather strap "to let them know they've done wrong," for "a few licks with that will learn them." The chief of police once said that "thirty days" wouldn't do a certain woman any good, and that he "had a mind 'to work her over' . . . . , to give her something she wont forget." According to him, there were "plenty of good Negroes around" who had been "worked on" to make them that way. Direct punishment can sometimes be as crudely ingenious as it is effective, as in the case of a number of Negro boys who were stealing chickens.

The bunch of kids stole about sixty chickens one night when we caught them. They were all too small to do anything with so we put them in a cell with all the chickens. It was several days before the owners got all the chickens, and it was the —est mess you ever saw. We then whipped the kids and turned them out. That cured all but one, and they have never been in trouble since.

Much of the beating of Negroes by the police is based on the general belief that formal punishments by fine or jail sentence fail to act as deterrents to Negro criminals. This belief is combined with the feeling that legal technicalities frequently prevent Negro lawbreakers from being punished through the courts. Thus, the police tend to revert to direct action and to administer punishment themselves. They claim that their action is justified because it reduces crime.

Crime prevention.—Many activities of the police are directed toward preventing crime rather than toward the arrest of lawbreakers. This is true in their dealings with both Negroes and whites. If a Negro man and woman are having trouble, quarreling, and fighting, the police frequently do not wait for an overt infraction of the law but order them to separate and stay apart as a means of preventing trouble. If they suspect that a strange Negro may be a potential criminal, they order him to leave town and then see that their order is obeyed.

The same holds for white vagrants or prostitutes who are suspected of being trouble-makers. Also, the police will pick up any Negro whose actions appear suspicious. In certain sections of the city, a Negro on the streets late at night is viewed with suspicion and may be arrested on sight. On one occasion, a Negro suspect, arrested at midnight, looked "surly" when he came to court. The chief cursed him and asked him what he was doing "prowling around so late." The Negro explained that he "got off late" from the factory where he worked and that the blanket which he had been suspected of stealing was his own. He had been compelled to change his lodgings and only found time to do it after midnight. The story checked, so the chief just cursed him again and said that, if he "had his way," all Negroes found "prowling late at night" would be locked up for investigation.

Caste attitudes of policemen.—Despite the treatment of Negroes described above, the police, in general, do not show violent antagonisms toward Negroes *as Negroes.* Individual policemen, however, often express strong antagonisms toward particular Negroes—those who "give them trouble," who are "uppity" in manner, or who do not show proper respect for their authority. They are, however, firmly convinced of the Negro's inherent inferiority, of his lack of control, of his proneness to lie and steal; and they regard any Negro who resists a policeman as a "bad nigger," one who must be "taken care of" unofficially. Except for these concepts of "racial" inferiority, their attitudes toward Negroes are much the same as their attitudes toward lower-lower-class whites. Most of the policemen live in mixed lower-class neighborhoods, where they are in frequent contact with Negro neighbors and appear to be on good-natured terms with them. A number of them have kept Negro women, usually on a more or less temporary arrangement, and are on a friendly footing with Negro proprietors of illegal establishments. The asperities of caste are thus mitigated.

Police-court trials.—Although Negroes are not subject to arrest any more than lower-class whites, their treatment in the police court is decidedly different. Analysis of the police-court records in Old City shows no significant differences in the percentage of total convictions obtained: Negroes, 59 per cent; whites, 60 per cent. Nonetheless, there was a considerable difference in the number of convictions in those cases in which the police were prosecuting witnesses. It appears that when the Negro is brought into court on the testimony of the police, the probability of his conviction is much higher than that of a white under the same circumstances. The white man, even though prosecuted by the police, has available means by which he can avoid punishment. Through political connections he may bring influence to bear upon the police to withdraw the charges or modify their evidence, or he may bring white witnesses whose testimony will be accepted by the judge. On the other hand, the Negro is, from the very beginning, in a position subordinate to both the police and the court. His testimony will not be accepted if contradictory to that of the police. His witnesses carry little weight with the court, and he can wield no political influence. Furthermore, although there is no attempt to prevent it, the Negro is less apt to have legal assistance in the police court or to appeal his case to the higher courts. Many of the whites escape a penalty by hiring a lawyer, who, if necessary, takes the case to the higher courts. Whites, moreover, even though convicted, often escape a penalty by appealing to the board of aldermen, who may remit the fine or jail sentence. While this occurs in a few Negro cases, it is much less common than among whites, since Negroes are not potential voters. In fact, in the type of offense carrying the heaviest fine, operating a car under the influence of liquor, only 46 per cent of the whites so charged were convicted; and, of these, 80 per cent had their fines remitted by the aldermen. Of the Negroes so charged, however, 100 per cent were convicted, and only 17 per cent had their fines remitted.

CASTE, CLASS, AND LOCAL GOVERNMENT

Mixed cases in the police court.—Negro cases in which the prosecuting witness is white are comparatively few. Most of them are cases of theft or shoplifting from local merchants, and the Negro is almost always convicted. It is very unusual to find both Negroes and whites involved in cases of assault and battery or fighting. When such cases occur, the odds are decidedly against the Negro, since any defense forces him to step out of the "proper" Negro role. For the same reason, Negroes seldom prefer charges against whites. The police usually discourage such actions; and in trying such cases, the court protects the whites by technicalities and by attacking the truth of the Negro testimony. In one case, when Negro witnesses testified against whites, the judge was quite evidently annoyed, continually abused and found fault with the prosecuting witnesses, and finally threw the case out of court on technicalities.

Occasionally, a case is interpreted as an affront to white people, even where there was no direct intent to commit aggression against the superordinate caste. The case cited below was one of this type. It is also significant because it indicates the value of securing a competent white lawyer.

A Negro woman was arrested for disturbing the peace and for using rude and profane language. She had hired a lawyer; and before court opened, he tried to get the judge to let her off with a small fine. The judge said: "I am going to give her a ten-dollar fine. She was in here just a month ago, and I told her not to come back or I would stick her plenty. She is getting off light at that. If it wasn't for you, she would get more. I wont stand for her being brought up so often after I have warned her."

The lawyer continued to plead with the judge, but the judge refused to fine her any less and kept insisting that the lawyer was helping her as it was, and could show that he had earned his fee. Finally the judge said: "Why you haven't got any defense at all." The lawyer replied: "Certainly not. That's why I am here begging. If I had any defense, I wouldn't have to plead with you."

Finally the lawyer asked that the charge be reduced to just disturbing the peace, which would draw a fine of seven dollars. The judge said that was up to the cops, he could only try her on the charges that they brought. The lawyer then turned to the cops, but the chief said: "No, sir, she gets the whole thing and it should be more. She has been causing trouble and acting up a long time. She was cussing and raising hell and wouldn't quit when told to."

The lawyer said: "She wasn't cussing in public there." The chief said: "Like hell she wasn't. There was a white lady there and she heard it all but I didn't want to bring her into court. When these Negroes get so they don't show no respect for a white lady and use profane language in their presence, they ought to be punished. That charge is going to stand as it is."

The judge said: "Yes, and the next time she comes in I'm going to give her thirty days." The chief said: "Thirty days won't do no good. What she needs is a good beating, and I have a good mind to work her over the next time she comes in. I will give her something she won't forget, and it will do her more good than a jail sentence."

After this the lawyer agreed to the ten-dollar fine. The case was called but was merely a formality, with the judge not even asking for evidence. The lawyer then appealed the case and arranged to have her released on bond.

All-Negro cases.—In those arrests in which the prosecuting witness is another Negro (usually charges of assault and battery) the percentage of convictions is very low. One reason for this is the custom among Negroes of using the police court as a means of revenge. If a Negro quarrels with his wife or beats her, she often retaliates by preferring charges against him in the police court. The police arrest the man; but either at the trial or before, a reconciliation takes place and the woman withdraws the charges. In a fight between two men, each attempts to bring charges before the other can do so. A policeman, speaking of this practice, said:

They will watch a chance to file charges and get even that way. Usually when they want revenge, they go to Gilmore, a justice of the peace; and the first that gets to him to file charges is the one that wins. I had a Negro man Saturday come to me and tell me that he had just hit another Negro and knocked him down and now wanted to file charges.

He wanted to make a complaint before the other did, just to protect himself.

This practice is so common that the police judge made a ruling that $3.75 in court costs must be paid by either the defendant or the prosecuting witness. Nevertheless, it was frequently noticed that, when cases of this type were called, especially when a woman had filed the charges, the prosecuting witness announced that she wished to "withdraw" and paid the costs. In the event that the prosecuting witness refused to pay the costs, the defendant paid them or was held in jail for three days. In these instances the Negro defendant found himself penalized without benefit of trial and without regard for his guilt or innocence.

Even when the charges are not withdrawn, the percentage of convictions is not overhigh. The judge attempts to interpet the evidence in terms of the white concepts of Negro behavior, with the result that the cases are often dismissed on evidence which would bring conviction in a white case. The judge, in dismissing the defendant, does not necessarily believe him innocent but merely disbelieves the testimony presented and feels unable to make what he considers a fair decision. With all attempts at fairness, however, he remains a white judge questioning and judging Negroes, continually asserting his superordinate caste and judicial position and expecting the Negroes to remain properly subordinate.

Many of the cases presented before the police-court judge develop into contests between the defendant and his witnesses and the prosecuting witnesses, with both groups attempting to prevent evidence interspersed with strong opinions regarding Negro veracity, honesty, and morality. The result is often a tangled mass of facts and opinions from which the judge can draw no conclusions. He dismisses these cases with a verbal castigation frequently delivered in dialect, such as the following:

DEEP SOUTH

The way I see it is, this is just a case of a squabble between two men over a woman. It's another one of these cases of a man and woman living together unlawfully, and then another man getting her away from him, and they get into a squabble about it. Now you know how I look at these cases. When you come in here and have been living together like you do, you needn't expect that I'm going to give you the same consideration that I'd give to married, respectable people. That's all there is to it. You-all will live together like this unlawfully. I suppose it's just your custom. Half of you get married, and half of you don't. And I don't guess there's any way to stop you, and we'll never be able to change it. But don't expect any consideration when you come up here with your squabbles.

You girl. Look at me. You're living with this man, and you won't marry him. So leave him alone. I don't want to ever hear of you coming up here with any more complaints against him. And, you, boy. Don' you ever, so long as you live, let me see you here again charged with botherin' this girl. Don' you go near that house. She's payin' the rent, an' it's her house. Boy! You hear me? If any of these officers tell me you ben there, I'm going to put you under the jail! Don't forget that now. I'll put a heavy sentence on you. Now both of you get outtuh here! Go on!

PUNISHMENT

"Laying out" and "working out" fines.—Jail sentences are the exception in the police court for either Negroes or whites; but since many of the Negroes are unable to pay their fines, they are required to "lay them out" in jail. While in jail, they are confined in a small "cage" with cells accommodating two people. Whites and Negroes, men and women, are confined in the same "cage" but in separate cells. They are fed one hearty meal a day, sent in from a near-by restaurant. If a prisoner with a long sentence or a large fine behaves himself, he is frequently released by order of the chief of police before he serves his full term. Shortening the sentence seems to depend both on good behavior and upon the crowded conditions of the jail. If room is needed for new prisoners, some of the old ones are released.

CASTE, CLASS, AND LOCAL GOVERNMENT

The law makes no provision for the length of a jail sentence to be served in lieu of a fine. In theory, a prisoner can be held indefinitely or until he pays the fine. In practice, he is allowed $1.00 for every day in jail. One variation commonly followed is to allow the prisoners to work out their fines with the city street commissioner or to work around the city hall. If the prisoner is willing and able to work, he may either act as janitor and run errands around the courthouse or may work with the regular laborers on city streets or improvements. When the prisoner works, he receives three meals a day, is allowed to sleep at home, and receives $1.00 a day credit on his fine. Thus, in effect, he works for his meals under the same conditions and restrictions as the regular paid laborers, since no guards are used and there is no special control over his movements.

The chief of police mentioned working the prisoners and said:

> When they can't pay their fine, we just keep them in jail [letting them "lay it out"]; or, if they are able-bodied, we let them work it out on the streets. We don't have a regular chain gang but just put them out to work. We don't worry with guarding them, but they seldom run off. If they run off, we just wait until they show up again and make them finish working it out. Mostly we have local Negroes; but sometimes we get one from out of town, and if he runs off we are glad to be rid of him.

The interviewer observed a Negro prisoner cleaning the cell block. When it was finished, he was sent across the street to get a pail of coffee for the desk sergeant, the officer explaining that

> our regular janitor is sick and we are using this boy in his place. He was fined $150 for something, and we are letting him work it out at $1.00 a day. He does all the cleaning and runs errands. He isn't much good, too dumb to know what you tell him. He will be through in a few more days now. He has a wife who comes to see him at times.

A Negro came in while the interviewer was present, with a police club which he said the deputy sheriff wanted to return. The officer said that this was one of the boys arrested for chicken-stealing in a case previously referred to: "That is a bad boy. . . . . He was sent to the pen and recently came back and was arrested for chicken-stealing again. He is now working out a fine at the county jail."

The extent of freedom allowed to prisoners was well illustrated by a story which the desk sergeant told of a Negro prisoner who committed a robbery while he was presumably confined in the jail for burglary. The prisoner stole a gun from the police station and robbed the same filling station where he had committed the original crime. "The chief worked on him a little, rapped him on the head with his fist, and the boy told where the pistol and the money were hid in the basement of the city hall."

CASTE, CLASS, AND THE LOWER COURTS

The policemen themselves are drawn principally from the upper-lower class with a few from the lower-middle class, and their behavior patterns are characteristic of these groups. In effect, the system of law enforcement places in a position of considerable authority some members of these classes subordinate in the white social structure, with the first stages of law enforcement almost entirely in their control. They not only are in a position to officially subordinate persons below them, but, because of the sanctions of the law, may also arrest persons above them in social class. Yet, except for periodic waves of enforcement of minor traffic regulations, the police seldom arrest upper-class or upper-middle-class whites. It is recognized that these groups are generally immune from police control except in very flagrant violations of the laws under unusual circumstances. Thus, an upper-class individual may be drunk on the streets, and the police will either ignore him or escort him home. If an upper-class individual is drunk very frequently, the police may keep him in jail over night, but only rarely is he booked and tried for the offense. One police officer described the treatment of an unusual elderly upper-class individual who as a young man had

been in jail hundreds of times and paid plenty of fines. Usually we just make him pay the costs and dismiss the charge, keep him in jail awhile to worry him plenty, and then let him out. He has paid plenty of fines. He was a good boy but would get drunk. He is usually quiet, but he used to fight the cops when they arrested him, would try to kick them. Finally some cop beat him up bad for doing that, and he hasn't tried it since.

It's a wonder we don't get him for driving drunk. Several times we have found him at night sitting in his car dead drunk. We would pick him up and take him home and push him out at his place and drive off and leave him there. He would often run along behind trying to catch us until we could get away from the house.

He has had a number of accidents when drunk but would always settle the damages, and the cases would be dropped. He was always good about that; any damage he caused he would pay for.

The enforcement of minor traffic and parking rules is generally very lax. Periodically, however, there are many accidents or complaints, and the mayor or aldermen will issue orders for police to enforce the regulations. There is then a drive on traffic-violators; and any individual, regardless of color or class, is brought into court and fined. Even in these cases, however, Negroes are much more likely to be convicted than whites. Among the whites themselves, upper-class and upper-middle-class persons are noticeably less subject to arrest and conviction than others. In fact, upper-class women told of ignoring tickets for violation, and nothing was done about it. In other cases the chief of police dismissed charges against upper-class people.

Class position, therefore, does influence the treatment of white offenders by the police and by the courts. To some extent among Negroes, too, class position is a factor in the relation of Negroes to the law. Upper-class Negroes are arrested for lower-court offenses much less frequently than lower-class Negroes; but they are not, by any means, immune to the same extent that upper-class whites are. Upper-class Negroes who are arrested may not ignore a court summons, nor do they have recourse to the board of aldermen or to the mayor, as whites do. When arrested, an upper-class Negro, like any other Negro, goes to court and may be punished for his offense. He can, however, defend himself more adequately than a lower-class Negro, through his ability to secure a lawyer and sometimes through the influence of whites.

The activities of the lower courts, particularly the justice-of-the-peace courts, vary little as between rural and urban areas. The difference, however, between rural Negro-white relations and urban Negro-white relations has a decided effect upon the cases appearing in court. In rural areas the planter not only has strong control over his Negro tenants but is expected to exercise it. That is, he is expected to take over those duties of law enforcement and control of behavior which, in the city, are handled by the police and courts. In some cases a rural justice was known to advise planters to whip Negroes for theft rather than to bring them into court. In other cases planters were known to take it upon themselves to settle fights and disputes among "their Negroes" which might otherwise be taken into courts.

As was pointed out earlier in this chapter, the Negro is excluded from participation in the political system and the activities of law enforcement—an exclusion which, though not formally recognized, is implicit in the operation of both formal and informal social controls. There are no Negro officers, judges, lawyers, or jurymen. The only role a Negro can take is that of defendant or witness, except in a few types of civil cases. Furthermore, the Negro has no part in making the laws which the court system enforces. As a defendant, he faces the white man's laws in the white man's court; he is tried not only on the evidence but also on the basis of the white man's concept of how a Negro would and should act. If he is found guilty, his sentence and punishment are determined by the same factors. The Law is white.

THE HIGHER COURTS

The operation of the circuit court is in sharp contrast to that of the lower courts. Ceremony and ritual are highly formalized, and the court structure is so elaborate that individual differences among officials in any one position have little effect upon the total activity. The circuit courts reflect the total structure of the whole society and symbolize the operation of the highest power in the community.

The judge.—During a murder trial, such a court is one of the most dramatic spectacles in the whole society. The characters in the courtroom drama are a varied lot, drawn together by the functioning of the governmental system, with their roles clearly defined by it. The judge who presides over the court is the symbol of the society and its governmental organization. Toward him the entire ritual is directed. He is expected to maintain the dignity of the court, to decide or interpret points of law, and to see that the action proceeds according to legally established forms. The judge of the circuit court is elected for a four-year term not only by the voters of Old County but by the voters of several counties which comprise the circuit. Thus, he represents the people of several communities. In consequence, he is not dominated by any local political clique, although, since Old City is the largest community in the area, local politicians can affect his chances of re-election. At the time of this study the judge of the circuit court was a member of the upper-middle class, over fifty years of age, and a lawyer by profession.

The jury.—Although the judge is ritualistically and formally the most important personage, the principal action is addressed to the jurors. They are the ones who evaluate the evidence in the case and who decide the guilt or innocence of the defendant. To them are directed the words of the witnesses, the questions of the cross-examination, the final pleas of the lawyers. They are not merely symbols of the society, but its selected agents who must judge the acts of an individual in terms of the society's concepts of right and wrong. Theoretically, the jurors must be free from bias or preconceptions regarding the case and must not have had any relations with the defendant or with other individuals who might influence their judgment. Jurors tend to be drawn, however, from a relatively small and select group whose membership is, to a large extent, determined by the political clique and by the right of lawyers to challenge any juror for "cause" and a certain number for no stated reason. Thus it is possible for lawyers to fill the jury box with people who will be friendly to them and their case and who will respond to their evidence and their arguments in the manner desired. As a result, the selection of a jury in an important case is of crucial significance, with the struggle between the prosecution and defense unstated but clearly evident to the audience.

To the stranger the process of selecting a jury may be a routine and boring affair. To the members of the community, the audience, it is an engrossing drama. They see clearly the conflict between the lawyers; they watch closely the way in which each is trying to assemble, not merely a group of individuals, but a configuration of relations which, drawn from the total society, are fitted together into a courtroom pattern. One man is selected or discarded because of an ancient antagonism to the defense lawyer; another because he is a "hanging juror," who always wants the death penalty; another is a supporter of the political ring; another can be depended upon to oppose any majority. Watching the lawyers, listening to their questions, and evaluating the patterns of relations in the situation, the local onlooker can anticipate the tactics of each side and predict the possibilities of success or failure, a process indicated in the comments of several local officials. On one occasion for instance, Tillman, a county official, was, as usual, sitting across from the jury box, whittling, while the lawyers were picking the jury for a murder case. He said: "I am especially interested in getting all this killing stopped, and so I am here for this case. When they pick a jury, the prosecution comes to me for advice about different men. It is quite a help for them to have someone to consult with who knows all the people."

In another instance, a jury on the case of a suit against a railroad reported that they could arrive at no decision and were dismissed. The lawyer for the plaintiff said: "I expected that from the time I saw the jury. I used all my challenges but couldn't get the jury I wanted. The deputy sheriff and the clerk of the court both said, as soon as they saw the jury, that it would not reach a verdict. In these small places you get to know just what everyone thinks and how they will react in a case."

Once when a Negro was being tried, while the lawyers were selecting the jury for a murder case, other lawyers, officers, and spectators sat around guessing as to which jurors would be accepted by each side. One spectator pointed out two prospective jurors and said: "Mollison will throw those two off. They are the kind that would hang a Negro on general principles." However, the defense accepted the two and the spectator said: "Apparently, Mollison has some hold on them or knows something we know nothing about."

Class position of jurymen.—The average jury is predominantly lower-middle class and upper-lower class, with an occasional upper-middle-, upper-, or lower-lower-class individual. The upper and upper-middle classes are generally scornful of the "type of person" commonly found on juries, but they seldom consent to serve themselves. They usually manage to be excused from jury service by means of political connections, or, if those fail, they may plead a fixed opinion in the case.

A number of factors are present in the open avoidance of jury duty by the upper and upper-middle classes. The common excuse is that business interests would suffer in their absence. Obviously, this is not the sole factor, for they frequently absent themselves from business for several days on hunting trips or other recreations. For the lower-middle-class individual, jury service is an opportunity to be temporarily in the public eye as representative of the society and to be placed in a desirable superordinate position. This factor has little meaning for a person of the upper classes; he is normally in a superordinate position, to which jury duty can add nothing. Furthermore, jury service places him in a continual relation of equality with jurors of lower social status; and in their deliberations over the case he may even be forced to subordinate himself to lower-class individuals.

Even when concepts of civic duty bring an upper-class person to assent to jury duty, the lawyers rarely accept him. Although the lawyers themselves, usually upper-middle class, complain about the type of people who serve on juries, they, nevertheless, when faced with the problem of winning a case, are more concerned with the problems of interrelations and the probable behavior of jurors than with problems of civic virtue. Because of their own class position, the lawyers all have intricate sets of relations with most members of the upper and upper-middle class, relations which definitely affect the actions of such men when jurors. Any man who is closely tied in with one lawyer will be refused by the other. Then, too, the lawyer who hopes to appeal to lower-middle-class sentiments does not want an upper-class person, who may react differently. Nor does a prosecutor want an upper-class person, who, by his superordinate behavior and attitudes, might array the other jurors against him.

The lawyers.—The lawyers have the most dramatic role in the courtroom. They select the jury; they question the witnesses; their impassioned pleas are the climax of the trial. They not only must know the law but, to be successful, must also know the social structure and the place of individuals in it; they must know the concepts and verbal symbols of the society; and, above all, they must be able to use this knowledge so as to arouse the jury to action.

The prosecuting attorney is an essential part of the court structure; and, although the defendant may dispense with the services of a lawyer, he does so only at grave risk. Without a lawyer he is at the mercy of legal technicalities; he is unable to observe many of the minor rituals involved in a trial; and he is unable properly to invoke the higher legal authorities.

Although most defendants know that they have the right to a trial without a lawyer, they realize the futility of such a gesture and seldom attempt it. In a very large number of cases, Negroes who cannot afford a lawyer plead guilty and accept whatever sentence the court imposes. In one case, a Negro made a plea of not guilty, and the court followed the formal procedure of selecting a jury and presenting the evidence. However, without a defense lawyer, the cast was incomplete and the whole play lost its significance and savor. Everything proceeded according to form, but in a perfunctory manner. In fact, the participants seemed annoyed at the defendant for forcing them to go through with it. The inevitable result was the conviction of the defendant.

Counsel appointed by the court.—The importance of a defense lawyer is also recognized by the law; and in cases involving the death penalty or life-imprisonment, the court furnishes a lawyer if the defendant so desires. In such cases, the court instructs a lawyer to take the case, and the county pays a small fee for his services. Any lawyer who has refused the case in his private capacity cannot be appointed by the court. This eliminates the leading criminal lawyers, since they are usually approached first by the defendant. The judge usually appoints a young lawyer who needs experience; and, if one is available, an older lawyer to work with him. Only rarely is the most competent defense obtained. Even where experienced lawyers are appointed, they seldom have the opportunity to prepare the case thoroughly, obtain witnesses, or hire technical experts. Consequently, the defendant's chances of freedom are somewhat limited.

The court system thus tends to operate against indigent defendants and Negroes. In one session of court there were two murder trials—one involving a Negro who was defended by a leading firm of criminal lawyers, and the other a white man for whom the judge had appointed counsel. The lawyer who had the Negro case remarked: "The Negro raised five hundred dollars, and so we are defending him. The white boy couldn't raise the money, and so we didn't want it."

As a rule, however, it is the Negro who cannot obtain a lawyer and the white person who can. This is due primarily to the fact that the Negro generally cannot pay, whereas the white, even if he cannot afford legal advice, may get some one who will take the case for reasons other than monetary reward. To be successful, a lawyer must build up a reputation for success so that people will bring their cases to him. Therefore, he must have favorable patterns of relationships throughout the community. To build up this reputation, a young lawyer may take cases, either Negro or white, merely for the experience and to create a favorable opinion. A few successes, then, will bring him cases from people who cannot afford the older, established lawyers. Also, if he wins white cases, especially for lower-class and lower-middle-class persons, he establishes relations which may assist him in future cases, since from these groups come the bulk of the juries and law-enforcement officers.

The defendants.—The defendants in the higher court, just as in the police court, are predominantly Negro. There is, however, a somewhat larger proportion of whites brought to trial, since Negroes often cannot afford lawyers and so plead guilty on minor charges. Many whites, too, attempt to escape severe sentences in the lower courts by appeals. It is, for example, a well-recognized fact that, while the city ordinance prescribes a minimum fine of $100 for driving under the influence of liquor, such cases, when carried to the circuit court, usually go free or receive a fine of about $25.

The white defendant plays an active part in his trial. He sits beside his lawyer at the table facing the judge; he continually consults with his lawyer regarding the jurors, the witnesses, the questions to ask, the testimony to be given; and finally, he usually takes the witness stand in his own behalf. Throughout the trial he is an active participant in the fight for his freedom or his life. The Negro defendant, on the other hand, plays a comparatively passive role. He sits behind his lawyer, outside the circle of activity; he rarely speaks to his lawyer unless asked a question; he seldom consults about the jury and the evidence; he frequently is not even called to the witness stand. The black man waits, a humble spectator, while the drama of the white man's court determines his fate.

Types of cases handled.—The cases tried in the circuit court are predominantly crimes of violence occurring within either caste. Occasionally a Negro is tried for some crime against a white, but almost never is a white tried for a crime against a Negro. As is to be expected, the odds are against the Negro in a mixed case, especially if the Negro is accused of attack upon a white person. A Negro who has killed a white is generally considered a case for the hangman. However, in two cases in the past, Negroes who killed whites escaped the death sentence. One was acquitted, and one received seven years for manslaughter. According to the judge who tried both cases, in each one the whites had been planters who "didn't know how to treat niggers," and the Negroes had fired in self-defense. Speaking of one of these cases, the judge said:

The white man was from the North and didn't know how to handle Negroes. Always went around with a gun and telling them to do this and do that. [Someone said the planter was from Virginia.] Anyway he never could get along with Negroes, just didn't understand them. He went out to this Negro's cabin, on his place, of course, but still it was the Negro's home, and crowded him—talking rough, trying to get him to do something and swaggering around with a big gun on. When he crowded the Negro too much, the Negro got scared and shot him down. The Negro was tried and acquitted.

From other comments like the above, it seems that the whites who were killed had not been completely accepted by the local white group and had failed to conform to the accepted standards of behavior in their relations with their Negro tenants.

Crime among Negroes.—With Negro defendants the jury tends to evaluate the evidence and the crime in terms of the white concepts of Negro behavior. The injury or death of a Negro is not considered by the whites to be a serious matter, since the Negro has little social value and is not a member of the superordinate group. The white idea of Negro immorality and lack of emotional restraint, too, frequently acts to mitigate the punishment for an act of violence. Since the Negro knows no better and can act no differently, he should not be punished too severely, as long as he restrains himself in his relations with whites.

White protection of certain groups.—It is evident that the Negro, as a Negro, is relatively helpless and at the mercy of the courts and the law. If, however, he has a strong relationship with the whites, they often protect him. This is an accepted element in the relationship between planter and tenant or between master and servant. The white person will usually assist the Negro in any trouble with the law. If a house servant is arrested, she immediately appeals for aid to her white employer, who feels under strong compulsion to assist her. He furnishes bail, hires a lawyer, pays her fine, or even testifies in her behalf. Planters in the same manner assist their tenants and frequently use all their power and influence to defend them in court. This was described by the district attorney, who said:

> If a Negro kills another or something serious like that and is guilty, the planter will frequently come in and say: "Look here, this nigger is guilty as hell and he ought to be hung but I hate to see him hung. If he will plead guilty, will you give him a life sentence instead of hanging him?" I will agree to that, and he will go out and talk to the Negro, and he will come in and plead guilty all right. Sometimes, however, a man will come in and say: "That Negro is guilty but the other Negro should have been killed. He is going to fight." When they say that, it means I am going to have a fight on my hands to get a conviction because they will do all they can to save the Negro.

A white planter also described the manner in which the system works:

> I have often been on the grand jury investigating some cases when a planter would fix up some case in the jury-room. They come in and tell what they know about the Negro and the case; and if they think the Negro is all right and not guilty, the grand jury will usually drop the charges.
>
> Ike, a Negro on my place, killed his wife and was sent to the pen. I could have gotten him off, but I didn't attend to it in time, so they sent him up. I felt sort of bad about it. The way it was, Ike had this wife, and another Negro had been going to see her. Ike came in one night, maybe he was suspicious, because he had a gun, and found this Negro in the cabin. He shot at him and killed his wife by mistake, and he never did get the Negro. Anyhow, when the grand jury investigated, I could have gone in and told the straight of it, and they would have dropped it. As it was, I talked to the D.A. and to the judge, and I figured it would do him good to spend a year in the pen because he had been getting troublesome. Anyhow, when the case came up, he pleaded guilty and the judge gave him three years. It seems to have done him good. He has been a good steady Negro since he came back.
>
> Wash, another Negro on my place, lied about that case. That's one

reason why Ike was sentenced. The grand jury had Wash into question him, and he told it so as to put Ike in the wrong. I sent word to the grand jury that I would come in if they wanted me, but later the foreman told me that after they had Wash in they didn't see any use in bothering me because they thought he was telling the straight of it. They knew Wash was a white man's nigger, and they thought that he would tell the truth.

The protection which the white man extends to his tenants, servants, or other employees may become a permanent element, persisting even after the primary relation no longer exists. This is especially true of servants who become identified with a white family. Even if they cease to function as servants, they may retain the identification with the white family and receive protection in times of crisis.

This type of protection extends only to those Negroes who are in direct subordinate relation to white people. It is therefore limited to the lower-class and middle-class Negroes who are employed by whites. Negroes of the upper class, who may be planters, businessmen, or professional men, lack the necessary relations with the whites and do not receive this direct support. Their high class position is recognized by the police, however, and by the courts and definitely operates to modify their treatment. Upper-class Negroes are recognized as having greater social status in their relations to both the Negro and the white groups and are treated accordingly. They are less subject to abuse, either verbal or physical; their legal rights are more freely recognized; and they are generally not so strongly subordinated by the white officials. They are known to the whites as leading Negroes; they have a large number of business relations with whites through the stores, the banks, and other economic enterprises; they are the ones who represent the Negro group in relations with the whites as a group. As a result, in case of any trouble they often receive the support of middle-class or upper-class whites. This was well shown in the case of a prominent Negro who accidentally ran down and killed a lower-class white. While there was some talk of a trial or other punishment, a number of leading whites assured him of their protection. If he had been a lower-class Negro, these whites would have done nothing for him unless he were their own employee.

The retaining of a lawyer.—Another type of relationship which, as has been previously mentioned, is extremely important to the Negro in his contacts with the police and courts is that in which he retains a lawyer. Many Negroes, especially those involved in bootlegging, have one lawyer whom they consult in all their affairs. Much of the consultation is not on a fee basis, the Negro turning to the lawyer for advice on business, on his relations with whites or other Negroes, and even on family matters. If the Negro has money or if a court appearance is involved, the lawyer may charge accordingly; otherwise he may advise the client free of charge. However, in serious cases, such as a murder charge, the capable criminal lawyers demand a good fee and collect it, often before they take the case. Once a lawyer accepts the case, he does his best to win. He does not merely make the gesture of fulfilling the legal forms. A definite contest develops, with the result that a good lawyer often obtains freedom or a light sentence for his Negro client, even when many of the whites believe he should be punished.

Sometimes lawyers are accused by whites of having no interest in preserving the white caste position but only an an interest in their fees. Thus, a white planter told of a group of whites whipping a Negro for stealing, and said:

I wanted to have the Negro prosecuted, as he confessed; but they all said it was no use, as the confession had been obtained by force and the court would throw it out. Some of these cheap lawyers up town would just get the Negro off. So we just whipped him and turned him loose.

I fell out with a local lawyer over that too. He said he had a family to support; and if the Negro was brought into court, he would defend him if the Negro wanted him. He said that the Constitution of the United States gave the Negro the right to legal protection in court. I said that the people here needed to be protected and that should come first. He got real sore over the things I said, and we didn't speak for some time.

However, when a Negro crime is one which is believed to be directed toward the white group as a whole and is one which is generally condemned by the whites, the lawyers refuse the case rather than place themselves in direct opposition to white sentiment.

Mixed cases.—Occasionally, however, lawyers accept a case in which the conflict is between a Negro and a white. In such instances they attempt to shift the emphasis from the caste element to the point where the case becomes a conflict between various elements within the white society. They may array class against class, country against city, old against young, until the caste element becomes relatively unimportant.

In one case of this type a Negro woman sued a white man who had run over her son, and was awarded $7,500. Usually cases of this type do not reach the courts. The lawyers refuse to accept them; other whites discourage the litigant and use direct pressure to prevent the cases going to trial. In this instance, however, the woman had the support of a white planter on whose land she was a tenant, and she retained a prominent lawyer. The case itself was a relatively simple one. The white man, while driving along a country road, had struck and killed the Negro boy. Several whites, who were in the car, claimed that the boy stepped in front of the car which was going at a high speed. Negro witnesses claimed that the car swerved and struck the boy from behind.

An important element in the case was the fact that the defense attorney, a competent local lawyer, was hired by the insurance company with which the car was insured. Thus it was known beforehand that the insurance company would pay the bill, since the white man had no property and was working on a W.P.A. project. This undoubtedly influenced the prosecuting lawyer who accepted the case and the jury who awarded the verdict. Besides this, the woman's lawyer was a prominent politician and a member of the political ring, and he managed to obtain a jury composed principally of middle-aged white farmers. He showed that the defendant, a young city man, had aroused the antagonism of rural whites in the neighborhood of the accident by his reckless driving and arrogant manner. The Negro woman, on the other hand, was a "good nigger," deferential and hard working, who was share-cropping a small tract of land, where her son had helped her. Her relations to the local whites and also the relations of her attorney to them were shown by the fact that a number of prominent white planters testified in her behalf.

The defense was based on the testimony of the whites in the car, all young men, and on the testimony of one or two others who were not eyewitnesses. The defense had one surprise witness who tried to prove that the Negro eyewitnesses were lying. However, the prosecution showed that this white man was antagonistic to the local whites and Negroes and, more-over, was living with a Negro woman. This evidence so discredited the witness that his testimony had no effect. A description of the part this witness played reveals the tactics of lawyers in their manipulation of caste attitudes:

> The surprise witness of the case was a white railroad section foreman who testified that one of the Negro witnesses had told him, just after the accident, that the boy had run in front of the car. This testimony was to show that the other witnesses were lying about the car swerving into the boy. The prosecuting attorney then called the Negro who had seen the accident back to the stand, and he swore that he had never talked to the white man on the day of the accident and had never told him of another version. He also testified that the white had been mad at him and hadn't been speaking to him for two years.

> The lawyer asked why, and he squirmed and finally said because the white had taken up with a Negro woman and they "fell out" over it. The lawyer then asked him when he had talked about the accident to the white. He said that several days after the accident he was at the house of

a Negro woman, and the white had asked about the accident. The lawyer asked if the woman had said anything; and the witness, after some hesitation, replied: "She said to him: 'Sweetheart, you shouldn't take so much interest in colored folks affairs'. " There was no cross-examination.

The white man had quarreled with the other whites in the neighborhood when they had criticized him. Obviously, he was antagonistic to the others, and it showed in his attitude on the witness stand. Later the defense lawyer said that he hadn't known about the situation before it was brought out in court or he would not have used the white as a witness. The other lawyer was asked how he got the Negro to give that testimony, and he said: "I knew about the situation, so I just put a little fire under him before I put him on the stand and made him bring it out. He is all right, as he has the support of the better-class whites around there, so nothing will come of it. The white has no friends there and is sore at everyone."

Prison as a deterrent to crime among Negroes.—Although the whites generally insist that the objective in meting out punishment is to discourage crime, they are convinced that their treatment of Negro crime fails in this objective. They insist that a penitentiary sentence is no punishment to a Negro, that in some cases it may even give him a certain social prestige within his own group. This much is true, that while on a prison-farm where chain gangs no longer exist, the man is fed, is permitted to have a woman on certain visiting days, and, unless he runs afoul of prison regulations, works no harder and is treated no worse than when he is working on a plantation or on the levees. Although a penitentiary record does carry a certain amount of social stigma among the middle-class and lower-class Negroes, it is not sufficient to make a man an outcaste among his friends. A killer is often received not only with fear but with admiration in the lower class. In one case, a Negro said:

If you bothered by nigguhs . . . . you gottuh tek uh stan', de firs' time enything happens. If you have to kill him, go awn to the pen for three years, an' come back, and you won't nevuh have no mo' trouble in dat neighborhood. Of course, soon ez you move into an othuh section or county, you gottuh have mo' trouble. Dey gonnuh try you out, an' you gottuh give um hell de firs' time. You jes' gottuh tek yo' nerve an' tek uh chance on shootin' him or gittin' shot. I got three in my day. May have to git another one today, too.

Since there is this widespread belief that prison sentences are not effective deterrents to crime, there is a tendency, periodically, to single out a Negro for hanging—to make a lesson of him that the community will not soon forget.

The prisoner as symbol.—Periodically the white caste becomes conscious of a "crime wave" among the Negroes. There has been an unusually large number of fights, resulting in injuries or killings. The white community begins to deplore conditions. People begin to blame the courts for being too lenient, and to say: "It's time we had a hanging, that's the only way to stop all these killings." (Even the sheriff and the judge explain that an occasional hanging is necessary to keep down Negro crime, and that following a hanging there is always a great decrease in the number of killings.) When that point is reached, the attitude of the juries and courts begins to shift, the penalties become heavier, and the first murder is likely to bring a death sentence.

One such situation of this kind occurred during the research. The whites had begun to talk about the prevalence of killings among the Negroes and the ineffectiveness of prison sentences as a deterrent to Negro crime. At the next session of the circuit court, there were two Negro murder cases. There were no acquittals; no light sentences. The defendants were sentenced to hang. But the trials were no mere perfunctory gestures. The defendants were both represented by competent counsel—in one case appointed, in the other, hired. The drama of the conflict was intense. The defense lawyers felt their responsibility keenly and did their best, and at no time were the verdicts certain. There was, however, a general belief among the officials and lawyers that a hanging was due and that "it was a hanging jury." The odds were against either acquittal or light sentences.

These two Negroes thus became more than convicted murderers. They were, in a sense, scapegoats paying the penalty for those before them who had gone unpunished, and were serving as a warning to the entire Negro group. As soon as the death sentence was pronounced, their role became one of great symbolic importance to the entire society. They were the focus of constantly increasing attention and interest, which mounted during a period of several months to culminate in the ceremony of execution.

Preparing the prisoner to die.—Although the whites considered the men vicious killers deserving of their punishment, and although one was a "bad" Negro because of his surly manner, there was no feeling that the two men should be punished by brutal treatment before the hanging. In fact, the jailer, the sheriff, and the other officials who came in contact with them felt that the period of waiting, and the very execution itself, should be made as easy as possible for them. While they were not allowed the freedom of other prisoners, who could mingle with one another during the day, act as helpers in the kitchen, or run errands on the outside, still they were granted any "reasonable" requests. They were supplied with tobacco and special food (chicken was frequently served them); verbal messages to friends or relatives were delivered; and visitors were freely admitted. The officials often chatted with them and inquired about their feelings and desires, seldom or never taking the rough, jocular attitude which conversations with other prisoners assumed. None of the officials cursed the two Negroes or told them they were "just getting what they deserved."

Furthermore, the prisoners were expected to "get religion," to "make their peace with God," thus symbolically absolving the white community of any guilt or injustice, while taking it upon themselves. The white officials were particularly solicitous about the prisoners' spritual welfare. Negro preachers were invited to talk to them, and other prisoners were invited to pray with them.

Only one of the prisoners, however, acted his role properly by accepting the consolation of religions. He confessed his sin, prayed for forgiveness, and was "ready to go." He had been visited frequently by preachers, friends, and relatives, who talked and prayed with him. This was welcomed by the jailer and deputies, who would admit any Negro who wanted to pray with the prisoner. One deputy said, on the night before the execution:

I guess all the preachers around here have been in with him today. I have talked with him a lot, he has told me all about the crime several times; he says the Devil got in his path, and he lost his temper and killed his wife. He admits he did it all right.

Another official said that he

wouldn't let two niggers in to see him just now. They were coming out of curiosity, and I don't like to have them go in and stare at him like he was a monkey in a cage. I asked them if they were relatives or friends, and they said they didn't even know him. I asked if they came to pray with him, but they said they didn't, so I wouldn't let them in.

There were certain practical values, too, in the prisoner's "getting religion." In this case the Negro was suspected of another murder, and the sheriff was anxious to find out if he had actually committed it. A deputy said, on the morning of the execution:

I have talked to him a number of times, and he always denies that he did it. I went in to see him this morning and asked him if he realized that this was his last morning with us and he said he did. I told him he was paying the supreme penalty and that it wouldn't be any worse for him if he told us the truth about that other murder. We couldn't do any more to him, and he would go with a clear conscience; but he said: "Afore Gawd I didn' do that killin'. I am going to Him telling you the truth."

I asked if he was going to tell me the same thing when he got on the trap, and he said he was.

Another official added: "Well, that settles it; he is telling the truth. He isn't the kind who would lie at this time."

The hanging of an "unprepared man."—The other prisoner, however, was a "hard sinner" and would not "get religion," and there was a general sense of uneasiness among the white officials at this stubborn refusal to assume, in full, his guilt. The evening before Roy was to be hung, a small group of whites, mostly county officials, were gathered at the jail. The conversation was about Negro behavior generally, and everyone was interested in the prisoner. One deputy began to talk about Roy.

He has never gotten religion; there have been several preachers in there, but they say they can't help him. I asked him the other day if he was ready for the long journey, told him it would be a mighty long trip and he ought to pray and make his peace before he started. He said he had tried to pray but just didn't seem able. I asked if he wanted me to get a preacher, and he said I could if I wanted to, but it didn't make any difference to him. We had a preacher in the same cell with him for a while; Ben Tolliver was a preacher and we put them together. Tolliver tried to work on him and pray with him, but he said he "couldn't do no good, the Devil had sealed Roy's mouth so he couldn't pray."

I have given him candy from time to time, and he was crazy about it. I asked him today if there was anything special he wanted, and he said there was nothing. I asked if he wanted some candy, and he said he didn't care for any. He has seemed sort of quiet all day and hasn't had much to say.

Even the justice of the peace attempted to get the Negro to pray. He came to the jail where the officials were gathered and asked if he could see Roy. The deputy offered to take the whole group in. He asked if they had guns, and then the jailer locked them in the cell block. A group of Negro trusties were in the entrance-room, and the judge asked them if they were the ones he had sent to jail and joked with them about it. The deputy and judge then went to the Negro cell block where the two condemned men were kept in the same cell. The deputy asked how they felt, and they replied that they didn't "feel so good." Judge Foster asked Roy if he were ready for his journey and advised him to pray.

The next morning a group of officials and others began to gather an hour before the execution was to take place. Conversation was very subdued, usually about minor everyday matters, greetings to new arrivals, comments on business or the weather, with an occasional question or comment about the behavior of the condemned man, to which they all listened intently. A deputy said: "He seems rather quiet this morning. The Catholic priest came down last night to see him and stayed quite a while; but they said they couldn't do much with him, he wouldn't pray or repent."

The sheriff and deputies discussed the procedure and instructed two Negro trusties who had been running errands outside to be ready to help put a straight jacket on the prisoner. One deputy said: "It is bad when they fight and you have to carry them by force. A big strong man like Roy is mighty hard to handle if he resists, and *you don't want to hurt or abuse* him in any way."

A Negro preacher had been with the prisoner for some time but finally came out and sat on a bench in the office where everyone was gathered. The deputy asked how Roy was, and the preacher said: "I talked to him and tried to get him to pray, and finally he turned his face away and I think he was crying. I think he has been praying."

The deputy said: "If he has, no one has seen him; he hasn't gotten down on his knees yet. Reverend, don't you think you had better go back and stay with him until the end? It won't be long now. Don't you think you had better baptize him, not immerse him, but just pour a little water over him?" The preacher didn't think Roy wanted that; so the conversation ended.

As the hour approached, the crowd increased until about thirty were gathered in the jail office. Finally the two trusties and a group of officials went into the cells to put him in a strait jacket. They reported that he was perfectly calm and walked out of his cell and held out his arms so they could put the jacket on. The crowd, principally policemen, deputies, various officials, and doctors, then moved into the scene of the hanging. The trap was set in the floor of a second-story room, and part of the group gathered around the trap and others stood in the room below. While waiting, they either stood quietly or chatted in very low tones.

After a few minutes the prisoner was brought in. He walked calmly up the stairs and took his position on the trap with no show of emotion. Following him were two preachers, who stood to one side of the trap. The deputy placed a black hood over Roy's head and then adjusted the noose, but his hands were trembling so that he had great difficulty in handling the rope. He asked if the rope were too tight, but received no answer and then moved Roy's jaw back and forth as if to test the tightness. He asked if the prisoner had anything to say, but there was no reply. They then shouted down the stairs to know if all was clear, and the sheriff asked the preacher if he were ready.

The preacher prayed for the condemned man while the whites stood with uncovered, bowed heads. As the prayer ended, the sheriff sprang the trap and turned quickly and stared out the window. The group above crowded around the trap to watch the scene below. The trustees placed stepladders beside the body, and the doctor mounted to examine it. Apparently the neck was not broken, and it was five or ten minutes before the doctor pronounced him dead. Four Negro trustees then mounted the ladder, and, amid admonitions from the crowd to handle it gently and not to drop it, the body was taken down and placed in the undertaker's basket.

There was considerable interest in whether the neck had been broken, and the witnesses criticized the sheriff for not having a longer drop. He, in turn, insisted that the drop was sufficiently long and that he didn't want to risk pulling the head off, as had recently happened in a near-by town. He even had the doctor examine the body after it was taken to the undertaker to make certain that the neck had been broken.

DEFIANCE OF THE SUPREME POWER

Reaction of whites.—To the whites the execution ceremony is much more than the punishment of a Negro by a group of whites. It is a ritual sanctioned by God, that is, by the most important power of the total society, whereby the complete subordination of the individual to the society is upheld. The proper role of the victim is one of complete subordination to the caste society and to God. He must confess his crime and seek for forgiveness, not of individuals who have been harmed, but of the total society. He must accept the rightness of this supreme white power which takes his life. If he fails in this role, if he does not pray and ask forgiveness, if he does not "get religion," he is denying the supreme authority and is rebelling against the society. He is a "bitter" Negro.

Reaction of Negroes.—With the Negro group the situation is somewhat different. To them the courts and the law are primarily an expression of the authority of the white group rather than that of the total society. Even though the crimes were strictly within the Negro group, and the group itself considered the punishments as justified, the actual hangings were viewed as a caste matter more than as a matter of punishment or control of crime. To them the Negro murderer who confesses and makes his peace with God accepts the white authority and acquiesces in his subordinate caste role. On the other hand, the Negro who refuses the consolation of religion achieves the heroic role of one who dares to defy and deny the white authority even in the face of death. Since the Negroes conceive of God as white, both God and heaven symbolize, to them, the superordinate white caste. The condemned man who refuses religion and prayer, in spite of the desires of the white group, maintains his Negro identity to the end. He is a brave man who "knows how to die."

This attitude of the Negroes was well shown in many comments and incidents following the two hangings. The one who refused religion was to the whites a "bad nigger who deserved to hang," but to the Negroes he became a hero about whose death there arose a number of stories to show his courage and defiance of the whites. While most of the tales were false or exaggerated, they became almost a body of mythology about a group hero. An observer reports:

I brought up the subject of Roy's refusal to repent before he was hanged, and Jerry said: "A man tol' me that when Reverent Daniels wuz prayin' ovah him jus' befo' they hung him, he asked Roy: 'Brother, will I see you again?' [meaning in heaven]. Roy tol' him: 'I see you now.' That's all he said. Course I don' know ef that's true or not, but that's what a man tol' me."

Another said: "They tell me that when they tol' Roy about the Devil he said he wuz goin' to hell an' bus' in de do' and break off de Devil's horns." [*Great laughter.*]

The keeper of the undertaking parlor said: "People were coming in all day to see the body of Roy. It was just like a circus."

"Dey tell me dat when the preacher as'ed him 'Brother, will you see me again in Heaven?' Roy tol' him, 'I see you now.' That's whut he tol' the preacher."

Jerry said that he kept hearing that Nathan, who is to be hanged next week, is "melancholy" and keeps thinking of ways he could have got out of the death penalty.

After the hanging of Nathan, who got religion, Jerry praised the nerve of Roy, who did not pray. He said: "Aw man, dat felluh las' Thursday wuz jus' the same right up to the las' minute. Dey couldn' mek him talk about no religion or nuthin' lak dat. You gottuh hand it to that man, I declare. It wuzn' none of that religious stuff that carried him through. [Yet Jerry is deacon and treasurer of his church and frequently a delegate to the conference.] That man went up on dem galluhs with jes' what he had in himself, you see whut I mean. Not whut preachin' an' a lot of singin' and prayin' an' stuff had put in him, but jes' with whut he had of his own. Why, dey tell me dat aftuh they put that black cap over his head dey as'ed him again if he had anything to say; all he said wuz: 'It's tight enuf'. " [*Exclamations of admiration from his hearers.*]

After each hanging, the body was taken to a Negro undertaker's establishment, where it lay in state until the funeral a day or two later. Apparently, most of the local Negroes viewed the bodies, and many came in from the country. Although there were more expressions of admiration for the man who refused religion and "died brave," and more interest in his body, it seemed that just as many visited the second one. In any case, it was a very serious matter to the Negro group, whatever the manner in which the men had gone to their deaths.

An observer visited the MacIntyre Undertaking Parlor after the hanging. About thirty-five or forty men and women, men predominating, were waiting for the body of Nathan to be "laid out" for public inspection. Comments and the whole atmosphere were hushed and very serious. Two hours before, Nathan had been alive and the center of great solicitude, praying, and encouragement; now he was laid out in state, and the same people were waiting to see if he looked "natural" and "peaceful." The most talkative group consisted of four old women, four girls in their teens, and an effeminate man of about twenty-five. He was acting as the transmitter of the authentic canon of Nathan's last day. He insisted upon distinguishing between what he had heard him say and seen him do and what had been reported to him. The following was overheard:

DEEP SOUTH

MAN: He said to me himself when I was in there yesterday, he said: "I had a dream a long time ago, before any of this happened, and I dreamed I saw myself dead." He saw his own self dead.

OLD WOMAN: Well, dat's fine. If he dreamed dat, he couldn't he'p it. I feel bettuh about it now. I'm glad ef dat's de way it wuz. [Other women agreed.]

MAN: I talked with him, and he said he was ready to go. He went down like a man all right. And he said that since he'd seen himself dead, he knew he couldn't have helped it.

WOMAN: I'm glad it wuz like dat befo' he died. Dat makes it bettuh.

MAN: There were a lot of people coming in to see him, and I couldn't ask him all I wanted to, but he did tell me before I left that he didn't kill that boy. He said he did kill his wife but he didn't kill that boy.

WOMAN: Well, I'm glad he didn't kill the boy. You know, maybe he didn't kill his wife either. Maybe they jus' hung that man for nuthin'.

MAN: On no, he admitted all right that he killed his wife. He admitted that to me, and he told the sheriff he did kill her. A man who wuz at the hanging told me that he said this just three minutes before he died. I don't say he told me this, but I'm going to ask the preacher if he did say it and find out definitely. This man said he told the sheriff when the sheriff asked him if there was anything he wanted to say, and after he had admitted that he killed his wife, he said to the sheriff: "No, sir, I'm ready to go, but you know you didn't hang that white man for killing the other white man. You know you didn't hang him but you're hanging me." He told the sheriff that. Oh, he went down like a man all right.

The women were very indignant about the failure to sentence the white man to hang. One said: "They jus' sent that white man to the pen. They didn't hang him. They won't hang any white man, you know that." Another woman: "You know, that this ain't never happened in this town befo'. This is terrible. Two of them in one week [*frightened and ominous*]." A man said:

Well, that's two of them in a week. They tell me this felluh Nathan wuzn' nervy lak the firs' one. The firs' didn' change at all, but a man at the jail tol' me that this felluh wuz jus' about dead when they went to get him this morning. They say he jus' folded right up an' they had to lift him up.

CASTE, CLASS, AND LOCAL GOVERNMENT

The group of women who had been discussing the case came out of the "parlor," and one had tears in her eyes. She said: "I don' keer. I can't he'p feelin' sorry fuh him. I jus' cain't." Another woman said: "Well, I raly can't feel sorry fuh him, I tell the truth now. I can't make muse'f feel sorry fuh him, knowning how he kilt his wife and that boy. He got jus' what he 'served. I don' feel sorry fuh him." The woman who was crying said: "Mary, you ough'n' say that, you know you ough'n'. You got sons of yore own. An' you don't know what one of them might do. You cain't tell. His mother loved him; she feel sorry fuh him right now, don't keer whut he did. He wuz her son jus' lak yore sons."

Nor did the Negroes discuss only the current hangings; they also related accounts of previous hangings and even of lynchings and other killings, especially cases where the Negroes had rebelled against the white power. In some cases even the present legal hangings were unconsciously referred to as "lynchings." One man told of a "nervy" Negro, a young man who went to his death on the gallows some years ago without showing fear:

The minister who wuz beside him wuz jus' shaking and scared to death. When he come up the steps to the gallows, the minister wuz jus' sinking in the knees an' everything, and this boy jus' as calm! He caught the preacher's arm an' hel' him up and tol' him: "Hol' up, elder!"

Another Negro would not name the hanged man,

becuz his people still live here, an' you all know um. But that thing got me. The minister come to me and as' me to go to the jail with him at midnight when they wuz goin' to hang him, but I tol' him: "Man, no, I can't do that. I jus' can't do it." But you know at twelve o'clock that night I had to git up outtuh my baid. I wuz so nervous I wuz just shaking. I couldn't get myself together, an' I didn't sleep a bit that whole night.

A listener entered the conversation and said: "None of the rest of us. We all knew that boy, an' his fam'ly too. I reckon

we didn't sleep. That wuz a terrible thing, hangin' that boy."
The others were all quiet, faces tense, while John looked and
talked as if he were on the point of weeping.

Another man spoke of Nathan:

"Dis man wuz chicken-hearted and scary. But dat Roy wuz de man.
He went down like uh man. Did you evuh hear of the Kiah boys?"
[*proudly*]. [The Kiah brothers had killed a white man and fought a posse
until they were killed.]

Dis guy Nathan, he war chicken-hearted lak, 'n he wuz sorry aw right.
Dey tell me he couldn't get enough religion. But dat other guy, he war
hard, jus' born hard, 'n ben lak dat all his life, didn't care about nuthin'.
He never been sorry for nuthin' he done. Yo read whut he say? 'N dey tell
me dat on his way to die he stop by dis guy's cell 'n say: "I'll see you
some'ere dis time next week, buddy." He say dat on his way to die!
'N ef 'twas me, dey'd have to be draggin' me!

Yo evuh heard of de Kiah boys up whar I cum from? Dey knowed
how to die.

The hanging of a Negro under the circumstances described
in this chapter is the most dramatic method which the white
community has of reaffirming its title to power—its superordinate caste position. It is a reaffirmation of the fact that
caste is a reality and that any variations from the pattern will
be severely punished.

CASTE AND CLASS

THE SOCIAL MATRIX

Life in the communities of Deep South follows an ordered pattern. The inhabitants live in a social world clearly divided into two ranks, the white caste and the Negro caste. These color-castes share disproportionately in the privileges and obligations of labor, school, and government, and participate in separate families, associations, cliques, and churches. Only in the economic sphere do the caste sanctions relax, and then but for a few persons and in limited relationships. Within the castes are social classes, not so rigidly defined as the castes, but serving to organize individuals and groups upon the basis of "higher" and "lower" status, and thus to restrict intimate social access. Both the caste system and the class system are changing through time; both are responsive to shifts in the economy, in the social dogmas, and in other areas of the social organization. Both are persisting, observable systems, however, recognized by the people who live in the communities; they form Deep South's mold of existence.

INDEX

INDEX

543

INDEX

Cash-tenants—*continued*
cotton, 371; supervision of, 285–86; as tenant managers, 320; *see also* Cotton cultivation; Credit; Lint-rental; Rental agreements; Tenants, farm

Caste: class, contrasted with, 9–10; definition of, 9; "race," contrasted with, 7–8; *see also* Caste behavior; Caste controls; Caste dogmas; Caste sanctions; Caste solidarity; Caste system; Caste taboos; Negro-white sex relations

Caste antagonisms: during caste crises, 48–49, 476–77; and church, colored, 414; economic competition, 463–75; and economic groups, upper, 476; and leaders, Negro, 249; manipulation of, by lawyer, 525; and moderation of: by miscegenation, 38–39, 407–8; necessity for, 404; of Negroes, vicarious expression of, 249, 533–38; and rape, 25–27; of white middle class, 52, 56–57; of white policemen, 503–4; *see also* Caste behavior; Caste solidarity; Intimidation; Lynching

Caste behavior: and caste sex taboos, 26; and class behavior, comparison with, 50; deference as a form of, 22–24, 402; definition of, 15; effect of cross-caste kinship on, 39–40; landlord-tenant relation, similarity to 402; rural and urban, 54–57; and titles of respect, 22; variations in: by class, 49–50, in occupational relations, 49; of white workers at planing-mill, 431; *see also* Caste sanctions; Caste solidarity; Caste taboos

Caste code, relation to general moral code, 7; *see also* Caste dogmas

Caste controls, *see* Caste behavior; Caste dogmas; Caste sanctions; Caste taboos

Caste dogmas: caste system, relation to, 57; conflicts of: of Christianity and democracy, 229, 414–16, with dogmas of "chivalry," 399; and division of labor,

426; economic behavior, 455–61; modification of, by presence of: Negro upper economic groups, 457, of Negro consumers, 457, of Negro employers, 459, of Negro laborers, 457; reinforcement: by Christian dogmas, 414–15, 530–33, by economic dogmas, 324–25; variations from, 53, 58; *see also* Caste dogmas, Negro; Caste dogmas, white; Caste sanctions; Caste taboos

Caste dogmas, Negro: caste solidarity desirable, 230–31, 247, 446–47, 472–73; "depression" a leveling influence, 463–66; education will "advance the race," 420; idealization of "bad nigger," 249, 527–38; light-skinned Negroes are superior, 21, 41, 232–35, 236 n.; miscegenation prevents caste antagonisms, 39; Negro business will relieve economic subordination, 420, 420–21 n.; whites display interest in Negro kin, 39–40; *see also* Caste dogmas

Caste dogmas, white: blacks "primitive," 21; crime: intra-caste, Negro not serious, 499, 520, jailing will not prevent, 46, 526–27, whipping will prevent, 46, 502–3; educated Negroes dangerous, 418–19; on handling Negroes, 46, 55, 489, 520; on industrial inefficiency of Negroes, 428, 431 n.; about mobility of tenants, 339, 341–42; mulattoes: dangerous to caste system, 41–42, superior to blacks, 21, 41; "Negro jobs," 425–27; Negro traits: childlike, 19, inferior, 4, 15, 16–17, 414, rapists, 25–26, 490, unclean, 16, 233, un-socialized, 17, 324; use of, by politicians, 488–90; responsibility of whites for Negroes, 20, 408–9, 447–51; *see also* Caste dogmas

Caste role, *see* "Bad Negro"; Caste behavior; Caste sanctions; "Good Negro"

INDEX

INDEX

INDEX

Race, inadequacy of concept, 7–8; *see also* Caste system
Race pride, *see* Caste solidarity
Race relations, 7–8; *see also* Caste system
Rape, 25–27, *see also* Caste dogmas; Negro-white relations
Raper, Arthur F., 293 n.
Rations, 350, 354, 382–83; *see also* Advances; Credit, Standard of living, tenants
Relief, caste differentials, in, 465
Religion, and caste sanctions, 529–34; *see also* Church, Negro
Rental agreements: and amount of supervision, 286, 330–32; contracts and liens, 290–92; and degree of subordination, 327; factors determining type of, 284–86; rates of rental, 286–90; types of, 281–92; variations in: with landlords' interest, 282–83, with price of cotton, 284–86; *see also* Cash-tenants; Half-tenants, Quarter-tenants; Share-tenants; Sharecroppers
Residential areas: and caste, 21–22; and social class, 81–82
Rural County: labor turnover, 340; lack of urbanization, 340; location of, 3, 260 n.; reason for studying, 260 n., 267; types of plantations in, 340, 350–51

Scapegoat, 49, 528
Schools: for Negroes, 417–18; and social mobility, 198; *see also* Education
Settlements, 325; and debt-peonage, 371–74
Share-tenants: A.A.A., rights of, under, 283–84; degree of subordination, 281–82, 330–32; net income from cotton, 366; one-third rental, 282; selling cotton of, 371–73; stealing cotton, 374–76; three-fourths rental, 282; *see also* Half-tenants; Quarter-tenants, Rental agreements; Tenants, farm

Sharecroppers, 283; *see also* Half-tenants; Quarter-tenants; Share-tenants
Skin color: ambivalence of Negroes toward, 247–48; black disliked, 21, 24, 233–36; and colored class system, 244–48; of the colored artisans, 437; dark, as bar to colored women's mobility, 247; light: antagonisms to, 235, economic advantages of, 437; *see also* "Blue-vein" society; Class system, colored; Miscegenation; Passing for white
Slavery: colored artisans, 437–38; favored position of domestic servants, 451; free Negro families, 245; purchase of property after, 296–97; size of rations, Old County, 383 n.; social organization during, 3–4; *see also* Civil War
Social anthropology: frame of reference, 13, 266 n., 267–68; methods of, 7–8; scope of, 7–8; 266, 266; *see also* Economic system; Social logics; Social organization
Social logics, 267; *see also* Caste dogmas; Caste sanctions; Dogmas, Christian; Dogmas, economic; Dogmas, political
Social mobility: characteristic of class system, 171; and cliques, 138–39, 161, 170, 191; downward, 202–7; nature of process, 172–73; rate of, 171, 203–4; upward, 173–202; *see also* Class; Cliques
Social mobility, colored society: antagonisms toward mobile persons, 225, 231; by associational and church leadership, 220–21, 222–24, 230–32; dark women, difficulty of, for, 217; mobile persons as clique core members, 217; upper class, rate of, into, 216; *see also* Class system, colored; Cliques, colored
Social mobility, white society: associational membership, change in, 197, 194–95; of children, 187–88, 199; church membership, change

555

AFTERWORD

I AM the last survivor of the team that set out in 1933 to study the social organization, behavior, and beliefs of a community which represented a culture that reached its peak in the first half of the nineteenth century. This book can be considered an artifact of an earlier time, a picture of the society with a glamorous past, which had adjusted to the buffeting of the war between the states and, at the time of the study, was suffering in the depths of the Great Depression of the 30s. Within two decades the Civil Rights movement would force major readjustments in a major element of the social order.

As the title indicates, this was a community in the "Deep South," where a dominant element in the social structure was the systematic subordination of Negroes to whites and the exclusion of Negroes from any participation with whites that implied equality.

To digress a bit, I want to give some of the background of the study and explain why Old City was chosen. The beginnings go back to the experience of Professor W. Lloyd Warner, who after three years of studying the Murngin tribes in Northern Australia, joined the faculty of anthropology at Harvard University.[1] He dreamt of applying the methods of social anthropology to the study of modern society. At Harvard, his ideas attracted the interest of Professor Ernest A. Hooten in physical anthropology, Professor Elton Mayo, and Dean Wallace Donham of the Graduate School of Business Administration of Harvard. Through them Warner was able to obtain foundation support to start such studies. The first community chosen was in New England, convenient to Boston, and Warner was able to recruit students from his classes to do much of the field work. This study has been

---

[1] W. Lloyd Warner, *A Black Civlization: A Social Study of an Australian Tribe.* New York: Harper & Bros., 1937.

reported at length in the six volumes referred to as "The Yankee City Series," published by Yale University Press between 1941 and 1959.

I entered the scene in the fall of 1930 when I came to Harvard as a graduate student in anthropology, having received my B.A. and M.A. in anthropology at the University of Texas. My primary interest had been archaeology, but I soon came under the influence of Warner and became a volunteer in the Yankee City study. For over a year I spent most weekends in Yankee City studying the Poles and Greeks in the community, and learning the method and concepts needed for a social anthropological study. (Social anthropology, a relatively new field then, had been established by the work of A. Radcliffe-Brown in his study *The Andaman Islanders* [1922], and reported by Bronislaw Malinowski in *Argonauts of the Western Pacific* [1922] and Margaret Mead in *Coming of Age in Samoa* [1928].)

Funds were tight in those days; as volunteers we were paid only out-of-pocket expenses. Only Elliott Chapple, who lived in Yankee City to serve as field supervisor, received a stipend; but he was on the job full time and, with his wife, became thoroughly integrated into the social life in the community.

Among the Yankee City researchers were two Negroes, Allison Davis and his wife, Elizabeth. Allison was also a graduate student, having decided to change careers from literature to anthropology in spite of having established himself at Hampton Institute. We soon became good friends as well as colleagues.

With the Yankee City study well under way, Warner sought to expand his study to include another old community in a different part of the American culture. In 1932, he received a grant for the new study from the Committee on Industrial Physiology of Harvard University. This was made possible by the enthusiastic support of Professor Mayo and Dean Donham.

With the funding arranged, Warner then began selecting a site and the research team. He soon settled on the city referred to here as Old City in the "Deep South." The well-recognized rigidities of Negro-white separation that had existed since the days of slavery made it clear that the research team had to be composed of both Negroes and whites, each sharply restricted to studying their own group. Allison and Elizabeth Davis were then in London where Allison had a year's grant to study at the London School of Economics. He was fortunate to work with Malinowski and Radcliffe-Brown. However, Allison was to return to teach during the summer at Hampton Institute and enthusiastically accepted Warner's offer for him and Elizabeth to join the team.

I expected to complete my course work in the spring of 1933 and, of course, jumped at the chance to join the Davises. I was also courting Mary, who had specialized in anthropology at Smith College and was then assistant to a young instructor, Dr. Carleton Coon.

With this opportunity to participate in a major field study, Mary and I agreed to become the white contingent on the study. We were married July 1, 1933, and by August were on our way to the South. En route, we spent about a week visiting the Davises at Hampton Institute and were surprised at the reactions of their friends to this venture into the wilds of the Deep South. Although I grew up in south Texas, I had not realized the problems and fears of an educated Negro venturing into the hostile world of the South. We learned that in driving through the South the Davises' friends always planned their journey so that they could spend the night with friends or take refuge at one of the Negro colleges. Otherwise they could stay only in Negro accommodations often little better than "flop" houses filled with vagrants.

To their university associates the Davises were starting an expedition into a world where any white man could be an enemy and a danger. When I think that this was only fifty-two years ago, I wonder if, off the beaten path of modern expressways, there have been any major changes, except that now a good car could take one swiftly from one safe house to the next.

AFTERWORD

I learned a little of this condition firsthand when Warner wanted us to attend a conference at the Negro university in Atlanta, Georgia. Warner and a colleague, Paul Lunt, drove down to Old City, and I went on to Atlanta with them and met the Davises, who drove their own car. I rode back with the Davises, and they arranged for us to spend the night at Tuskegee Institute on the way since we could not make the trip in one day.

On the drive back I rode beside Allison, who drove, and for any stops we picked small filling stations away from the towns. At each stop I played the proper white man's role, giving the attendant instructions, asking questions, and even requesting keys to the restrooms for the Davises to use. We kept a close watch on the usual gangs of whites sitting in the shade and wasted no time in conducting our business and leaving. They eyed us ominously but we acted as any tourists. Tuskegee was a welcome sight. The Davises had friends on the faculty there, and we were able to relax until starting again in the morning. We arrived at Old City without any incidents.

As I look back on the trip, even at the time I was surprised at my own reactions. The worst that could have happened was that we would be stopped and questioned by some sheriff or deputy. Clearly the Davises were not the usual local Negroes, and we might have had to show proof of residence in Old City. Moreover, our reason for living there would have sounded implausible and to explain that we were sent out by Harvard University would not have made us welcome.

Warner had been advised that we should spend some time in a smaller community near Old City, whose economy was completely dependent on cotton plantations, to give us a better understanding of planters and their life. After visiting the Davises at Hampton we went directly to the community, about twenty miles from Old City. The newspaper owner had arranged for us to room in one of the old mansions in the town with an elderly couple who formerly managed a plantation. He also had us meet the leading planters and businessmen in the community.

So far, I have presented a sketchy description of how this

study developed and the start of our venture into the wilds of the Deep South. This leads us to discussion of the methodology and problems of such a study.

As I have mentioned, Warner at the start had decided that a Negro team and a white team were essential. Remember, this was in 1933, when everyone was preoccupied with the Depression and civil rights had not become an issue. The Roosevelt Administration gave some attention to the plight of the Negro and ruled that there be no racial discrimination in pay on any federally funded work. (While we were in Old City a national minimum wage of twenty cents an hour was put in force that raised wages in the local box factory from five cents for women and ten cents for men to the "outrageous" twenty-cent level.)

Some of the conditions I feel were essential to our acceptance and to the success of the study were: First, Warner gained acceptance for the study among key community leaders. He contacted the newspaper editors in both the small cotton-planting community and Old City. He also met with the mayor of Old City, a prominent lawyer whose partner was the Democratic committeeman and the key political leader. Through them Warner met the county sheriff and the city chief of police. Our acceptance by the political leaders dispelled any of our doubts.

Next, we had to have an acceptable reason for being there and prying into all sorts of information. The explanation given was that we were doing a study of Old City as a typical Southern society to compare it with a Northern society, Yankee City. Many, especially the old aristocracy, were delighted to tell us of the city's long and illustrious background and how things had changed.

Finally, it was essential that we become accepted socially in the community. It was important that we be able to participate in both formal and informal gatherings and see people in spontaneous interaction. Of course, we could not reach all groups on this basis because there were too many activities for us to cover. However, the Davises through their sponsorship soon made contacts with most of the Negro upper and upper-middle class. We did the same with the white groups. Mary was sufficiently accepted to be invited to act as a hostess in one of the old mansions during their annual Garden Pilgrimage when, for a fee, the mansions were open to the public. No one commented on the incongruity of a young woman with a strong Boston accent acting the role of a Southern belle complete with hoop skirts and the traditional Southern costume.

When we participated in any event we tried to memorize and record the names of all in attendance. We soon found distinct social groupings of those who tended to come together frequently in informal activities. With the help of the social news items in the local paper we were able to create a map of the informal as well as formal groupings, especially for the upper and upper-middle classes. (These are discussed in chapter VII, Social Cliques of the White Society, and chapter IX, Social Cliques in the Colored Society.)

After a couple of months in the small town, Mary and I suggested that the Davises not attempt to come there but that we move the whole study to Old City. There were several reasons for this move:

1. The town was too small to provide a good comparison with the larger New England site, Yankee City.
2. The Davises would be too conspicuous in a small town where all the Negroes were servants, laborers, or farm hands.
3. There would be no decent housing available to the Davises in a town where all Negroes lived in one- or two-room houses without plumbing or electricity.

Warner and the Davises agreed, and we immediately arranged to move to Old City. We were able to rent a small bungalow across the street from one of the old mansions. I at once met with the mayor, and he introduced me to various key officials and explained the research. This gave me access to the police and the sheriff's office and to the various officials in City Hall. We also met with the local editor and managed to get a carefully worded announcement of our research in the newspaper. We wanted to make our presence known, but without fanfare.

The Davises found rooms with a leading Negro doctor. They were quickly accepted into the upper-class Negro society and met the educated Negroes and a number of successful Negro planters.

It was important that we abide by the local customs. Although we considered Allison Davis the senior member of the team, we had to play the proper Negro-white roles, explaining that he was working for me.

While we had no problems in interviewing the upper- and middle-class whites, we had no reasonable access to the lower class, especially the "po-whites" at the bottom of the status system. To reach them, Mary volunteered to serve as a case worker with the Federal Emergency Relief. They were glad to have her services as an unpaid volunteer. She requested that they give her a case load of lower-class whites. The other case workers were mostly lower-middle-class women whom the "po-whites" tended to resent, and there was often friction between the case workers and the families. The other case workers, therefore, were glad to turn the white cases over to Mary.

Mary managed to keep a reasonable case load and was able to call on each family once a week. She was trained as an interviewer, and always interested in getting the informants to talk about themselves, which made her popular with her clients. Often they would invite her to have a cup of coffee and would talk freely, and she could observe the families in action. Most of them lived in two-room shacks on the lowland beside the Mississippi. To supplement their meager welfare payments they fished or occasionally found temporary work. These contacts proved very important to our understanding of the whole social system.

Another major source of information were the police and the courts. I spent considerable time visiting in the police station and getting to know the policemen as well as the police chief.

AFTERWORD

I also attended the courts, especially the police court and the lower court presided over by the justice of the peace whom we met at some upper-middle-class social gatherings. The circuit court was also useful; here more serious crimes, such as murder or robbery were tried. One of Mary's client families had a son tried for murder and she attended with the family, who treated it as an exciting event in a dull life rather than as a serious threat to the family. (Incidentally, he was convicted and sentenced to twenty years in prison; before he left, Mary took snapshots of the family so he could have pictures of them all to carry with him to prison.)

We had a servant, a young woman who came in six days a week for the typical wages of $3.00 per week and "carrying privileges" (which meant carrying home any leftovers from our meals). When the street peddlers came by selling vegetables in season we would send her out with a little change to bargain with them. Sometimes she would come in and announce we couldn't have any vegetables because the peddler wanted too much money.

In our work we used no questionnaires but relied on personal interviews and observation. We did keep a card file with information on everyone we interviewed, and files of newspaper clippings. We tried to interview at all levels of the society, but used no formal sampling methods. We sought out informants and information where we could. In this way we took no notes, and to everyone the contacts were seen as normal social interactions rather than as "research." In fact, we were often asked what we were doing even by people we had known quite well for many months. The less people thought of us as "making a study," the more open they were in telling us about themselves and others.

Mary and I typed all interviews and observations; for security we kept our copies in locking files and sent one copy to Warner in Cambridge. This was to prevent the loss of all our data in case something went wrong and we had to leave hurriedly.

Because of the Negro-white social separation, we found it difficult to confer with the Davises. At first we rented an office on an upper floor of the one high-rise office building, a bank with eight stories of offices. After one or two visits Allison felt too uncomfortable as the only Negro in the elevator with whites, and we gave up that effort. We also tried to have Allison come to our house, but we heard of rumors of his visits and they were discontinued. From then on, one of us would call the other on the phone and arrange for me to pick him up at a certain corner. Then we would drive out to some sheltered country road where we could sit and talk unobserved. Toward the end of our stay I heard that the sheriff knew of these meetings, but because of our sponsorship he said nothing.

Burleigh B. Gardner

Chicago, Illinois
1986